D0201478

SANDRA GUSTAFSON

GREAT SLEEPS ITALY

FLORENCE • ROME • VENICE
FIFTH EDITION

CHRONICLE BOOKS
SAN FRANCISCO

Copyright © 2005 by Sandra A. Gustafson.
Maps copyright © 2005 by Ellen McElhinny.
Cover photograph copyright © 2002 by INDEX STOCK PHOTOGRAPHY/Peter Adams.

All rights reserved. No part of this book may be reproduced in any form without
written permission from the publisher.

Printed in the United States of America.

FIFTH EDITION

ISBN: 0-8118-4565-6
ISSN: 1074-5076

Cover design: Ayako Akazawa
Book design: Words & Deeds
Typesetting: Jack Lanning
Series editor: Jeff Campbell
Author photograph: Marv Summers

Distributed in Canada by
Raincoast Books
9050 Shaughnessy Street
Vancouver, B.C. V6P 6E5

10 9 8 7 6 5 4 3 2 1

Chronicle Books LLC
85 Second Street
San Francisco, CA 94105

www.greateatsandsleeps.com
www.chroniclebooks.com

*For Rosmarie Diletti and her daughter Patrizia...
delightful friends, and always the perfect hostesses*

Contents

To the Reader

Italy is my magnet.
> —*Lord Byron*

I realize that every day my heart is Italian.
> —*Stendhal*

Italy has played host to visitors for more than two thousand years, and in that time, tangled red tape, long lines, and the Italian penchant for complicating simple issues have endured. However, you will survive with your humor intact if you come with a healthy does of *pazienza* (patience), a sense of adventure, and a copy of *Great Sleeps Italy* in hand. Italy is nothing short of marvelous, and it is my aim to help make your trip equally so.

Great Sleeps Italy is written for those travelers who want to save money without sacrificing comfort, convenience, and well-being in the bargain. As many travelers know, value is not always measured by how much you spend. There are times when spending the least amount possible is necessary and smart. Then there are times when spending just a little more can yield a great deal of extra comfort and enjoyment, and *Great Sleeps Italy* will help you make that distinction by leading you to the best hotel values for your particular taste and budget, ones I hope will make your stay truly special and set the stage for many return visits. But first, decide for yourself what comforts you can and cannot do without, and what trade-offs you will accept to hold down costs, then pack lightly and with an open mind. All travel should be an adventure, a chance to learn new things about the world and about yourself. You may find you need less than you thought, or more, but either way, enjoy all the new sights and people, sample new foods, make an attempt at a few Italian words if you don't already know the language, and remember that a smile is understood worldwide. If you can do these things, you will come home a more knowledgeable person with a lifetime of happy memories.

Not long ago the hotel situation in Italy was relatively easy. If you wanted luxury, you got it without breaking the bank. If you wanted a simple, clean pensione with charm, character, and a low rate, you could find one. Things have changed dramatically. Because Italy is part of the European Union (EU), hotels are required to meet certain safety standards, and the effort to comply has driven many to near bankruptcy. The result of course is higher prices passed on to you, the hotel guest. Remodeling and redecorating worn-out hotels has become almost a growth industry in Italy. What used to be cheap and cheerful is now more expensive and modern, with extras such as minibars, hair dryers, Internet connections, and color televisions, many of which beam CNN around the clock. These features may add little or nothing to your trip, but they are the justification for doubling or tripling the rates. The result: that once-affordable family hotel is now inching perilously close to $200 per night for two. On the positive side, new on the scene, especially in Florence and Venice, are renovated lodgings with fewer than a dozen rooms, often located in old *palazzos*. Many of these *affitta camere* are opulent, others are very basic. Because of their small size, they do not qualify for hotel or star status and have limited extras (that is, no room service, no twenty-four-hour staffs, no large buffet breakfasts), but they are often a far better value than their big hotel neighbors.

Almost every hotel tacks on a few extra costs that the savvy Great Sleeper must watch out for. First is breakfast. This is a real moneymaker for the hotel and an absolute budget-killer for you. If the strong coffee does not wake you, the high cost of the hotel breakfast will. Convenience is the reason why so many eat at the hotel, but the cost is usually exorbitant, if not downright extortionist, when you pay between 5€ and 15€ per person for food that may cost the hotel 1 to 2€. The guest seldom sees this charge because it is hidden in the room cost. As you can imagine, hotels are very reluctant, and some flat out refuse, to deduct the cost of breakfast, but sometimes in the low season it is negotiable. Also watch out for hotel laundries, which often charge more than a garment is worth, and in-room minibars: these drinks and snacks are real budget-blowers. Finally, telephone surcharges in some hotels can be as much as 250 percent of the cost of the call.

Some of the hotels in *Great Sleeps Italy* are cozy, quaint, and rustic, full of charm and personality and boasting unforgettable views. Others are just right for romantic stays, a few are a bit faded around the edges but have enough redeeming virtues (most especially price) to be acceptable, while others are fully renovated, sporting the latest word in room amenities and bathroom plumbing. What can you expect almost anywhere you stay? The concept of the shower curtain has not been universally embraced by hoteliers in Italy, even in some three-star hotels. "The water eventually evaporates" is the answer I get when I ask why this civilized invention is so often missing. Also, a large majority of Italian hotels are in historical buildings that, by law, cannot be changed. This may mean you will carry your own luggage up and down several flights of stairs and do without air-conditioning—or else pay a supplement for it, only to find that it is available only during a few short hours in the morning and again late in the afternoon and not at all at night.

It is important for readers to know that I do not include any hotel or shop, no matter how highly recommended it may be elsewhere, that I have not personally visited. Other guidebooks, when revising an edition, may send a questionnaire to be filled out by someone at the hotel, or they employ a few on-site stringers to stop by a random selection of the entries. I do not do this. For all of my books, I do all of the research, on-site inspections, and evaluations and descriptions. I have been to every address in this book—plus hundreds of others I tossed into the rejection pile. On all of my unannounced visits, I decide whether a hotel is a true Great Sleep value by assessing not just the rate but the facilities, the attitude of the management and reception staff, and the hotel's overall cleanliness and ambience. I am on the lookout for dust, mold, mildew, bugs, thin towels, scratchy or waxed toilet tissue, creaking floors, peeling paint, no-watt bulbs, strange smells, depressing views, and cigarette burns on the bedspreads. I evaluate a room's livability: Is there somewhere to store the luggage, a place in the bathroom to put a toothbrush and cosmetics, enough chairs for the number of people the room holds, and closet space to hold the contents of more than a carry-on flight bag? Then I pass on my findings to you.

In addition to offering budget-minded travelers advice about the best hotel values in Florence, Rome, and Venice, *Great Sleeps Italy* provides Great Chic shopping addresses for the smart consumer who feels, as I do, that no trip is complete without at least a few hours spent browsing and buying—and if at all possible, not paying top price.

One of the benefits and joys of my job is discovering hidden treasures and passing them along to you. For me, it is the perfect job, and I love every minute—I can't wait to return to Italy and do it all over again. I want to thank all of my faithful readers and extend a warm welcome to those of you who have picked up *Great Sleeps Italy* for the first time. I encourage all my readers to write to me and tell me about your experiences, whether to disagree with something I have said, to pat me on the back, or to point me toward some new or special place you want me to check out on my next trip. For contact information, see "Readers' Comments," page 399. Your comments and suggestions are very important to me. In the meantime, I wish you *buona fortuna* and *buon viaggio*.

Tips for Great Sleeps in Italy

All saints can do miracles, but few of them can keep a hotel.
—Mark Twain (sign in a hotel in Florence)

1. For a successful trip, you must plan ahead. Research where you want to go, how to get there, and the things you want to do. Most of all, make hotel reservations in advance to ensure that you get the hotel of your choice in the location you want—and at the price you can afford.

2. Try to go in an off-season, when rates are lower and tourists are fewer.

3. Where are the discounts? Always check the hotel Website for special offers and last-minute deals. Some hotels in Rome offer lower weekend rates, while in Venice, discounts are given for midweek stays. Ask about extended stays, cash versus credit card, *Great Sleeps Italy* reader prices . . . anything you can think of that might apply. Be sure the quoted rate includes taxes and service charges, and get the rate you have agreed to pay in writing—then take it with you to show when checking in. If a hotel has an 800 number, forget it. The operators are merely telephone order takers with no authorization to grant discounts.

4. Ask to have the cost of the hotel breakfast deducted from your total bill, even if the hotel policy states that breakfast is included. In some cases, hotels charge up to 15€ per person per day for a breakfast consisting of a roll, coffee, jam, and butter—and, if you are lucky, a glass of processed juice and prepackaged cheese. Multiply this by two or three people over several days, and it becomes a ridiculous amount of money poorly spent. It is a much better value, and more interesting, to have a cappuccino and *cornetto* (roll) at the corner *caffè* with the locals.

5. If you do eat the hotel breakfast, remember that this is the only meal you are having: breakfast only. Please do not take advantage of the buffet and load your pockets and bags with enough extra food to sustain you and your family for the rest of the day. Hoteliers take a very dim view of this cheap trick.

6. A room with a double bed (*letto matrimoniale*) and shower on the back of the hotel will be cheaper than a twin-bedded room (*due letti*) with a bathtub and a balcony or a view. Don't be surprised if the shower, whether stall or over the tub, has no curtain. Note that two-star hotels are required to provide clean towels twice a week and sheets once weekly, not daily.

7. Don't expect to control the heat and air-conditioning yourself. Many hotels in all categories turn on the heat or air-conditioning only from 7 to 9 A.M. and again from 5 to 11 P.M., turning them off completely during midday and after midnight, no matter how high or low the temperature might be.

8. Major Italian cities are not known for their peaceful tranquillity. In fact, Rome has the dubious distinction of being the noisiest city in Europe. Florence has the most motor scooters per capita, and in Venice, narrow walkways echo with the voices of late-night revelers. If you are a light sleeper, bring earplugs and ask for a quiet room—but be prepared for a dark space with no view and limited ventilation on the back of the hotel.

9. Find out what the hotel refund policy is should you have to cancel a reservation or cut short your stay. Some have only one policy: No refunds, period. This is a critical point if you are renting an apartment. (For more on apartment rentals, see page 15.)

10. Insist on checking out the room before checking in: make sure everything works, it is clean, there are towels, and it is what you reserved. This is the time to reconfirm the room price and discuss extra charges such as telephone calls. Pleading ignorance to extra charges at checkout time is no excuse not to pay them.

11. Italian law states that hotel guests are not allowed to have any unregistered guests or visitors in their rooms, no matter how short a time they may be staying. In small hotels, this is strongly enforced.

12. Hotels detest any kind of eating in the room, so if you do have room snacks, please dispose of your papers, crumbs, and cores discreetly.

13. It is not the washing of clothes that hotels object to, it is the dripping while they dry. Wet clothes have ruined many carpets and stained walls. Place clothes to drip-dry over the tub, sink, or bidet. If you have jeans or other heavy articles, go to the nearest coin-operated laundromat. Hotel laundry services are sky high, and so are finish laundries. Who knows, mixing with locals at the local laundromat could turn out to be one of your more interesting encounters in Italy.

14. If you are staying in Florence or Venice from spring through fall, bring mosquito repellent. The mosquitoes during this time of year are lethal, and very few hotels have window screens. Hotels do provide a *macchina per zanzare* (mosquito-zapping device), but often this is not enough.

15. Italians must have developed the power to read by the light of the moon! I have never seen so many low-watt bulbs masquerading as proper lighting. I travel with a folding halogen light, but you can pump up the watts by buying stronger bulbs at an Italian corner convenience store and carrying them with you.

16. Never change money in a hotel, restaurant, or shop. Go to a bank or the American Express office, or use an ATM.

17. While not a routine practice, some hotels overbook or move you to another less-desirable location. This happens especially during large exhibitions or conventions. Because of this it is extremely important that you guarantee your room with a credit card as far in advance as possible and get a written confirmation stating the exact accommodations, rate, and dates of your stay. Written confirmation of the price is especially crucial if you have been quoted a special off-season rate.

18. In Italy, a *piano* is not always a musical instrument; it is also a floor in a building. *Piano terra,* or T, as you will see it on elevator indicators, means ground floor. *Primo piano,* or 1, means the first floor above the ground level (or what Americans would consider the second floor).

19. To wish someone good luck, never say *auguri* (best wishes). This brings bad luck. Say instead, *in bocca al lupo* (in the mouth of the wolf), and the response will be, *crepi il lupo* (may the wolf die). If you give flowers, avoid chrysanthemums, which are exclusively placed on graves.

Tips for Renting an Italian Apartment

1. MOST IMPORTANT: *Know the cancellation policy and buy cancellation insurance.* It is beyond the scope of this book to detail the various apartment rental policies you will encounter, but I can assure you they are not favorable to you and always hit the hardest when the chips are down. To protect yourself, purchase trip insurance (see page 38).

2. While the apartment definitely should be clean and habitable, owners cannot control views, stairs versus an elevator, the weather, street noise, or the Italian economy. Italians have a much higher cost of living than we do; as a result, many make do with a great deal less in terms of square footage, modern appliances, and other conveniences most Americans take for granted. You will encounter oddities in electricity, plumbing, and even linens. Therefore, it is imperative that you spell out your needs in specific detail. The more specific you are, the better you will be served, and the less chance for a ruined trip. But be reasonable. For 300€ a week, don't expect a penthouse with a doorman, live-in maid, plasma-screen television, and data ports in every room.

3. Evaluate what's important to you: How much square footage do you need? Does everyone need their own individual bed, or can some share and some make do on a sofa bed? Must you have a stall shower, or can you live with a handheld shower nozzle in a tub with no curtain? How important is air-conditioning? Do you need a view? Zero street noise? CNN, or will you be happy watching Italian TV?

4. Is there a telephone specifically for your unit, and how much are you charged per call? Is there an answering machine available, a fax, sufficient wiring to support your computer?

5. In an individual rental, it is almost certain that you will pay for all utilities. How much will this be? Chances are that heating and/or air-conditioning will be needed, and charges are handled in two ways. Either they will be deducted from a hefty security deposit—which is collected upon reserving, and the remainder of which will be refunded as long as three months *after* you have gone home—or they will be charged at a fixed rate you will be required to pay when reserving or upon arrival.

6. How far is the flat from what you want to see in the city? Ask for photos of the apartment inside and out and a city map with the flat location and nearest mode of public transportation marked on it.

7. How far is the nearest market, laundry and dry cleaner, pharmacy, restaurant, and so on?

8. Is maid service included, and if not, is it available and for how much extra? How much is the final cleaning fee? (Even if you leave the flat surgically clean, you will almost always pay a final cleaning fee.)

9. Who is responsible for laundering sheets and towels? If you are, you will probably want a washing machine in the flat, or at least in the building.

10. Is the apartment childproofed? Is it suitable for someone with special needs? Is there a park or playground nearby?

11. Is there an elevator to your flat? That fifth-floor penthouse may have a million-dollar view, but do you really want to lug suitcases up and down, as well as daily bags of groceries, bottles of wine and water, and all those Great Chic shopping finds? Think about this one carefully—stairs get old in a hurry.

12. Upon arrival, will someone meet you at the apartment to show you the ropes, or do you have to go to an office somewhere to get the keys?

13. What back-up services are provided? Is there a twenty-four-hour hot line to call if the heater blows up (don't laugh, it happened to me), the plumbing quits (that, too), or you face some other household crisis?

14. Upon arrival, check out the equipment: Are the pots and pans clean and serviceable, the dishes and glassware chip-free, and the sheets and towels in good condition? Do all the appliances work? Check the furniture carefully for any rips, tears, or damage that you might be charged for if not noted upon arrival. If the answer is no to any of the above, insist on immediate replacements or repairs.

How to Use Great Sleeps Italy

The great adventure of a hotel is that it is a refuge from home life.

—*George Bernard Shaw*

Big Splurges and Cheap Sleeps

Most of the hotels in this guide are in the midrange price category. However, some fall into the Big Splurge category because of their higher prices; others are true budget accommodations and designated as Cheap Sleeps. Big Splurge hotels are included for readers with more flexible budgets, exacting tastes, greater needs, or a special occasion to celebrate. Even though the prices are higher, these hotels all offer the same good value for money as the other accommodations in this guide. It is important to point out that while these hotels are considered Big Splurges during the various high seasons, many of them offer significantly lower rates during the low seasons, making them affordable to a wider group of travelers. In text, Big Splurge hotels are marked with a dollar sign ($). The index includes a separate list of these special hotels.

Those looking to maximize their travel dollar without sacrificing cleanliness and a good night's sleep should look for the Cheap Sleep hotels, which are marked with a cent symbol (¢) and are also listed separately in the index. These budget-priced accommodations are in safe locations and maintain excellent quality for their price category. Those on a budget should also consider hostels, Holy Hotels, or if you qualify, student accommodations, which are listed under "Other Options" in each city.

Stars

Hotels in Italy are controlled by a government rating system that ranks them from no stars to five-star deluxe. The star rating depends on things like the number of lights in a room, whether or not the hotel has an elevator, the number of private showers and toilets, and the size of the rooms. It has nothing to do with service, attitude of management, decor, ambience, cleanliness, or cross-ventilation, so don't always judge a hotel by its stars.

Indeed, a growing number of exceptionally nice, small boutique hotels, particularly *affitta camere,* do not participate in the star system because a "no-star" ranking is automatically given to any hotel under ten rooms. In this guide, hotels that don't participate in the star system have no ranking by their name, and those that do participate and are officially rated as "no stars" are so noted.

No-star and one-star hotels have minimum facilities and seldom an elevator. Two stars means a comfortable room with a telephone, but not necessarily an elevator or private bathroom. Three stars usually guarantees a private bathroom, a color television, possibly air-conditioning, maybe a room safe, and perhaps an elevator. A four-star hotel has most luxuries you need, including an elevator and usually a uniformed staff and sometimes a restaurant. An Italian five-star deluxe hotel is a slice of heaven on earth. Please note that many Italian hotels do not have elevators. This does not mean that the hotel is not a good one. It usually means that the hotel is in a historically designated building that does not allow the renovations necessary to install an elevator.

Reservations

People always ask me, "Do I need reservations? I am only going to be in Rome (or Florence or Venice) for a few days." The answer is absolutely yes, no matter how long or short your stay or the time of year. It is not unusual for hotels in the central parts of these cities to be fully booked, even in the off-season. Without reservations, you risk spending major portions of vacation time securing hotel accommodations, paying more than your budget allows, or staying on the fringes and commuting into tourist central. Today the best way to reserve is by email or telephone, and sometimes by fax; writing a letter to make a reservation has become an anachronism of another age.

When making reservations, be sure to say you are a *Great Sleeps Italy* reader and cover the following points.

1. Your dates, time of arrival, and number of people.

2. The size and type of rooms: a double means a double bed, a twin means two beds. State if you need a room with extra beds, adjoining rooms, and so on.

3. The facilities needed: private toilet and shower or bathtub, or hall facilities if these are acceptable to you.

4. The location of the room: view, on the street, on the courtyard, or on the back of the hotel (which may be quiet but have no view because it probably faces a wall).

5. The rates. Determine the nightly rate and state whether or not you will be eating breakfast at the hotel (you will save considerable money if you do not). If you do not eat breakfast at the hotel, be sure it is deducted from the quoted rate if possible. Most hotel rates include taxes and services: be sure your hotel rates do. Some apartment rentals do not, and these can run close to 10 percent.

6. Determine the deposit required and the form of payment. Also inquire about the cancellation policy.

7. Request a confirmation in writing from the hotel for both your reservation and deposit, and carry this confirmation with you to the registration desk when you check in. You may have to prove that there is a record of your reservation or that you are not booked into the presidential suite (or maybe that you are).

Email/Internet

More and more Italian hotels are plugging into cyberspace, but it is not quite comparable to the frenzied addiction we see in the States. Whenever applicable, each hotel's email or Website is listed.

Fax

If you and the hotel both have a fax number, this is a satisfactory way to make and confirm a reservation. To fax a message to Italy, you use the same country and city codes as when making a telephone call. See "Staying in Touch," page 34.

Telephone

For information on how to make a phone call to or within Italy, see "Staying in Touch," page 34. When you are telephoning for reservations, time the call during the hotel's weekday business hours to avoid talking to a night clerk who has no authority to make any sort of discount arrangements, and who perhaps cannot even accept a telephone reservation from abroad. Before calling, write down all your requests and questions. Ask the hotel to send you a written confirmation (by either email or fax) and, in turn, send them a confirmation of the conversation. In your confirmation, cite the reservation details, the name of the person you spoke with, and the date and time of the call.

Making Reservations in Italian

Most hotels in this guide have at least one person on staff who speaks English. However, if you want to try your luck with Italian, here are a few simple phrases (also see the Glossary, page 389).

Potrei prenotare una camera singola (doppia) con/senza bagno per il tre Aprile?
Can I reserve a single (double) room with/without bath for the third of April?

È compresa la prima colazione?
Is breakfast included?

Quanto costa?
How much is it?

Ha qualcosa che costa di meno?
Do you have anything cheaper?

Va bene, la prendo.
Okay, I will take it.

Mi chiamo _____.
My name is _____.

Arriverò alle sedici.
I will arrive at 1600 (that is, 4 P.M.).

Mille grazie.
Many thanks.

Deposits

After you make your reservations, most hotels require at least a one-night deposit, even if you have been a guest before. This is good insurance for both sides. It should mean you are guaranteed the room you want for the number of nights you requested. The easiest way to handle a deposit is with a credit card. If the hotel does not take credit cards for payment, some will take them for the guarantee. The next best thing for you is to send the hotel an international money order in U.S. dollars, which can be converted into European euros by the hotel. While this option is more convenient for you, it is added work, time, and expense for the hotel, and budget Great Sleeps usually will not do it. They will insist on a deposit made out to them in euros. Check with your local bank to find out where you can obtain a money order in euros.

If your local bank cannot provide you with a euro draft, then contact International Currency Express (Tel: 888-278-6628; Internet: www.foreignmoney.com), a currency specialist.

Checking In/Checking Out

Remember, it isn't always how you start your stay, but how well you finish it.

> —*Sam Matar, businessman and veteran world traveler*

When you arrive at the hotel, make sure you have your written confirmation and always ask to see the room before accepting it. If you are dissatisfied, ask to see another. After accepting the room, reconfirm the rate, and if you don't plan on eating breakfast at the hotel, be sure to request that the breakfast price be deducted (per day, per person) from the quoted room rate. If it is summertime, ask if there is a supplemental cost for air-conditioning; in some hotels it can be as much as 10€ extra a day. This advance work helps avoid unpleasant surprises at check out.

The Italian hotel day begins and ends at noon. If you have an early-morning arrival on an international flight, and the hotel cannot guarantee that your room will be ready before noon, you might consider booking the room for the day before. That way you can have a hot shower and regroup immediately after a long flight, rather than hanging out in a daze for several hours. Conversely, hotel guests are expected to arrive by 6 P.M. If you have a reservation, even with deposit and confirmation, the hotel does not have to hold the room for you beyond this time unless they have been forewarned that you will be late arriving.

If you are checking out at noon but have a later plane or train to catch, most hotels will be glad to hold your luggage for you at no additional cost. In fact, if you are making some side trips and don't want to take all the luggage you brought with you, arrangements can be made to store your luggage at the hotel. A few hotels may give a day rate, or offer an extended checkout time, if you need the use of your room until your plane or train leaves. Make these arrangements as early as possible. Otherwise, if you overstay without notifying the desk, you could be charged the price of an extra day.

In most hotels, you pay for the room, not for the number of people in it. Thus, if you are alone and occupy a triple, you could end up paying the triple price. Most hotels have two kinds of single and double rooms. First there is the usual single, which can too often be nothing more than a cell on the back of the hotel with no view, poor ventilation, and very little living space. If you are a solo Great Sleeper and are willing to pay extra for a better room, ask for a double that is sold as a single. These rooms are usually the smaller doubles with one double bed (*letto matrimoniale*) rather than twin beds (*due letti*). If you ask for a room with a bath, specify if you want a bathtub or will settle for a shower (but remember, even some three-star Italian hotels may not have a shower curtain or door). Prudent Great Sleepers also know that a room with one double bed and a shower will cost less than a room with two twins and a bathtub.

Rates: Paying the Bill

Hotel rates and the number of stars must be posted, and the rates must include all services and taxes. In some residence hotels, services and taxes are extra (sometimes up to 10 percent).

Italian hotel rates are no longer tightly controlled by the government. As a result, hotels now offer different rates at different times of the year, getting the most they can even in the off-season. It always makes Great Sleeping sense to ask for the lowest rate possible, and to go in the off-season if your schedule permits.

All of the rates listed in *Great Sleeps Italy* are for full price and do not reflect any discounts or deals. The listings state if lower off-season rates apply, if there are special weekday or weekend prices, and when discounts are granted to readers of *Great Sleeps Italy*. These special rates can vary widely depending on the time of year, demand, length of stay, and in some smaller hotels, if you pay in cash or by credit card. *No matter when you go, ask for a discounted rate.* You never know, you may get lucky.

The hotel listings state which credit cards are accepted. In most Great Sleeps listings, payment is required one night in advance to hold your room. Some low-priced hotels, and almost all youth hostels and Holy Hotels, do not take credit cards. It is cash up-front, in advance, in euros only. The following abbreviations are used to denote which credit cards a hotel or shop will accept:

American Express	AE
Diners Club	DC
MasterCard	MC
Visa	V

Hotel money exchange rates are terrible and never in your best interest. If you must pay your bill in euros, convert your money at a bank.

Before leaving the hotel, go over your bill carefully, question anything you do not understand, and get a receipt marked paid before leaving.

Breakfast

Most hotels listed in *Great Sleeps Italy* serve at least a Continental breakfast consisting of a roll, butter, jam, and coffee, tea, or chocolate. Hotels stand to make an enormous profit on this meal, and in some cases the cost per person, per day, can exceed 10 to 15€, which is an unwritten hidden cost in your hotel bill. If you want anything extra, it costs dearly and is usually not worth the additional outlay. Many three-star hotels now offer a buffet breakfast with cereals, yogurt, meat, cheese, and fruit added to the basic Continental offering. Sometimes the buffet may be worth the price if you plan to skip lunch. However, it is never anything but a show of very poor manners to load your purse or sack with enough food from the breakfast buffet to sustain you through the day. Please refrain from taking advantage of your hotel in this way.

Some hotels present breakfast as an option, and some include it in the room rate no matter what. Others include it in the room rate but allow you to deduct it if you don't want it. If you are trying to save money, omit every hotel breakfast you can. Even if a hotel doesn't present it as an option, insist that the cost be deducted from your bill; not every hotel will agree, but it's worth the effort to ask.

English Spoken

All the listings in this guide say whether English is spoken. If you can dust off a few Italian phrases, smile, and display goodwill, most hotel staffs will respond with warmth and friendliness and go out of their way to serve you. However, if all you know are a few polite phrases, try to choose hotels where at least someone can speak English. While it is fun to practice your broken Italian, it is definitely not fun to be unable to communicate when facing a crisis. See the Glossary, page 389.

Nonsmoking Rooms

Will wonders never cease? Believe it or not, the Italian government has recently passed a law prohibiting smoking in public places. For hotels, it means no smoking is allowed in the hotel's common areas. That is the good news. The bad news is that the law does not extend to the rooms, because they are considered to be private places once a guest enters and shuts the door. Further, Italians have a great distaste for this type of behavioral mandate, and they prefer to think of the no-smoking law as more of a "suggestion" rather than a rule cast in cement. Many hotels have smoking and no-smoking rooms, and a surprising number prohibit smoking altogether throughout the hotel. If the hotel does provide specific nonsmoking rooms, it is noted under Facilities and Services. If you are a nonsmoker, always ask for a nonsmoking room. This doesn't always mean a smoker has never occupied it, but at the very least, it will be aired out and sprayed with room freshener before your arrival.

Facilities and Services

A brief summary at the end of each hotel listing tells what facilities and services the hotel offers, such as public Internet terminals for guests, air-conditioning, in-room safes, and so on. Generally, the more facilities, the more money you will spend. Also note that, particularly in Venice, elevators are not always available, even in nicer hotels, so expect to encounter stairs while in Italy.

Nearest Tourist Attractions

In each city, hotels are organized by neighborhood and then listed alphabetically. To assist you in planning your visit, each hotel listing notes the tourist attractions that are within a reasonable walking distance.

Transportation

It is beyond the scope of *Great Sleeps Italy* to note all of the available public transportation options in Florence, Rome, and Venice. Of the three, only Rome has a metro system, and it consists of two lines, which are designed to take people through or across the city, not around it. Since the system is only marginally useful as a way to travel to the hotels listed in this guide, metro stops are not mentioned. Rome's buses are a more comprehensive way to get around, though the city is small enough that you can walk comfortably to many places.

Florence and especially Venice are cities where walking is not just the most convenient but the preferred way to travel. Otherwise, Florence has a public bus system, and in Venice one travels by canal, whether on a vaporetto, in a gondola, or via a very expensive private boat or taxi.

Maps

The maps in *Great Sleeps Italy* are meant to help locate the hotels and shops in Florence, Rome, and Venice; they are not meant to replace detailed street maps. Most news kiosks and bookstores stock easy-to-follow city maps. Each hotel listing in *Great Sleeps Italy* has a number in parentheses to the right of its name that corresponds to the map key of the appropriate city map. Establishments located outside the boundaries of these maps have no number.

General Information

When to Go

Wouldn't it be wonderful to drop everything and fly to Italy whenever the spirit moved us? Unfortunately, most of us do not lead such charmed lives; we are bound by schedules, budgets, family considerations, and deadlines on all sides. The most important single thing you as a cost-conscious traveler can do is to schedule your trip to Italy in the off-season.

Throughout Italy, the high season is generally from the first of April through October (excluding mid-July to the end of August when it is too hot for most of the natives) and again for the two weeks around Christmas and New Year's. Venice has an additional high season during the two weeks before Lent, when Carnivale is celebrated and the city is filled with unbelievable hordes of partying tourists. As one wag put it, you could drop dead and still remain standing upright in the crowds that pack Piazza San Marco during the last few days of Lent. Having experienced this mad scene, I don't doubt it: you literally cannot move one inch in any direction, and it is scary. For most people, let alone anyone who is even mildly claustrophobic, it is beyond the beyonds—and in addition, prices for everything are out of sight.

August is the traditional vacation month for most in Rome, while Venetians vacation in the damp months of January and February. In Florence, vacations seem to be in July and August, when the heat, humidity, and mosquitoes are at their peak. At these times, services may be reduced and some restaurants may close for a week or more.

Holidays and Events

The following is a list of legal holidays (*giorni festivi*) in Italy, when banks and most stores are closed. Restaurants tend to go with the moment: if business is slow, they will close; otherwise they may be open. It is impossible to nail down exact policies. Hotels are always open, but the third-string staff may be on duty. On the eve of important holidays such as Christmas, New Year's, and the Feast of the Assumption, some stores close for the day at 1 P.M. and the banks close at 11:30 A.M. If the holiday falls on a Thursday or a Tuesday, the Friday and Monday may also be taken to create long weekends. This is called "building a bridge" (*ponte*) from one holiday to another. For example, if May Day falls on a Thursday, many shops will close from Wednesday afternoon until Monday afternoon or Tuesday morning.

January 1	New Year's Day	*Capo d'Anno*
January 6	Epiphany	*La Befana*
March/April	Easter Sunday	*Pasqua* (dates vary)
March/April	Easter Monday	*Lunedì Pasqua* (dates vary)
April 25	Liberation Day	*Venticinque Aprile*

May 1	Labor Day/May Day	*Primo Maggio*
June 2	National Day	*Festa della Repubblica*
August 15	Assumption of the Virgin	*Ferragóst*
November 1	All Saints' Day	*Tutti Santi*
December 8	Feast of the Immaculate Conception	*Festa dell'Immacolata*
December 25	Christmas	*Natale*
December 26	Boxing Day	*Santo Stefano*

Patron Saints' Days

Florence:	June 24	St. John the Baptist's Day (*San Giovanni*)
Rome:	June 29	St. Peter's and St. Paul's Day (*San Pietro e San Paolo*)
Venice:	April 25	St. Mark's Day (*San Marco*)

Tourist Information

For more information about specific events and festivals, or any tourist-related information, contact the Italian tourist offices in the United States. They are on the Internet at www.italiantourism.com. Or write or call them at 630 5th Avenue, Suite 1565, New York, NY 10011 (Tel: 212-245-5618); 500 N. Michigan Avenue, Suite 1850, Chicago, IL 60611 (Tel: 312-467-1550); 12400 Wilshire Boulevard, Suite 300, Los Angeles, CA 90025 (Tel: 310-820-0622).

What to Bring

On a long journey, even a straw weighs heavy.
—Spanish proverb

I hate a room without an open suitcase in it . . . it seems so permanent.
—Zelda Fitgerald

Here is the rule I follow on any trip: take twice as much money as you think you will need, and half as many clothes. Start by laying out all the clothes you want to bring, then put at least half of them back into the closet. Trust me on this, particularly in Italy, where charming little pensiones are often five floors up with no elevator in sight. Coordinate around one color, and use every nook and cranny of your suitcase to its fullest: stuff your shoes, roll your sweaters and underwear, lay plastic garment bags between layers to prevent wrinkling, and pack the suitcase full so things will not slide to a pile at one end. Take the same clothes you would wear in any major metropolitan city. Short shorts, baseball caps, jogging outfits (when not jogging), and bare midriffs, no matter what the temperature, will label you as a gauche tourist. Backless, low-cut, or otherwise abbreviated dresses are always unwelcome in restaurants, many museums, and churches. In fact, St.

Peter's in Rome and St. Mark's Basilica in Venice have dress codes: women must not have bare shoulders, but heads may be uncovered.

If you are in Italy during the hot summer, bring comfortable, light cottons. Synthetics do not breathe and will add to your discomfort. Even though the days can be very hot, nights are often cool, so include a sweater or lightweight jacket. In winter, you will want a warm coat or lined raincoat, a hat (70 percent of body heat goes out through your head), extra sweaters for layering, and perhaps a set of silk underwear and warm nightwear. Many hotels turn off the heat or air-conditioning around midnight, and central heating in many buildings and restaurants is antique at best.

Pack your toiletries and cosmetics in a waterproof bag for their trip in the airplane. Most people learn to do this only after having experienced the mess of uneven airplane pressure blowing off the top of their shampoo bottle.

Most of all, remember: You are not going to a desert island but to Italy, where hundreds of shops sell life's little necessities. No matter what you're looking for, shopping in Italy is a fun cultural experience, and you might even find something unusual to bring back home.

The following list of useful items to pack has been compiled over the years by veteran travelers.

- an extra pair of walking shoes, a pair of flip flops (if you've booked a room without its own bath), walking socks, and a hat
- a plastic bag for damp or dirty laundry
- several inflatable hangers (for in-room laundries) as well as a few hangers you can throw out at the end of the trip
- a bar or bottle of your favorite bath soap and your own shampoo and conditioner
- antiseptic hand wash
- packaged wipes for shoe cleaning, make-up removal, and nail polish removal
- Italian dictionary or phrasebook
- a portable radio with earphones
- a pedometer to keep track of the number of miles you walked (you will be amazed)
- a first-aid kit, a sewing kit with good scissors, and a Swiss army knife
- sunscreen and sunglasses
- copies of vital prescriptions and an extra pair of eyeglasses; Tylenol or something similar
- a rubber doorstop as a security measure
- an adapter plug and transformer for electrical appliances (see "Voltage," page 39)

- a suction hook for the back of the bathroom or bedroom door
- a magnifying mirror with suction attachment
- an alarm clock
- mosquito repellent
- a good book
- an umbrella
- a camera
- extra batteries
- flashlight
- calculator
- extra fold-up travel bag for new purchases and a few sheets of bubble wrap to enclose breakables

Finally, pack common sense and good cheer. They weigh nothing, cost nothing, and no security check can confiscate them.

Disabled Travelers

Italy is slowly improving its services for travelers with special needs. However, while many hotels have rooms they advertise as handicapped accessible, that often means little more than a wide door, a grab-bar by the tub, or a room on the ground floor. Please see the Florence, Rome, and Venice chapters for specific information for disabled travelers in those cities.

General information for disabled travelers can be obtained from the following U.S. companies and organizations:

Directions Unlimited—Empress Travel and Cruises
Bedford Hills, NY 10507
Tel: 800-533-5343
Email: info@cruisesusa.com
Internet: www.empressusa.com

Society for Accessible Travel and Hospitality
347 Fifth Avenue
New York, NY 10016
Tel: 212-447-7284
Email: info@sath.org
Internet: www.sath.org
This is a full-service travel agency with a division specifically for meeting the needs of disabled travelers.

Access-Able Travel Source
www.access-able.com
This is an excellent resource that links disability organizations with individuals worldwide.

Discounts

Hotels

Every *Great Sleeps Italy* hotel listing states if any discounts are offered. The amounts of the discount can vary with the time of the year, room availability, and often the whim of the owner. In most cases, you can count on a 10 to 15 percent discount in the off-season, sometimes a whopping 40 percent. In Rome, discounts are more prevalent on the weekends, whereas in Venice, they are frequently offered during the week. In Florence, it is the luck of the draw. In some cases, discounts are granted specifically to *Great Sleeps Italy* readers who mention the book when reserving and show a copy upon arrival. These hotels are indicated. Finally, just because a hotel doesn't advertise any sort of discount doesn't mean they won't offer one if you ask. Don't be timid about this . . . always ask.

Senior Citizens

It is great to be young, but it pays to be older. Today, more and more people over fifty find themselves with extra time and money on their hands. Statistics show that the bulk of travelers are between forty-five and seventy years of age. Italy is not the best place to find senior citizen discounts, but there are a few savings to be had.

Travelers over sixty can buy the senior citizen's Silver Card (*Carta d'Argento*), a state rail pass good for a 20 percent reduction on Italian train tickets. There are some blackout periods.

Any person sixty or older is given free or reduced admission to state and some private museums, national monuments, cultural events, and cinemas. The key is to ask at the ticket booth and to be prepared to show a passport.

Travelers over fifty-five years young who are willing to bunk in hostels can save significantly on accommodation costs by purchasing an International Youth Hostel Card for $18; this is good for one year. For more, see "Students," below.

The following two U.S.-based organizations are aimed at seniors and are worth contacting if you are planning any trip, not just one to Italy.

American Association of Retired Persons (AARP)
601 E Street NW
Washington, D.C. 20049
Tel: 202-434-2277, 800-424-3410

Elderhostel
75 Federal Street, Third Floor
Boston, MA 02110
Tel: 617-426-7788

Students

If you have youth and energy on your side and are twenty-six years old or younger, bargains abound.

Youth hostels are the cheapest beds around, but you will need an International Youth Hostel Association card. The card is valid for one year and costs $28 for those between eighteen and fifty-four years old; it's $18 for those over fifty-five and free for those seventeen and under. Contact Hostelling International/American Youth Hostels (HI/AYH), which can also provide books listing all the European hostels.

Hostelling International
8401 Colesville Road
Silver Springs, MD 20910
Tel: 202-783-6161
Internet: www.hiusa.org, www.hihostels.com

For discounts on transportation, museums, and other attractions, it is smart to buy the International Student Identity Card (ISIC) if you are a student, or the International Youth Card (IYC) if you are not a student but still under twenty-six. They are also deals for teachers. The cards cost around $22 and are available through STA Travel (see below). In addition, holders receive hotel, restaurant, and cultural discounts at participating establishments as well as accident and medical emergency benefits. Don't leave home without it! Another discount card is the Euro<26 card (www.euro26.org), which is accepted worldwide and available to everyone under age twenty-six.

STA Travel main office
7890 South Hardy Drive, Suite 110
Tempe, AZ 85284
Tel: 800-777-0112
Internet: www.sta.com

The Centro Turistico Studentesco Giovanle (CTS) is a student travel agency in Italy dedicated to furthering travel opportunities for students. This organization has offices in major Italian cities and helps students find accommodations and low airfares, and it's a good place to get connected with the travel-on-a-shoestring crowd.

CTS main office
Via Genova, 16
Rome
Tel: 06 462 0431
Fax: 06 4620 4326
Internet: www.cts.it

Tours and Classes

Whether this is your first visit to Italy or you are a seasoned veteran, time spent with a knowledgeable guide can enhance your trip to Florence, Rome, and Venice in ways you never thought possible, giving you a deeper understanding of these marvelous cities. I have discovered very special people in each city whom I recommend without hesitation: Frank Peters, Ann Reavis, Simone Gaddini, Gabriella Ganugi, and Judy Witts Francini in Florence (see page 48), Scala Reale in Rome (see page 156), and Samantha Durell in Venice (see page 248). In addition to being bilingual, extremely knowledgeable, and well-qualified, they are all passionate about what they do.

Money Matters

If you will be a traveler, have always two bags very full . . . one of patience and another of money.
—*John Florio*

The heaviest baggage for a traveler is an empty purse.
—*German Proverb*

No aspect of your trip has the potential to cause you more grief than money, even if you have enough of it. If you are on a limited budget, try to have a little cushion that will enable you to enjoy a cappuccino on Piazza San Marco in Venice, to stay in a romantic pensione in Florence with a view to the Tuscan hills, or to splurge on a great meal in Rome. Life is too short not to have the happy memories that come from just enjoying the moment without trying to squeeze every penny.

As a practical matter, carrying large amounts of cash, even in a money belt, is risky business. If you bring a few traveler's checks, charge big items on your credit card, convert euros as you go, and use ATMs, you will do well. Also, remember to carry some of your own personal checks. If you suddenly run out of money, you can use them to get cash advances or buy traveler's checks, provided the credit cards you have allow you to do this. Also, try to have a few euros on hand when you arrive. You may pay more for this convenience, but if you change $200 or so before you leave home, you gain the peace of mind and convenience of being able to get to your hotel and get comfortable before having to find a bank or ATM. Airport and train station change booths have long lines and poor rates, and they should be used in emergencies only.

Banks offer the best exchange rate, much better than hotels or exchange windows, which are identified by signs reading "Cambio," "Wechsel," or "Change." Avoid these commercial money-changing operations even if they say "no commission." Believe me, they are getting their commission, and you're paying for it. Estimate your needs carefully. If you overbuy euros, you will lose twice, both in buying and in selling. Every time you change money, someone is making a profit, and I can guarantee that it is not you.

NOTE: Italian banking hours are Monday through Friday from 8:30 A.M. to 1:30 P.M., and 3 or 3:30 P.M. to 4 or 4:30 P.M. All are closed on holidays and sometimes on the afternoon before a major holiday.

ATMs (or Bancomats)

Most major Italian banks have 24-hour automatic teller machines (ATMs), which in Italy are known as Bancomats. If your ATM card is part of an international network, you are in business. I recommend going to a Bancomat during banking hours in case there is a mistake. Sometimes machines will issue a correct receipt, but not the correct amount of money.

Italian Bancomat machines work the same way as ATMs in the United States: you first punch in your personal identification number (PIN) and then the amount of cash you want. It is essential that you check in advance on the limits of withdrawals and cash advances within specific time periods. Also ask whether your bank card or credit card PIN number will need to be reissued for use in Italy, since Italian machines only accept four-digit PIN numbers. Your U.S. bank debit or credit card will also charge you for using a foreign ATM; on the other hand, you will be getting a wholesale conversion rate that is usually better than you would get at a bank or currency exchange office.

Finally, plan ahead. Find out the ATM locations and the names of corresponding affiliated cash machine networks before you leave home. For MasterCard Cirrus locations, call 800-4-CIRRUS. For Visa Plus locations, call 800-THE-PLUS. To enroll in the American Express foreign ATM program, call 800-CASH-NOW.

Credit Cards

Despite the fact that Italy is the world's fifth-largest industrial nation, some smaller hotels—especially in the student, hostel, and Holy Hotel categories—have not kept pace with the rest of the world in accepting plastic instead of cash. Quite often a place will accept a particular credit card and then stop accepting it for no apparent reason, only to start again. All the *Great Sleeps Italy* listings indicate which credit cards, if any, are accepted.

I recommend using a credit card whenever possible; it's convenient, quick, safe, and means delayed billing of up to four to six weeks after purchase. American Express, Diners Club, MasterCard, and Visa convert foreign purchases at a wholesale market rate, then add a conversion fee. On top of that, many issuing banks (with the exception of Capital One and MBNA) add their own foreign purchase charges. Before you leave home, contact the credit card companies whose cards you will be using and find out whether they charge additional fees (it can be up to 4 percent) for transactions in foreign currencies, and then use the card that charges the least. Even with the added charges, the currency conversion rates of most major credit companies are far better than those offered by exchange kiosks, which charge between 5 and 8 percent to convert cash or traveler's checks. Remember, though, that the currency conversion rate is made at the time of processing, not at the time of purchase—which will work for or against you depending on currency rates.

In Italy and all of Europe, MasterCard is Eurocard, and Visa is Carte Bleu. Here are a few other credit card tips:

1. Before using your credit card, ask the store or hotel if there is any discount or incentive to pay in cash.

2. Keep a copy of all your credit card numbers with you and leave another copy at home.

3. Save your receipts to check against the statement when it arrives. Errors are all too frequent.

4. Finally, emergency check cashing is a benefit for many cardholders, as is free car-rental insurance. Check with your issuing bank to determine the list of benefits you have; you may be pleasantly surprised.

If your card is lost or stolen, report it immediately. Contact the local police, then report the loss to the credit card company. When you get home, contact your insurance agent to see if the loss is covered. Please note that you must have a police report if you are filing an insurance claim.

American Express (U.S.) 800-233-5432; toll-free in Italy 800 874 333, 800 864 046 (card emergencies), 1678-72000 (traveler's check emergencies); www.americanexpress.com

Diner's Club   (U.S.) 800-234-6377; toll-free in Italy 800 864 064; www.dinersclubus.com

MasterCard (U.S.) 800-307-7309; toll-free in Italy 800 870 866; www.mastercard.com

Visa (U.S.) 800-877-232; toll-free in Italy 800 877 232; www.visa.com

Traveler's Checks

ATMs have almost driven traveler's checks to extinction. However, traveler's checks can be preferable because if they are lost or stolen, there is some recourse and they will be replaced. You will always get a better exchange rate for traveler's checks than for cash, but the real cost lies in what you spent to get the traveler's checks in the first place and what commission you pay to cash them.

American Express provides the most convenient services. Cardholders can order traveler's checks by phone, at participating banks, or at credit unions free of charge with a gold card, or for a 1 percent commission with a green card. Nonmembers also pay the 1 percent commission. You can exchange American Express traveler's checks to euros without paying a commission at any American Express office, which are located in Rome, Florence, and Venice (and twelve other Italian cities). American Express cardholders can also write a personal check for traveler's checks at any of these offices. For a directory of American Express services and offices, ask for the American Express Traveler's Companion. Call 800-673-3782 to order checks or get further information.

In addition, Citicorp banks sell traveler's checks that give the holder access to a twenty-four-hour SOS line that provides travel-related services. For information, call 800-645-6556. Thomas Cook/MasterCard International (Tel: 800-223-7373) issues traveler's checks that are widely accepted. And Visa (Tel: 800-227-6811) sells traveler's checks through many U.S. banks and at AAA offices, but there can be a limit.

REMEMBER: Always keep a separate record of your traveler's check numbers and the receipt of purchase. On the back of this receipt will be emergency numbers to call in case they are lost or stolen.

Wiring Money to Italy

Sometimes we need a little help from home—and fast. One way is to have someone send you an American Express MoneyGram (Tel: 800-926-9400). You do not have to be an American Express cardholder to send or receive a MoneyGram. You can send up to $10,000 using a credit card, or if you only have cash, you can send up to $1,000. A MoneyGram can be sent and ready for you to pick up in less than an hour! Fees vary according to the amount of money sent, but they average from 3 to 10 percent. When you pick up your money, you will have to know the transaction number from the sender at home and show ID.

Another option is Western Union (Tel: 800-325-6000).

Tipping

Tipping is definitely part of the Italian way of life and is expected on almost all levels of service. However, you are not required to tip if the service is poor or rude.

Hotels	
Maids	1€ per day
Doorman for calling a taxi	1€
Bellboys and porters	1€ per bag; 2.50–5€ for extra services
Concierge	2–5€ for each service given
Room service	1€
Restaurants	15 percent service is often included in or added to the bill—this is the tip. If service has been exceptional, leave 5–10 percent more or round off the total.
Caffès and bars	0.30–0.50€ for whatever you drink standing at a coffee bar; 0.50–1€ for table service in a sidewalk *caffè*
Museum and church offerings	1€ per person
Theater usher	0.50€ per person
Service stations	Nothing expected
Taxis	Nothing expected, but always pleased with 5–10 percent of metered fare
Train station and airport porters	They charge a fixed rate per bag. Tip an extra 0.50–1€ per bag, more if they have been very helpful.
Washroom attendants	0.20–0.30€
Beauty parlors and barber shops	10 to 15 percent for each person who serves you, plus 1–2€ for the shampoo girl

NOTE: Beware of the restaurant credit card tipping scam. Many Italian restaurants automatically add a 12 to 15 percent gratuity (or service charge) to every bill, or they will include the service charge in the cost of the meal; however, when you charge your meal to a credit card, some will write the total amount of the bill at the top of the charge slip and leave the boxes marked "gratuity" or "tip" and "total" empty, hoping that you will forget that the gratuity has already been included and add it again. Do not fall for this. If the service has already been added or included, draw a line from the top figure to the total at the bottom of the sheet, then write in the total figure yourself. If you are leaving a tip on top of this total, leave it in cash. Tips left on credit cards are not properly distributed. It is better to leave any tip in cash.

Staying in Touch

Telephone

It has been said that even the pope is at the mercy of the Italian telephone system. The wide range of digits is just the start of the fun, fascination, and challenge of dialing in Italy. Note that when calling (or faxing) a land-line telephone number in Florence, Rome, and Venice, you must always dial the entire city code (which is equivalent to an area code), including the 0, no matter where you're calling from. For instance, if you are in Rome and want to call or fax across the street, you must still dial 06, Rome's city code, before the number. The same is true if you are calling from the United States, or from anywhere. See "Calls Made to Italy," page 35, for a list of all the city and country codes. However, this being the Italian phone system, logic takes a backseat to whimsy: when calling an Italian cell phone within Italy, the city code is omitted.

Italy has three types of public telephones, two of which are obsolete: token (*gettoni*) phones, coin telephones, and card phones. The *gettoni* are holdovers from the days of Caesar and are antique curiosities, and coin telephones are also dinosaurs. (If you get a handful of *gettoni* coins as change in a bar, insist on real coins.)

It is easy to make a call from a public telephone using a phone card (*schede telefoniche*). You can buy these phone cards from *tabacchi,* post offices, some bars, and news agents, and they come in denominations of 5 to 20€. When you insert the card, a meter subtracts talk time from it as you speak and displays the remaining value. Don't leave your card behind; chances are you will still have time left on it. Some phones will also take credit cards. Please remember that unless you are calling a toll-free number, all calls made from any phone in Italy, even if it is just next door, cost the caller. Toll-free numbers (*numeri verdi*) begin with 167, 1678, or 800; cell phone numbers begin with a three-digit prefix such as 330. U.S. toll-free numbers are not toll-free from Italy. When dialing them, you must first dial 880, and then the call is no longer free. Domestic Italian telephone charges are highest between 8 A.M. and 6:30 P.M. Monday through Friday and 8 A.M. to 1 P.M. Saturday. A local call from a public phone will cost from 0.10 to 0.20€ for a three-minute call during peak time.

If you need help making a local call in Italy, dial 12 for National Directory Assistance. English-speaking operators are reached by dialing 170.

Calls Made from Italy

The cheapest and easiest way to make an international call is to use an international telephone card. These are sold for face value from change kiosks (the only time you should do business with these places) or from a *tabacci* (tobacconist shop). These are easy to use from your hotel room or a public phone booth and come in denominations of up to 20€. You can also use an international phone card purchased before leaving home from a warehouse club (Costco, Sam's Club), or use your own telephone calling card. No matter what method of payment you use, calls to the United States and Canada are lowest between 11 P.M. and 8 A.M. from Monday through Friday and 11 P.M. to 2 P.M. on weekends.

Hotels are well known for sticking guests with as much as a 200 percent surcharge for long-distance and international calls. Check with the hotel desk, and if they do add a surcharge, go to a public phone to make the call.

If you want to make a collect call, or bill a call to your calling card (which will be cheaper than billing it to a credit card), dial 172-1011. An English-speaking operator will come on the line to assist you. To call the United States and Canada from any place in Italy, you must dial the following sequence: 00 plus the country code (1 for the United States and Canada), then the area code and the number you are calling (thus, 001-213-123-4567). For an international, English-speaking operator, dial 170. For international directory assistance, or if you are having a problem dialing out of the country, dial 4176.

Calls Made to Italy

To call or fax Italy direct from abroad, dial 011, the country code, the city code (including the 0 preceding it), and then the number you are calling. For example, for a call to Florence, dial 011 39 055 123 4567.

Country code for Italy	39
City code for Florence	055
City code for Rome	06
City code for Venice	041

Email and the Internet

Using the Internet and sending email is rapidly becoming an integral part of daily life in Italy. However, bringing a laptop and the necessary adaptors can be a hassle, and logging on in your hotel room can be expensive. To avoid this, leave the laptop at home and go to a cybercafe. They are everywhere, even in laundromats. It makes perfect sense. You can accompolish two things at once: get clean and get connected. More and more hotels have an Internet-ready terminal where guests can send free emails or log on to the Internet with a credit card. If you are going to be in one place for more than a few days and know you will be doing a lot of digital communicating, buy a subscription card; these are good for anywhere from a couple of hours to up to 250 hours.

If you do bring a laptop, you need the correct telephone adaptor plug; contact Magellan's (Tel: 800 962 4943; Internet: www.magellans.com) for assistance.

Safety and Security

Caution and common sense should be exercised on a trip to Italy, just as they should be when traveling anywhere. Keep your eyes open, be aware of your immediate surroundings, and do not take any chances you would not take back home. The biggest menaces are pickpockets and bands of gypsies, particularly children who are well-versed in the art of distraction and diversion. These thieving groups operate in a swarming mass, fluttering newspapers to divert your attention as they get in and out of your pockets before you know what hit you. Extreme caution should be exercised on crowded buses and the metro during the morning and evening rush hour. If you are on a bus and know you have been robbed, immediately alert the driver, who will lock the doors and drive to the nearest police station. In Rome, it is also wise to avoid the Via Veneto in the evening.

In general, keep the following advice in mind while traveling in Italy.

1. Make two copies of your passport, credit cards, airline tickets, hotel and car rental confirmation letters, and any other documents without which, if they were to be lost or stolen, you would be either in trouble or very inconvenienced. Take one copy with you and leave a second copy with someone at home. This one precautionary step could save you hours of time should you lose these vital papers.

2. Try to blend in. Leave at home all jewelry, expensive watches, high-visibility wardrobes, and anything else you cannot bear to lose.

3. Do not carry all your valuables in one place . . . distribute them. Use the hotel safe for everything but a photocopy of your passport, one credit card, and the amount of cash you think you will need for the day, and carry these in separate places on your person—and never in a hip wallet or fanny pack.

4. Use a money belt or a necklace purse worn inside your clothing, even if it feels bulky and uncomfortable. Money belts and necklace purses will also protect you against skilled thieves who use razors to slash open backpacks and fanny packs. The fanny pack is the biggest giveaway that you are a tourist, and it is especially vulnerable in a distraction theft, when it can be cut from your waist in seconds. Large, bulging backpacks are another red flag that says "tourist." If you are carrying a backpack, buy a small combination padlock and slip it through the zippers. If you don't have a lock, use a safety pin.

5. If you carry a purse, buy a sturdy one with a secure clasp, and carry it crosswise with the clasp against you and on the side of your body away from the street. Better yet, keep it under your jacket or coat, if posssible. Thieves on darting Vespas ride through the streets searching for likely victims, and they simply yank the purses from women's shoulders.

6. Keep a hand on your bags at all times. Don't drape your bag over a restaurant chair, or leave it in a dressing room if trying on clothes.

7. Don't flash cash. At any time, but especially when leaving a bank, ATM, or other change facility, never count money in public.

8. In cars, do not leave luggage locked inside, and open the door of the glove compartment to show potential thieves that nothing is there. Remove the radio when you leave your car. Never travel with your car unlocked. The U.S. State Department warns that any car, whether parked or moving, can be a potential target for armed robbery.

9. At night, stay on brightly lit streets and walk with purpose. It is also smart to walk in groups at night.

10. If you are a victim of theft, always file a report (*denunciare*) with the police. You will need it for your own insurance, and it is helpful in case anything is eventually found.

11. There is a zero-tolerance law in Italy regarding drugs, and possession of even the smallest amount of any narcotic, including marijuana, is now illegal. All foreigners are subject to Italian law. If you are caught with drugs, the U.S. government can do little to help you: they send consular officers to visit you in jail, provide a list of attorneys, and inform your family. They cannot repatriate you to a prison on U.S. soil, and they have nothing to do with your sentencing, let alone your trial. For further information, read Travel Warning on Drugs Abroad, a free pamphlet put out by the Bureau of Consular Affairs, Department of State, Washington, D.C. 20520; Tel: 202-647-1488.

12. Anywhere in Italy, if you find yourself in a dangerous situation, call 113, the Public Emergency Assistance number for the State Police and First Aid. The military police, at 112, might be of help, and so could the Italian automobile club (ACI), at 116, if you need immediate assistance due to a crisis on the road.

Hotel Security

Hotel security centers around theft. Note that hotel liability tends to be limited and often provides absolutely no compensation for a traveler's losses incurred at the hotel. If something is stolen from your room, you may have little recourse unless you can prove gross negligence on the part of the hotel, which is also an apt description if you leave your valuables in plain sight in the first place. Here are some points to keep in mind:

1. Avoid rooms on the ground floor and those near fire escapes.

2. Never leave valuables exposed, even when sleeping. Valuables include more than just money and jewelry. Consider camcorders, cameras, computers, personal and travel documents, and CD players.

3. Nothing is gained by locking valuables in your suitcase. What is to prevent someone from just taking the entire suitcase? It has happened often. When you leave your room, close and lock the windows and lock up valuables. There are no hiding places thieves do not know about. Almost all hotels have office or in-room safes. Use them both.

4. If you are a victim of a theft, file a complete report with the local police immediately. This police report is required if you are filing for compensation from your own insurance company, or worse yet, involved in a lawsuit.

5. Finally, if you don't need it on your trip, leave it home.

Insurance

No one plans on a crisis, whether medical or otherwise, that requires cutting a trip short or abandoning it altogether. Travel insurance is seldom a great bargain, but it does buy you protection and, just as important, peace of mind should these unfortunate circumstances occur.

Hotel cancellations less than forty-eight hours prior to arrival can result in charges unless the room can be relet. This is, frankly, not worth covering with an insurance policy. However, if you have prepaid a large portion of your trip, such as rented a flat and paid a big chunk in advance, you are crazy not to buy cancellation insurance. Italian serviced apartments, individual apartment owners, and the agencies representing them are merciless when it comes to refunds. Their policy is very simple: No refunds. Period.

Before your departure, check with your health-care plan to see what, if any, medical coverage you will have, and seriously consider taking out a supplemental policy to fill in the gaps. The amount you spend in supplemental insurance will be nothing compared to a foreign medical emergency with you picking up the tab. If you do need medical attention, most medical facilities will require that you pay for your treatment in full at the time of service. Do not assume that they will file claims for you or participate in any medical plan you may belong to. It will be up to you to get your claim processed and be reimbursed.

Read through your homeowner's policy and see if it covers you in any way when you are traveling, and if it is lacking, again consider adding a floater policy for the duration of your trip, especially if you are traveling with a laptop or other expensive equipment.

Finally, if you are an American Express Card member, call 800-297-2900 to find out about their Travel Medical Protection Insurance coverage for members. American Express Global Assist (Tel: 800-554-2639; Internet: www.americanexpress.com) is another service for cardholders who need emergency medical, legal, or financial assistance while traveling.

There are many ways to purchase travel insurance: through travel agents, apartment rental agencies, and from specialized travel companies. The Automobile Club of American has a complete list of carriers. For a comparison of many companies, visit www.insuremytrip.com or www .quotetravelinsurance.com.

Here are a few companies:

Access America, Inc.: 800-284-8300, www.accessamerica.com
CSA travel protection: 800-554-2639, www.csatravelprotection.com
Medex Insurance Services: 800-732-5309, www.medexassist.com

Travelex: 800-228-9792, www.travelex-ins.com
Safeware (will insure laptops): www.safeware.com
Wallach: 800-237-6615, www.wallach.com

Time

Italy is one hour ahead of Greenwich Mean Time (GMT), six hours ahead of Eastern Standard Time, and nine hours ahead of Pacific Standard Time. Daylight Savings Time is observed from April 1 to October 31. In Italy, time is based on the twenty-four-hour clock (often referred to as military time); thus, 0700 is 7 A.M., 1200 is noon, and 1600 is 4 P.M.

Standards of Measure

Italy uses the metric system. Here are the conversions.

$$
\begin{aligned}
1 \text{ inch} &= 2.54 \text{ centimeters} \\
1 \text{ mile} &= 1.61 \text{ kilometers} \\
1 \text{ ounce} &= 28 \text{ grams} \\
1 \text{ pound} &= 0.45 \text{ kilograms} \\
1 \text{ quart} &= 0.95 \text{ liter} \\
1 \text{ gallon} &= 3.8 \text{ liters} \\
1 \text{ centimeter} &= 0.4 \text{ inch} \\
1 \text{ kilometer} &= 0.62 \text{ miles} \\
1 \text{ gram} &= 0.04 \text{ ounces} \\
1 \text{ kilogram} &= 2.2 \text{ pounds} \\
1 \text{ liter} &= 1.06 \text{ quarts}
\end{aligned}
$$

How much is that in miles, feet, pounds, or degrees? Here is how to do the conversions.

Kilometers/miles: To change kilometers to miles, multiply the kilometers by .621. To change miles to kilometers, multiply the miles by 1.61.

Meters/feet: To change meters to feet, multiply the meters by 3.28. To change feet to meters, multiply the feet by .305.

Kilograms/pounds: To change kilograms to pounds, multiply the kilograms by 2.20. To change pounds to kilograms, multiply the pounds by .453.

Celsius/Fahrenheit: To change Celsius to Fahrenheit, double the Celsius figure and add 30. If the Celsius figure is below zero, double the subzero number and subtract it from 32.

Voltage

Italian electrical circuits are wired at 220 volts. You will need a transformer and an adapter plug for appliances you bring that operate on 110 volts. Things such as hair dryers and hair curling irons may have switches that convert the appliance from one voltage to another. This only eliminates the need for a transformer, not for the adapter plug. If you are bringing your laptop, be sure to have a surge protector, otherwise you could end up damaging your machine. Magellan's (Tel: 800-962-4943; Internet: www.magellans.com) is a travel mail-order company that carries everything you will ever need.

FLORENCE

There is a catch to Florence; no matter how many times you visit, you are never satisfied. Everyone leaves longing to return.
—Fulvia Ferragamo

Of all the places I have seen in Italy, it is the one by far I should most covet to live in. It is the ideal of an Italian city, once great, now a shadow of itself.
—William Hazlitt, Notes of a Journey through France and Italy, *1826*

Florence, the world's greatest celebration of the triumph of the human spirit, has long been regarded as the birthplace of the Renaissance and the Athens of modern civilization. Under the ruling of the powerful Medici family, Florence was decorated with churches and palaces, making it one of the most incredible living museums in the world. In testimony to this, her four hundred thousand residents are host to five million yearly visitors.

If you like to walk, Florence is your city. Almost everything a visitor wants to see and do is easy to manage on foot. Explore her beautiful history by wandering down medieval streets and narrow lanes that have not changed in centuries. Wherever you turn, elegant Florence is a feast for the eyes and the soul, whether you are admiring the River Arno from the Ponte Vecchio, strolling through the Boboli Gardens with the hazy Tuscan hills in the distance, or losing yourself for hours in one of her many churches and museums.

The good news about accommodations is that whatever your budget—from palatial to penny-pinching—you will be able to find a room in Florence, thanks to the relaxing of hotel licensing. In the last few years, Florence has added 1,200 to 1,500 new rooms; for the fifty years prior, only a handful of new-room licenses were granted. Many of the grand old villas of Florence have now been converted into hotels. These range from simple, fourth-floor pensiones (no elevator, of course) to grand luxury palaces. One of the most welcome additions to the Florence hotel scene has been the *affitta camere,* a concept that has taken the city by storm and given many one- and two-star hotels a serious run for their money. Their philosophy is "less is more." *Affitta camere* are small operations that by law can have no more than ten to twelve rooms and thus do not qualify for the star-rating system. There is seldom a proper lobby or breakfast room, often no elevator, never a porter, and the reception desk is not staffed around the clock. What they do offer are charming, well-decorated rooms, usually with private facilities, the usual hotel maid services, and prices to fit almost all budgets.

Whenever possible when visiting Florence, take advantage of lower rates between November and February, with the exception of Christmas and New Year's, and again during July and August. If you come in July or August, be prepared to share your stay with swarms of tourists and very aggressive mosquitoes. To aggravate the mosquito nuisance, only a handful of hotels have screens; however, with the exception of the low-end budget hotels, air-conditioning is standard.

More and more people are discovering the year-round charms and beauty of the Tuscan countryside. If your time allows, consider at least a day trip to this lovely region. Better yet, plan an extended stay, To help you get started, consult "Villas in Tuscany," page 139.

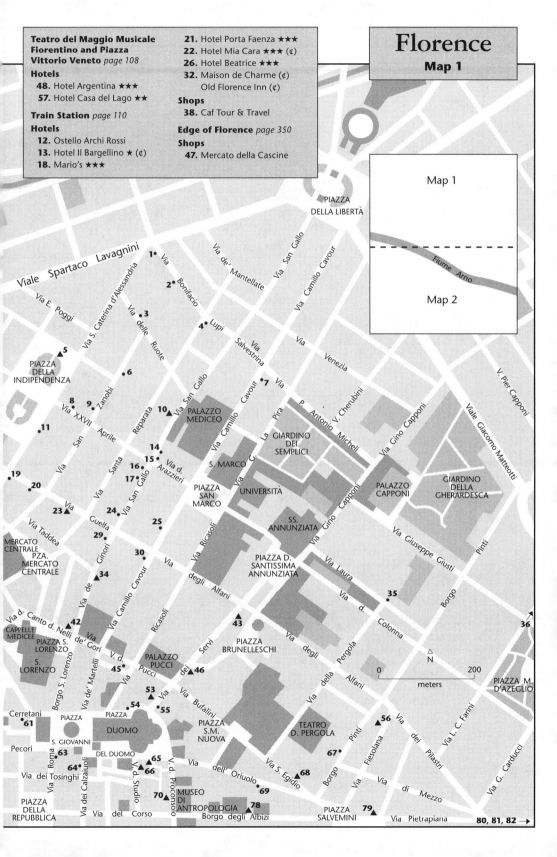

Florence
Map 1

Map 1

Map 2

Fiume Arno

Viale Spartaco Lavagnini

PIAZZA DELLA LIBERTÀ

Via E. Poggi

Via S. Caterina d'Alessandria

Via delle Ruote

Via Bonifacio

Via de' Mantellate

Via San Gallo

Via Camillo Cavour

1•

2•

•3

4• Lupi

•5

PIAZZA DELLA INDIPENDENZA

•6

Via Salvestrina

•7 Via

Via Venezia

V. Pier Capponi

8• 9• Zanobi

Via XXVII Aprile

Reparata

San

10▲ PALAZZO MEDICEO

Via Camillo Cavour

La Pira

P. Antonio V. Cherubini

GIARDINO DEI SEMPLICI

Via Gino Capponi

Viale Giacomo Matteotti

•11

14•

15•

16•

17•

Via Santa

Via San Gallo

Via d. Arazzieri

S. MARCO

PIAZZA SAN MARCO

UNIVERSITÀ

PALAZZO CAPPONI

GIARDINO DELLA GHERARDESCA

•19

•20

23▲

24•

25•

Via Guelfa

Via San Gallo

Via Ricasoli

SS. ANNUNZIATA

Via Gino Capponi

Via Giuseppe Giusti

Pinti

MERCATO CENTRALE PZA. MERCATO CENTRALE

29•

30•

34▲

Via de Ginori

Via Camillo Cavour

Via degli Alfani

PIAZZA D. SANTISSIMA ANNUNZIATA

Via Laura

Via d.

35•

Borgo

Via d. Canto d. Nelli

42▲

CAPPELLE MEDICEE

PIAZZA S. LORENZO

S. LORENZO

Via de' Gori

Borgo S. Lorenzo

Ricasoli

43▲

Servi

PIAZZA BRUNELLESCHI

Via degli

Colonna

Via della Pergola

Alfani

36

N

0   200

meters

PIAZZA M. D'AZEGLIO

Via de' Martelli

45•

V. d. Pucci

PALAZZO PUCCI

▲46

Cerretani

•61

PIAZZA

S. GIOVANNI

DUOMO

PIAZZA

53•

54•

•55

Via Bufalini

PIAZZA S.M. NUOVA

TEATRO D. PERGOLA

56▲ Via dei Pilastri

Via L. C. Farini

Via G. Carducci

Pecori

•63 Via Roma

64• 65•

•66

DEL DUOMO

V. d. Studio

V. d. Proconsolo

Via dell' Oriuolo

Via S. Egidio

•67

Pinti

Fiesolana

Borgo

Via

Via di Mezzo

Via dei Tosinghi

Via dei Calzaiuoli

70•

MUSEO DI ANTROPOLOGIA

•69

•68

78▲

79▲

PIAZZA SALVEMINI

PIAZZA DELLA REPUBBLICA

Via del Corso

Borgo degli Albizi

PIAZZA S.M. NUOVA

Via Pietrapiana

80, 81, 82 →

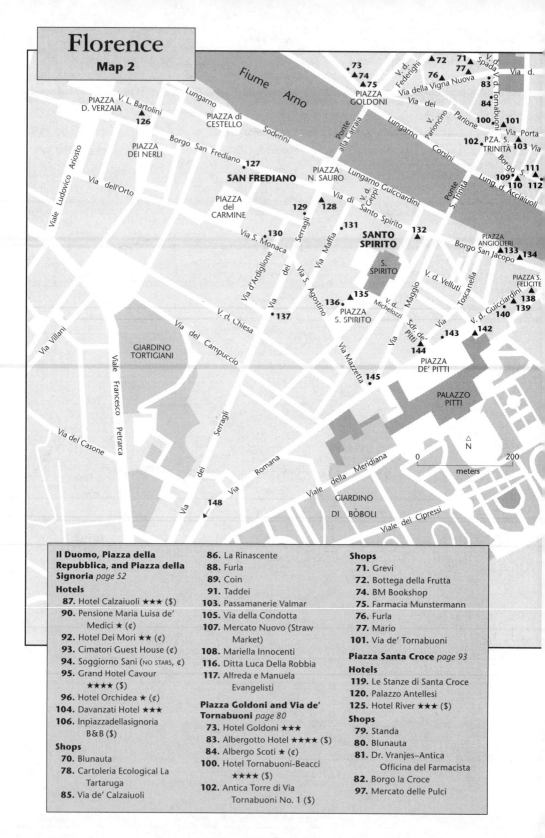

Florence
Map 2

Fiume Arno

PIAZZA D. VERZAIA
V. L. Bartolini
• **126**

Lungarno

PIAZZA di CESTELLO

Soderini

Borgo San Frediano
• **127**

PIAZZA DEI NERLI

SAN FREDIANO

PIAZZA N. SAURO

• **73**
▲ **74**
▲ **75**

V. d. Federighi
▲ **72** **71** ▲
76 ▲ **77** ▲

PIAZZA GOLDONI

Via della Vigna Nuova
Via dei

V. d. Spada
Via d.
83 ▲

84 ▲

V. Parioncino Parione
100 • ▲ **101**

V. d. Tornabuoni

Lungarno Corsini

Lungarno Guicciardini

Ponte alla Carraia

Via **Porta**

102 • PZA. S. TRINITÀ **103** Via

Borgo S.

Via dell'Orto

Viale Ludovico Ariosto

Via dell'Orto

PIAZZA del CARMINE

• **129** ▲ **128**

131 •

Serragli

Via di Santo Spirito

V. d. Geppi

SANTO SPIRITO

▲ **132**

Ponte S. Trinità

Lung. d'Acciaiuoli
109 ▲ ▲ **111**
110 ▲ **112**

PIAZZA ANGIOLIERI
Borgo San Jacopo ▲ **133** ▲ **134**

Via S. Monaca • **130**

Via d'Ardiglione

Via dei

Via S. Agostino

Via Maffia

S. SPIRITO

▲ **135**
136 •
• **137**

PIAZZA S. SPIRITO

V. d. Michelozzi

V. d. Velluti

V. d. Maggio

Toscanella

PIAZZA S. FELICITE
138 ▲
139 ▲

V. d. Guicciardini
140 ▲

Via del Campuccio

V. d. Chiesa

GIARDINO TORTIGIANI

Viale Francesco Petrarca

Via Villani

Via del Casone

Serragli

Via dei

Sdr. de' Pitti

Via

• **143** ▲ **142**

144 •

PIAZZA DE' PITTI

• **145**

Via Mazzetta

PALAZZO PITTI

△ N

0 _____ 200
meters

Romana

Viale della Meridiana

GIARDINO DI BÒBOLI

• **148**
↙

Viale dei Cipressi

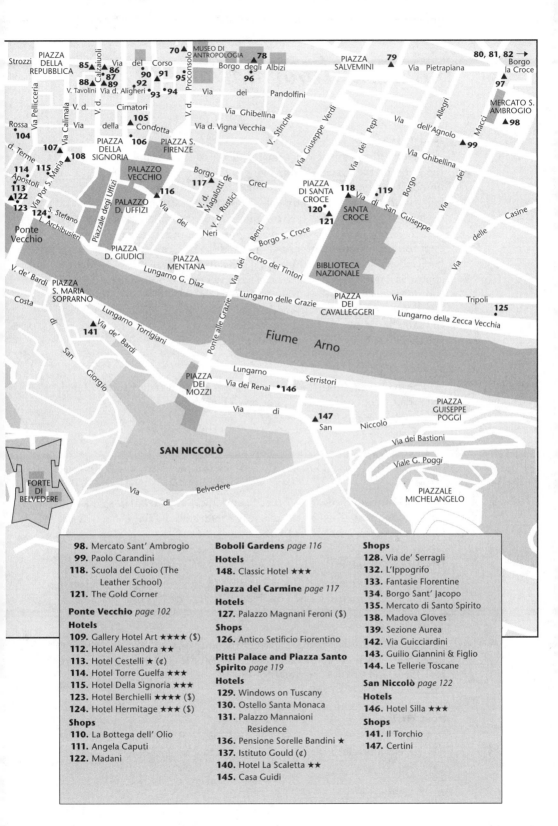

98. Mercato Sant' Ambrogio
99. Paolo Carandini
118. Scuola del Cuoio (The Leather School)
121. The Gold Corner

Ponte Vecchio *page 102*
Hotels
109. Gallery Hotel Art ★★★★ ($)
112. Hotel Alessandra ★★
113. Hotel Cestelli ★ (¢)
114. Hotel Torre Guelfa ★★★
115. Hotel Della Signoria ★★★
123. Hotel Berchielli ★★★★ ($)
124. Hotel Hermitage ★★★ ($)

Shops
110. La Bottega dell' Olio
111. Angela Caputi
122. Madani

Boboli Gardens *page 116*
Hotels
148. Classic Hotel ★★★

Piazza del Carmine *page 117*
Hotels
127. Palazzo Magnani Feroni ($)

Shops
126. Antico Setificio Fiorentino

Pitti Palace and Piazza Santo Spirito *page 119*
Hotels
129. Windows on Tuscany
130. Ostello Santa Monaca
131. Palazzo Mannaioni Residence
136. Pensione Sorelle Bandini ★
137. Istituto Gould (¢)
140. Hotel La Scaletta ★★
145. Casa Guidi

Shops
128. Via de' Serragli
132. L'Ippogrifo
133. Fantasie Florentine
134. Borgo Sant' Jacopo
135. Mercato di Santo Spirito
138. Madova Gloves
139. Sezione Aurea
142. Via Guicciardini
143. Guilio Giannini & Figlio
144. Le Tellerie Toscane

San Niccolò *page 122*
Hotels
146. Hotel Silla ★★★

Shops
141. Il Torchio
147. Certini

General Information

Addresses

Street addresses in Florence are difficult to understand until you get the hang of the system. Unknowing visitors, faced with a sequence of numbers that makes no apparent sense, have been known to collapse into hair pulling and serious arguments out of sheer frustration. However, once deciphered, the system is easy to follow: Addresses follow two numbered sequences, one in red and one in black. The red numbers are for commercial establishments (restaurants and shops), and the black are for residences and hotels. Black addresses usually appear as a number only, while red addresses appear as a number followed by the letter *r*. The two numbered sequences run independently of each other, so that you will see 21r, 45, 23r, 47, and 49 all running next to one another on the same side of the street, or on the same building. To find your destination, you just have to remember whether you are looking for a red or a black number.

Tourist Offices

The main tourist office also takes reports of unfair treatment at a hotel, restaurant, shop, or any other location in Florence:

Via Cavour, 1/r
Tel: 055 29 08 32
Internet: www.firenze.turismo.toscana.it
Open: Mon–Sat 8:15 A.M.–7:15 P.M., in summer also Sun 8:30 A.M.–1:30 P.M.

Other tourist offices are at Borgo Santa Croce, 29/r (Tel: 055 23 40 444; Open: Mon–Sat 9 A.M.–2 P.M.) and at the train station (Tel: 055 21 22 45; Open: Daily 8:30 A.M.–7 P.M.).

Disabled Travelers

For train information, call 055 235 2275 (daily 7 A.M.–9 P.M.). English is spoken. At the train station, a disabled assistance desk is near platform 5.

Consulates

The U.S. Consulate is at Lungarno Amerigo Vespucci, 38r; Tel: 055 266 951; Open: Mon–Fri 9 A.M.–12:30 P.M., 2–3:30 P.M. The British Consulate is at Lungarno Corsini, 2r; Tel: 055 28 41 33; Open: Mon–Fri 9:30 A.M.–12:30 P.M., 2:30–4:30 P.M.

Post Office

Florence's main post office is at Via Pellicceria, 3, first floor; Tel: 055 27 361; Open: Mon–Fri 8:15 A.M.–7 P.M., Sat 8:15 A.M.–12:30 P.M.

Lost Property

If you lose anything while in Florence, call the Ufficio Oggetti Ritrovati, via Circondaria, 19; Tel: 055 328 3942/3943; Open: Mon–Sat 9 A.M.–noon. See "Transportation," page 51, for who to call if you lose something in a plane, train, or taxi.

Telephone

The Florence city code is 055, and this must be dialed before any land-line number in Florence. However, when dialing a cell phone number, the city code is omitted. If you need assistance making an international call, you can dial 4176 from 7 A.M.–9 P.M. For further information on Italian telephones, see "Staying in Touch," page 34.

Emergency Numbers

General emergency	113
Ambulance, medical emergencies, night doctor	118
Fire	115
Police	112
Central Florence Police Station	055 49 771

Medical Treatment

In a medical emergency, dial 118 for an ambulance. For other problems, resources in Florence include the Tourist Medical Service (Via Lorenzo Il Magnifico, 59; Tel: 055 47 54 11), which is a private medical group with multilingual doctors who will make house or hotel calls, or see you by appointment. Home visits are available 24/7; a walk-in service is open six days a week: Mon–Fri 11 A.M.–noon, 5–6 P.M., Sat 11 A.M.–noon.

Dr. Stephen Kerr, a private English-speaking doctor, takes appointments Mon–Fri 10 A.M.–3 P.M., and walk-ins from 3–5 A.M. (Via Porta Rossa, 1; Tel: 055 288 055, cell 335 836 1682; Email kerr@iol.it; Internet www.dr-kerr.com).

You can make appointments to see a homeopathic doctor at Ambulatorio Santa Maria Novella, Piazza Santa Maria Novella, 24; Tel: 055 28 01 43. There is an English-speaking homeopathic pharmacy at Via dei Banchi, 18/20r; Tel: 055 21 11 59; Open: Mon–Sat, 9 A.M.–1 P.M., 4–8 P.M.

Pharmacies

For problems that are not serious, pharmacists in Italy dispense informal medical advice and nonprescription drugs. You can identify a pharmacy by a large, lighted green cross hanging outside.

Twenty-four-hour pharmacies include Farmacia Communale, inside S. M. Novella Train Station, No. 13 (Tel: 055 21 67 61); Farmacia Molteni, Via Calzaiuoli, 7r (Tel: 055 21 54 72); Farmacia S. Antonio, Piazza San Giovanni, 17r (Tel: 055 21 07 36). The last two speak some English.

Money Matters

For commission-free currency exchange and other travel-related matters, the multilingual staff at American Express is helpful. There is no commission fee for student card holders on cash advances or wiring money.

American Express
Via Dante Alighieri, 22/r
Tel: 055 50 981; lost or stolen traveler's checks, 800 872 000; lost or stolen credit cards, 06 722 80371
Open: Mon–Fri 9 A.M.–5:30 P.M.

Travelex
Lungarno Acciaiuoli 6/12
Tel: 055 28 97 81
Open: Mon–Sat 9 A.M.–6 P.M., Sun 9:30 A.M.–5 P.M.

To report lost credit cards besides American Express:

Diners Club	800 864 064
MasterCard	800 870 866
Visa	800 877 232

If you need to wire money while in Florence, call Western Union (Tel: 800 220 055 or 800 464 464).

Museum Tickets

Every visitor to Florence wants to see the world-famous art collection in the Uffizi Gallery and the statue of David at the Accademia Gallery. As such, the line starts forming at daybreak and by 9 A.M. is snaking several blocks along the river. Who needs this on a vacation? No one, and you can avoid it by buying your tickets ahead of time. The Uffizi Gallery sells tickets ahead for a specific day and time (Tel: 055 47 19 60; Internet: www.musa.uffizi.firenze.it), as does the Website www.weekendafirenze.com. There is a nominal charge for advance bookings, but you'll consider it money well-spent when you see the throngs standing in line.

Another very useful number, which handles general advance bookings for these and other museums, is 055 29 48 83.

Tours and Classes

Apicius: The Culinary Institute of Florence
Via Guelfa, 85, 50129

In 1997, after many years as a successful architect, Gabriella Ganugi changed courses and careers and opened Apicius. With thirty-five teachers and twenty chefs, it is now recognized as one of the foremost cooking schools in Italy. As the brochure states, "Apicius is a cooking school which associates cooking with the historic and artistic background of Italy." The school is divided into two teaching sections: one for professionals and the other for nonprofessionals. The programs for nonprofessionals range from a one-day hands-on experience for one person to weekly, monthly, and yearly programs. In addition, individuals may request customized programs and/or tours of gourmet shops, famous food markets, cooking supply shops, olive oil tastings, wine classes, a dinner in a Tuscan home, and a field trip to Chianti, among others. All nonprofessional classes are conducted in English. For details and all prices, please consult the Website.

Telephone: 055 265 8135
Fax: 055 265 6689
Internet: www.apicius.it
Credit Cards: AE, DC, MC, V

Art History Tours by Frank Peters

Frank Peters has lived in and loved Florence for many years and has a deep knowledge of its art and history that makes Florence come alive. His in-depth, very scholarly private tours are for a maximum of four (unless it is a family) and last at least four to five hours. However, Frank's expertise isn't limited to Florence; he also offers excellent tours of the Tuscan countryside.

Reservations are mandatory and can be made through the Hotel Morandi alla Crocetta (page 73; Tel: 055 234 4747; Fax: 055 248 0954; Email: welcome@ hotelmorandi.it); you do not need to be a guest of the hotel to book one of Frank's tours. Credit cards are not accepted. Rates on request.

Divina Cucina

If you love good food and long to be Italian, even for a day, treat yourself to one of Judy Witts Francini's wonderful Divina Cucina cooking classes in Florence. Judy is an enthusiastic, dynamic American with an extensive culinary background who came to Florence, met and married her Italian husband, and has never looked back. She is a hands-on cook and teacher, who invites her students into her colorful kitchen and teaches them the art of eating and cooking, Tuscan-style. Classes are limited to six students, and Judy's programs range from one to five days. The one-day class includes a guided shopping trip to the Mercato Centrale, preparation of a meal, and finally, savoring the fruits of your labor. Her five-day program includes a full-day trip to Chianti, three days of cooking classes, plus shopping and walking tours of Florence. To help you re-create the dishes, everyone takes home one of her recipe books and a Divina Cucina apron.

Telephone & Fax: 055 29 25 78
Internet: www.divinacucina.com
Credit Cards: MC, V
Rates: Prices start at $250 per person for a one-day class

Florentia: Historical Walking Tours
P.O. Box 9679, Berkeley, CA 94709

Simone Gaddini organizes art and history walking tours of Florence and Tuscany that are recommended for anyone. In Florence, you can select from six city tours and seven museum tours. The Tuscany tours cover Lucca and Chianti (the area between Florence and Siena), or you custom design an itinerary. Florence walking tours are conducted three times a day and last approximately two and a half hours. The Tuscany tour lasts all day. All arrangements are handled by Simone in the United States, and the tours are led in Florence by a select group of English-speaking, Florentine scholars.

Telephone: U.S. 510-549-1707, Florence 055 22 55 35

Internet: www.florentia.org

Credit Cards: None

Rates: Per group, walking tours 175€, Chianti tour 625€, including private transportation

Tuscan Traveler

Ann Reavis, owner of Tuscan Traveler, is the perfect person to heighten your enjoyment of Florence and Tuscany. A former San Francisco trial attorney, Ann has lived in Florence since 1998 and now spends her time writing about Italy and designing private tours of the region based on the sometimes off-beat interests of her clients. One asked to see all of the Last Supper frescos in Florence, while an eight-year-old asked to see all the sights connected with stories where people had lost their heads. Ann's curiosity and enthusiasm are infectious no matter what your interests. One of her most popular tours is of the Chianti Classico region, visiting village markets, ceramic artisans, local butchers, wineries, trattorias, medieval hill towns, and castle villas. Ann is available most of the year in Florence, but to arrange for her services, contact her as far in advance as possible.

Email: ajrev@tiscal.it.

Internet: www.TuscanTraveler.com

Credit Cards: AE, MC, V

Rates: Varies with tour, but generally 50–75€ per hour

Walking Tours of Florence

Piazza Santo Stefano, 2

The groups are small, and the guides are native English speakers who really know their facts and impart them in an interesting and very enjoyable way. In addition to all the famous sights and museums, you will find out little known, sometimes shocking Florentine history, such as who was buried alive near Il Duomo, hear fascinating stories about the difficult genius Michelangelo . . . and much more. Also available are day trips to Siena, San Gimignano, the Leaning Tower of Pisa, Cinque Terre, the Tuscan countryside, bike tours, and shopping excursions to the designer discount malls outside of Florence. As one tour participant said, "And, more importantly, you don't feel like a sheep in a flock, herded around town." Private tours can be arranged, but frankly, you'll have more fun on one of the small group tours.

Telephone: 055 264 5033

Fax: 055 272 8680

Internet: www.artviva.com

Office Hours: Tues–Fri 8 A.M.–6 P.M.; Mon, Sat, Sun 8:30 A.M.–1 P.M.

Credit Cards: minimum 150€, otherwise cash only

Rates: 3-hour walks from 25€ per person (children under 6 free); day trips from 49€ per person

Transportation

Airports: In Florence, contact the Amerigo Vespucci-Peretola; Tel: 055 30 615 (main office), 055 30 61 300 (national flight information), 055 30 61 702 (international flight information); Internet: www.safnet.it. For lost luggage, call 055 30 61 302, 055 21 60 73 (air terminal in Florence Santa Maria Novella Train Station). In Pisa, contact Aeroporto Galileo Galilei; Tel: 055 84 911 (main office), 055 849 300 (flight information), 055 849 400 (lost luggage); Internet: www.pisa-airport.com.

Taxi: Never get into a private taxi. How do you spot the authorized taxis in Florence? The name of an Italian city and a telephone number are written on the side of the taxi, and if you have ordered a taxi, the dispatcher will give you that information: "In five minutes, 'Firenze 4242' will pick you up." Before you get in the taxi, determine the rate, and then make sure the starting rate is showing on the meter or you may find yourself paying for someone else's ride. If possible, keep your bags, or at least your most important pieces of luggage, with you in the cab. In case of fare confrontation, you won't be at the further mercy of a dishonest cabdriver. To order a taxi, call 055 42 42, 055 43 90, 055 47 98, or 055 49 99.

Train: For general information on train stations and railways, call 055 893 021; for luggage service and lost luggage, call 055 23 52 190. For online booking, go to www.fs-on-line.it.

Bus: To contact the shuttle bus from the airport to the train station, call 800 37 37 60. For public bus information in Florence, call 055 56 50 222.

Car: The Automobile Club of Italy, Viale Amendola, 36, operates a twenty-four-hour, English-speaking information line: Tel: 055 24 861.

Parking

If you drive *to* Florence, fine, but do yourself a favor and do not try to drive *in* Florence. The narrow one-way streets, lack of parking, speeding mopeds, tailgating, and just general crazy mentality of Italian drivers is not conducive to a stress-free vacation. Instead, park your car and forget it until you are ready to leave town. Of course, this is its own challenge. Most hotels have valet parking arrangements (for a fee) with car parks, and this is the easiest solution. Prices depend on the size of your car, but in general, plan on paying the equivalent of around 20 to 35€ per day.

For a more time-consuming, yet cheaper, parking solution, the Parterre Parcheggio parking company (Tel: 055 50 01 994) has special rates for motorists who spend at least one night in a Florentine hotel (and show a receipt). The cost is around 15€ per day. The lot is in Piazza della Libertà, about a twenty- to thirty-minute walk to Il Duomo. They will also loan you a free bike to get back to your hotel or issue you a one-way taxi voucher. For more information, call them directly or ask at your hotel reception desk.

Hotels *Di Qua d'Arno*

The Florence hotel listings have been organized into two main sections: those on the Uffizi Gallery and Il Duomo side of the Arno, known as *Di Qua d'Arno* (which literally means "this side of the Arno") and those across the Ponte Vecchio on the Pitti Palace side of the Arno, *Di La d'Arno,* or *Oltrarno* (literally, "the other side of the Arno").

Il Duomo, Piazza della Repubblica, and Piazza della Signoria

Il Duomo, or the House of God, was begun in 1296 by Arnolfo di Cambio. His goal was to create a cathedral of "the greatest lavishness and magnificence possible." Today it reigns supreme as the heart, soul, and symbol of Florence. Indeed, most visitors begin their tour of the city by coming to the Piazza del Duomo to admire the soft pink, white, and green marble cathedral, the octagonal baptistry, and the splendid bronze doors Michelangelo called the "gates of paradise." The massive dome, designed by Brunelleschi, dominates the city landscape for miles around and is the model for the larger but not more beautiful dome of St. Peter's in Rome.

The large Piazza della Repubblica was once the Roman Forum and, until 1888 when the surrounding medieval buildings were torn down, the Mercato Vecchio. The huge square is now ringed by outdoor *caffès* and expensive shops.

Just off the Piazza della Signoria is the Uffizi Gallery, the most glorious Renaissance art museum in Europe. It includes masterpieces of Italian painting from every age, including works by Giotto, Fra Angelico, Botticelli, Leonardo, Raphael, Michelangelo, Titian, and Tintoretto, to name only a few. Two of the most famous paintings in the Uffizi Gallery are in Room 10, Botticelli's *Birth of Venus* and *Primavera*. But remember, the lines outside the Uffizi are as legendary as the art inside; to make reservations, see Museum Tickets, page 48.

HOTELS

($) indicates a Big Splurge; (¢) indicates a Cheap Sleep

CIMATORI GUEST HOUSE (¢, 93)
Via Dante Aligheri, 14

5 rooms, all with shower and toilet

Domenico Cuiuli's Cimatori Guest House B&B makes a strong case for the adage "good things come in small packages." The five-room, completely nonsmoking, budget walk-up near Piazza della Signoria is well turned out with cream-colored walls and coordinated fabrics and furnishings. Two rooms have terra-cotta flooring; the other three have polished wood. All bathrooms have enclosed showers. From the fourth floor, guests are treated to views of Il Duomo, and thanks to the extra steps, cost a fraction less than those on the second floor. In the common area is an old sewing machine, still in working condition, that belonged to Domenico's grandmother. She also gave him the beautiful hutch that graces the small dining area. The artwork hanging in the hotel is by Domenico's sister and another local artist. Credit cards are accepted, but in the low season, paying cash nets you a 5 percent discount.

FACILITIES AND SERVICES: Air-conditioning, direct-dial phone, hair dryer, no elevator (4 floors), in-room safe, communal refrigerator, TV, reception desk open 8 A.M.–8 P.M., nonsmoking hotel

NEAREST TOURIST ATTRACTIONS: Central Florence, within walking distance to almost everything

TELEPHONE
055 26 55 000
FAX
055 23 99 145
INTERNET
www.cimatori.it
CREDIT CARDS
AE, MC, V
RATES
1–2 people: 90–110€,
triple 140€; 5% cash discount
in low season
BREAKFAST
Packaged Continental breakfast
included
ENGLISH
Yes

DAVANZATI HOTEL ★★★ (104)
Via Porta Rossa, 5
21 rooms, all with shower or bath and toilet

TELEPHONE
055 28 66 66
FAX
055 26 58 252
INTERNET
www.hoteldavanzati.it
CREDIT CARDS
MC, V
RATES
Single 75–105€, double 110–
165€, triple 165–195€, quad
185–215€
BREAKFAST
Buffet breakfast included
ENGLISH
Yes

A good location, value-priced rates for a three-star, and very nice owners add up to a Great Sleep in Florence. The hotel has been family-owned and -operated for sixty years and recently underwent a massive renovation project with impressive results. A wonderful collection of black-and-white photos of Florence lines the corridors, and Florentine family flag paintings add interest and color to the breakfast room. All the soft yellow rooms and light blue tiled baths have something to offer: In No. 206 it is an exposed wall of the original tower of the Davanzati Palace, one of the oldest in Florence. Number 304, a suite, offers space plus two satellite TVs, a balcony, and a bathroom with a double sink and a glass-enclosed shower. Free high-speed Internet connection is available in the rooms and lobby, and the front desk will loan a laptop (for a fee).

FACILITIES AND SERVICES: Air-conditioning, bar, direct-dial phone, elevator from first floor, hair dryer, free high-speed Internet in rooms, laptop to loan (small fee), laundry service, minibar, in-room safe, satellite TV, nonsmoking hotel

NEAREST TOURIST ATTRACTIONS: Central Florence, within walking distance to almost everything

GRAND HOTEL CAVOUR ★★★★ ($, 95)
Via del Proconsolo, 3
103 rooms, all with shower or bath and toilet

TELEPHONE
055 28 24 61
FAX
055 21 89 55
CREDIT CARDS
AE, DC, MC, V
RATES
Single 187€, double 218€,
triple 233€; lower off-season
rates
BREAKFAST
Buffet or Continental breakfast
included
ENGLISH
Yes

If you like elegant surroundings with all the services and extras, you will love the Grand Hotel Cavour, directly opposite the Bargello Museum in the heart of Florence. It is also close to Il Duomo and the Piazza della Signoria and within walking distance of the Uffizi Gallery and the Ponte Vecchio.

The hotel is a former thirteenth-century palace built by the Cerchi family. The palace's chapel is now an independent restaurant, where the air of luxury is enhanced by the beautiful hand-painted ceilings, stained-glass windows, and the original altar and confessional. The main lounge of the hotel has a polished marble floor, a fountain, massive gold mirrors, and sectional sofas designed specially for the room. In the center pillar of the lobby you can see the high-water mark from the disastrous 1966 Florence flood.

The comfortable bedrooms in the original section keep pace with the rest of the hotel. They are uniformly done with carpets, walnut furniture, and coordinated bedspreads and curtains. They have large closets, good drawer and luggage space, and fully stocked baths outfitted with fluffy towels. On every floor there is a room with a handicapped-accessible bathroom. Views from most of the rooms are not spectacular, and those facing front will have some noise. However, single guests will like No. 409, which has a view of the Bargello, and couples will enjoy No. 411, a double with a large bathroom that has the same view. If you want quiet, book the rooms on the interior courtyard, but they have no views at all. Twelve rooms have been added in a new wing where traditionalism has been replaced by swaths of brown and orange on the walls, awning-striped bed coverings, and contemporary art in the halls. There is no elevator access to these rooms, yet they have inexplicably higher prices.

The terrace on the sixth floor offers a breathtaking panorama of the city. A large buffet breakfast is served here in warm weather, or in the cooler months in the Michelangelo breakfast room. If you prefer, a Continental breakfast can be brought to your room.

FACILITIES AND SERVICES: Air-conditioning, direct-dial phone, hair dryer, elevator to most rooms, laundry service, minibar, parking (35€ per day), satellite TV, in-room and office safes, tea and coffeemakers in some rooms, porters

NEAREST TOURIST ATTRACTIONS: Within walking distance of central Florence

HOTEL ALDINI ★★ (64)
Via dei Calzaiuoli, 13

15 rooms, all with shower and toilet

The Aldini receives Great Sleeps honors for its comfortable accommodations and desirable location at the corner of Piazza del Duomo, which is about as central as you will find in Florence. The clean white rooms are freshly painted and have dark Italian country reproduction furniture and terracotta floors. Bright floral spreads add a needed splash of color, and matching fabric-covered headboards tie everything together. There is enough wardrobe and drawer space for longer stays. To help buffer the noise along Florence's major pedestrian thoroughfare, the windows are double-glazed, and to keep you cool in the sizzling summer months, the rooms are fully air-conditioned. Still, earplugs wouldn't be a bad idea. Room 101, a huge double or triple with a fabulous view of Il Duomo, has a large bathroom suitable for handicapped guests. Number 109 has a peek at Il Duomo, but the shower leaves something to be desired. Same goes for the bathroom in No. 108. Perennial favorites are the

TELEPHONE
055 21 47 52, 055 21 24 48

FAX
055 29 16 21

INTERNET
www.hotelaldini.it

CREDIT CARDS
AE, DC, MC, V

RATES
Single 85€, double 135€, triple 170€; 10% discount if pay in cash; lower off-season rates

BREAKFAST
Continental breakfast included

ENGLISH
Yes

Tower Room (No. 102), a triple with a long-necked view of Il Duomo and a better shower, and No. 105, which has two streetside windows with a view of the patchwork of Florentine rooftops and a sweet old fireplace painted pink and gilded in gold. All rooms display a selection of the owner's impressive print collection, which is also hung throughout the rest of the hotel.

FACILITIES AND SERVICES: Air-conditioning, direct-dial phone, elevator to hotel (which occupies one floor), hair dryer, minibar, TV, office safe

NEAREST TOURIST ATTRACTIONS: Central Florence, convenient walking distance to everything

HOTEL BELLETTINI ★★ (44)
Via dei Conti, 7

28 rooms in main building, 6 in annex, all with shower and toilet

Without inside information, chances are slim that you would find this outstanding Great Sleep. While central to the action in Florence, it is tucked away through a court-yard entrance near the Medici Chapel by the San Lorenzo Central Market. Originally it served as a lodging for work-ers at the Medici Palaces. For decades it was a very basic one-star operated by two aged sisters. Several years ago, a new page was turned: two stars now shine, and they are polished to a bright luster by the present owners.

From the moment you enter the attractive reception area there is a sense of comfort, which extends down the halls scattered with antiques. An old mantel has an original papal insignia hanging over it, which serves as the hotel's logo. Before you leave, be sure to take a peek at the kitchen to admire the lovely ceiling. In the rest of the hotel, you can admire the Florentine oil paintings, stained-glass windows, and more painted ceilings.

The bedrooms are very nice. One of their best features, from an American standpoint, is that most of the bath-rooms have stall showers with doors (there are no tubs). Number 20, a twin with hand-painted furnishings and a courtyard view, has red-tiled floors and a huge bathroom with a separate enclosed toilet. In one of the singles, No. 25, you feel as though you can almost touch the dome of the Medici Chapel, but the shower here has no base, only a drain in the floor. It does, however, come with a curtain. Numbers 28 and 45 have views of Il Duomo, the Medici Chapel, and the Library of Lorenzo the Magnifico. In No. 45, you can lie in bed and watch the sun rise every morn-

TELEPHONE
055 21 35 61, 055 28 29 80
FAX
055 28 35 51
INTERNET
www.hotelbellettini.com
CREDIT CARDS
AE, DC, MC, V
RATES
Hotel: single 80–105€, double 110–140€, triple 150–180€, quad 180–220€; annex: single 95–115€, double 150–175€, triple 180–210€; lower off-season rates
BREAKFAST
Buffet breakfast included
ENGLISH
Yes

ing over Il Duomo. Room 44, the only one with a balcony, has nice reproduction furniture and watercolors of Florence decorating the walls.

For a three-star experience at two-star prices, check into one of the six beautiful rooms in the annex around the corner. These rooms offer more space, larger closets, more luxurious furnishings, frescoed ceilings, and five-star marble bathrooms, two of them with bathtubs. The drawback, if you can call it that, is that you will have to go to the hotel for your breakfast.

The owners of the hotel also own several short- or long-term apartments and student rooms on Via Cavour. The student rooms share a communal kitchen; the apartments are self-contained. Rates on request.

FACILITIES AND SERVICES: Same for hotel and annex: air-conditioning, bar, direct-dial phone, elevator to reception (hotel on two floors), hair dryer available, guest Internet terminal, minibar in annex, parking (35€ per 24 hours), satellite TV, in-room safe, tea and coffeemakers

NEAREST TOURIST ATTRACTIONS: Within easy walking distance of central Florence

HOTEL CALZAIUOLI ★★★ ($, 87)
Via dei Calzaiuoli, 6

45 rooms, all with shower or bath and toilet

If you wanted to pinpoint the best location in Florence, anything on the pedestrian-only Via dei Calzaiuoli would come up a winner. At this forty-five-room hotel, you begin in the boring commercial lobby and lounge and continue up the original stone staircase through handsome halls lined in muted wallpaper. In addition to space, a rarity in most hotels in this old section of Florence, the streamlined rooms have coordinated colors and tiled bathrooms. Room 205, a nicely done double in cream with floral prints for interest, has good luggage space and light. If you are a single traveler and space is a priority, one of the best choices is No. 215, but you will sacrifice a view to get it. I would avoid No. 105 on the back—the high-ceilinged room is large, but the dated bathroom is too small for comfort. Many of the rooms have good views directly onto the street below. Unless you count horse-drawn carriages, this is a traffic-free zone where you can people-watch from your open window instead of having to seal it shut against honking horns and backfiring mopeds.

FACILITIES AND SERVICES: Air-conditioning, bar, direct-dial phone, elevator, hair dryer, laundry service, minibar,

TELEPHONE
055 21 24 56/7/8
FAX
055 26 83 10
INTERNET
www.calzaiuoli.it
CREDIT CARDS
AE, DC, MC, V
RATES
Single 185€, double 255€, triple 307€; lower off-season rates
BREAKFAST
Buffet breakfast included
ENGLISH
Yes

parking (35€ per day), room safe, satellite TV, some non-smoking rooms

NEAREST TOURIST ATTRACTIONS: Central Florence, easy walking distance to everything

HOTEL DALÌ ★ (¢, 69)
Via dell' Oriuolo, 17
9 rooms, 3 with shower and toilet

TELEPHONE & FAX
055 23 40 706
EMAIL
hoteldali@tin.it
INTERNET
www.hoteldali.com
CREDIT CARDS
V
RATES
Single 40€ (no private facilities), double 60–75€; lower off-season rates
BREAKFAST
Not served
ENGLISH
Yes

"Here, you are home," say Marco and Samantha, the enthusiastic, young owners of the Hotel Dalì. Thanks to their warm hospitality, the hotel attracts a savvy group of budgeteers who know how to cut corners in style. If you are here in the low season and opt for one of the bathless rooms, you will enjoy a very contented cheap sleep, saving an additional 10 to 20 percent off the already low rates. Each room is different and showcases the artistic whimsy of the owners. Number 4 is a good example. It is a double on the quiet side of the hotel, with an old-fashioned sun-bonnet over the antique-style bed, two chairs and a little table, and detailed hand-painting around the sink. The spotless bathroom is down the hall. In No. 6, you walk across linoleum, hang your clothes in an armoire done in decoupage, and sleep in a pretty wrought-iron bed. If you feel like springing for a room with private facilities, check into No. 7, which can sleep three in beautiful antique beds. Dog lovers will appreciate the paintings of dogs walking their owners. The only drawback here is that the view is over the car park below. Which reminds me, if you are driving, you can park here free. Considering that most hotel and public car parks in Florence start around 30€ per day, this may be reason enough to check into the Hotel Dalì.

FACILITIES AND SERVICES: Elevator, fans, hair dryer available, free parking, office safe, nonsmoking hotel
NEAREST TOURIST ATTRACTIONS: Il Duomo

HOTEL DEI MORI ★★ (¢, 92)
Via Dante Aligheri, 12
11 rooms, all with shower and toilet

TELEPHONE
055 21 14 38
FAX
055 23 82 216
EMAIL
deimori@bnb.it
INTERNET
www.bnb.it/deimori
CREDIT CARDS
MC, V

The Hotel Dei Mori has eleven quiet rooms, all nicely furnished with individual touches. Nine have en suite facilities, two have private facilities located in the hall outside the room. Rooms have air-conditioning (5€ extra per day and controlled by the front desk) and come equipped with duvets on orthopedic mattresses. On a warm afternoon, you can sit on the side balcony and read; note that this balcony area is also the only place you are allowed to light up in this otherwise nonsmoking hotel. The sitting room displays a fine collection of books, which are available to guests, but for some inexplicable reason, the television set here is off-limits. Also, be aware that there is no elevator, and the hotel is up two long flights of stairs (forty-seven steps in all!). While some might find a few amenities are missing, other guests applaud what the hotel does offer: "a smile, service, and a willingness to make your time at Dei Mori and Florence special." If you are planning on spending time in Tuscany, inquire about their country house with two guest apartments.

FACILITIES AND SERVICES: Air-conditioning (5€ per day), direct-dial phone, no elevator, hair dryers available, office safe, nonsmoking hotel

NEAREST TOURIST ATTRACTIONS: Central Florence, great shopping

RATES
Single 80–90€, double 90–110€, triple 135€, quad 160€; lower rates for longer stays year-round; 5% discount for cash
BREAKFAST
Continental breakfast included (no pastry; bread and tea cakes only)
ENGLISH
Yes

HOTEL DUOMO ★★★ (54)
Piazza del Duomo, 1
24 rooms, all with shower or bath and toilet

The prime position on the Piazza del Duomo guarantees views from each of the sixteen rooms in this rather modern, surprise-free, twenty-four-room hotel. Front desk duties are well-managed by Alberto Pasi, who has been here since the hotel opened in 1991. In addition to air-conditioning and a lift to the hotel, there is a bar, no-smoking rooms on request, and parking facilities available at a nearby garage. The blue-and-gold rooms are definitely nondescript in look and feel, but they are clean, well-kept, and comfortable.

Room 33 has a balcony in addition to a view, but the shower, like most in the hotel, is just a spout on the wall and a drain in the floor with a curtain around it. In No. 40, a bright double or triple, guests can lie in bed and see Il Duomo. The room also has comfortable seating, a large double closet, and a better bathroom because the shower is in the corner (therefore, when in use, it won't soak the entire room). Solo Great Sleepers will be happy in No. 41, a view room with two windows, a balcony, and a double bed. In No. 42, the view is of Fiesole and a corner peek of Il Duomo. To commemorate your stay, you can purchase a ceramic plaque with your room number and a design of Il Duomo on it.

FACILITIES AND SERVICES: Air-conditioning, bar, direct-dial phone, elevator to hotel (which is on one floor), hair dryer available, laundry service, minibar, parking (30€ per day), office safe, satellite TV, nonsmoking rooms on request, desk open 8 A.M.–9 P.M.

NEAREST TOURIST ATTRACTIONS: Everything in central Florence

TELEPHONE
055 21 99 22, 055 29 32 64
FAX
055 21 64 10
INTERNET
www.hotelduomofirenze.it
CREDIT CARDS
AE, DC, MC, V
RATES
Single 82–95€, double 120–163€, triple 160–180€, quad 180–200€
BREAKFAST
Buffet breakfast included
ENGLISH
Yes

HOTEL IL PERSEO ★ (¢, 61)
Via dei Cerretani, 1

TELEPHONE
055 21 25 04
FAX
055 28 83 77
INTERNET
www.hotelperseo.it
CREDIT CARDS
MC, V
RATES
Single 40–55€, double 55–95€,
triple 70–120€, quad 75–140€;
lower off-season rates
BREAKFAST
Continental breakfast included
ENGLISH
Yes

19 rooms, 7 with shower and toilet

It is what it is—a one-star near Il Duomo, cheerfully run by Louise and Giacinto, a friendly Australian/Italian couple, along with Louise's mother, Susan. Giacinto and Susan are artists whose paintings hang in the hotel (and are for sale). Other paintings scattered throughout the hotel were left by cash-strapped guests.

The bright, tile-floored rooms have Florentine wrought-iron furnishings mixed with dark wood pieces. In the winter, guests sleep under duvets. The hall facilities, which are cleaned several times a day, are just fine if you are trying to cut costs by occupying a bathless roost. Only five rooms are viewless, and the views from the others are of Forte Belvedere, Santa Maria Maggiore, and Il Duomo.

NOTE: The hotel is closed for four or five days at Christmas.

FACILITIES AND SERVICES: Bar, direct-dial phone, fans available, elevator to hotel (which is on one floor), hair dryer, guest Internet terminal, in-room safe, reception open 8 A.M.–8 P.M.

NEAREST TOURIST ATTRACTIONS: Il Duomo, Medici Chapel, San Lorenzo Market, Piazza Santa Maria Novella

HOTEL ORCHIDEA ★ (¢, 96)
Borgo degli Albizi, 11, first floor

TELEPHONE & FAX
055 24 80 346
EMAIL
hotelorchidea@yahoo.it
INTERNET
www.hotelorchideaflorence.it
CREDIT CARDS
None, cash only
RATES
Single 55€, double 75€
BREAKFAST
No breakfast served
ENGLISH
Yes

7 rooms, 1 with shower only

For twenty-plus years, Maria Rosa Cook, a former English teacher, and her daughter, Miranda, have been welcoming guests at their cozy Hotel Orchidea. The twelfth-century building overlooks Gemma's Tower, named after Gemma Donati, the wife of Dante, Italy's greatest poet. This tower can be seen from the nearby S. Pier Maggiore square, which is one of the most character-istic in this part of Florence.

The seven-room, first-floor lodging offers exceptionally clean, large rooms painted in soft pink. Several—including No. 7, with a shower and sink; No. 5, a great single; and No. 4, with a balcony—have quiet views of the garden below, which is especially wonderful when the wisteria vines are in bloom. Some disagree, but the only room I would personally avoid is No. 6, because of its opaque window. However, when that window is open, the view to the garden and its one-hundred-year-old statue is ap-pealing. The hall facilities have been redone and are just fine. The area around the hotel is interesting: in addition to being close to all the tourist musts, there is good shopping and browsing, especially in artists' and clothing boutiques. Reservations during high season are difficult to get, so if this is your spot, plan far in advance. Early-morning risers take note: they do not serve breakfast.

FACILITIES AND SERVICES: Elevator to hotel (which is on one floor), fans, hair dryer available, office safe, desk open from 8 A.M.–11 P.M.

NEAREST TOURIST ATTRACTIONS: Il Duomo, Santa Croce, Palazzo Vecchio, Piazza della Signoria, good shopping

INPIAZZADELLASIGNORIA B&B ($, 106)
Via dei Magazzini, 2

10 rooms and 3 apartments, all with shower or bath and toilet

Alessandro and Sonia Pini have magnificently transformed their fifteenth-century home into a stunning bed-and-breakfast overlooking the Piazza della Signoria. During the restoration process, the Pinis uncovered a niche that held a small feminine shoe made of wood and leather, which has been documented as over six hundred years old. Meticulous care was also taken in cleaning the original frescoes and ceilings, refinishing period antiques, and selecting the finest fabrics and amenities. The result is that guests feel they are staying in a luxurious noble home.

The spacious bedrooms have half-tester or canopy beds, plasma-screen televisions, marble bathrooms with aromatherapy toiletries, and antique furnishings. I like them all … but I especially adore Beatrice, a well-done double with frescoes, a small dressing area, and a Jacuzzi in the modern bathroom with a mosaic glass backdrop and gold highlights. Another favorite is Botticelli, a double or triple with a sleigh bed and a view onto the Piazza della Signoria and Il Duomo. In the deluxe Leonardo room, angels anchor the curtains over the bed, and in the bathroom, the sink is set in an old door that was salvaged during the restoration. In the morning, a substantial breakfast that includes fresh fruit and pastries is served in the dining room at a baronial table seating twenty.

The three fully equipped apartments are named after the Pinis's sons: Giulio, Umberto, and Matteo. From their windows on the fourth floor, one can see not only the lovely piazza but Giotto's bell tower, Brunelleschi's dome, and the Bargello tower. The smallest, Giulio, can sleep four under a pitched roof. Umberto has a separate bedroom and loft that can accommodate five. The three-level Matteo has two bedrooms, two bathrooms, and a wonderful view of Il Duomo. The apartments can be reserved either by the

TELEPHONE
055 239 95 46
FAX
055 267 66 16
INTERNET
www.inpiazzadellasignoria.com
CREDIT CARDS
AE, DC, MC, V
RATES
B&B: single 140–200€, double 200–260€, triple 230–280€, suite 280–360€; apartment (2–4 people): daily 290–380€, weekly 1,200–1,400€; yacht: 900€ per day (1,100€ in Aug)
BREAKFAST
Continental breakfast included (except for weekly apartment rentals)
ENGLISH
Yes

day (with daily maid service) or by the week (with weekly maid service).

For a memorable experience on your trip to Italy, consider chartering the Pinis's fifty-two foot yacht, "Old Salt," which has three bedrooms (sleeping up to six), three bathrooms, and a crew cabin for the skipper. Guests either eat out or trade KP duties, as there is no cook aboard. The yacht is available year-around for charters lasting from a day to a week.

FACILITIES AND SERVICES: Air-conditioning, bar, direct-dial phone, elevator, hair dryer, guest Internet terminal, equipped kitchens in apartments, in-room safe, satellite plasma-screen TV, no smoking except in living room

NEAREST TOURIST ATTRACTIONS: Central Florence, within walking distance to almost everything

PALAZZO NICCOLINI AL DUOMO ($, $$)
Via dei Servi, 2

7 rooms and suites, all with shower, bath, and toilet

TELEPHONE
055 28 24 12
FAX
055 29 09 79
INTERNET
www.niccolinidomepalace.com
CREDIT CARDS
AE, DC, MC, V
RATES
Single 240€, double 250–310€, suites 350–500€; lower off-season rates
BREAKFAST
Buffet breakfast included
ENGLISH
Yes

The Palazzo Niccolini al Duomo is a landmark for discerning visitors who want to be surrounded during their stay by the beauty and fabled past of historic Florence. The magnificent fourteenth-century *palazzo* was handed down over the centuries among members of the Naldini family, who were wealthy merchants and bankers in Tuscany. It remained in the family until 1879, when the last descendant, Cristina, married Marchese Eugenio Niccolini di Camugliano and the palace was included as part of her dowry. Today, it remains in the Niccolini di Camugliano family and has been carefully restored by them to preserve its features and history. The result is breathtaking and worthy of a front-cover feature in *Architectural Digest*.

The grand living areas are a study in serene elegance created by beautiful frescoes, handsome family antiques, luxurious fabrics on comfortable sofas and chairs, gracefully draped floor-to-ceiling windows and masses of fresh floral arrangements. The sumptuous deluxe rooms and suites, all with large marble bathrooms, are designed to create an environment that goes beyond mere comfort and convenience. Number 5 is a deluxe double with beamed ceiling and thick Oriental rugs in shades of Florentine red, where the unusual feature is the library wall of family-owned leatherbound books. In No. 2, a junior suite, allegorical frescoes wrap around the splendid heavily beamed room, which has a romantic four-poster bed and two large windows that let the light flow in. The crown jewel of the palace is No. 7, a handsomely furnished, two-room green-and-white suite surrounded by view windows that handsomely reflect the same colors as those in Il Duomo.

FACILITIES AND SERVICES: Air-conditioning, honor bar, direct-dial phone, elevator, laundry service, in-room data port, minibar, in-room safe, satellite TV, reception desk open 7:30 A.M.–8 P.M.

NEAREST TOURIST ATTRACTIONS: Central Florence, within walking distance to almost everything

PENSIONE MARIA LUISA DE' MEDICI ★ (¢, 90)
Via del Corso, 1

9 rooms, 2 with shower or bath and toilet

Welsh-born Evelyn Morris and her partner, Angido Sordi, bought this property with the intention of developing it into a rehabilitation facility for the elderly. These plans never materialized, and the rooms stood empty for twelve years until they decided to open it as a pensione in 1986. Those not well-versed in sixteenth-century Baroque art or early-twentieth-century furniture designers may think the second-floor pensione is a mishmash of odds and ends exemplifying the kind of faded elegance that appeals to artistic types who love retro clothing discovered in cluttered thrift stores. How wrong that impression turns out to be.

Angido Sordi has been a lifelong collector of Baroque paintings and statuary as well as early- to mid-twentieth-century furniture. Every item you see standing, hanging, or squeezed into a corner is original, authentic, and has artistic merit. I will admit I thought the plastic chairs were patio quality and dismissed the metal lights altogether. Wrong and wrong again. The plastic chairs were designed by Gae Aulenti, the most famous Italian female architect, who was commissioned to redo one of the train stations in Paris. The red-and-blue chair you see at the entrance cost the equivalent of more than a thousand dollars thirty years ago! Designed by Gerrit Rietveld and represented in the permanent collection of the New York Museum of Modern Art, it is considered to be one of the finest chair designs of the twentieth century.

Each eccentric room is named after one of the last dukes of the Medici, is adorned with one of their portraits, and displays an eclectic mixture of almost-antiques, dorm classics, and some of the modern pieces from Sr. Sordi's collection. The overall atmosphere of the hotel is chummy, especially for the residents of the seven bedrooms sharing the four hall bathrooms; only the two large family rooms have private facilities. In order to keep in close contact with her guests, Ms. Morris serves breakfast to them in

TELEPHONE
055 28 00 48

CREDIT CARDS
None, cash only

RATES
Single rates on request, double75–90€, triple 103–118€, quad 126–150€

BREAKFAST
Continental breakfast included, served in the room (breakfast cannot be deducted)

ENGLISH
Yes

their rooms. The meal includes juice, cereal, yogurt, eggs, a choice of breads, and a piece of cheese. For a one-star hotel, this is a good value.

Usually hotel rooms along this traffic-free patch of real estate cost a pretty penny, but for three or four friends or a family willing to share either of the enormous family rooms with its own bathroom (plus a Ping-Pong table in No. 5), the price is very attractive, especially since the big breakfast is included. Ms. Morris only takes telephone reservations; she doesn't send faxes or emails or answer letters. She also locks the front door around midnight and does not give out keys.

FACILITIES AND SERVICES: No elevator (one-floor hotel is up 2 flights of stairs), office safe, reception open 9 A.M.–9 P.M.

NEAREST TOURIST ATTRACTIONS: Piazza della Repubblica, Il Duomo, Palazzo Vecchio, Uffizi Gallery

RESIDENZA DEI PUCCI (45)
Via dei Pucci, 9

12 rooms, all with bath or shower and toilet

One of the most popular concepts in Florentine hotels is the *affitta camere*, a small hotel that offers somewhat larger rooms but limited guest services. That is not to say that guests are left on their own, since there is maid service and someone usually on duty during the day to check people in and out. Missing are concierge services, porters, buffet breakfasts, room service, and lobbies with twenty-four-hour receptionists. The Residenza dei Pucci, located between Il Duomo and the Piazza San Lorenzo, is one of Florence's nicest *affitta camere*.

The ample rooms are all different and very nicely decorated, but given my first choice, I would reserve No. 12. This sunny, yellow room has a wonderful four-poster bed with white cotton linens, a nice writing area, and two armchairs. Brass curtain rods hold the tassled curtains and sheers. The black-and-white tiled bathroom has a marble sink and a stall shower. Rooms 22 and 23 also have four-poster beds. Number 21, a double, does not have a four-poster, but the big bathroom has a tub and shower and its own window. If you require twin beds, ask for No. 25, which has a zebra motif and a marble bathroom with a recessed stall shower. There is no breakfast room, but a prepackaged breakfast is available for guests to eat in their rooms.

FACILITIES AND SERVICES: Air-conditioning, direct-dial phone, hair dryer, TV, no elevator (3 floors, 27 steps), office open daily 9 A.M.–8 P.M.

TELEPHONE
055 28 18 86
FAX
055 26 43 14
CREDIT CARDS
AE, MC, V
RATES
Single 91–130€, double 105–145€, triple 116–165€; lower off-season rates
BREAKFAST
Prepackaged Continental breakfast included, served in room
ENGLISH
Yes

NEAREST TOURIST ATTRACTIONS: Il Duomo, Medici Chapel, Accademia

RESIDENZA GIOTTO (63)
Via Roma, 6

6 rooms, all with shower and toilet

The Residenza Giotto is an *affitta camere* discreetly housed in a fourth-floor flat that has the advantage of an elevator and a common terrace facing Il Duomo and the Campanille de Giotto, from which it takes its name. The stylish, soft yellow rooms are sprinkled with antiques, have wooden floors and have gold-striped fabrics on the spreads and curtains. The best views of the Campanille are from Rooms 3 and 6. Hotel amenities are sparse, but there is a communal guest refrigerator and microwave, both handy for keeping and preparing money-saving light snacks in your room. Cheap sleepers will be happy to know that discounts in high season are given for cash payments. The Residenza dei Pucci, described below, is under the same management.

FACILITIES AND SERVICES: Air-conditioning, direct-dial phone, elevator, hair dryer available, guest refrigerator and microwave, reception desk open Mon–Sat 9 A.M.–5 P.M., Sun & holidays 9 A.M.–1 P.M., 3–8 P.M.

NEAREST TOURIST ATTRACTIONS: Central Florence, walking distance to almost everything

TELEPHONE
055 21 45 93
FAX
055 26 48 568
EMAIL
residenzagiotto@tin.it
INTERNET
www.residenzagiotto.it
CREDIT CARDS
AE, DC, MC, V
RATES
Single 90–120€, double 105–130€, triple 115–145€; discounts in high season for cash
BREAKFAST
Prepackaged Continental breakfast included, served in room
ENGLISH
Yes

SOGGIORNO SANI (NO STARS, ¢, 94)
Piazza del Giuochi, 1

6 rooms, 4 with shower and toilet, 2 with shower and sink

Talk about a primo location! This little six-room bed-and-breakfast is halfway between Il Duomo and the Uffizi Gallery, next to Dante's house, ten heartbeats away from the city's only American Express office, and a mere five- to twenty-minute walk from everything on a tourist's must-see and -do list in Florence. It is presided over by Remi Sani, who has worked diligently to transform it from an old, rundown backpacker's crash pad to a neat and tidy Great Sleep that should appeal to anyone not wanting to spend big bucks on lodging. The only remnants of the past are the original tiled floors—everything else is new. Plus, most of the rooms have a view, particularly those on the ends. In No. 1, you will see the Bargello Museum, which is famous for its sculpture collection. From the No. 6 perch, the view is of St. Michael's Church, Dante's house, and a fourteenth-century medieval tower. Public parking is a five-minute walk. If you are coming from the train

TELEPHONE
055 21 12 35
FAX
055 26 54 386
INTERNET
www.sanibnb.it
CREDIT CARDS
None, cash only
RATES
Single 35–70€, double 65–110€
BREAKFAST
Prepackaged breakfast 3€ per person
ENGLISH
Yes, also French and Polish

station, take bus No. 14 or 23 and get off at the second stop. Breakfast is optional.

FACILITIES AND SERVICES: Air-conditioning (7€ per day), in-room phone (receives calls only), public hall phone, elevator, hair dryer, minibar, in-room safes, TV, electric mosquito-repellent machines

NEAREST TOURIST ATTRACTIONS: Heart of Florence, easy walking distance to everything

Piazza della Indipendenza and Piazza della Libertà

Piazza della Indipendenza is a wide green space populated by retirees who gather on benches to gossip and while away the day. On the third Sunday of the month there is a flea market that is worthwhile. Not far away, on the northeastern edge of Florence, is the Piazza della Libertà, which serves as a good exit point if you're driving out of the city.

HOTELS

OTHER OPTIONS
Apartment Rentals

(¢) indicates a Cheap Sleep

HOTEL BONIFACIO ★★★ (1)
Via Bonifacio Lupi, 21

19 rooms, all with shower and toilet

TELEPHONE
055 46 27 133/4

FAX
055 46 27 132

INTERNET
www.hotelbonifacio.it

CREDIT CARDS
AE, DC, MC, V

RATES
Single 80–90€, double 100–130€, triple 120–140€, quad 130–150€; lower off-season rates (subject to availability)

Maria-Laura Muntoni has taken this old villa and created a pleasant hotel that emphasizes comfort and service. It is a good choice for motorists because it has easy access to several public car parks and to roads providing a quick getaway to the north. Everything about the hotel is well done in a clear-cut, simple way. Beige sponge-painted hallways lead to the rooms, which are nicely furnished with modern, light wood built-ins that add a sense of space. The serviceable bathrooms all have showers (no tubs) and roomy shelves. Sra. Muntoni wisely kept the colored modern skylights and ironwork over some doorways, as well as the charming breakfast room, which opens onto a colorful garden. This space is especially beautiful in March and April when the wisteria is blooming. Scattered throughout the hotel are framed pictures taken in France by Sra. Muntoni's husband, a pediatrician and amateur photographer.

NOTE: The hotel is closed for two to three days at Christmas and three weeks in August (dates vary).

FACILITIES AND SERVICES: Air-conditioning, direct-dial phone, elevator, hair dryer, minibar, in-room safe, TV, 4 nonsmoking rooms

NEAREST TOURIST ATTRACTIONS: Brisk 20-minute walk to Il Duomo, 30 to the Ponte Vecchio

BREAKFAST
Buffet breakfast included

ENGLISH
Yes

HOTEL CARAVAGGIO ★★★ (11)
Piazza della Indipendenza, 5
37 rooms, all with shower or bath and toilet

The Caravaggio offers its guests thirty-seven renovated rooms that present a balanced mixture of classic design and modern conveniences. The uncluttered abodes are simply appointed, yet tastefully decorated with tone-on-tone fabrics accented by block prints on the curtains and bedspreads. Only the wall colors change from green, light orange, or beige. Modern bathrooms are a welcome plus, thanks to the use of mirrors, heated towel racks, and top-notch housekeeping standards. Six of the superior doubles offer Jacuzzis; six more have Il Duomo views. A guest Internet terminal in the lobby makes it easy to stay in touch. Breakfast is laid out on a huge marble buffet in a room set with high-backed, coral-covered chairs. The hotel is part of a small family-owned group of hotels in and around Florence. However, the only other one listed in *Great Sleeps Italy* is the Hotel Colorado, a one-star near Piazza San Marco (see page 90).

FACILITIES AND SERVICES: Air-conditioning, bar, direct-dial phone, elevator, hair dryer, guest Internet terminal, laundry service, minibar, in-room safe, satellite TV, Jacuzzis, 2 handicapped-accessible rooms

NEAREST TOURIST ATTRACTIONS: Train station, Mercato Centrale, 20-minute walk to Il Duomo

TELEPHONE
055 49 63 10

FAX
055 46 28 827

INTERNET
www.hotelcaravaggio.it

CREDIT CARDS
AE, MC, V

RATES
Single 70–150€, double 100–200€, triple 150–250€

BREAKFAST
Buffet breakfast included

ENGLISH
Yes

HOTEL CELLAI ★★★ (8)
Via 27 Aprile, 14
57 rooms, all with bath or shower and toilet

The family-owned and -run Hotel Cellai has a poignant history. During World War II, the grandfather who ran the hotel had to flee Florence to escape from the Germans, and

TELEPHONE
055 48 92 91

FAX
055 47 03 87

INTERNET
www.hotelcellai.it
CREDIT CARDS
AE, DC, MC, V
RATES
Single 110–150€, double
135–185€, suite 225–275€;
lower rates subject to season and
availability
BREAKFAST
Buffet breakfast included
ENGLISH
Yes

in the process he lost the hotel. After the war, the family was able to get the hotel back, and now it bears the name of the grandfather who began it, and it is in the capable hands of his grandson, Francesco Cavallo. Francesco, an inveterate collector, has restored it beautifully, and the pieces he has gathered over the years add to the charm and richness of his hotel. He found the lights in the main salon in a local shop and fashioned the one in the winter garden breakfast room from pieces of iron he found in the cellar. In the second sitting area, there is an interesting display of old Florentine photos and revolving exhibitions of local artists' work. Another welcome part of the hotel is La Terrazza, a roof terrace with a half dozen comfortable cushioned armchairs, a wonderful collection of old maps, and a view of Il Duomo and the beautiful hillside town Fiesole in the distance.

The well-lighted bedrooms have plain white walls that offset the blue, gold, and red Florentine fabrics used on the beds and curtains. Number 303 is a quiet choice with a typical rooftop view, good luggage space, a white tiled bath, and an entryway large enough to accommodate a sofa bed. Number 414, a roomy double deluxe, has a safari curtain surrounding the bed and windows opening onto Il Duomo. I would avoid No. 216, which has the smallest bathroom in the hotel and a dreary view of the service roof.

FACILITIES AND SERVICES: Air-conditioning, bar, direct-dial phone, elevator, hair dryer, laundry service, minibar, guest Internet terminal, parking (25€ per day), office safe, satellite TV, 2 nonsmoking floors

NEAREST TOURIST ATTRACTIONS: Piazza San Marco, Accademia

HOTEL CIMABUE ★★ (4)
Via Bonifacio Lupi, 7 (at Via Zara)
15 rooms, all with shower or bath and toilet

TELEPHONE
055 47 56 01, 055 47 19 89
FAX
055 46 30 906
INTERNET
www.hotelcimabue.it
CREDIT CARDS
AE, DC, MC, V
RATES
Single 60–98€, double 75–
140€, triple 90–175€,
quad 105–195€; discount for
Great Sleeps Italy readers
BREAKFAST
Buffet breakfast included

The Cimabue is owned by Igino Rossi, a former director of Trusthouse Forte Hotels, and his son, Régis. The hotel is about twenty minutes by foot from most touristy things to do, but this neighborhood is quiet, appealing, and also safe—the main police station is nearby.

A few well-placed pieces of vintage furniture and interesting photos of old Florence decorate the hallways. Wood-framed doors open onto well-proportioned bedrooms, which have cool terra-cotta or wood floors, frescoed ceilings in five rooms, and a balcony in one. All have an interesting assortment of marble-topped dressers, carved wooden headboards, and mirrored armoires, as well as tiled baths with showers or tubs. A buffet breakfast is served in a pink-and-green room with banquette seating and changing art exhibits. And I have saved the best for last: you will receive a discount if you mention *Great Sleeps Italy* when reserving.

NOTE: The hotel is closed for two weeks at Christmas.

FACILITIES AND SERVICES: Air-conditioning in 10 rooms, bar, direct-dial phone, no elevator (2 floors), fans, hair dryer, guest Internet terminal, parking nearby (25€ per day), in-room safe, TV

NEAREST TOURIST ATTRACTIONS: A 20-minute walk or a 10-minute bus ride to central Florence

ENGLISH
Yes

HOTEL ROYAL ★★★ (3)
Via delle Ruote, 50/54

41 rooms, all with shower or bath and toilet

The Hotel Royal was built in the 1800s as the private villa for a noble Florentine family. After World War II, it became a hotel, and since then it has aged beautifully. Set off the street in a large garden not far from the train station and exhibition halls, it is considered one of the better three-star hotels in Florence.

Light gray and soft blue walls accented with white moldings, massive crystal chandeliers, highly polished hardwood floors with Oriental rugs, and a circular bar and sitting area strategically arranged for intimate conversations make up the downstairs portion of the hotel. In spring and summer, drinks are served in the garden, which is filled with roses and other blooming plants. For breakfast, guests are served in a glass-enclosed dining room overlooking the garden. Motorists will appreciate the free parking on the hotel grounds.

The bedrooms are well planned and comfortable. Those in the garden annex are newer and a bit smaller but have all the amenities of those in the main building. All of these are large and invite lingering stays. Most have generous shuttered windows with floor-to-ceiling white linen curtains gently pulled back to let in just enough sunshine. Number 24 has big windows framing a fireplace and its own little terrace. The rooms are all quiet, and most have views of the gardens. Framed botanical prints, excellent lighting, and roomy, marble bathrooms add the touches that make the difference between a place to sleep and a memorable hotel stay.

FACILITIES AND SERVICES: Air-conditioning, bar, direct-dial phone, elevator, hair dryer, minibar, free parking, in-room safe (1.55€ per day), office safe (free), satellite TV

TELEPHONE
055 48 32 87, 055 49 06 48
FAX
055 49 09 76
INTERNET
www.hotelroyalfirenze.it
CREDIT CARDS
AE, DC, MC, V
RATES
Single 115€, double 190€, triple 235€, quad 280€; lower off-season rates
BREAKFAST
Buffet breakfast included
ENGLISH
Yes

NEAREST TOURIST ATTRACTIONS: Accademia, other sites are a 15- to 30-minute walk or a bus ride away

RESIDENZA JOHANNA (¢, 2)
Via Bonifacio Lupi, 14, first floor (off right entrance to building)

11 rooms, 9 with shower or bath and toilet

TELEPHONE
055 48 18 96

FAX
055 48 27 21

INTERNET
www.johanna.it

CREDIT CARDS
None, cash only

RATES
Single 50€, double 80€, extra bed 18€

BREAKFAST
Continental breakfast included

ENGLISH
Yes

Savvy Great Sleepers in Florence who have stayed at the Residenza Johanna prefer to keep it a closely guarded secret. They do not want their favorite place spoiled by eager tourists who cannot appreciate it or, worse yet, to find it full when they want to return. I do not blame them—this is a find. But it is not for corporate climbers who must remain plugged in wherever they go or for those looking to paint the town red. This is a true getaway—no telephones, no radios or televisions, and no noise—that's about a half-hour walk from the heart of Florence. In this residential neighborhood, children play after school, matrons shop for dinner, and retirees sit in the small parks to gossip and feed the pigeons. Motorists will be minutes away from the main arteries leading in and out of Florence. Is it expensive? Not especially. Is it a good deal with value? I think so. Is it attractive? Positively.

The hotel, an *affitta camere,* is in a nineteenth-century villa that has been restored by Evelyn Arrighi, a transplant from France, and her business partner, Lea Gulmanelli, who is Italian. They combined their native French chic and Italian élan to create a hotel with the warmth and charm of a private home. The rooms are coordinated in pastels and small print fabrics and feature antiqued furnishings, comfortable seating, good beds, and in those without private bathrooms, a sink and a bidet hidden behind a screen. The hall facilities are first-class. Numbers 3, 6, and 10 have a balcony, and every room has an electric kettle with complimentary coffee and tea packets. There is also a small library for guests. The prepackaged breakfast is prepared on a tray and set out in the rooms.

NOTE: There are now five *affitta camere* in this group, four of which are run by Lea and her husband. The second, called Residenza Johanna II, is a six-room pensione that is every bit as nice, but the location, at Via delle Cinque Giornate, 12, is quite frankly beyond Mars for most visitors in Florence, and the distant neighborhood holds absolutely nothing of interest. For more information, visit the Residenza Johanna Website or call 055 47 33 77. Also see Residenza Johlea I (page 92), Residenza Johlea II (page 92), and Antica Dimora Firenze (page 88).

FACILITIES AND SERVICES: Cellular telephones available to rent (no room phones), elevator to hotel (which is on one floor), fans, office safe

NEAREST TOURIST ATTRACTIONS: At least a 30-minute walk to nearest attractions; 15 minutes to Il Duomo on bus nos. 1 or 17

RESIDENZA LE RONDINI (¢, 9)
Via San Zanobi, 43
5 rooms, all with shower and toilet

I will be honest: if I had not been tipped off about this five-room *affitte camere*, I never would have stopped, let alone climbed three flights of stairs (75 steps in all) to reach the front door. But it was worth the hike for me, and it will be for all other card-carrying cheap sleepers, because this cozy, clean, affordable den is designed to please. Residenza le Rondini, which means "residence of the swallows," is run by a hands-on husband and wife team—Giovanni and Elisabetta. Giovanni is a motor-racing buff and took all the framed photos you will see hanging about. The simple rooms are clean and, if you are traveling light, they will be big enough. Number 5 is a sunny double nest that makes up for its smallness with a balcony that accommodates a table and pair of chairs. Number 4 has space and a rooftop view of trees. Number 1 can fit three or four budgeteers; it faces the street but is high enough to escape most of the noise. I also like No. 3 with a corner fireplace and a bright green-and-beige striped bedspread. The room amenities include a piece of candy on your pillow each night.

FACILITIES AND SERVICES: No elevator (three floors), fans, office safe, TV

NEAREST TOURIST ATTRACTIONS: Mercato Centrale, Medici Chapel, shopping at San Lorenzo Market

TELEPHONE
055 46 20 226
FAX
055 48 23 59
INTERNET
www.residenza-lerondini.com
CREDIT CARDS
MC, V
RATES
Single 40–45€, double 60–80€, triple 90–110€; discount for *Great Sleeps Italy* readers
BREAKFAST
Not served
ENGLISH
Yes

Piazza della SS. Annunziata

The Piazza della SS. Annunziata is surrounded on three sides by lovely arcades and distinguished in the center by an equestrian statue of the Grand Duke Ferdinando I. The Ospedale degli Innocenti, designed by Brunelleschi in 1419, was built as a hospital for foundlings, who were the abandoned babies of domestic slaves. The blue-and-white medallions of babies are by Andrea della Robbia. The SS. Annunziata church, with a frescoed Baroque ceiling, was founded by the Servite Order in 1250, and rebuilt by Michelozzo between 1444 and 1480.

HOTELS

Hotel Monna Lisa ★★★★ ($)	72
Hotel Morandi alla Crocetta ★★★	73

($) indicates a Big Splurge

HOTEL MONNA LISA ★★★★ ($, 67)
Borgo Pinti, 27

TELEPHONE
055 24 79 751
FAX
055 24 79 755
INTERNET
www.monnalisa.it
CREDIT CARDS
AE, MC, V
RATES
Single 155–185€, double 240–360€, triple 430€, quad 515€, suite 515–725€; lower off-season rates
BREAKFAST
Buffet breakfast included
ENGLISH
Yes

45 rooms, all with bath, shower, and toilet

Part of the Renaissance palace that is now the Hotel Monna Lisa was built before 1300 as a convent or house of prayer. Joseph, the patriarch of Constantinople, lived here, along with twenty-three bishops from Greece and a number of other theologians and scholars. The palace is now owned by the Ciardì Dupré family, who turned it into a hotel in 1956. Over the years, they have added their own collection of antiques and paintings and made improvements gradually in order to avoid spoiling the original and ancient atmosphere of the building, which itself qualifies as a tourist attraction. The floors date from the 1500s, as does the ceiling in the sitting room, which was painted by Bernardino Poccetti Barbatelli when he lived in the palace some time between 1542 and 1612. The neoclassical drawing and sculpture collection is the work of Giovanni Dupré, who lived in Florence in the late 1800s, and from whom the family is descended. In the sitting room, you will find the first model of Giambologna's statuette Rape of the Sabines, which is displayed in its finished form in the Piazza della Signoria.

The public areas of the hotel are luxuriously appointed with deep red wall coverings, Oriental rugs, beautiful antique furniture, original art, a lovely fireplace, and a wall of windows in the breakfast room that opens onto a glorious garden, which is framed with boxwood hedges and filled with lemon trees, camelias, rhododendrons, azaleas, and colorful seasonal plantings.

Most of the rooms and suites have a dated elegance that many guests adore. Red-carpeted No. 19, a superior that can sleep four, has a narrow blue-and-white-tiled bathroom with a handheld shower over a tub with no curtain. The baronial furniture includes claw-footed twin beds, an enormous gold-trimmed mirror hanging over a large dresser, a lighted desk, and a 1960-style television set. Number 4, opening onto the hotel patio adjacent to the garden, is a small standard double with heavy floral fabric–covered walls, headboard, and curtains. Number 56, a double, is in the section at the back of the garden. It has an Art Deco feel to it that is carried out in the maroon, white, and gray-tiled bathroom. Until there is a complete facelift, please avoid No. 21, which surrounds occupants with busy green floral wall covering. It also has a sofa bed with a hideous pea green stretch cover over it that blocks the doors to the armoire, which has hangers positioned the wrong way. On a much more positive note, fifteen garden-view rooms have been added in the Limonia. Three of these very appealing superior rooms have balconies; all have polished floors, the right coordinated fabrics and furnishings, plus tiled baths (some with Jacuzzis) and easy access to a small gym, sauna, and rooftop solarium. The hotel is discreet, professional, and always helpful to their many devoted guests, who consider this gracious hotel to be a beautiful refuge in Florence.

FACILITIES AND SERVICES: Air-conditioning, bar, direct-dial phone, elevator in new section, hair dryer, guest Internet terminal, some Jacuzzis, laundry service, minibar, private parking (15€ per day), room service, satellite TV, free baby cot, some nonsmoking and handicapped-accessible rooms

NEAREST TOURIST ATTRACTIONS: Short walk to the Accademia and Il Duomo

HOTEL MORANDI ALLA CROCETTA ★★★ (35)
Via Laura, 50

10 rooms, all with shower or bath and toilet

The Morandi alla Crocetta is an absolute jewel that combines the best of modern comfort with the warmth of antique furnishings in an exquisitely restored convent dating from 1511. At this quiet and distinguished hotel, staff members pride themselves on giving four-star service and personal attention to all of their guests. Owner Paul

TELEPHONE
055 23 44 747
FAX
055 24 80 954
INTERNET
www.hotelmorandi.it
CREDIT CARDS
AE, DC, MC, V

RATES
Single 120€, double 177€,
triple 220€, quad 260€; lower-
off season rates depend on time
and availability
BREAKFAST
Continental breakfast 11€
ENGLISH
Yes

Doyle, who is also the architect responsible for this stunningly restored hotel, has worked diligently to keep the spirit of the original building alive. By ingeniously blending exposed parts of the original structure with pieces from other old buildings and authentic antiques, he has created a charming hotel with a definite sense of its past.

From the street, you pass by two large red clay pots and walk up a red-carpeted stairway to the front door. In the comfortable sitting room, easy chairs are well placed for conversation or for sitting and reading the morning papers. The unique rooms vary in size and magnitude. One of the best is No. 29, the chapel, with original frescoes that show the artist's brush strokes. Number 1 is a double, with four pieces of Mass vestments framed and hung as a backdrop for the bed. In No. 23, the bedroom is hung with Victorian prints and ten vestment pieces over the bed and has an armoire dating from the 1700s. Room 25 has an 1800s theme, with a wrought-iron bed and side tables accented in mother-of-pearl. The sitting area has a mirrored armoire and a mahogany desk with beveled-glass doors. Two rooms have a terrace, No. 26 and No. 30, the spacious suite. Room 26 can serve as a double or triple, thanks to a sofa bed. Two doors from the 1700s have been placed together and add interest to the room, as does the framed Greek icon over the bed. Number 30 has a dressing area and tiled bath (complete with a full-length mirror and heated towel rack) off the entry. The large bedroom, which opens onto a terrace with an antique fountain, has a brick fireplace with a painting of the owner's mother hanging above it. A comfortable sofa, a glass writing table, and a series of antique Florentine prints add to the enjoyment of this special suite.

Once people discover the Morandi, they never consider staying elsewhere. With only ten rooms, reservations fill up months in advance, so you must plan far ahead to get a spot.

NOTE: If you want to appreciate and understand Florence beyond what the usual tourist sees, please consider a private tour with one of the Morandi's own staff, Frank Peters, an extremely knowledgeable and personable American-born guide who conducts scholarly private tours. Reservations are mandatory and can be made through the hotel, but you do not need to be a guest of the hotel to schedule a tour. For more information, see "Tours and Classes," page 48.

FACILITIES AND SERVICES: Air-conditioning, bar, direct-dial phone (both in room and bathroom), no elevator (hotel is on first floor), hair dryer, guest Internet terminal, magnifying mirror in bathroom, minibar, two parking spaces (must request in advance, 16€ per day), radio, satellite TV, in-room safe

NEAREST TOURIST ATTRACTIONS: Accademia, Piazza della SS. Annunziata, Museo Archeologico

Piazza del Mercato Centrale

Inside the Mercato Centrale, a nineteenth-century food market hall, you will find the beautiful bounty of Tuscany: fruit, vegetables, meat, fish, and dairy products displayed in stalls covering two floors. Surrounding it is the San Lorenzo Market, which is teeming with stands selling the good, the bad, the indifferent, and the ugly—most particularly, clothes, gloves, bags, paper and leather goods, and of course, T-shirts.

The San Lorenzo Church, built between 1419 and 1469, was the parish church of the Medici family, and its massive dome is almost as big as that of Il Duomo. The inside of the basilica is a pure example of Renaissance art, exhibiting as it does the genius of Brunelleschi and Michelangelo, who designed the interior facade. Also of great interest are the Old Sacristy and the Medici Chapels, designed by Michelangelo as a Medici mausoleum.

HOTELS

Albergo Hotel Nazionale ★ (¢)	**75**
Hotel Accademia ★★	**76**
Hotel Basilea ★★★	**77**
Hotel Centro ★★	**77**
Hotel Globus ★★★	**78**
Hotel Nuova Italia ★★ (¢)	**78**
Hotel Palazzo Benci ★★★	**79**

(¢) indicates a Cheap Sleep

ALBERGO HOTEL NAZIONALE ★ (¢, 19)
Via Nazionale, 22, second floor
9 rooms, 5 with shower and toilet

Although not luxurious by any stretch of the imagination, the rooms at the second-floor Albergo Hotel Nazionale are pleasing to the eye, with freshly whitewashed walls, plain but scratch-free furniture, good wardrobe space, and clean bathrooms. Those facing the frantically busy Via Nazionale are noisy, but the windows are double-glazed to help quell the roar. Of course, if you open them, you will not have the soundproofing. For better sleeping prospects,

TELEPHONE
055 23 82 203
FAX
055 23 81 735
INTERNET
www.nazionalehotel.it
CREDIT CARDS
MC, V
RATES
Single 50–60€, double 80–90€, triple 115–125€

BREAKFAST
Continental breakfast included
ENGLISH
Yes

request a quiet room on the back with a sunny exposure. If it is a view of Il Duomo you want, ask for either Room 8 or 9, which also have the decided benefit of screens.

FACILITIES AND SERVICES: Air-conditioning in 5 rooms, direct-dial phone, no elevator (hotel on second floor), fans, parking (20€ per day), office safe, satellite TV

NEAREST TOURIST ATTRACTIONS: Mercato Centrale, Medici Chapel, shopping at San Lorenzo Market, train station, 20 minutes to Il Duomo

HOTEL ACCADEMIA ★★ (40)
Via Faenza, 7

TELEPHONE
055 29 34 51
FAX
055 21 97 71
INTERNET
www.accademiahotel.net
CREDIT CARDS
AE, MC, V
RATES
Single 50–90€, double 80–150€, triple 100–180€, quad 120–210€; special Internet rates and lower off-season rates
BREAKFAST
Buffet breakfast included
ENGLISH
Yes

20 rooms, all with shower or bath and toilet

The Accademia—with twenty rooms spread on three floors in a distinguished building—is located in an area known as "hotel heaven," because no matter what your price range or needs you have many choices. This hotel is family run and one of the prettiest two-stars in the neighborhood.

Many of the best features of the old hotel were kept and improved upon during the last renovation. The original eighteenth-century stained-glass windows and a painted ceiling create a dramatic entry area. Past this entry and up red-carpeted stone stairs, you will be impressed by the breakfast room, which also has a frescoed ceiling, corner fireplace, huge gilt mirror, stained-glass doors attributed to the Bernardo Cennini school of design (Cennini designed the magnificent door of the baptistery on Il Duomo), and a collection of framed photos of Florence mixed in with watercolors of Tuscany.

Room 6, for two or three, has hardwood floors, matching colors, and a tiled bathroom with a shower and curtain. Number 5 looks great, all in yellow with a cherub pattern on the bedspreads, and so does No. 4, a large twin with plenty of space. If you don't mind being near the reception area, No. 3, which overlooks a little garden, might appeal to you. Rooms 18, 19, and 21 open directly onto the garden.

FACILITIES AND SERVICES: Air-conditioning, bar, direct-dial phone, no elevator (2 floors), hair dryer available, guest Internet terminal, some minibars, satellite TV, in-room safe

NEAREST TOURIST ATTRACTIONS: Mercato Centrale, shopping at San Lorenzo Market, Medici Chapel, train station

HOTEL BASILEA ★★★ (20)
Via Guelfa, 41

38 rooms, all with bath or shower and toilet

The Hotel Basilea is owned and managed by the Abolaffio family. Their expert touch is evident everywhere, from the upstairs sitting room, nicely set with wingback chairs and polished wood floors, to the sunny terrace with a rooftop view of the Mercato Centrale and a series of working art studios. A generous buffet breakfast is served in a welcoming room with an original floral painted ceiling. The tables are set with yellow tablecloths and a bouquet of fresh flowers. The wall-papered bedrooms, most of which have been redecorated, are furnished with quality reproductions, including brass beds with new mattresses and bedspreads. Five have private terraces, and an additional two have balcony views of Il Duomo. Bathrooms are undergoing renovations, so some still have those odd half-tubs with a seat across the back. Newer ones have enclosed showers. In addition, guests are just a click away from cyberspace, as there is a free Internet terminal in the lobby.

FACILITIES AND SERVICES: Air-conditioning, direct-dial phone, elevator, hair dryer, guest Internet terminal, laundry, minibar, parking (25€ per day), office safe, TV, 10 nonsmoking rooms

NEAREST TOURIST ATTRACTIONS: Mercato Centrale, shopping at San Lorenzo Market, Medici Chapel, Piazza San Marco, Accademia, train station

TELEPHONE
055 21 45 87
FAX
055 26 83 50
EMAIL
basilea@dada.it
INTERNET
www.florenceitaly.net
CREDIT CARDS
AE, DC, MC, V
RATES
Single 80–110€, double 110–150€, triple 150–210€, quad 170–250€, family suite for 3–5 people 170–310€
BREAKFAST
Continental breakfast included
ENGLISH
Yes

HOTEL CENTRO ★★ (29)
Via de' Ginori, 17

16 rooms, 14 with shower and toilet

The Hotel Centro is in a former palace that was Raphael's favorite residence during his time in Florence. In 1996 the hotel was redone, and it now offers moderately priced Great Sleeping options between the Mercato Centrale and Il Duomo. The hotel is attractively dressed with light colors, which create a nice background for the collection of modern paintings done by a local artist and friend of the owner. In the rooms, good mattresses, modern furniture, individual safes, air-conditioning, and CNN should help to make your stay more comfortable. In No. 203, expect some noise and heat in the summer, since it has no air-conditioning. In No. 211, you will have your own balcony, and in No. 207, one of the best doubles, there are built-ins, luggage space, and a small but servicable bathroom. If there are three of you, ask for No. 104, a triple with a shower, and if four, request No. 201, a huge room with two windows on the street.

TELEPHONE
055 23 02 901
FAX
055 21 27 06
INTERNET
www. hotelcentro.net
CREDIT CARDS
AE, MC, V
RATES
Single 55–95€, double 70–140€, triple 90–180€, quad 120–220€
BREAKFAST
Buffet breakfast included
ENGLISH
Yes

FACILITIES AND SERVICES: Air-conditioning in 6 rooms (otherwise fans, same room rate), direct-dial phone, elevator from first floor of hotel, hair dryer, guest Internet terminal, radio, satellite TV, in-room safe

NEAREST TOURIST ATTRACTIONS: Shopping at San Lorenzo Market, Mercato Centrale, Medici Chapel, Il Duomo

HOTEL GLOBUS ★★★ (37)
Via Sant' Antonino, 24, third floor
23 rooms, all with shower and toilet

TELEPHONE
055 21 10 62
FAX
055 23 96 225
INTERNET
www.hotelglobus.com
CREDIT CARDS
AE, DC, MC, V
RATES
Single 70–95€, double 130–175€, triple 130–195€, quad 150–210€; 10% discount to *Great Sleeps Italy* readers
BREAKFAST
Buffet breakfast included
ENGLISH
Yes

If you want to be *centralissimo,* stay at Michele and Serena's three-star Hotel Globus, which was reopened in 2002 after a six-month complete overhaul. The hotel was redone in a minimalistic way, using cool muted colors, accented with stylized orchids and lucky bamboo plants. The simple bedrooms are all the same, only the color of the bedcovers (brown, green, cocoa, and blue) and the dimensions change. Each has a free computer keyboard that operates on the television. Number 304, a double, is a grand-slam winner, with a peek at the tip of the Medici Chapel and a little balcony. Numbers 209 and 309 are not so fortunate; they overlook the cluttered back of a discotheque (with the Medici Chapel beyond), but they do have bathtubs and a bit more space. Breakfast is served on glass tables positioned along cushioned beige banquettes in an airy room that doubles as a bar during the day.

FACILITIES AND SERVICES: Air-conditioning, bar, direct-dial phone, elevator from first floor, hair dryer, in-room and lobby Internet services, satellite TV, in-room safe, 2 handicapped-accessible rooms, 12 nonsmoking rooms

NEAREST TOURIST ATTRACTIONS: Mercato Centrale, shopping at San Lorenzo Market, Medici Chapel

HOTEL NUOVA ITALIA ★★ (¢, 27)
Via Faenza, 26
20 rooms, all with shower or bath and toilet

TELEPHONE
055 28 75 08, 055 26 84 30
FAX
055 21 09 41
EMAIL
hotel.nuova.italia@dada.it
INTERNET
www.hotel-nuovaitalia.com
CREDIT CARDS
AE, MC, V
RATES
Single 70–90€, double 90–120€, triple 110–140€; lower off-season rates

During all of my trips to Italy, I have seen literally hundreds and hundreds of hotels. I will tell you that I have seen fewer than a dozen in all of the star categories combined that provide something as simple as screens on their windows. It may not seem like much, but Italy, especially Florence and Venice, is invaded in the warm months by over-sized, relentless, carnivorous mosquitoes. Many hotels provide mosquito coils and bug repelling plug-ins, but I have not found them to be 100 percent effective, so I always warn readers to pack plenty of extra-strength mosquito repellent—and even then, you can expect to be awakened at some point by an elusive buzzing near your ear. However, at the Hotel Nuova Italia, peace and sleep replace the nightly insect battle. Why? Because in addition to air-conditioning in every room, they provide screens on the windows! I cannot emphasize this enough in terms of comfort during your stay.

Okay, so they provide screens, but what about the rooms and the rest of the hotel? At the Nuova Italia, owned by Luciano Viti, his Canadian wife, Eileen, and their daughter Daniela, care and personal attention are extended to all their guests. Their motto is, "Just ask and we will do our best to accommodate you." Pride of ownership is evident from the reception desk onward. The stone stairway, lined with art exhibition posters collected by Eileen, leads guests to the unadorned rooms, which are repainted annually, uniformly carpeted, and done in easy-care laminated wood furniture. All the rooms have private bathrooms, and the showers have curtains. Some of the rooms along the front can be noisy, especially in the early morning when market vendors pull their carts along the cobblestones. There are triple-glazed windows—called Airport Windows—but for ensured quiet, reserve an inside room, perhaps No. 18, which is one of Luciano's favorites. A downstairs sitting room showcases the family's collection of Italian paintings. This is where you will be served a Continental breakfast in the morning. The hotel is close to many good restaurants (see *Great Eats Italy*), interesting shopping (see Great Chic, page 330), and most of the places visitors have on their Florence itinerary.

FACILITIES AND SERVICES: Air-conditioning, direct-dial phone, no elevator (2 floors), hair dryer available, parking (20€ per day), satellite TV, office safe, and...screens on the windows

NEAREST TOURIST ATTRACTIONS: Mercato Centrale, shopping at San Lorenzo Market, Medici Chapel, train station, most other tourist sites within a 20- to 30-minute walk

BREAKFAST
Continental breakfast included
ENGLISH
Yes

HOTEL PALAZZO BENCI ★★★ (41)
Piazza Madonna degli Aldobrandini, 3 (at Via Faenza, 6/r)

35 rooms, all with shower or bath and toilet

The Hotel Palazzo Benci is a renovated sixteenth-century mansion of the Benci family of Florence. It is now an attractive uptown hotel owned and personally run by the Braccia family. The service they provide is cordial and always discreet, appealing to many government officials and top businesspeople when they are in Florence. Assisting

TELEPHONE
055 21 70 49, 055 21 38 48
FAX
055 28 83 08
INTERNET
www.palazzobenci.com
CREDIT CARDS
AE, DC, MC, V

RATES
Single 83–140€, double 130–195€, triple 155–220€, quad 180–245€
BREAKFAST
Buffet breakfast included
ENGLISH
Yes

the staff with greeting guests is the hotel mascot, Oliver, a West Highland terrier who operates from his command post in the front window.

The compact, well-decorated bedrooms provide guests with all the creature comforts and are quiet, soothing retreats after a long day of sightseeing or shopping in Florence. The rooms along the back overlook the Medici Chapel. All the rooms have double-glazed windows and air-conditioning. They also have another invaluable feature, especially in summer when the mosquitoes arrive in full force: screens on the windows. The hotel's enclosed, flower-filled garden has tables with umbrellas for summer alfresco breakfasts or afternoon drinks. The comfortable lounge area has turquoise leather sofas and chairs and a marble floor. Also on view is a glass-covered eleventh-century well, which is older by far than the building. To get to the breakfast room, guests cross the ornate upstairs sitting room, with a handsome, heavily scrolled ceiling, which served as a guest room in the mansion in the 1700s. In the breakfast room guests can admire the wooden ceiling, which once graced a room on the third floor of the palace, and they can enjoy direct views of the Medici Chapel.

FACILITIES AND SERVICES: Air-conditioning, bar, direct-dial phone, elevator, hair dryer, laundry service, minibar, satellite TV, room safe, window screens

NEAREST TOURIST ATTRACTIONS: Mercato Centrale, San Lorenzo Market, Medici Chapel, Il Duomo, 10- to 30-minute walk to most other destinations

Piazza Goldoni and Via de' Tornabuoni

Named after the playwright Carlo Goldoni, Piazza Goldini is a crossroads leading from Via dei Fossi across the Ponte alle Carraia to Piazza Santo Spirito on the Oltrarno. Via de' Tornabuoni is an elegant street lined with houses of the Florentine nobility, the most famous of which is Palazzo Strozzi, whose golden stone facade dominates the street. This stretch of pavement is sheer mecca for true shoppers—all the premier designer shops, including Prada, Gucci, Hèrmes, Ferragamo, Tiffany's, and Yves St. Laurent, are within a block or two of one another, and many more top names are nearby on side streets.

HOTELS

($) indicates a Big Splurge; (¢) indicates a Cheap Sleep

ALBERGO SCOTI ★ (¢, 84)
Via de' Tornabuoni, 7
11 rooms, 10 with shower and toilet

For cheap sleeps in one of the toniest sections of Florence, Doreen and Carmelo's Albergo Scoti is a popular choice that seldom has a vacancy. What you will save by sleeping cheaply you can apply to your purchases at the famous fashion boutiques lining Via de' Tornabuoni. The hundred-year-old *albergo* is located in an ancient Florentine palace that still has remnants of original frescoes and intricately tiled floors. As Doreen proudly told me, "Having a place that has a past gives one a sense of belonging, and we have guests who stayed here years ago, and now come by to say hello, whenever we are full and don't have a room for them." The eleven bedchambers are furnished with a collection of this-and-that furniture mixed in with wrought-iron beds and some great family Art Deco pieces. The ten new bathrooms boast heated towel racks and enclosed showers. Those staying in No. 2 will look out on the bell tower of Santa Trinita. In No. 10, the floor has been retiled, the bathroom upgraded, and the quadruple-size wardrobe is big enough for the contents of a large suitcase. Breakfast is extra and served in your room or in the dining room, where guests sit on copies of fifteenth-century red-velvet chairs.

FACILITIES AND SERVICES: Elevator, fans, hair dryer available, office safe

NEAREST TOURIST ATTRACTIONS: Shopping, shopping, shopping, plus Il Duomo and the core of Florence

TELEPHONE & FAX
055 29 21 28
EMAIL
hotelscoti@hotmail.com
INTERNET
www.hotelscoti.com
CREDIT CARDS
AE, MC, V
RATES
Single or double 105€
BREAKFAST
Continental breakfast 6€ extra
ENGLISH
Yes (Doreen is Australian)

ALBERGOTTO HOTEL ★★★★ ($, 83)
Via de' Tornabuoni, 13
22 rooms, all with bath, shower, and toilet

Carlo Martelli's single-minded purpose for his twenty-two-room hotel in the heart of Florence's premier shopping and sightseeing district is to offer stylish hospitality and tasteful, comfortable accommodations. On all accounts, he succeeds very well. The lift is on the first floor, so

TELEPHONE
055 23 96 464
FAX
055 23 98 108
INTERNET
www.albergotto.com
CREDIT CARDS
AE, DC, MC, V

RATES
Single 130–170€, double 178–253€, Mansarda suite 240–312€

BREAKFAST
Buffet breakfast included

ENGLISH
Yes

when you arrive, ring the bell at street level for the porter to come help with your luggage. When walking up, be sure to admire the collection of Zocchi prints, one of the most well-known artists of the 1700s. The reception area is small but leads into a sitting room with a bar and two very pretty breakfast areas, which display a collection of antique plates in floral and bird motifs.

The rooms have uniform cream-colored walls, floral fabrics on the curtains and spreads, and hardwood floors. Number 31 is a huge deluxe double, with a choice of a king or twin beds, two large windows, and copies of antique furniture purchased in London. The spacious Florentine green mosaic-tiled bathroom has heated towel racks and a three-tiered cart for toiletries. Number 28, a standard double, has less space but still has plenty of light and a serviceable bathroom with a stall shower. Number 25 is a pleasant, light single with a view of the Palazzo Strozzi. The only room with a view of the city is No. 40, the fourth-floor Mansarda suite with a beamed ceiling. Wingback chairs, a large pigeon-hole desk, and a chest of drawers add to its overall appeal.

FACILITIES AND SERVICES: Air-conditioning, bar, mini-bar, direct-dial phone, elevator from the first floor, hair dryer, laundry service, valet parking (from 26€ per day), porter, in-room safe, tea and coffeemakers, satellite TV

NEAREST TOURIST ATTRACTIONS: Heart of Florence, premier shopping, walking distance to everything

ANTICA TORRE DI VIA TORNABUONI NO. 1 ($, 102)
Via de' Tornabuoni, 1

12 rooms all with bath, shower, and toilet

TELEPHONE
055 265 81 69/1

FAX
055 21 88 41

INTERNET
www.tornabuoni1.com

CREDIT CARDS
AE, DC, MC, V

RATES
Single 180–200€, double 230–250€, suite 300–350€; lower off-season rates

BREAKFAST
Buffet breakfast included

ENGLISH
Yes

The Antica Torre is a sublime residence located in the heart of Florence, where guests are a heartbeat away from designer shopping, smart wine bars, romantic restaurants, and all the most important tourist destinations. Guests have access to the tower and two terrace lounges, which have spectacular panoramic views of the city both day and night. The spacious bedrooms are streamlined with every convenience to please a male traveler, yet decorative and seductively comfortable to appeal to women. Three of them have private terraces, one is a junior suite, and all are nonsmoking and have ISDN lines and large, well-lit marble bathrooms. Customer care and satisfaction are main objectives of the owner, Jacopo d'Albasio, and are competently carried out by his reception staff.

FACILITIES AND SERVICES: Air-conditioning, bar, direct-dial phone, elevator, hair dryer, data ports, laundry service, minibar, in-room safe, satellite TV, tea and coffeemakers, all nonsmoking rooms, reception open 8:30 A.M.–8 P.M.

NEAREST TOURIST ATTRACTIONS: The heart of Florence, within easy walking distance to almost everything

HOTEL GOLDONI ★★★ (73)
Borgo Ognissanti, 8
20 rooms, all with shower or bath and toilet

If you cannot afford the over-the-top prices at the nearby Excelsior and Grand Hotels, then check into this moderate three-star, competently run by Daniela Nerozzi. All twenty rooms are done in soft blue, from the quilted bedspreads on brass beds to the tiled bathrooms. The rooms are not created equal, other than having the same color scheme. For instance, only one room, No. 27, has a tiny balcony, but it is spacious enough to house four. All rooms have a shower, and three of these have additional bathtubs. Several others, notably Nos. 22, 23, and 28, face walls, but they are very quiet. So is No. 25, which also has lots of light. The best buys here are the family rooms, which go for 210€ for four people. Couple that price with the discount offered to readers who mention *Great Sleeps Italy,* and you have a Great Sleeping deal.

FACILITIES AND SERVICES: Air-conditioning, bar, direct-dial phone, elevator, hair dryer, laundry service, minibar, parking (20€ per day), in-room safe, satellite TV

NEAREST TOURIST ATTRACTIONS: River Arno, Piazza Santa Maria Novella, shopping

TELEPHONE
055 28 40 80
FAX
055 28 25 76
INTERNET
www.hotelgoldoni.com
CREDIT CARDS
AE, DC, MC, V
RATES
Single 98€, double 155€, family rooms (4 people) 210€; discounts to *Great Sleeps Italy* readers
BREAKFAST
Buffet breakfast included
ENGLISH
Yes

HOTEL TORNABUONI-BEACCI ★★★★ ($, 100)
Palazzo Minerbetti-Strozzi, Via de' Tornabuoni, 3
40 rooms, all with shower or bath and toilet

"Just what we have been looking for." "It is nice to feel at home so far away from home." "Every room is different, but they are all full of joy."

These are only three of the many enthusiastic comments written by visitors in the guest book, which dates back to 1917, when Sra. Beacci's parents opened this Florentine hotel. One of my favorites was written on November 29, 1928, and reads, "We the undersigned guests of the Hotel Tornabuoni-Beacci deem it to be in the interests of future American visitors to Florence to know of the perfection of the cuisine, the rare courtesy and the refinement of this hotel." This praise is followed by nine signatures. Over the years, the devoted clientele of writers (including John Steinbeck),

TELEPHONE
055 21 26 45
FAX
055 28 35 94
INTERNET
www.tornabuonihotels.com
CREDIT CARDS
AE, DC, MC, V
RATES
Single 150–180€, double 180–260€, suite 300–360€; extra person 50€; 3-course dinner 35€; lower off-season rates and Internet specials
BREAKFAST
Buffet breakfast included

ENGLISH
Yes

actors, models, heads-of-state and their wives (including Barbara Bush on several recent occasions), and just plain folks have returned time and again largely because of the warmth of the staff and the way they make everyone feel right at home. Francesco Bechi, who took over the reins from Sra. Beacci, along with the help of longtime manager Angelo and his delightful wife, Patricia, have clearly maintained Sra. Beacci's standards of excellence, while at the same time, they have breathed new life into the forty rooms so perfectly located in the heart of Florence.

Everything about the hotel is gracious and discerning without being pretentious. The sitting room, with its wood-burning fireplace, is comfortable and classically furnished with antiques, big sofas, easy chairs, and rare antique wall tapestries. Everywhere you look there are beautiful fresh flower arrangements and lush green indoor plants, which are cared for by Antonio Bechi, an attorney whose hobby is horticulture. The large, refreshed bedrooms, done in pastels, with painted furniture mixed with vintage wood, are so inviting that you may want to settle in and stay forever... or at least longer than intended. They are all fitted with comfortable reading chairs, dressers with a mirror, good beds with extra pillows, and large, sunny windows. Some come with original frescoes, others with a view of Il Duomo or San Miniato al Monte Church, which dates from 1127 and is the oldest in Florence. The bathrooms are slowly being redone in a more modern mode, but even those that are vintage are wonderful. The twelve new rooms don't quite have the charm or the views of the older ones, but they are large, very well-furnished, and two have dressing rooms and marble bathrooms. Rates vary depending on the size of the room.

A jasmine-filled rooftop terrace and the tower terrace are perfect places for afternoon drinks or a leisurely breakfast. They both offer splendid views of neighboring rooftops and churches and a Florentine sunset to behold. In addition to breakfast, guests can eat dinner three nights a week at the hotel, on Monday, Wednesday, and Friday. Snacks at the bar or on the terrace are available at lunchtime, but for dinner there is a well-selected à la carte menu.

FACILITIES AND SERVICES: Air-conditioning, bar, direct-dial phone, elevator to most rooms, guest Internet terminal, minibar, satellite TV, in-room safe, dinner three nights a week

NEAREST TOURIST ATTRACTIONS: Central to everything

Piazzale di Porta al Prato

This is one of the oldest gates of Florence, but today the area is a bit of a visitor's no-man's-land. However, there is good public transportation, and the location provides easy access to the highways out of the city.

HOTEL VILLA AZALEE ★★★
Viale Fratelli Rosselli, 44
25 rooms, all with shower or bath and toilet

It is always hard to be objective when you are in love, and I fell head over heels for the Villa Azalee the minute I arrived. After every visit, I must admit, I am even more in love than the last time. This romantic hotel is simply without peer in Florence.

The hotel was once the private family home of its present owner, Sra. Ornella Brizzi, who in transforming it has spared no effort to create an elegant haven of beauty and charm. Villa Azalee has that small-hotel look and feel, which is achieved through Sra. Brizzi's imaginative personal touch honed from her world travels and reinforced by her dedicated staff. Both are willing to go the extra mile to provide service and attention to each valued guest.

It is absolutely impossible to select a favorite room because each is unique and works perfectly in its own harmonious way. Number 28, on the first level, streetside, has a marvelous net canopy over a pink quilted headboard and an eyelet-ruffled duvet cover. Two chairs plus a long sofa provide the seating. The bath has a big tub and plenty of sink and shelf space. Number 21 has a violet flower theme carried out on the quilt spread, rug, settee, and two wing chairs. Over the bed is a lacy white canopy appliquéd with pink flowers. The bathroom is divine, with the convenience of a four-line drying rack hung over a walk-in shower. Number 24 is also fabulous, with a frescoed ceiling and a crown-held drape over the twin or king-size beds. There is a large double dresser to hold all of your clothes, a comfortable armchair, a terrace on the back, and a marble-tiled bathroom with a stall shower. Number 26, with a garden view, has its original inlaid floor and a great white headdress of net over the quilted bedspread, plus matching curtains and bedside table covers. If noise is a problem for you, consider reserving a room in the annex in back, which Sra. Brizzi calls a "cottage." Some cottage! The eight rooms here are slightly smaller but offer no shortage

TELEPHONE
055 21 42 42
FAX
055 26 82 64
EMAIL
villaazalee@fi.flashnet.it
INTERNET
www.villa-azalee.it
CREDIT CARDS
AE, DC, MC, V
RATES
Single 115€, double 175€, triple 234€; lower off-season rates
BREAKFAST
Buffet breakfast included
ENGLISH
Yes

of appeal, especially No. 29, a romantic room where you will be sleeping in an iron canopy bed from the 1800s and showering beneath a nozzle the size of a dinner plate. Number 36 has a jacaranda vine–covered terrace and a beamed bedroom.

The garden surrounding the villa is a beautiful oasis, filled with seasonal blooming plants and flowers, including azaleas and camellias in late winter. On the entry level of the villa is a glass sunroom and another, more formal sitting room around the corner. The sunroom, filled with light and attractive furnishings, is accented with multitudes of green plants and fresh flowers. To the side of it stands a wonderful telephone booth that was once a sedan chair. The sitting room has a working fireplace, old paintings, and an arrangement of comfortable, overstuffed chairs and sofas. Be sure to notice the antique Chinese glass screen.

In the adorable pink-and-white-striped breakfast room, your meal will be served on Richard Ginori china and your hot beverages poured from the family's collection of silver coffee and tea pots. Breakfast, which can also be brought to your room, is served until 11 A.M. This is because, as Sra. Brizzi told me, she likes the luxury of sleeping late whenever she takes a holiday, and she wants her guests to feel at home to do the same here.

The location may seem distant from the heart of Florence, but there is excellent bus service just around the corner; Nos. 1 and 17 go directly to Il Duomo. Or, for around 4€ per day, rent one of the hotel's bicycles and pedal your way around Florence.

FACILITIES AND SERVICES: Air-conditioning, bar, direct-dial phone, no elevator (2 floors), hair dryer, minibar, clothes drying racks, laundry service, parking (25€ per day), room service, satellite TV, office safe, bicycles for rent (around 4€ per day, BYO helmet)

NEAREST TOURIST ATTRACTIONS: Opera house; otherwise must take bus, car, or bicycle, or walk about 30 minutes to central Florence

Piazza Massimo d'Azeglio

This pretty green square on the eastern edge of Florence anchors a residential neighborhood a few blocks north of the Sant' Ambrogio market.

HOTEL VILLA LIANA ★★★ (36)
Via Alfieri, 18
24 rooms, all with shower or bath and toilet

The Hotel Liana is in a nineteenth-century villa that once served as the British Embassy. When you see the public areas of the hotel, with their inlaid Florentine-tile floors, magnificent frescoes, and a bygone air of casual elegance, it is easy to imagine formal parties and receptions being held here and in the gardens behind. I think the prime rooms face the garden. One of these is Number 1, a large duplex done in seafoam green and gold with twin beds on the mezzanine; another is No. 6, a second-floor double with a balcony and a pink-tile bathroom. Number 24 is a majestic choice with cupid frescoes, Florentine painted furniture, and a needlepointed child's chair that, while admittedly useless, is adorable. Number 5, known as the Count's Room, is as regal as the name suggests thanks to its almost overpowering mural of a man arriving in a swan-propelled boat to meet his lover waiting on the shore. Cupid also reigns over the breakfast room, which is enhanced further by a marble fireplace and carved doorframes.

All in all, it is quite appealing if you don't mind staying on the fringes of Florence, or if you are in a car and want to be by the ring road, thereby avoiding the impossible driving conditions in central Florence.

FACILITIES AND SERVICES: Air-conditioning in most rooms, bar, direct-dial phone, no elevator (3 floors), hair dryer available, guest Internet terminal, laundry service, some minibars, private parking (15€ per day), office safe, TV

NEAREST TOURIST ATTRACTIONS: None, 30-minute walk to most tourist spots, 20-minute trip on buses 31 or 32 to train station and near Il Duomo

TELEPHONE
055 24 53 03/4, 055 23 44 595

FAX
055 23 44 596

INTERNET
www.hotelliana.com

CREDIT CARDS
AE, DC, MC, V

RATES
Single 135€, double 175€, extra bed 55€; lower off-season rates

BREAKFAST
Buffet breakfast included

ENGLISH
Yes

Piazza San Marco

Cosimo il Vecchio (a Medici) built the Dominican monastery of San Marco and funded a public library full of Greek and Latin classical works. This is now the Museo di San Marco, which occupies the convent beside the church and is dedicated to the works of Fra Angelico of Fiesole, a fifteenth-century spiritual artist.

HOTELS

Antica Dimora Firenze	**88**
Hotel Casci ★★	**89**
Hotel Colorado ★ (¢)	**90**
Hotel Il Guelfo Bianco ★★★ ($)	**90**
Hotel Orto de' Medici ★★★ ($)	**91**
Residenza Johlea I & II (¢)	**92**

OTHER OPTIONS
Apartment Rentals

Residenza Sangallo	**130**

($) indicates a Big Splurge; (¢) indicates a Cheap Sleep

ANTICA DIMORA FIRENZE (24)
Via San Gallo, 72

TELEPHONE
055 46 33 292
FAX
055 46 34 552
INTERNET
www.anticadimorafirenze.it
CREDIT CARDS
None, cash only, or euro traveler's checks
RATES
1–2 people 130€, extra bed 25€
BREAKFAST
Buffet breakfast included
ENGLISH
Yes

6 rooms, all with shower or bath and toilet

Antica Dimora Firenze is the latest jewel in the crown of Lea Gulmanelli, who also owns a number of recommended properties in this guide: Residenza Johanna (page 70), Residenza Johanna II (page 70), Residenza Johlea I & II (page 92), and Villa il Poggiale in the Tuscan countryside (page 144).

Antica Dimora is a carefully restored palace that offers great value for money. Its six individually decorated bedrooms have pastel upholstery and beautiful antique furniture, and generously displayed throughout is the owner's impressive art collection of botanical prints and watercolors. The Blue Room is almost a private art museum: botanical art prints decorate the turquoise entryway, while in the bathroom are paintings of Santa Spirito, Uffizi Gallery, Ponte Vecchio, and the doors of the city at Porta al Prato and Porta San Gallo. The bedroom has a four-poster canopy bed and opens onto a small balcony. The Yellow Room overlooks the Palazzo Pandolfini, home of one of Florence's most famous families. The Green Room is also called "the room of the water" because all of the prints concern water and ships. The Pink Room is a large double with good desk space, a nicely lit bathroom, and prints of Florentine gardens and monuments. The Peach Room has a Moroccan theme carried out in the lacy lights and colorful throw rugs spread over the terra-cotta floor. The two windows overlook a beautiful terrace. Buffet breakfast and afternoon apéritifs are served in a stylish sitting room, which has more interesting prints and a fanciful painting of an Italian train.

FACILITIES AND SERVICES: Air-conditioning, direct-dial phone, elevator, hair dryer, guest Internet terminal, minibar, laundry service, in-room safe, satellite TV with DVD, reception open daily 8:30 A.M.–8 P.M.

NEAREST TOURIST ATTRACTIONS: Accademia, Medici Chapel, Mercato Centrale, shopping at San Lorenzo Market

HOTEL CASCI ★★ (25)
Via Camillo Cavour, 13

25 rooms, all with shower or bath and toilet

The Casci is owned and managed by the Lombardi family: Armando, Carla, and their son, Paolo. All are fluent in several languages and do a fine job of taking personal care of their guests. While I was at the hotel, Carla's comment to me proved true: "We say kindness and cleanliness go a long way." Obviously, many Great Sleepers in Florence agree and have endorsed her philosophy by becoming devoted regulars.

The hotel is centrally located in a fifteenth-century palace that was once home to the famous nineteenth-century musician Gioacchino Rossini. From the doorstep, guests are close to Il Duomo, countless museums, good Florence shopping, and many restaurants listed in *Great Eats Italy.* The comfortable rooms are upgraded and maintained on a regular schedule. All have private bathrooms, luggage and closet space, and pleasing colors. Number 6 is called the Honeymoon Room because it overlooks a garden with a lovely magnolia tree. Number 21 is a good double with a pink cloudlike tiled bathroom with both a tub and shower; however the most ooh-la-la tub in the hotel is the corner one with pink floral inlaid tile found in No. 24, a family room for four. Breakfast is served in a large dining room with its original frescoed ceiling and a colorful collection of Carla's vibrant plants, which provide evidence of her green thumb. When going back and forth to your room, be sure to notice the framed collection of geographical jigsaw puzzles that Paolo assembled as a boy, and in the process learned geography and developed his keen desire to travel throughout the world.

TELEPHONE
055 21 16 86

FAX
055 23 96 461

INTERNET
www.hotelcasci.com

CREDIT CARDS
AE, DC, MC, V

RATES
Single 105€, double 145€, triple 185€, quad 225€; excellent lower off-season rates

BREAKFAST
Buffet breakfast included

ENGLISH
Yes

FACILITIES AND SERVICES: Air-conditioning, bar, direct-dial phone, hair dryer, elevator, guest Internet and email access, laundry service, unstocked room refrigerator, satellite TV, individual safe-deposit boxes in the office for each guest

NEAREST TOURIST ATTRACTIONS: Il Duomo, Piazza San Marco, and all of central Florence

HOTEL COLORADO ★ (¢, 7)
Via Camillo Cavour, 66

TELEPHONE
055 21 73 10
FAX
055 28 37 83
INTERNET
www.hotelcoloradofirenze.com
CREDIT CARDS
AE, MC, V
RATES
Single 70€, double 90€, triple 120€, quad 140€; lower off-season rates
BREAKFAST
Buffet breakfast included
ENGLISH
Yes

10 rooms, all with shower and toilet

Hotel Colorado is a perky one-star not far from the Accademia. It is run by a young couple, Franco and Donata, who say, "We are everything from owner and manager to plumber and cleaning person." Thanks to a recent renovation, everything from top to bottom is in good order, including new doors with brass handles, and all the furniture, fabrics, and bathrooms. The only remnants of the past are the original mosaic floors in Nos. 18 and 20, which are pretty choices on the quiet side of the hotel, overlooking a garden. Those facing front, especially No. 2, are noisy and do not have double-glazed windows. However, when you look at the cheap sleeping prices, ear plugs are a sensible investment.

FACILITIES AND SERVICES: Air-conditioning, direct-dial phones, hair dryer available, no elevator (hotel is on fourth floor, 55 steps), office safe, TV in lounge

NEAREST TOURIST ATTRACTIONS: Accademia, Piazza San Marco, 15-minute walk to Il Duomo

HOTEL IL GUELFO BIANCO ★★★ ($, 30)
Via Camillo Cavour, 29

TELEPHONE
055 28 83 30
FAX
055 29 52 03
INTERNET
www.ilguelfobianco.it
CREDIT CARDS
AE, DC, MC, V
RATES
Single 135–180€, double 150–235€, triple 265€, quad 285€, apartment 420€; lower off-season rates
BREAKFAST
Buffet breakfast included
ENGLISH
Yes

43 rooms, all with shower or bath and toilet

Il Guelfo Bianco is an ideal upmarket, midtown choice for those wanting to be a heartbeat away from the artistic and architectural treasures of Florence. For businesspeople, it is a short taxi ride to the convention center.

The hotel is skillfully owned and run by Lusia Ginti and Sr. Bargiacchi, whose good taste and decorating talents are evident at every turn. The imaginative rooms are impeccably done in soft colors that show off the original parts of the building; perhaps a pair of antique doors or beam-and-brick ceilings, hand-painted bathroom tiles, large windows, or a fireplace. The beautiful bathrooms have nice fixtures and good lighting and are large enough to turn around in and lay things out. Number 101, a deluxe, is a perfect example. The huge room has two armchairs, the original marble fireplace, old doors, and a cherub-motif ceiling. The pink-and-white-tile bathroom is a dream, with its long tub, good shelf space, and light. Room 42, with a balcony, has the best view of Il Duomo. Number 46, a nice single, overlooks the courtyard and is quiet. The large balcony in No. 24 increases the size of the room, which has a set of antique doors on a built-in wardrobe and a blue-and-white-tile bath with a glass-enclosed shower. Reaching No. 55 requires climbing a few steps, but you are rewarded with views of the San Lorenzo Chapel and the rooftops of Florence. Wherever you look, it is clear that the owners care about the details that make a stay memorable. Scattered in the hotel and annex are warm touches of their welcome...a hall table with current magazines, a dish of fragrant potpourri, a bouquet of fresh flowers, a lovely painting, or a comfortable chair.

Breakfast for all hotel guests is served in an Art Deco–style room highlighted by modern artwork. In summer, umbrella-shaded tables are placed in the courtyard for your morning meal.

FACILITIES AND SERVICES: Air-conditioning, bar, direct-dial phone, elevator, hair dryer, guest Internet terminal, minibar, parking (20–30€ per day), radio, satellite TV, some VCRs, some hydro-massage showers, in-room safe, 6 nonsmoking rooms, 2 handicapped-accessible rooms

NEAREST TOURIST ATTRACTIONS: Piazza San Marco, Piazza SS. Annunziata, Mercato Centrale, San Lorenzo Market, Il Duomo

HOTEL ORTO DE' MEDICI ★★★ ($, 14)
Via San Gallo, 30
31 rooms, all with shower, bath, and toilet

The Hotel Orto de' Medici evokes the feeling of grandeur and elegance of a bygone era. One of the cornerstones of the hotel is the magnificent garden room where breakfast is served each morning. This palatial room is surrounded with eight paneled murals of tropical plants, giving the feeling of being in a lush garden. This leads to an umbrella-shaded terrace where guests gather at the music bar for late afternoon and evening cocktails. Another popular gathering spot is the frescoed television room with its plasma-screen TV and assorted plush sofas and chairs that invite all-day lounging.

The bedrooms offer guests both comfort and traditional warmth in their classic design, and every one can be recommended, including the three singles. These have gold-and-orange sponged walls and both a shower and tub in the bathroom. For something larger and more lavish, ask for

TELEPHONE
055 48 34 27

FAX
055 46 12 76

INTERNET
www.ortodeimedici.it

CREDIT CARDS
AE, MC, DC, V

RATES
Singles 140€, doubles 200–240€, triple 300€, quad 290€; lower off-season rates

BREAKFAST
Buffet breakfast included

ENGLISH
Yes

No. 45, a superior room with its original nineteenth-century floral tiled floor and views of Il Duomo, San Marco, and Fiesole. For a sunny balcony with a view of the garden below, request No. 40, a spacious superior double with hand-painted closet doors and a marble bathroom. Another quiet choice is No. 14, featuring ruby red wrought-iron beds, inlaid wood floors, and a view of the Medici Chapel.

For the stay of a lifetime in Florence, ask about La Casa Dell'Orto, the stunning penthouse apartment on top of the hotel. A long wood parquet floor connects the rooms: a bedroom with two view windows, two marble bathrooms, a state-of-the-art kitchen, and a dining room overlooking Il Duomo. In addition there is a fully equipped office, including a computer, satellite television, and DVD player. The pièce de résistance, however, is the wraparound terrace with a 360-degree view of Florence. This is a perfect setting for a romantic dinner for two or a party with friends. Prices are quoted on request.

FACILITIES AND SERVICES: Air-conditioning, bar, direct-dial phone, elevator, hair dryer, laundry service, minibar, in-room safe, satellite TV, all rooms nonsmoking, 2 handicapped-accessible rooms

NEAREST TOURIST ATTRACTIONS: Accademia, Medici Chapel, shopping at San Lorenzo Market, Mercato Centrale

RESIDENZA JOHLEA I & II (¢, 17, 16)
Via San Gallo, 76 & 80

Residenza Johlea I, 6 rooms; Residenza Johlea II, 10 rooms; all with shower or bath and toilet

Residenza Johlea I and II adhere to the *affitta camere* philosophy that less spent in the staff department means more money can be spent on guest room amenities. The rooms in both residences are tastefully done in soft colors and comfortable furnishings. In Johlea I, dog fanciers will appreciate the prints of man's best friend that hang along the hallways and in some of the bedrooms. The rooftop terrace is a pleasant place to enjoy a bird's-eye view of Florence. I also like No. 4's 360-degree, wraparound view, which takes in everything from Fiesole to Il Duomo and San Miniato Church. This duplex is also the biggest room, and it has a brass bed, a marble bathroom, and a mezzanine sitting area with a skylight, sofa bed, and a mosaic-tiled floor with Oriental-style rugs. Framed prints from old botanical books give the well-appointed No. 2 a bit of panache. The view from this room, as well as from No. 1, is of a big tree next to a parking area.

TELEPHONE
055 46 33 292
FAX
055 46 34 552
INTERNET
www.johanna.it
CREDIT CARDS
None, cash only
RATES
Single 70€, double 95–105€, suite 115€
BREAKFAST
Prepackaged Continental breakfast included
ENGLISH
Yes

Just down the street is the ten-room Residenza Johlea II, with the same warmth and charm found in Johlea I. All the rooms are appealing, especially the romantic one on the top floor with a view of a small garden next door. Other rooms, including the antique-furnished suite, have views of the Palazzo Pandolfini, trees, and in the spring, masses of light violet-colored wisteria vines.

NOTE: Also under the same ownership is Antica Dimora Firenze (page 88), Residenza Johanna (page 70), Residenza Johanna II (page 70), and Villa il Poggiale in the Tuscan countryside (page 144).

FACILITIES AND SERVICES: Air-conditioning, honesty bar, direct-dial phone, elevator, hair dryer, minibar, parking (15€ per day), in-room safe, TV, office open 8:30 A.M.–8 P.M.

NEAREST TOURIST ATTRACTIONS: Piazza San Marco, Accademia

Piazza Santa Croce

The piazza was once the site of tournaments, games, and spectacles, including Florentine football in the sixteenth century. Today it is filled with hawker stalls and serves as a meeting place for neighborhood residents and dog walkers who live in the old *palazzos* ringing the square. Shops selling leather goods line the streets leading to the piazza, and in back of the church is the well-known Leather School, which was founded by priests but is now a privately run commercial business. The Santa Croce Church began as a Franciscan order in 1228. By the thirteenth century, the Gothic church was considered inadequate, and it was replaced by a building that was supposed to be the largest in Christendom. It is not, but it is the richest medieval church in Florence, with a chapel by Brunelleschi, frescoes by Giotto, and the tombs of Michelangelo, Galileo, and other famous Florentines, including a memorial tomb to Dante (who is actually buried in Ravenna).

HOTELS

OTHER OPTIONS
Apartment Rentals

($) indicates a Big Splurge

HOTEL RIVER ★★★ ($, 125)
Lungarno della Zecca Vecchia, 18

TELEPHONE
055 23 43 529/30
FAX
055 23 43 531
INTERNET
www.hotelriver.com
CREDIT CARDS
AE, DC, MC, V
RATES
No single rates; double 191€,
extra bed 50€; lower off-season
rates
BREAKFAST
Buffet breakfast included
ENGLISH
Yes

38 rooms, all with shower or bath and toilet

The Hotel River is perfectly positioned along the River Arno, only a short walk from Santa Croce, the Uffizi Gallery, and across the Ponte Vecchio to the Pitti Palace. The hotel consists of two buildings: the oldest housed sisters from the Santa Croce Church and dates from 1380, and the "newer" one dates from 1856. Today, everything has been refurbished and is definitely up to twenty-first-century code. Wherever possible, original beam ceilings and frescoes have been lovingly restored and kept in place. All the rooms are done in shades of blue and green and offer all the creature comforts. Naturally, the most popular have river vantage points, but those that do not overlook the pretty hotel courtyard or a small back street leading to Piazza Santa Croce. On the third floor, two rooms have private terraces, but there is also a covered terrace for all hotel guests that faces Piazza Michelangelo. Eight rooms on the ground floor open onto a winter conservatory filled with tropical plants. Breakfast includes homemade pastries and is served in a well-appointed dining room that has high-back bamboo chairs and tables covered in blue striped fabric. Housekeeping standards are remarkable. On one of my visits, a uniformed maid was painstakingly working her way down the 150-year-old stone staircase dusting the hard-to-reach corners with a small paint brush!

FACILITIES AND SERVICES: Air-conditioning, bar, direct-dial phone, elevator, hair dryer, guest Internet terminal, laundry services, valet parking (21€ per day) or special street parking voucher (8€ per day), in-room safe, satellite TV

NEAREST TOURIST ATTRACTIONS: Piazza Santa Croce, Santa Croce Church, easy walk to Uffizi Gallery and Ponte Vecchio

LE STANZE DI SANTA CROCE (119)
Via delle Pinzochere, 6

TELEPHONE
055 200 13 66
FAX
055 200 84 56
INTERNET
www.viapinzochere6.it
CREDIT CARDS
MC, V

4 rooms, all with shower and toilet

For an experience similar to living in a Florentine home, where you will be warmly welcomed and made to feel you actually *are* at home, check into Mariangela's attractive *affitta camere*. After years of doing PR work for her artist husband, Paolo Carandini (see "Shopping: Great Chic," page 330), she wanted to do something on her own, so she decided to open the type of personal bed-and-breakfast she always hopes to find on her own travels.

She has succeeded beautifully, using her gracious style to create four artistic bedrooms named for well-known bells in Florence. The Bell of Bargelo has a wrought-iron canopy bed with a floral cover and coordinated linens, two comfortable chairs, terra-cotta flooring, and a lavender mosaic-tiled bathroom with a basket of Etro toiletries. In La Montannia (an ancient bell no longer in existence), the room has a pitched roof and is done in Florentine oranges and reds. La Trecca is a twin- or king-bedded room with a little balcony ringed with jasmine plants; it doesn't really have a view, but it provides a nice extension to the room. La Squilla is up another flight of stairs, but the payoff is the bathroom with a Jacuzzi, which is just outside the room but private to it. Four skylights flood the lime green and lavender room with sunshine. Mariangela and Paolo have apparently passed their artistic genes along to their son, whose son is responsible for the interesting photography of flowers hanging in the hotel. Breakfast is served on a plant-filled glass-covered terrace and includes only natural products: homemade jams, organic honey, fresh fruit, a large selection of bread, cheeses, and Tuscan salami.

In addition to running her B&B, Mariangela has put her impressive cooking skills to good use and offers one- or two-day cooking lessons. Participants start with a morning visit to the Sant' Ambrogio Market (see page 351) to buy the ingredients and wine for the afternoon cooking class, which is followed by a dinner composed of the results.

All in all, when your stay is finished, I hope you will agree that this is the sort of small, friendly Great Sleep one always hopes to find in Florence.

FACILITIES AND SERVICES: Air-conditioning, no elevator (3 floors), private telephone line in each room, hair dryer

NEAREST TOURIST ATTRACTIONS: Santa Croce Church, leather shopping, Sant' Ambrogio Market

RATES
Single 140€, double 160€, triple 195€; sometimes winter discounts for three days or more
BREAKFAST
Buffet breakfast included
ENGLISH
Yes

Piazza Santa Maria Novella

The Santa Maria Novella Church was the headquarters of the Dominicans, a fanatical order that urged followers to strip and whip themselves before the altar. The oldest part of the convent in the cloisters dates from 1270, and the square in front is one of the largest in the city.

HOTELS

($) indicates a Big Splurge; (¢) indicates a Cheap Sleep

HOTEL ABACO ★ (¢, 60)
Via dei Banchi, 1

7 rooms, 3 with shower and toilet

TELEPHONE
055 23 81 919

FAX
055 28 22 89

EMAIL
abacohotel@tin.it

INTERNET
www.abaco-hotel.it

CREDIT CARDS
AE, DC, MC, V

RATES
Single 60€, double 65–90€, extra bed 30€; discounts for cash; lower off-season rates

BREAKFAST
Continental breakfast 5€ extra per person

ENGLISH
Yes

Each of the seven spotless rooms in this money-saving Great Sleep are dedicated to a famous artist who has a painting hanging in the Uffizi Gallery. Naturally, since it's a one-star, you would think it would be bare-bones simple, but it's quite the opposite. These rooms are shipshape and without a trace of the usual one-star garage-sale school of decorating. Several have lovely beamed ceilings and polished hardwood or marble floors; others have gold-trimmed furniture and brocade fabrics. One room even has a fireplace. Three have a private shower and toilet, and the rest have sinks and share hall facilities. An optional Continental breakfast is served on wooden café tables. Bruno, the sympa owner, is here every day until 3 P.M. making sure that his guests are happy campers.

FACILITIES AND SERVICES: Air-conditioning (5€ daily supplement), direct-dial phone, no elevator (2 floors), fans, desk open daily 8 A.M.–9 P.M.

NEAREST TOURIST ATTRACTIONS: Il Duomo, shopping along Via de' Tornabuoni, easy walking distance to the train station, Santa Maria Novella, and countless restaurants

HOTEL APRILE ★★★ (50)
Palazzo dal Borgo, Via della Scala, 6

36 rooms, all with shower or bath and toilet

TELEPHONE
055 21 62 37

FAX
055 28 09 47

The Hotel Aprile has been preserved by the Commission of Fine Arts as a historic monument. Converted from a fifteenth-century Medici palace, it retains its original frescoes and hand-decorated vaulted ceilings. Because of its busy location, there is some noise, but if you are on the back side, uninterrupted sleep is possible. Next to the flower-filled reception area is a lounge and arched-ceiling bar filled with healthy green plants and comfortable chairs scattered among leather couches. Breakfast is served in two rooms: one is starkly modern with brown and black leather high-back chairs and stainless-steel tables; the other is a more traditional room, with a ceiling dating from the 1700s. On warm mornings, you can enjoy your cappuccino and rolls in the adjacent garden.

Wide halls with sitting areas lead to the rooms, many of which have marble-tiled baths, walnut or wrought-iron furnishings, frescoed ceilings, mosaic-tiled floors, and a view of the Piazza Santa Maria Novella. Number 5 is a ground-floor single with an orange faux finish that opens onto the hotel courtyard. Number 4 is a roomy twin with a high ceiling and wrought-iron beds wrapped in safari curtains. Number 15 is really something. In addition to a cathedral ceiling with gold highlights and two angels looking over the gauze-draped bed, it has a sitting area with a sofa bed, two white leather armchairs, and a full marble bathroom. Number 64, another suite, has a sunny exposure with a view of Santa Maria Novella Church and the hills beyond. Sharing this same view to the Florentine hills is No. 63, a twin with a new bathroom. Plus, three times a week the hotel management hosts a complimentary evening lecture in English on Florentine history.

FACILITIES AND SERVICES: Air-conditioning, bar, direct-dial phone, elevator, hair dryer, minibar, satellite TV, office safe

NEAREST TOURIST ATTRACTIONS: River Arno, Santa Maria Novella, Il Duomo

HOTEL SANTA MARIA NOVELLA ★★★★ ($, 59)
Piazza Santa Maria Novella, 1

75 rooms, all with shower, bath, and toilet

The classic Hotel Santa Maria Novella has quite a history. Originally built as the Hotel National, it closed its doors in 1974, and after almost thirty years of scandals and a four-year renovation, it reopened on December 31, 2003, under the direction of Claudio Delli. Today, the magnificent hotel offers guests gracious service with a comfortable air of cosmopolitan dignity, and despite its size, provides the intimacy and pleasant surroundings one expects to find in a luxurious private residence.

INTERNET
www.hotelaprile.it
CREDIT CARDS
AE, DC, MC, V
RATES
Single 140€, double 220€, triple 240€, quad 260€, supplement for suite 35€; 20% lower off-season rates
BREAKFAST
Buffet breakfast included
ENGLISH
Yes

TELEPHONE
055 27 18 40
FAX
055 27 18 4199
INTERNET
www.hotelsantamarianovella.it
CREDIT CARDS
AE, DC, MC, V
RATES
Single 156–260€, double 175–275€, triple 225–325€, junior suite and Bella Vista 275–375€

BREAKFAST
Buffet breakfast included
ENGLISH
Yes

The elegant marble entrance , with a tufted velvet seat and a pair of sofas flanking the fireplace, is further enhanced by matching highboy chests and deep burgandy walls. Large stylized fresh floral arrangements add interst and color. In the Napoleon room is another working fireplace and comfortable seating, where guests can thumb through the daily papers, catch the news on the large plasma-screen television, or do a bit of work at the fine writing desk. Electric oil lamps frame the entrance to the intimate hotel bar, which faces the piazza and the church. During the extensive renovation, part of the original walls of Florence, dating from 1078, were uncovered, as were Roman tubs that were used to dye clothes. These have been glass encased and are on view on the lower ground level near the gym and sauna.

Two elevators, both with white-and-green marble floors (reflecting the colors of the church), take guests to the wide gray-green halls that lead to the rooms—no two of which are alike in size or decoration. Most face the church; however, all have monogrammed linens, at least two windows in addition to the one in the bathroom, and a specific color-coordinated palate that extends from the walls and fabrics to the toiletry tray (filled with products from the famed Farmacia Santa Maria Novella), the do-not-disturb sign, and the bottle opener in the minibar. It would be impossible to select a favorite, so I will start from the top: the sixth-floor Belle Vista penthouse suite is just what its name implies. In addition to its own breathtaking view terrace, it has a magnificent marble bathroom with the floor design copied from the church below, regal furnishings, and enough space to move in and never leave. Number 601 is a romantic favorite, with shimmering handmade taffeta-lined draperies held back from the view windows by tassle cords. I also like No. 504, which is filled with light and has a view from the bed of the majestic green-and-pink marble Santa Maria Novella Church.

The breakfast room has its original high ceilings and is hung with oil paintings of the monuments in Florence. Tables are set with linens, fresh flowers, and a card with the weather forecast. Not to be forgotten is the two-level rooftop terrace on the sixth floor, which offers guests a dramatic view of Florence stretching from Il Duomo to the Boboli Gardens, Forte Belvedere, and the Pitti Palace.

FACILITIES AND SERVICES: Air-conditioning, bar, direct-dial phone, 2 elevators, hair dryer, data ports, guest Internet terminal, laundry service, minibar, in-room safe, satellite plasma-screen TV, gym, sauna, porter, room service for light snacks, tea and coffeemakers, slippers, and robes

NEAREST TOURIST ATTRACTIONS: Santa Maria Novella Church, train station, most of Florence within a 5- to 20-minute walk

J. K. PLACE ★★★★ ($, 58)
Piazza Santa Maria Novella, 7
20 rooms, all with shower, bath, and toilet

J. K. Place was the cover story for the August 2003 Italian edition of *Architectural Digest*. This alone tells you the hotel is special, and indeed it is, and it attracts an international blend of intellectuals and artists who demand—and receive—nonstop care and service. The concept of J. K. Place is to create the same atmosphere you would find in a luxurious, contemporary Italian home. This is carried out most forcefully in the public rooms, especially the glass-roofed breakfast room, where a long, polished communal table is beautifully made up each morning with starched white linens, silver place settings, crystal glassware, lovely china and linens, and fresh flowers. Later in the day, complimentary afternoon tea and coffee along with a tray of sweets are served here. If you want something stronger, the first glass of wine is offered. In one of the sitting rooms, a large wall-mounted plasma-screen television dominates the scene, while soft, off-white cashmere throws are placed over the ottomans in front of the cushioned couch. A guest laptop sits on a broad desk decorated with a single rose floating in a crystal bowl. In another sitting room, a pair of creamy wing-back chairs with zebra-covered footstools flank the wood-burning fireplace, and a large glass-enclosed bookcase displays beautiful art books (which are available for purchase). Candles flickering day and night lend a subdued romantic air.

Black-and-white prints of noble Florentines sit on each step of a wide stone stairway that leads to the perfectly planned bedrooms. Or, guests may ride to each floor in a bevel-mirrored elevator with a little seat in it. The rooms are simple yet elegant with tone-on-tone fabrics and few color highlights, except on throw pillows and wall hangings. All rooms have ample working desks, dark wood furnishings, and either striped carpets or polished wood floors; most come with flat-screen televisions. Chrome and mirrors abound, as do walk-in closets and marble baths with all the bells and whistles.

While the prices are assuredly in the Big Splurge column, lower off-season rates make it affordable for those who want streamlined luxury and personal service.

FACILITIES AND SERVICES: Air-conditioning, bar, direct-dial phone, elevator, hair dryer, minibar (soft

TELEPHONE
055 264 51 81
FAX
055 265 83 87
INTERNET
www.jkplace.com
CREDIT CARDS
AE, DC, MC, V
RATES
Single or double 315–470€, suite 610–681€; low-season rates drop by 100–250€ per room; children 12 and under are free
BREAKFAST
Buffet breakfast included
ENGLISH
Yes

drinks included), complimentary tea and coffee during the day, daily newspaper, welcome drink, ADSL Internet line in room, guest Internet terminal, satellite TV with CD/DVDs, in-room safe, robe and slippers, room service for light snacks

NEAREST TOURIST ATTRACTIONS: Santa Maria Novella Church, train station, central Florence within easy walking distance

PALAZZO CASTIGLIONI (52)
Via del Giglio, 8
15 rooms, all with shower and toilet

TELEPHONE
055 21 48 86
FAX
055 27 40 521
EMAIL
torreguelfa@flashnet.it
INTERNET
www.venere.it/firenze/
palazzocastiglioni
CREDIT CARDS
None, cash only
RATES
Single 100€, double 170€, suite 210€; lower off-season rates
BREAKFAST
Continental breakfast included
ENGLISH
Yes

The Palazzo Castiglioni defines a Great Sleep in Florence, and proves without a doubt that you cannot judge a hotel by its stars ... or the lack thereof. This is the type of wonderful accommodation nobody dares share with others for fear it will be constantly booked—and such fears are well-placed here. Sabina and her husband, Giancarlo, who also own the Hotel Torre Guelfa (see page 107), have tastefully restored this space, creating elegantly large bedrooms and townhouse suites. Recently they acquired the nine beautiful rooms below, formerly known as the Hotel Burchianti, which blend perfectly with the style of the Castiglioni.

It all begins the minute you step off the elevator into the beautiful sun-filled reception and sitting room, which is filled with overstuffed chairs around a large fireplace. In one corner is a dining area where breakfast is served. All the rooms have quality furnishings and fabrics. In No. 1, a junior suite, the original frescoed ceiling depicting romantic myths is in place. This room sleeps three comfortably and is the only one with a bathtub in addition to a shower. Sabina and I also like No. 2, with its romantic soft pink and lavender pastoral wall scenes and a bed that seems to float in the center of the room. Because the building is a historic site, no interior structural changes are allowed. As a result, Room 3, done in rich Florentine red and gold, is enormous. It has three big windows, a wonderful decorative ceramic wood-burning heater, a cushy armchair, and a setee that can be made into a single bed. A Gothic coat of arms is the centerpiece of Room 4, which also has its original frescoes beautifully restored. Room 5 is a long room with two windows and is decorated with a collection of pretty prints of French castles.

NOTE: Sabina and Giancarlo also run the Pitti Gola Cantina, a wine bar across from the Pitti Palace, and the Villa Rosa, a fifteen-room country hotel serving breakfast and dinner and located forty kilometers from Florence on the way to Radda in Chianti. For more information, see "Villas in Tuscany," page 139.

FACILITIES AND SERVICES: Air-conditioning, bar, direct-dial phone, elevator, hair dryer available, office safe, TV

NEAREST TOURIST ATTRACTIONS: Midway between Piazza Santa Maria Novella and the Medici Chapel, train station

PENSIONE OTTAVIANI ★ (¢, 62)
Piazza Ottaviani, 1
20 rooms, all with shower, 2 also with toilet

A lift from the ground floor takes you to the second floor, where this nineteen-room pensione is located. The best part about this choice is the prices, which are very kind to those on a budget. If you stay in Sra. Cartei's cheap sleep, you can count on clean rooms, with no musty odors, that are uniform in their total simplicity. You can also count on student groups invading your space. In small, lower-priced hotels with little or no discount margin, many have been forced to take groups, which can lead to noise and lines in the bathrooms. However, if you are a student yourself, can schedule your stay around the students, or can live with this...read on.

The sparse rooms are painted regularly, the linoleum floors are washed daily, and the only colors in them are on the bedspreads. All have a shower and sink, and for the eighteen that do not have private toilets, those on the hall are pristine. Some of the rooms overlook the tip of the Santa Maria Novella Church, but if you value sleep, reserve a back location on the top floor—otherwise the traffic roars like a racetrack day and night. Breakfast is served in a cheery dining area facing the street. If requested when reserving, Sra. Cartei will cook lunch and/or dinner for small groups.

NOTE: The pensione is closed for two to three weeks at Christmas.

FACILITIES AND SERVICES: Elevator to hotel, fans, TV in reception, office safe

NEAREST TOURIST ATTRACTIONS: Within walking distance of almost everything, including train station

TELEPHONE
055 23 96 223
FAX
055 29 33 55
EMAIL
pensioneottaviani@hotmail.com
INTERNET
www.pensioneottaviani.com
CREDIT CARDS
None
RATES
Single 40–50€, double 60–70€, extra bed 25€
BREAKFAST
Continental breakfast included
ENGLISH
Yes

Ponte Vecchio

Crossing the narrowest point of the Arno, this stone bridge was built in 1345 to replace a twelfth-century structure swept away by flood in 1333. Its shops were originally for tanners, but in the sixteenth century, butchers occupied them. The butchers were thrown out in 1593 by Grand Duke Ferdinandi I, who objected to their foul smells and replaced them with goldsmiths and jewelers, whose picturesque and very expensive shops still line the bridge.

HOTELS

($) indicates a Big Splurge; (¢) indicates a Cheap Sleep

GALLERY HOTEL ART ★★★★ ($, 109)
Vicolo dell Oro, 5

74 rooms, all with shower, bath, and toilet

TELEPHONE
055 27 26 4000, 055 27 263

FAX
055 272 64 444, 055 26 85 57

INTERNET
www.lungarnohotels.com

CREDIT CARDS
AE, DC, MC, V

RATES
Single 345€, double 380–480€, suite 660€, penthouse 1,150€; lower off-season rates

BREAKFAST
Buffet breakfast included

ENGLISH
Yes

Hotel art gets hip at the Gallery Hotel Art, the first design hotel in Italy and owned by Florence's first family of fashion, the Ferragamos. The boutique hotel doubles as a modern art gallery with changing exhibitions showcasing artists working on the cutting edge of today's contemporary art scene. The seventy-four ultra chic rooms and suites are as of-the-moment as the rest of the hotel. Varying shades of sand, off-white, gray, and beige define the rooms, which are as minimalist in look as they are in spirit. Those on the seventh floor overlook Florence. Everything is placed with precision, making an open suitcase or a magazine tossed on the bed feel like an insult to the overall design. Hand-crafted pigskin straps serve as pulls on the closet doors, which open onto neatly arranged built-ins. Moody black-and-white pictures of Florence hang on the walls, gray-and-white-checked curtains frame the windows, and bathrooms showcase the latest in chrome, mirrors, deep tubs, and halogen lighting. The penthouse suites offer over-the-top comfort, including cashmere blankets, linen sheets with high thread counts, high-tech TVs, and private terraces with drop-dead views of Florence. Data ports? Of course. Room service? Certainly. As soon as you want your champagne and sushi sent up to your room, just notify the front desk. Don't know what souvenir to buy for the person who has everything? Stroll through the hotel shop where everything you see in your room, and more, is for sale and can be shipped. You don't have far to go to eat or drink...just book a table in the hard-edge Fusion Bar, which serves potent drinks and has a four-page tea menu, in addition to Italian, French, and Japanese food with all sorts of twists. Yes, you are in Florence, but you have to look out the window to make sure.

FACILITIES AND SERVICES: Air-conditioning, bar, direct-dial phone with voice mail, elevator, hair dryer, fax and modem lines, laundry service, minibar, private valet parking, in-room safe, room service for light snacks, nonsmoking rooms, satellite and pay TV, stereos in all suites

NEAREST TOURIST ATTRACTIONS: Ponte Vecchio, Arno River, Uffizi Gallery, walking distance to central Florence

HOTEL ALESSANDRA ★★ (112)
Borgo S.S. Apostoli, 17
27 rooms, 19 with shower or bath and toilet

The Gennarini family's hotel is an excellent value that provides old-fashioned charm in a friendly setting. It is clear to me that the family cares about the hotel and all of their guests. The rooms are not plush, but they are retreats that are easy to recommend because they are larger than average, have matching colors, and are spotlessly clean. Four have views of the top of Il Duomo: Nos. 15, 16, 16bis, and 18. And four rooms have views of the Arno: Nos. 11, 21, 22, and 27. The best of the river-view rooms is No. 21, a double with a tango-size bathroom and coordinating fabrics on the little round table and chairs, bedspread, and window detailing. Number 27 is a two-room suite with a balcony view of the river and the belltower of SS Apostoli Church, the oldest in Florence. I like the desk that is hidden away in a mezzanine alcove and the large lavender-tiled bathroom with a deep tub suited for long bubble baths. Number 6 is a big single with a glass-topped desk, spacious armoire, and pink-tile shower. The row of makeup lights over the bathroom shelf is another pleasing touch. For a quiet choice, No. 9 is a double on the back that overlooks a church. Room 10 is a double with air-conditioning and a rooftop view but no private facilities. Don't worry about booking a bathless room: the hall facilities are excellent.

To reach the hotel, you must walk up one flight of stairs (twenty-eight steps) and then take an elevator to the hotel, which is spread out over three floors. The public rooms are

TELEPHONE
055 28 34 38, 055 21 78 30
FAX
055 21 06 19
INTERNET
www.hotelalessandra.com
CREDIT CARDS
AE, MC, V
RATES
Single 75–115€, double,115–150€, triple 150–196€, quad 165–220€, suites 165–265€
BREAKFAST
Buffet breakfast included
ENGLISH
Yes

all gracious. Soft sofas and chairs in the sitting rooms are comfortable places to watch television, read the newspaper, or access email on the guest Internet station. Breakfast is served in a room with matching yellow linen tablecloths and window curtains.

If you are staying in Florence for a week or more, inquire about their two apartments on the Oltrarno that rent on a weekly basis. For further information, contact them via the hotel's fax number or visit the Website www.florenceflat.com.

NOTE: The hotel is closed for ten to twelve days around Christmas; it reopens on December 27.

FACILITIES AND SERVICES: Air-conditioning, direct-dial phone, elevator to hotel (which is on 3 floors), hair dryer, guest Internet terminal, laundry service, minibar in 4 rooms, parking (25€ per day), satellite TV, office safe, 20 nonsmoking rooms

NEAREST TOURIST ATTRACTIONS: Between Piazza Santa Trinità and the Ponte Vecchio, a 10- to 20-minute walk to almost everything

HOTEL BERCHIELLI ★★★★ ($, 123)
Lungarno Acciaiuoli, 14 (at Piazza del Limbo)
76 rooms, all with shower or bath and toilet

TELEPHONE
055 26 40 61
FAX
055 21 86 36
INTERNET
www.berchielli.it
CREDIT CARDS
AE, DC, MC, V
RATES
Rates for low-high season:
single 123–245€, double
173–345€, triple 223–445€,
extra bed 95€; no surcharge for
view rooms
BREAKFAST
Buffet breakfast included
ENGLISH
Yes

The Hotel Berchielli is a typical conservative, traditional hotel with comfortable, surprise-free accommodations and an excellent location. Furnishings and colors are predictable, with lots of blue and burgandy. Twenty-five rooms face the Arno, six of these have balconies, and the rest have a variety of outlooks. Naturally, any room with a balcony facing the river is a premier pick, and no wonder, when they cost the same as a room on the back. Everyone likes No. 512, a double with large French twin beds and a great river view. Number 106 is another room with a balcony and river view. In addition, it has space, two comfortable chairs, and a double sink in the bathroom. It is billed as either a twin, triple, or quad, but should be reserved as a twin because the third and fourth beds are futon folding chairs, which I find an unacceptable sleeping arrangement for anyone over ten. The same uncomfortable sleeping situation for three exists in Number 418, which has a small entry, an interesting rooftop view of Florence and a nice bathroom in sandy beige. Breakfast is served in a formal room with a large self-service buffet table in the center.

FACILITIES AND SERVICES: Air-conditioning, bar, direct-dial phone, elevator, hair dryer, guest Internet terminal, laundry service, parking (30€ per day), porter, in-room safe, satellite TV

NEAREST TOURIST ATTRACTIONS: Located between Piazza Santa Trinità and the Ponte Vecchio, and within walking distance of central Florence

HOTEL CESTELLI ★ (¢, 113)
Borgo S.S. Apostoli, 25
8 rooms, 3 with shower and toilet

The building is a twelfth-century palace that was the studio of Cosimo II de Medici. The approach, up two flights of stairs, is not inspiring, but once you reach the small entrance hall, with its pretty interior stained-glass window at the back, and are welcomed by the enthusiastic young owners, you will know you have arrived in a special place.

The Hotel Cestelli has gone through several lives, and it is now in the capable hands of Alessio Lotti and his sweet wife, Asumi Igarashi. The two met while attending college in Southern California. After marrying, they decided to return to Alessio's homeland and open this little B&B. After moving in, they worked night and day: cleaning, painting, tossing out, and streamlining the rooms, which had suffered from years of benign neglect and accumulated clutter. The result is a clean, friendly, low-cost Great Sleep in the very heart of Florence. Number 3, a double with morning light, and No. 4, another double, both have private bathrooms. Number 5, facing the street, is a colossal room that can house up to five and still not feel crowded. It has two velvet wing chairs, a great gold mirror, and a still-intact three-hundred-year-old floor. In No. 6, the sink and bidet are in the room, but guests sleep in a bed with an inlaid headboard. I would not check into No. 8 for two reasons: it is too far from the bathroom, and the delapidated tufted sofa full of scratches and holes is an eyesore. Perhaps it will be removed soon. Breakfast is not included, but the engaging charm and friendly smiles of Alessio and Asumi definitely are.

FACILITIES AND SERVICES: Fans, no elevator (one floor), hair dryer available, nonsmoking hotel

NEAREST TOURIST ATTRACTIONS: An easy walk to all tourist destinations and shopping

TELEPHONE & FAX
055 21 42 13
INTERNET
www.hotelcestelli.com
CREDIT CARDS
AE, MC, V
RATES
Single 45€ (none with shower or toilet), double 65–80€, extra bed 20€
BREAKFAST
Not served
ENGLISH
Yes, and Japanese

HOTEL DELLA SIGNORIA ★★★ (115)
Via delle Terme, 1
27 rooms, all with shower or bath and toilet

Judging from this hotel's wide audience of devoted regulars, owner Rita Lippoli's actions meet her words: "For more than thirty years it has been a pleasure to

TELEPHONE
055 21 45 30
FAX
055 21 61 01

INTERNET
www.hoteldellasignoria.com
CREDIT CARDS
AE, DC, MC, V
RATES
Single 95 163€, double 163
200€, extra bed 38€
BREAKFAST
Continental breakfast included
ENGLISH
Yes

welcome clients. The best thing we have to offer them is our service, and we try to satisfy all of them because this is out best publicity."

Joining Sra. Lippoli in receiving guests, and assisting them throughout their stay, is Fabrizio, who has been behind the reception desk since the first day the doors opened in 1970. Well-situated between the Ponte Vecchio and the Ponte S. Trinita, the hotel is ideally located for visitors wanting to explore all the beauty and shopping possibilities in Florence.

One of the hotel features guests appreciate most is the second-floor covered terrace, where they meet first for breakfast and then later on for afternoon drinks and conversation. While the rooms are not cutting-edge modern, they are individually decorated with sturdy, traditional furnishings and comforts that add up to a pleasing stay. Single travelers are not reduced to closet-size abodes. In No. 540, a viewless single, there is a desk, comfortable chair, luggage space, and a bright bathroom with an enclosed stall shower. For a bit more space, singles should request No. 429, which has a view of the corner of the Mercato Nuovo (Straw Market). A couple will feel at home in No. 325, which has twin beds (that can be zipped into a double), rose floral patterned walls, a pair of windows, cushioned wicker chairs, and a large shower. The rooms on the first floor have balconies.

FACILITIES AND SERVICES: Air-conditioned, direct-dial phone, elevator, hair dryer, laundry, minibar, office safe, satellite TV

NEAREST TOURIST ATTRACTIONS: All of central Florence within easy walking distance

HOTEL HERMITAGE ★★★ ($, 124)
Vicolo Marzio, 1, Piazza del Pesce
28 rooms, all doubles with shower or bath and toilet

One of my favorite hotels in Florence has always been the Hermitage, located in a building on the Piazza del Pesce overlooking the Ponte Vecchio and the Arno River. Everything about this charming hotel is appealing, from the plant-filled terrace with its spectacular top-floor views to the well-thought-out bedrooms and sitting areas. The cozy living room has a bar along one side and a fireplace for cool winter evenings. Oriental rugs are tossed on the tile floors, and yellow slipcovers add a touch of brightness to comfortable chairs and sofas, which are perfect for sinking into with a good book.

No two of the bedrooms are alike, but all are done with good taste and flair. They have muted wallpaper, a mixture

TELEPHONE
055 28 72 16
FAX
055 21 22 08
INTERNET
www.hermitagehotel.com
CREDIT CARDS
MC, V
RATES
No single rooms; double
for single use 221€, double
233–245€, suite for four 300€;
lower off-season rates
BREAKFAST
Continental breakfast included
ENGLISH
Yes

of antique and reproduction furniture, and double-glazed windows to buffer the noise along the river. Many are quite small. Of the eight rooms with river views, No. 409 is a twin with a corner Jacuzzi in the marble bathroom. My absolute favorite rooms are Nos. 601 and 602, located on the top floor and reached by a little stairway. However, aside from the comfortable, beautifully appointed rooms, twenty-two of which have Jacuzzis, the real payoff is the terrace, which has a spectacular wraparound view of Florence. To alleviate the area's impossible parking situation, the hotel has a garage for guests, but the hotel is so central to everything in Florence that a car would only be a nuisance.

FACILITIES AND SERVICES: Air-conditioning, bar, direct-dial phone, elevator (one flight of stairs to roof garden), hair dryer, laundry service, parking (25–30€ per day), porter, in-room safe, satellite TV, many rooms with Jacuzzis, nonsmoking rooms

NEAREST TOURIST ATTRACTIONS: Ponte Vecchio, River Arno, Uffizi Gallery, all of central Florence

HOTEL TORRE GUELFA ★★★ (114)
Borgo S.S. Apostoli, 8
29 rooms, all with shower or bath and toilet

If you are looking for one of the nicest three-star hotels in Florence, you have found it at Sabina and Giancarlo's Hotel Torre Guelfa. In this case, the hotel's brochure perfectly captures its great spirit: "What could be better than looking toward the twenty-first century from a thirteenth-century Florentine tower? Located fifty meters from the Ponte Vecchio in the tallest private building in Florence, the *Torre Guelfa* (Guelfa Tower) offers an incredible view, a beautiful atmosphere, and twenty-nine select rooms for a few, select clients."

Everything about this exceptional hotel is smart and sophisticated, and all rooms are recommended. Starting at the top, No. 15 is a twenty-two-step climb, but once you are seated on the massive terrace with its beautiful view, the only word that comes to mind is, Wow! The double room has a wrought-iron bed draped with sheer side curtains and a pleasing marble bathroom that looks onto the terrace. No stair-climbing is required to reach No. 3, done in shades of green with a marble bathroom and a detailed ceiling. One wall is faced with lovely seventeenth-century mirrors, the floor is parquet, and the double bed is outlined by a swagged curtain. Singles in cozy No. 2 will enjoy the original wooden ceiling. There is more room for a solo guest in No. 4, which has a four-poster metal bed and a small marble

TELEPHONE
055 23 96 338

FAX
055 23 98 577

EMAIL
torre.guelfa@flashnet.it

INTERNET
www.hoteltorreguelfa.com

CREDIT CARDS
AE, DC, MC, V

RATES
Single 110€, double 140€–180€, terrace double 230€, junior suite 210€

BREAKFAST
Continental breakfast included

ENGLISH
Yes

bathroom. Twin-bedded No. 13 has a view of the street and a small garden, and in No. 14, the two wrought-iron double beds have angels flying above and tassled side curtains. Finally, the nine rooms on the first floor are appealing for many because these simple hardwood-floor rooms are less expensive and do not have televisions or minibars, but they are still quite pleasant and offer guests all the other amenities of the hotel. For breakfast, all guests gather in a glass-enclosed winter garden with glass-topped tables surrounded by black wrought-iron chairs.

Two large rooms make up the impressive, baronial hotel living room, where stone columns frame the second room with a wall of wood-carved bookshelves along one side and comfortable sofa and lounge chair seating. In one corner is the guest Internet terminal; in another the honor bar. Glass doors open onto a long wooden (seventy-two-step) stairway that leads to the Guelfa Tower and its two view terraces. Once you reach the first landing, I urge you to go the additional sixteen steps to the top perch, which rewards your efforts with a spectacular 360-degree view of all of Florence and the surrounding hillsides. Don't forget your camera!

Please see page 100 for a description of their other Florence hotel, the Palazzo Castiglioni, and see page 145 their Villa Rosa in the Chianti countryside. Special prices are offered guests at Pitti Gola Cantina, their wine bar across from the Pitti Palace.

FACILITIES AND SERVICES: Air-conditioning, bar, direct-dial phone, elevator, hair dryer, guest Internet terminal, laundry service, minibar, parking (25€), satellite TV, office safe, nonsmoking rooms on request

NEAREST TOURIST ATTRACTIONS: Walking distance to almost everything

Teatro del Maggio Musicale Fiorentino and Piazza Vittorio Veneto

The Teatro del Maggio Musicale Fiorentino, formerly the Teatro Comunale, is the home of the city's opera, symphony, orchestra hall, ballet company, and theater productions. In May, the Maggio Musicale Fiorentino Festival, which is the oldest festival in Italy and one of the oldest in Europe, is held here. The Piazza Vittorio Veneto is on the edge of the city, leading to the Cascine, a park with a swimming pool, tennis courts, and a huge Tuesday morning market.

HOTELS

HOTEL ARGENTINA ★★★ (48)
Via Curtatone, 12

30 rooms, all with shower or bath and toilet

In addition to warm hospitality, the Scatizzi family delivers good value, comfortable accommodations, and a desirable location in their three-star hotel. The senior Scatizzi first opened the hotel in the late thirties. It is now run by his charming daughter, Maria Angela, and her nephew Lorenzo. The large lobby has Oriental rugs, tile floors, leather-upholstered barrel chairs, and all the necessary plants, paintings, and attitude to remind you this is Florence. A filling breakfast buffet is presented in an open dining room off the lobby, or you can order a Continental breakfast brought to your room.

Upstairs, the bedrooms are conservatively decorated in soft greens, grays, and corals, with classic furnishings, inlaid tile flooring, and plenty of space for luggage and impulse purchases. Two rooms have balconies: No. 101, a single with workspace and a corner, built-in wardrobe, and No. 104, a popular roomy double with an Art Deco feel and a small bathroom with a tub. The baths in the rest of the hotel are generally dated but functional.

FACILITIES AND SERVICES: Air-conditioning, bar, direct-dial phone, elevator, hair dryer, laundry service, minibar, parking (20€), TV, office safe

NEAREST TOURIST ATTRACTIONS: Train station, Arno River, about a 20- to 30-minute walk to Il Duomo

TELEPHONE
055 23 98 203, 055 21 54 08, 055 23 98 616
FAX
055 21 67 31
INTERNET
www.hotelargentina.it
CREDIT CARDS
AE, DC, MC, V
RATES
Single 130€, double 170€, extra bed 30€; lower off-season rates
BREAKFAST
Buffet breakfast included
ENGLISH
Yes

HOTEL CASA DEL LAGO ★★ (57)
Lungarno Amerigo Vespucci, 58

18 rooms, all with shower or bath and toilet

Views of the Arno or the hills of Florence can be savored from seventeen of the eighteen well-manicured rooms at the Ricciarini family's riverside Casa del Lago. You feel you can almost dive into the river from the ten rooms facing the Arno, all of which have white walls, sunshine, extra space, and nicely tiled bathrooms with a shower stall. For tranquil views toward Fiesole and Monte Morello along the back of the hotel, book No. 419, a large choice that has a floral appliquéd, white chenille spread on the double bed. The hotel is close to the Teatro del Maggio Musicale Fiorentino, so performers often stay here. The fifteen- or

TELEPHONE
055 21 61 41
FAX
055 21 41 49
INTERNET
www.hotelcasadellago.com
CREDIT CARDS
AE, DC, MC, V
RATES
Single 95€, double 145€; lower off-season rates
BREAKFAST
Buffet breakfast included
ENGLISH
Yes

twenty-minute walk along the river to and from the center is beautiful, and in the off-season when the rates drop, the hotel becomes an even better Great Sleeping value.

FACILITIES AND SERVICES: Air-conditioning, direct-dial phone, elevator, fans, hair dryer, parking (20–25€ per day), in-room safe, satellite TV

NEAREST TOURIST ATTRACTIONS: None; must use bus or walk 20 minutes to Ponte Vecchio

Train Station

Located on the western side of Florence, the train station provides easy access to city bus routes, almost all of which flow through the Piazza della Stazione in front. Just next to it is the Palazzo dei Congressi, the venue for big trade shows.

HOTELS

OTHER OPTIONS
Hostels

(¢) indicates a Cheap Sleep

HOTEL BEATRICE ★★★ (26)
Via Fiume, 11

TELEPHONE
055 21 67 90, 055 23 96 137

FAX
055 28 07 11

INTERNET
www.hotelbeatrice.it

CREDIT CARDS
AE, DC, MC, V

RATES
Single 65–90€, double 85–145€, triple 120–195€, quad 160–245€

BREAKFAST
Buffet breakfast included

20 rooms, all with shower or bath and toilet

Via Fiume is a pensione-packed street close to the train station. Five decades ago it was strictly residential. At that time, when Adriano Chinaglia opened his flat as a full- or half-board pensione, it was a scandal—neighbors were up in arms. Since then, they have joined the lucrative bandwagon, and you will be hard-pressed to find many single-family dwellings on Via Fiume today.

Since those early days, the pensione has expanded into a twenty-room hotel and is still run by Adriano's extended family. They are all undeniably proud of all the improvements, especially the dining room with custom-made, hand-painted ceramic wall lights and the welcoming yellow-clad sitting room with interesting opaque lighting.

The guest rooms are large and have light, coordinated colors, similar wall coverings, and the best mattresses available. Some have new Art Deco–style furnishings, while others retain the family's collection of beautiful 1920s bed frames, marble-topped dressers, and armoires. Two rooms have balconies, and all are scrupulously clean.

FACILITIES AND SERVICES: Air-conditioning, bar, direct-dial phone, elevator (some steps required), hair dryer, minibar, parking (22€ per day), room safe, satellite TV, 6 nonsmoking rooms

NEAREST TOURIST ATTRACTIONS: Train station, Palazzo dei Congressi, 15- to 30-minute walk to most everything else

HOTEL IL BARGELLINO ★ (¢, 13)
Via Guelfa, 87

10 rooms, 5 with shower or bath and toilet

Looking for a friendly Great Sleep in Florence, one that is also a well-deserved success story? If the answer is yes, then read on about this super one-star hotel, which is the end result of much hard work and dedication, plus pounds and pounds of elbow grease.

Carmel Coppola is an expatriate American from Boston who came to Florence to study. She met Pino, now her husband, and the rest is history and the Hotel Il Bargellino. They bought the hotel in 1992 and have slowly but surely brought it into the modern world. Pino is a one-man decorating team and construction crew, doing most of the renovations himself. He also haunts country auctions and picks up some amazing antiques and artwork, which he uses in the rooms. This is not to suggest that Carmel is idle. One of my favorite things about this hotel is the wraparound roof terrace, which is lovingly tended by Carmel and filled in spring and summer with tables, chairs, lemon trees, and roses. In summer, breakfast is served here, and guests are encouraged to enjoy the terrace all day long.

Rooms 8, 9, and 10 open onto the terrace. Number 8 has a ship-style bathroom, but at least you won't have to share. Number 9 showcases one of Pino's antique finds, a pine armoire. And No. 10 features a double bed with inlaid work and matching side tables; it also has a shower and sink but no toilet, which is just next door. Pino installed a new bathroom in No. 1 and painted the picture hanging over the bed. The best points about Room 6 are the

ENGLISH
Yes

TELEPHONE
055 23 82 658
FAX
055 23 82 698
INTERNET
www.ilbargellino.com
CREDIT CARDS
MC, V
RATES
Single 38–43€, double 65–75€, triple 85–90€, quad 90–110€
BREAKFAST
No breakfast served
ENGLISH
Yes

walnut twin beds and its vintage but clean and spacious bathroom. Number 7, with a shower and bidet (but no toilet), looks onto the terrace and is very quiet. All the beds have good mattresses and down comforters. Note that all singles are bathless, and there is only one public bathroom, but it is new.

To top it off, the neighborhood is full of favorite *Great Eats Italy* restaurants, and Carmel happily shares her knowledge of Florence to help make your time in the city even more wonderful.

NOTE: The hotel is closed for a week to ten days at Christmas.

FACILITIES AND SERVICES: Fans, no elevator (one floor), unstocked minibars, office safe, parking (15€ per day, must reserve in advance), TV in 3 rooms

NEAREST TOURIST ATTRACTIONS: Train station, Palazzo dei Congressi, Mercato Centrale, San Lorenzo Market

HOTEL MIA CARA ★★★ (¢, 22)
Via Faenza, 58

18 rooms, all with shower and toilet

TELEPHONE
055 21 60 53
FAX
055 23 02 727
INTERNET
www.hotelmiacara.it
CREDIT CARDS
AE, MC, V
RATES
Rates span low/high season: single 50–80€, double 65–120€, extra bed 20–50€
BREAKFAST
Continental breakfast included
ENGLISH
Yes

What a difference a new generation can make!

For decades, the Mia Cara was a no star–rated, bottom-rung cheap sleep for thrift-minded travelers who only needed a clean, decent place to sleep and change clothes. But remarkable changes have taken place. The hotel was closed for months and gutted to make way for eighteen new rooms boasting soft pink stenciled walls, walnut hotel-style furnishings, satellite televisions, and minibars. The shiny bathrooms have enclosed showers and good towels. Breakfast is now served, an Internet terminal has been installed in the lobby, and three stars have been added to the revised name on the marquee. But the best news is that the complete makeover did not do away with the value-packed rates or the warm and friendly hospitality so many cheap sleepers in Florence came to know and love.

FACILITIES AND SERVICES: Air-conditioning, direct-dial phone, hair dryer, elevator, guest Internet terminal, minibar, in-room safe, satellite TV, nonsmoking hotel

NEAREST TOURIST ATTRACTIONS: Train station, Mercato Centrale, Palazzo dei Congressi, San Lorenzo Market, Medici Chapel

HOTEL PORTA FAENZA ★★★ (21)
Via Faenza, 77
26 rooms, all with shower or bath and toilet

The Porta Faenza is the epitome of an ugly duckling transformed into a lovely swan. The hotel is in a restored eighteenth-century building, with all twenty-six sound-proofed rooms done in regal gold and dark royal blue. Downstairs, three-hundred-year-old brick archways, alcoves, and an old Roman well and wall are reminders of the past. Highlighting the newer side of the hotel is the glass-paneled elevator with bilingual computerized operating instructions and the free Internet and email services.

The rooms have all the perks, including significantly lower off-season rates. Number 102, with a ceiling fresco, is a large double or triple that has a bathroom suitable for the handicapped. Number 106, also with a frescoed ceiling, is a quiet choice that faces the back parking area and jacaranda trees in neighboring gardens. Number 207 is a basic double with an inside view; its blue-and-white bathroom has limited shelf space but enough room to move around in. A better view is from No. 303, a sunny top-floor double with a rooftop outlook from a flower-lined balcony. The roomy, blue-and-white-tile bathroom has both a tub and enclosed shower.

FACILITIES AND SERVICES: Air-conditioning, bar, direct-dial phone, elevator, hair dryer, laundry service, private parking (10€ per day, by reservation only), in-room safe, satellite TV, guest Internet terminal, nonsmoking rooms

NEAREST TOURIST ATTRACTIONS: Medici Chapel, Mercato Centrale, San Lorenzo Market, train station, Palazzo dei Congressi, 15-minute walk to Il Duomo

TELEPHONE
055 21 79 75, 055 28 41 19
FAX
055 21 01 01
INTERNET
www.hotelportafaenza.it
CREDIT CARDS
AE, DC, MC, V
RATES
Single 65–85€, double 85–130€, triple 110–150€, quad 120–160€
BREAKFAST
Buffet breakfast included
ENGLISH
Yes

MAISON DE CHARME (¢, 32)
Largo Fratelli Alinari, 11
6 rooms, all with shower and toilet

Marie-Claude Hanotel's six-room *affitta camere* lives up to its name—it is indeed a charming house, one that, just like Marie-Claude, is very nice and very French. She proves that you can make small spaces work by paring rooms down to basics and avoiding fussy details: walls are whitewashed, furnishings are plain, and everything is kept bright and clean. At the Maison de Charme, someone is on duty from 9 A.M. to 9:30 P.M. A packaged Continental breakfast is set out on a tray in each room, and you brew your own coffee or tea in an electric kettle. The location is a two-minute walk from the railway station and is close to the Mercato Centrale and the Medici Chapel.

TELEPHONE
055 29 23 04
FAX
055 28 10 14
EMAIL
maisondecharme@estranet.it
INTERNET
www.maisondecharme.it
CREDIT CARDS
MC, V
RATES
Single 50–65€, double 75–95€, triple 95–125€, quad 105–140€

BREAKFAST
Prepackaged Continental breakfast included

ENGLISH
Yes

FACILITIES AND SERVICES: Air-conditioning, direct-dial phone, electric kettle, elevator, minibar, in-room safe, satellite TV

NEAREST TOURIST ATTRACTIONS: Train station, Santa Maria Novella Church, Palazzo dei Congressi, Mercato Centrale, San Lorenzo Market, Medici Chapel

MARIO'S ★★★ (18)
Via Faenza, 89

16 rooms, all with shower or bath and toilet

TELEPHONE
055 21 68 01

FAX
055 21 20 39

INTERNET
www.hotelmarios.com

CREDIT CARDS
AE, DC, MC, V

RATES
Single 120€, double 165€, triple 210€, quad 240€; lower off-season rates

BREAKFAST
Buffet breakfast included

ENGLISH
Yes

While you can find rooms in Florence for less, you will not be able to top Mario Noce's fine establishment for general ambience and friendly staff. The hotel reflects the best in quality, value, and comfort, and many Great Sleepers have become devoted regulars. Everything is well executed, from the amenities to the decor, such as the Oriental runners cushioning the picture-gallery hallways. The attractive bedrooms might have a corner writing desk, a small balcony, ceiling beams, a canopy bed, or a stained-glass window. Mario's warmth and hospitality are evident at every turn, from the welcome in four languages to the bowls of fresh fruit and greenery that grace each guest room. On request, Mario will give personal day tours of Tuscany for one to four people. Guests are encouraged to mingle and get to know one another at the bar in the early evening or while seated at one of the three communal breakfast tables under the watchful eyes of the stuffed boar's head.

FACILITIES AND SERVICES: Air-conditioning, bar, direct-dial phone, hair dryer, no elevator (2 floors), parking (25–30€), satellite TV, in-room safe

NEAREST TOURIST ATTRACTIONS: Mercato Centrale, Palazzo dei Congressi, San Lorenzo Market, train station, 15-minute walk to Il Duomo

OLD FLORENCE INN (¢, 32)
Largo Fratelli Alinari, 11

6 rooms, all with shower and toilet

TELEPHONE & FAX
055 21 54 01

INTERNET
www.oldflorenceinn.it

CREDIT CARDS
AE, DC, MC, V

RATES
Single 75€, double 89–95€, triple 109–115€

BREAKFAST
Prepackaged Continenal breakfast in each room

ENGLISH
Yes

On my last research trip to Florence, I saw all six of Florio Manini's *affita camere*, and the Old Florence Inn is my favorite. An elevator takes guests from the street to the second-floor location. Inside, the small reception area and hallway is attractively done in Tuscan yellow faux finishing and unusual Venetian ceiling lights, which lend an Art Deco feeling. One of the best rooms is No. 5, a large choice with white walls that set off the dark wood armoire and writing desk. Electric window shades control the amount of light that flows in. Number 2, dressed in Florentine red, has a balcony and view of Santa Maria Novella Church. Three floral prints provide the backdrop over the bed, and six framed antique pictures of shoes, hats, dresses, and time pieces add amusing detail. All the bathrooms are new and offer a basket of Tuscan-produced toiletries.

FACILITIES AND SERVICES: Air-conditioning, direct-dial phone, elevator, hair dryer, minibar, satellite TV, office safe, reception open 9 A.M.–7 P.M., nonsmoking rooms

NEAREST TOURIST ATTRACTIONS: Train station, Palazzo dei Congressi, Santa Maria Novella Church, Mercato Centrale, San Lorenzo Market, Medici Chapel

Hotels *Di La d'Arno,* or *Oltrarno*

The other side of the Arno River from Il Duomo — called *Di La d'Arno,* or *Oltrarno*—is an area known for artisan workshops, trendy boutiques, bars, and restaurants, plus the vast Pitti Palace, Boboli Gardens, and the Brunelleschi-designed Santo Spirito Church.

Boboli Gardens

Designed for Eleonora di Toledo and Cosimo I, and extending over forty-five thousand square meters on the hill behind the Pitti Palace, the Boboli Gardens are one of the greatest examples of Italian-style gardens. One of the most famous parts of the gardens is the grotto with statues of Ceres and Apollo by Bandinelli and Michelangelo's cast of Dying Slaves. The beautiful site affords wonderful views of the city and is a good place to bring children to run and play and feed the ducks.

CLASSIC HOTEL ★★★ (148)
Viale Machiavelli, 25

20 rooms, all with shower or bath and toilet

TELEPHONE
055 22 93 51

FAX
055 29 93 53

INTERNET
www.classichotel.it

CREDIT CARDS
AE, MC, V

RATES
Single 110€, double 150–200€, suite 210€; lower off-season rates

BREAKFAST
Continental breakfast included

ENGLISH
Yes

Set in a residential area next to the Boboli Gardens, the Classic Hotel was a beautiful old villa until Connie Bernabei invested her heart, soul, and plenty of money to turn it into this alluring garden hotel. Some may not like the out-of-the-mainstream location, but those who love Florence know better. Here you have the best of everything: peace and quiet in elegant parklike surroundings, and all main tourist sites in Florence are an easy twenty- to thirty-minute walk or bus ride away. Motorists will also appreciate the free parking the hotel provides.

On my first visit to the Classic Hotel, I thought it offered the quintessential Florentine experience, with high molded ceilings, crystal chandeliers, inlaid hardwood floors, fireplaces, marble bathrooms, and well-appointed bedrooms perfectly in keeping with the hotel's history as a private home. On subsequent visits I have not changed my mind too much. The rooms, with their polished hardwood floors, are still lovely, and so are the bathrooms. Favorites include No. 105, a two-level garden suite with an upstairs sitting room and a double bed downstairs. Frescoed ceilings and antiques add to the charm. The bath is excellent, but it has a shower only, no tub. There are three suites similar to this. Number 204, which can sleep three in comfort, has a high-pitched roof with a skylight and windows on the garden. I also like No. 102 because of its private balcony, and Nos. 106 and 107 with their quiet garden views and private entry, which allows them to be combined for a family stay.

A Continental breakfast is served either in a vaulted breakfast room surrounded by a mural of the Boboli Gardens, at tables in the garden, or in your room. Later on, drinks are served in a glass conservatory overlooking the beautiful garden. However, questionable taste remains in the public sitting areas near the entrance. Why Sra. Bernabei has invested so much effort and money in the other parts of the hotel and continues to keep the ugly pea-green slipcovered couch in the entry remains a mystery to me. Because the bedrooms themselves are so nice, try not to judge the hotel from a few decorating blips.

NOTE: The Classic Hotel is closed for two weeks in August and sometimes around Christmas. To get to the hotel and Boboli Gardens from central Florence, take bus Nos. 11, 36, or 37 from Piazza Santa Maria Novella or the railway station to Porta Roma. The walk back and forth along Via Romana into central Florence provides interesting window shopping in local shops and artisan workshops.

FACILITIES AND SERVICES: Air-conditioning, bar, direct-dial phone, elevator, hair dryer, laundry service, free parking, TV, in-room safe, room service for breakfast and drinks during the day

NEAREST TOURIST ATTRACTIONS: Boboli Gardens, 20- to 30-minute walk or bus ride into central Florence

Piazza del Carmine

The neighborhood around Piazza del Carmine includes the baroque Santa Maria del Carmine Church and Brancacci Chapel, with frescoes by Masaccio and Masolino. It is also an area well-known for many artisan's workshops, trendy restaurants, and a popular yuppie bar scene.

PALAZZO MAGNANI FERONI ($, 127)
Borgo San Frediano, 5

12 suites

For one of the most memorable stays of a lifetime, the magnificent sixteenth-century Palazzo Magnani offers its privileged and pampered guests twelve 1,100-square-foot, luxurious suites with vaulted ceilings, thirty-foot windows,

TELEPHONE
055 239 9544
FAX
055 260 8908
INTERNET
www.florencepalace.it

CREDIT CARDS
AE, DC, MC, V

RATES
Standard 320€ (applies to one room), suites 440–590€; low-season rates drop by 110–250€

BREAKFAST
Buffet breakfast included

ENGLISH
Yes

and every conceivable amenity. The palace has been in owner Dr. Alberto Giannotti's family for 250 years, and great care was taken to maintain the building's original style and to save and highlight the many antique works of art. In fact, as Dr. Giannotti says, "During the nineteenth century, my great-grandfather was one of the most important European antique dealers. In honor of him, we have created a small exhibit in one of the palace galleries where guests can admire antique fabrics, costumes, and correspondence with the Italian Royal family."

No expense was spared during the two-and-a-half-year restoration, and today the family's masterful attention to detail is evident everywhere, from the fine antique furnishings, restored frescoes, rich brocades, and thick velvets to the marble bathrooms, glorious rooftop dining terrace, and state-of-the-art fitness room. Every place you turn, there is something of historical interest, starting with the mirrored elevator with its original seat. It was the forty-second elevator to be brought to Italy, of which only eight are still operating. In every suite, there are special family heirlooms: perhaps framed tassels and trims, a magnificent tapestry, or a museum-quality piece of furniture. The beautiful breakfast room is dominated by an antique Murano chandelier hanging from a hand-decorated ceiling from the *Palazzo Farnese di Roma* and gold-framed chairs covered in tiger and zebra prints. Service is, of course, discreet and beyond reproach... and nothing is left to chance. Even your soap can be personally selected by you according to type and fragrance, and then delivered to your room.

In addition to the amenities listed below, other services include light meals for guests who arrive after 9:30 P.M., dinner either en suite or on the terrace and served by a private butler, in-room massage service, beautician and hairdresser appointments, and a limousine and guide service for museums, shopping, wine tastings, and/or trips outside of Florence.

Of course, all of this falls into the Big Splurge category, but for the experience, especially during the low season when the rates are dramatically less, it offers great value—along with unforgettable memories.

FACILITIES AND SERVICES: Air-conditioning, bar, billiard room, direct-dial phones, elevator, hair dryer, gym, data ports, free laptops available, laundry service, minibar, private parking (30–50€ per day), in-room safe, CD player, two satellite TVs in each suite, 24-hour room service

NEAREST TOURIST ATTRACTIONS: Piazza del Carmine, Piazza Santo Spirito, Pitti Palace, Boboli Gardens

Pitti Palace and Piazza Santo Spirito

The Pitti Palace was built in 1457 for Luca Pitti, a rival of the Medicis, but less than a century later, the impoverished Pitti family was forced to sell the palace to the Medici family. The sprawling building now consists of six museums, including the royal apartments showcasing a huge collection of Medici paintings, silver, and art.

The Augustinian monks of Santo Spirito gave up one meal a day for fifty years to help pay for the construction of Santo Spirito Church. It was designed by Brunelleschi, but he died before his plans were completed. Inside is a series of thirty-eight chapels. The piazza in front is alive on the second Sunday of the month with a flea market, and on the third Sunday, an organic market. Many good trattorias and bars listed in *Great Eats Italy* dot the piazza and the streets surrounding it.

HOTELS

OTHER OPTIONS

(¢) indicates a Cheap Sleep

HOTEL LA SCALETTA ★★ (140)
Via Guicciardini, 13

14 rooms, 12 with shower or bath and toilet

Hotel guests here are a convivial mix of international travelers who know that obtaining a room at La Scaletta is no mean feat. The main draw is its pivotal location just over the Ponte Vecchio on Via Guicciardini, the street that leads to the Pitti Palace and Piazza Santo Spirito. There is a lift to the third-floor hotel, which is in an old *palazzo*. Once inside, the halls seem to go on forever, and numerous steps lead from one end of the rambling hotel to the other, which prompted the owner's son to jokingly say to

TELEPHONE
055 28 30 28, 055 21 42 55
FAX
055 28 95 62
INTERNET
www.lascaletta.com
CREDIT CARDS
AE, MC, V

RATES
Single 65–100€, double
115–150€, family room 150€,
extra bed 30€; lower off-season
rates; discounts to *Great Sleeps
Italy* readers, mention when
reserving; dinner by request
(15.49€ per person)
BREAKFAST
Buffet breakfast included
ENGLISH
Yes

me, "We give our guests a city map and a hotel map." The 360-degree view from the roof garden is nothing short of sensational. On a clear day, you can see all the way to Fiesole. Closer in, your view is of the Pitti Palace and the Boboli Gardens.

The hotel is frankly old-fashioned, with few upgrades or apologies. For its regulars, that is the appeal. Rooms facing the garden require reservations one month in advance. Some of the rooms are huge, with marble fireplaces and high ceilings; others are smaller but still sizeable. Two relatively new rooms are joined and share a bath, and thus would be suitable for a family stay. All rooms are furnished in assorted styles, colors, and fabrics. Only a few have full tubs; otherwise you get a shower or a half-size tub that you cannot sit in without having your knees under your chin. For longer stays, towels are changed every other day and sheets twice a week. A three-course dinner is available upon request. Just let them know in the morning if you will be staying for dinner.

And last but not least, *Great Sleeps Italy* readers will be given a discount if they mention the book when making their reservation—but not if they mention it when they are leaving and paying the final bill.

FACILITIES AND SERVICES: Air-conditioning in 8 rooms, fan, bar, direct-dial phone, elevator to reception, hair dryers on request and in some rooms, TVs on request, office safe, reception desk open 8 A.M.–11 P.M.

NEAREST TOURIST ATTRACTIONS: Ponte Vecchio, Arno River, Pitti Palace, Piazza Santo Spirito, 10-minute walk to central Florence

ISTITUTO GOULD (¢, 137)
Via dei Serragli, 49
97 beds in 41 rooms, 35 with shower and toilet

TELEPHONE
055 21 25 76
FAX
055 28 02 74
EMAIL
gould.reception@dada.it
CREDIT CARDS
None, cash only
RATES
All rates are per person: single
35–40€, double 24–30€, triple
20–23€, quad 20–22€; group
rates for lunch or dinner on
request

The Istituto Gould was founded by American Emily Gould in 1871 when she opened her Florence home to young victims of a flood disaster. Today it is run by a kind, gentle man named Paolo and is part of the Protestant Church of Italy. Also run by the same Christian Protestant organization is Casa Valdese in Rome (see page 203) and Foresteria Valdese in Venice (see page 328).

The mission and purpose of Istituto Gould is to provide a short- or long-term home for approximately fifteen boys and girls from ages six to eighteen who, because of severe family problems (but not drugs), cannot live with their own families. There are also two after-school programs; one is for children to come and stay until they are picked up in the evening, and the other provides care for boys and girls with serious emotional problems and mental illnesses. In addition, there is a special transition program for those who have lived here, reached eighteen, and have nowhere to go.

On the second floor of the main house, the institute operates a type of hostel, open year-round to guests of all ages. In doing my research for the Great Sleeps series, I have seen my share of hostels, but let me assure you, in the world of hostels, this is the Ritz. That is the reason it is listed here rather than under "Hostels" in "Other Options." The Istituto Gould is a place in which a Great Sleeper of any age can stay comfortably. One side is newer than the other, but all of the rooms are exceptionally nice, especially those facing the garden. Although not lavish, they are crisp and functional and kept neat and clean. You will not have to live with hideous mismatching colors, unsightly tears, or tacky, beat-up furniture. Four of the rooms open onto a lovely shared terrace; others overlook the mimosa trees in the institute's gardens and Fort Belvedere in the distance; and eight rooms share their own sitting room. Meal service is available for groups of twenty or more. I think the wonderful part about staying here is that the money goes directly to the institute to help the children. What better way to spend your hotel euros?

NOTE: Office hours are Monday to Friday 8:45 A.M.–1 P.M. and 3–7:30 P.M., and Saturday 8:45 A.M.–1:30 P.M. The office is closed Sunday and holidays.

FACILITIES AND SERVICES: No elevator (3 floors), fans, office safe

NEAREST TOURIST ATTRACTIONS: Piazza Santo Spirito, Arno River, brisk walk to Pitti Palace, 20- to 30-minute walk to Il Duomo

BREAKFAST
Breakfast is included only for groups, otherwise not served
ENGLISH
Yes

PENSIONE SORELLE BANDINI ★ (136)
Piazza Santo Spirito, 9

12 rooms, 5 with shower or bath and toilet

Warning: This hotel is not for everyone. Magnificent in its day, the *palazzo* was owned and occupied by the Bandini sisters until 1978. During their lifetimes, and certainly since, not much was or has been done to the building other than an occasional paint job. Guests who stay here either fiercely defend it or would not stay again for free. If you like shiny chrome and glass, slick bathrooms, and heel-clicking room service 24/7, skip this one. On the other hand, if you don't mind laid-back management; appreciate faded and wrinkled charm; long for huge, sunny, view rooms filled with oversize

TELEPHONE
055 21 53 08
FAX
055 28 27 61
EMAIL
pensionebandini@tiscali.it
CREDIT CARDS
None, cash only
RATES
Single 70–96€ (no singles in April), double 108–130€; extra bed 30€; lower off-season rates; lunch and dinner for groups by arrangement only

BREAKFAST
Continental breakfast 10€ extra
ENGLISH
Yes

antiques in varying stages of disrepair; and dream of reading or napping on a veranda with sweeping views of the Piazza Santo Spirito—then you might have what it takes to join the dedicated fans of the Pensione Sorelle Bandini. These fans now include the cast members from the film *Tea With Mussolini,* which was shot in part on the *loggia.*

From April to October, meals are served to groups in a baronial banquet dining room with a wrought-iron chandelier and oils hung on the walls. Breakfast is always extra and so overpriced my advice is to forget it . . . go to one of the bars on the piazza and start your day the Italian way. On the second Sunday of every month, a flea market (see page 351) is held on the square, and the neighborhood has some interesting artisan's workshops and trendy boutiques.

FACILITIES AND SERVICES: Elevator to pensione (which is on 2 floors), fans, office safe

NEAREST TOURIST ATTRACTIONS: Piazza Santo Spirito, Pitti Palace, Boboli Gardens, interesting shopping

San Niccolò

Legend has it that Michelangelo hid in the bell tower of the San Niccolò Church to avoid being rounded up with the other political activists during the fall of the Republic in 1529. Inside the church today are lovely frescoes, and in the sacristy, Madonna della Cintola from the fifteenth century. The streets in the area are dotted with the ateliers of working artists.

HOTEL SILLA ★★★ (146)
Via dei Renai, 5

TELEPHONE
055 23 42 888
FAX
055 23 41 437
EMAIL
hotelsilla@tin.it
INTERNET
www.hotelsilla.it
CREDIT CARDS
AE, DC, MC, V
RATES
Single 130€, double 175€, triple 230€; lower off-season rates
BREAKFAST
Buffet breakfast included

35 rooms, all with shower or bath and toilet

The stately Hotel Silla earns its laurels as one of the most comfortable hotels on this side of the Arno River. The riverfront location is next to the Giardino Demidoff, a small green space and statue commemorating a wealthy Russian who lived in the villa next to it. The hotel skillfully evokes the spirit of Florence by blending the charm and grace of its past as a fifteenth-century palace with the modern comforts that today's travelers appreciate. The street entrance is through a pretty courtyard and up a wide stone stairway padded with an Oriental runner. This gentle walk is the extent of the stair-climbing, as there is an elevator once you reach the hotel itself. Twelve rooms face the river, but in full foliage, the lime-scented trees banking the front of the hotel filter your outlook. Backside rooms look onto the medieval quarter of San Niccolò.

ENGLISH
Yes

The Florentine tiled rooms are open and spacious, with walnut furniture composed of a mirrored bureau, desk, comfortable chairs, and bedside lights. The baths are also roomy, with adequate light and heated towel racks, and many house a tub and separate enclosed stall shower. Breakfast is served in a formal room with a window onto the courtyard. Along the back wall, a china cabinet beautifully displays the owner's collection of hand-painted ceramic Tuscan plates. On warm days, the riverside terrace is a delightful place to have your breakfast or sip a cool early evening drink. Doing the honors at the reception desk is a delightful staff who speak beautiful English and take a genuine interest in all the guests.

NOTE: The hotel is closed in December.

FACILITIES AND SERVICES: Air-conditioning, bar, direct-dial phone, elevator, hair dryer, minibar, private hotel parking (18€ per day), satellite TV, in-room safe

NEAREST TOURIST ATTRACTIONS: Piazzale Michelangelo, 15-to 20-minute walk to Pitti Palace, Santa Croce, Ponte Vecchio, and Uffizi Gallery

Other Options

Hotels are not your only choice of accommodations in Florence. Travelers have numerous reasons for wanting to explore other options: they want even cheaper beds (and perhaps have youth or student status on their side); they will be staying at least a week and want a homier and more economical long-term choice; or they just want to get off the beaten tourist track and camp under the stars. For those who want to explore Tuscany, I've provided a few recommended villas.

Apartment Rentals

Those of you who have done it know—by staying in an apartment you will save money on meals, have more room, and get to know your neighborhood from a perspective never gained during a hotel stay. Living for a time in an apartment allows you to feel less frantic about seeing and doing everything. Instead, you are caught up in the adventure of exploring and getting to know your own neighborhood, which you will soon come to think of as your own, becoming a little bit Florentine in the process. In addition to individually owned apartment rentals in Florence listed below, there are agencies, located either in Florence or in the States, that are experts in short- and long-term apartment rentals that cater to almost all budgets. Several of the agencies can also find you an apartment in Rome, Venice, and the Italian countryside.

Before deciding on renting in Florence, you should refer to "Tips for Renting an Italian Apartment," page 15. After securing your apartment, please take out cancellation insurance (see page 38).

APARTMENT RENTALS

CASA GUIDI (145)
Piazza S. Felice, 8 (Pitti Palace)

Sleeps 6

The suite of rooms on the first floor of the Palazzo Guidi was the Florentine home of poets Robert and Elizabeth Barrett Browning. They lived here from 1847 to 1861, and it was here that they wrote some of their finest poetry. When Elizabeth Browning died in 1861, Robert commissioned a painting of the drawing room by George Mignaty, to commemorate the place in which she worked. After her death, Robert left Casa Guidi; he died in Venice in 1889.

In 1971, the apartment was purchased by the Browning Institute of New York, and it was later sold to the British Landmark Trust charity. The restoration process began in the drawing room, which was done as closely as possible to the original shown in the George Mignaty painting. The furnishings include the desk of the Brownings' son, Pen, as well as busts of Elizabeth and Robert, copies of the Mignaty painting, an original mirror, and brocade curtains that match those described in Elizabeth's letters. Her bedroom has also been redone as closely as possible to what it was during her time. Today, it has a beautiful bed, a crystal chandelier, and a baby grand piano that are similar to those during her occupancy. The original ceramic stove stands in one corner; the bathroom was the Brownings' kitchen. The new kitchen is enormous. It has two refrigerators, a large stove, a dishwasher, and every other piece of equipment and dish needed to turn out a fine feast. To the back of the kitchen, in what was once the servant's quarters, is a sleeping area with bunk beds that is reached through a wooden spiral staircase. The apartment is available to rent and accommodates up to six people for short- or long-term stays throughout the year. For anyone who loves the Brownings' poetry, I cannot imagine a more romantic and nostalgic place to stay in Florence.

TELEPHONE
011 44 1628 825 925
(Landmark Trust office in London); 802-264-6868 U.S.

INTERNET
www.landmarktrust.org.uk

CREDIT CARDS
MC, V

RATES
Rates are quoted in British pounds: per night £266, per week £1,329

NOTE: This is one of four Landmark Trust properties in Italy. Full details are published in the Landmark Trust Handbook, available on their Website. Reservations can be made by phone.

FACILITIES AND SERVICES: Air-conditioning in kitchen and Elizabeth's bedroom, elevator, equipped kitchen, weekly maid service and linen change

NEAREST TOURIST ATTRACTIONS: You are living in it! Also, Pitti Palace, Boboli Gardens, Piazza Santo Spirito

CONTESSA MARIA VITTORIA RIMBOTTI

For contact information, see Rentvillas.com, page 129.

CREDIT CARDS
MC, V

RATES
Studio apartments start at $1,000 for 2 weeks, $1,250 for 1 month (1-week rentals for studios); 1-bedroom apartments start at $1,875 for 1 week, $2,625 for 2 weeks, $3,250 for 1 month; 2-bedroom apartments start at $2,500 for 1 week, $3,750 for 2 weeks, $4,938 for 1 month; 3-bedroom apartments start at $4,750 for 2 weeks, $8,125 for 1 month; lower rates for longer stays; telephone and maid service extra; 1-week rentals include all utilities and final cleaning; for 2-week and longer rentals, all utilities and final cleaning are extra

ENGLISH
Yes

The Contessa Rimbotti's Florentine apartments top my list—worldwide. Nothing else even comes close. I could move into any one of them and feel as though I was in absolute heaven. In fact, I have lived in her apartments several times . . . and I can't wait to go back. One look at any of them will tell you that a person of distinguished elegance is in charge, and that describes Contessa Rimbotti to a T.

Her lovely flats, located in two buildings she owns in the middle of Florence, reflect her refined artistic taste and judgment, as she has personally designed and selected everything you see, employing her imagination and creativity at every turn. She once told me, "I always try to put myself in the guests' shoes and provide the best that I can for them." She succeeds beyond measure. From the smallest tower studio to a large impressive penthouse with wrap-around terraces—or an apartment with dreamlike views across the Arno to the Uffizi Gallery and the sparkling lights of the Ponte Vecchio—she has created beautiful living spaces furnished with lovely antiques, rich Italian fabrics, and interesting paintings.

Closet and drawer space abound. The linens are embroidered, the towels are thick and fluffy, and everything is color-coordinated. You will love her bathrooms and kitchens. The marble and tiled bathrooms all have a tub with a shower over it or an enclosed stall shower. Larger ones have double sinks; all have big mirrors and loads of space. In the kitchen there will be Richard Ginori china, quality cooking equipment, and beautiful marble workspaces. Of course, there will also be a dishwasher, a full-size refrigerator, a complete stove with oven, and a washing machine. Upon arrival, you will find water and perhaps a bottle of wine, a small jar of coffee, a few tea bags, and some crackers or cookies to tide you over until you can go food shopping. To help you do that, there will be a packet of information in each apartment listing the best shops and restaurants in the neighborhood as well as the major sites in Florence.

The Contessa maintains an office in Florence with a competent, English-speaking staff able to handle any problems that may arise. Absolutely no details are left to chance. I wondered after my last stay how the Contessa could improve on the perfection of her apartments. I know that by my next visit she will have thought of many beautiful ways.

I am saving the best for last. These apartments are affordable! Reservations and bookings are not made directly, but through Suzanne Pidduck's Rentvillas.com, page 129.

FACILITIES AND SERVICES: Air-conditioning, direct-dial phone (answering machine on request), hair dryer, elevator in most, fully fitted kitchen with dishwasher, clothes washer and dryer, TV, maid service on request (additional charge)

NEAREST TOURIST ATTRACTIONS: All perfectly located in central Florence

FLORENCE AND ABROAD (6)
Via San Zanobi, 58 (Piazza della Indipendenza)

Some agencies are from hell. Others, like Florence and Abroad, are pleasant to work with and honestly try to match an apartment with the budgets and needs of their clients. Bookings are taken for a minimum of one week, and rates vary depending on the size and type of apartment; a security deposit is required.

The office is open to make reservations Monday to Friday 10 A.M. to 5 P.M. The office is closed Saturday and Sunday and in August.

TELEPHONE
055 48 70 04, 055 49 01 43
FAX
055 49 01 43
INTERNET
www.florenceandabroad.com
CREDIT CARDS
None
RATES
Short-term studio apartments 600–900€ per week; long-term rentals (three months or more) start around 900€ per month; in short-term rentals, utilities (except telephone and air-conditioning) are usually included
ENGLISH
Yes; ask to speak with Karen Brennan Piemonte, who is English and very helpful

ITALIAN ESCAPES

Italian Escapes can plan your escape in upmarket apartments in Florence, Rome, Venice, Siena, Capri, and Positano, and in luxurious villas in Sicily and the Tuscan countryside. They can also make arrangements for cooking lessons, yacht charters, and personally guided tours. For further information and reservations, contact the U.S. number provided.

TELEPHONE
925-939-6346 U.S.
EMAIL
la.contessa@astound.net
CREDIT CARDS
None, cash only
RATES
From 800€ per week for a small one-bedroom
ENGLISH
Yes

PALAZZO ANTELLESI (120)
Piazza Santa Croce, 21/22 (Piazza Santa Croce)
14 apartments, all with shower or bath and toilet

TELEPHONE
Italy: 055 244 456;
New York: 212-932-3480
FAX
Italy: 055 234 5552;
New York: 212-932-9039
EMAIL
Italy: antellesi@dada.it
New York:
ciaomanfredi@aol.com
INTERNET
www.florencerentals.net,
www.palazzoantellesi.com
CREDIT CARDS
None, cash or bank checks in
U.S. dollars or euros
RATES
Florence (Palazzo Antellesi):
weekly from $1,600–$3,200;
Siena (Palazzo Piccolomini):
weekly from $1,400–$1,900;
lower long-term rates;
telephone, utilities, maid service
and final cleaning extra in both
locations; minimum stay is six
nights
ENGLISH
Yes

The Palazzo Antellesi was created in the second half of the sixteenth century by joining several medieval towers. The facade was painted in allegorical themes by Giovanni da San Giovanni, the foremost fresco painter of his time. Today it is considered to be the most famous and authentic Renaissance palace on the dramatic Piazza Santa Croce, the ancient site of colorful football games with costumed players. Today, the piazza is the site of summer football games and other sporting events. The palace has been completely restored and refitted into flats accommodating up to six people. Over the years it has attracted many international guests who consider their favorite flat at the Palazzo Antellesi to be their second home.

Aside from their historical significance and original architectural designs, the flats are furnished with a combination of modern pieces and antiques. The kitchens are equipped with dishwashers and washing machines in addition to all the pots, pans, and crockery you will need to perform any level of cooking. Some of the apartments have working fireplaces and sweeping views, not only of the piazza but of the famous sites of Florence and the surrounding hills. Several of the apartments have their own terrace or open onto a private garden. All have American-style bathrooms and are accessible by elevator. Maid service is available.

The dynamite location puts you within easy range of all that awaits you in Florence. From a practical point of view, excellent markets and food shops are minutes away. So are interesting shops, restaurants, cleaners, and a post office. Office hours in Florence are limited to telephone calls Monday to Friday, 1 to 7 P.M.

In addition to their Florence apartments, the owners of the Palazzo Antellesi have created five apartments on the top floor of Palazzo Piccolomini, their historic sixteenth-century Renaissance *palazzo* in the heart of Siena, which is an hour's bus ride or drive from Florence. Siena is an ideal base for exploring the wine regions of Chianti and Montalcino and the historic towns of San Gimigniano, Pienza, Montepulciano, and Monteriggioni. In Siena, the *palazzo*'s pivotal location in the old city allows guests to be within walking distance of the magnificent cathedral and all the necessary shops, and only two hundred yards from the central square, where the city's medieval past comes alive in July and August with the colorful Palio, a horse race in which teams of riders charge bareback around the cobbled Piazza del Campo.

Because of the nature of the *palazzo* and its historic importance, which prohibits structural changes, some skillful design techniques were necessary to create suitable living spaces, and this means there are very few windows at eye level. The bedrooms of two flats have no windows at all, only skylights. In another, Leocorno, there are no windows to speak of in the sitting area, only little peepholes at the floor level. I only mention it here because for some the lack of windows might be a problem. The air-conditioned flats are attractively furnished with rustic Tuscan reproduction antiques and have modern-designed, pastel-colored kitchens and bathrooms, complete with good-size dishwashers and washing machines. The closet space is excellent. Reservations are made through the Florence office.

FACILITIES AND SERVICES: Florence (Palazzo Antellesi): Air-conditioning in most apartments (otherwise portable units or fans available), direct-dial phone, elevator, gym, fully equipped kitchen, satellite TV, all with either or both washing machine and dishwasher, maid service extra; Siena (Palazzo Piccolomini): Air-conditioning, fully equipped kitchen, dishwasher, washing machine, direct-dial phone, elevator, satellite TV, maid service extra

NEAREST TOURIST ATTRACTIONS: Florence (Palazzo Antellesi): Santa Croce Church, Arno River, Il Duomo, museums, shopping; Siena: Central Siena, nearby wine regions, base for exploring Tuscany

RENTVILLAS.COM
700 East Main Street, Ventura, CA 93001

Suzanne T. Pidduck has devoted over thirty-five years to traveling and living in Italy. Her California-based company has now grown into one of the best organizations renting properties in Italy—as well as those in other European locations. Through Suzanne you can obtain anything from a studio in Venice to a magnificent Florentine apartment facing the Arno and Ponte Vecchio, from a farmhouse in Tuscany to a panoramic penthouse in Rome. In addition to rentals throughout Italy, she covers apartments in Britain, France, Spain, Portugal, and Greece, as well as yachts in Turkey. To learn more about the services she offers and to have a good look at the properties available, go to rentvillas.com, one of the most user-friendly Websites out there.

Once you are in your rental, someone who speaks English will be available via a toll-free telephone number, or on-site, should the need arise. I used Rentvillas.com during several research trips to Venice and Florence and found the staff to be competent professionals on every level, and I give them my highest praise.

TELEPHONE
805-641-1650, 800-726-6702
FAX
805-641-1630
INTERNET
www.rentvillas.com
CREDIT CARDS
MC, V
RATES
Depends on the apartment, but studios start at around $1,000 per week for 2 people

NOTE: For an in-depth description of two of their outstanding rental properties, see Contessa Maria Vittoria Rimbotti, page 126, in Florence, and Rosmarie Diletti's Villa Delros, page 222, in Rome.

RESIDENZA SANGALLO (15)
Via San Gallo, 28 (Piazza San Marco)
5 apartments, all with shower or bath and toilet

TELEPHONE
055 490 760
FAX
055 483 247
INTERNET
www.residenzasangallo.com
CREDIT CARDS
MC, V
RATES
Daily 130–200€, weekly 850–1,050€; rates for longer stays on request
ENGLISH
Yes

The Residenza Sangallo apartments are owned and operated by Mariangela Masoero and her family, who for forty-three years ran the Hotel Splendid next door, which has been refashioned into the Hotel Orto de' Medici (see page 91). The tile-floor apartments are not fancy, but they are comfortable, and once you move in, you will soon feel right at home. Family antiques, welcoming sitting and dining areas, adequate closet and storage space, working kitchens, well-lit bathrooms with shelf space, and sunny balconies with pretty garden views increase the desirability of staying here. The apartments do not have land-line telephones, but rental cell phones can be provided. The neighborhood is filled with shops that cater to the needs of everyday living, and you're centrally located for leisurely walks to the Accademia, the Medici Chapel, and Il Duomo. There is a minimum two-night stay. Prices are all-inclusive, which means, other than cell phone charges, you will not be paying for utilities, weekly maid service and linen change, or a final cleaning. Better still are the lower prices for longer stays.

FACILITIES AND SERVICES: Air-conditioning, elevator, fitted kitchens, satellite TV

NEAREST TOURIST ATTRACTIONS: Accademia, Il Duomo, Medici Chapel

SMALL & ELEGANT HOTELS INTERNATIONAL
9425 Whispering Sands, West Olive, MI 49460

TELEPHONE
616 844 6000
FAX
616 844 6402
INTERNET
www.smallandelegant
hotels.com
RATES
One-bedroom from 160€ per night, two-bedroom from 270€ per night; lower rates for longer stays
CREDIT CARDS
AE, DC, MC, V

American Bonnie Palutke knows what she is doing when it comes to hotel and apartment accommodations. As a former London hotel owner and a manager of apartments in major European cities, she understands what Americans want and need during their stays away from home. Bonnie personally reviews her properties regularly and always provides local contacts in case of emergency. Her apartments are upmarket, well-located, and fairly priced given the amenities offered.

FACILITIES AND SERVICES: Vary with each property

TUSCANY VACATION RENTALS
Casa Tizzano
Via Castiglionchio, 9
Rignano sull'arno 50067, Firenze

Tuscany Vacation Rentals has a selection ranging from cottages in the rustic countryside to fabulous villas that sleep ten people. Owner Marie Lyons offers personal service and is always available for her clients to smooth over any problems. The Website shows photos and lists the services and amenities for each location, but always be sure to inquire about all aspects of a rental before you sign on the dotted line.

It is also possible to have Marie and her staff organize entire weddings and romantic honeymoons of any size, kind, and budget. The ins and outs of Italian red tape are guaranteed to cool a romance in a hurry, but Tuscany Vacation Rentals seamlessly leaps the bureaucratic hurdles to allow for a beautiful walk down the aisle and a romantic honeymoon to follow. Marie has also co-authored *Views from a Tuscan Kitchen,* an appealing cookbook with charming illustrations and easy-to-follow Tuscan pasta recipes.

TELEPHONE
0039/830 3280; cell 39/328 19 11 508
INTERNET
www.tuscanyvacationrental.com
CREDIT CARDS
MC, V
RATES
Studio (2 people) 300–900€ per week; villa (10 people) 1,740–3,300€ per week; house (4 people) 876–1,256€ per week
ENGLISH
Yes

VIA TRAVEL DESIGN
7458 Devon Street, Philadelphia, PA 19119

James Dominic and his wife, Lori Redmond, offer three hundred hand-picked vacation homes in Italy and France. In addition, they have turned their extensive travel information, collected over the past two decades, into a vast database that clients can access on their Website and use to enrich their stay. They also publish a free email newsletter (see their Website for subscription details). Prices are quoted in U.S. dollars and depend on the season and the length of the stay.

TELEPHONE
215-248-2571, 888-477-2740 (toll-free in the U.S.)
FAX
215-248-1919
INTERNET
www.viatraveldesign.com
CREDIT CARDS
MC, V
RATES
From $2,000 per week, discounts in low-season and for longer stays

VILLAS INTERNATIONAL
4340 Redwood Highway, Suite D-309
San Rafael, CA 94903

David Kendall's Villas International offers a wide selection of rental properties of all types for the independent traveler who wants more than just a city hotel room. In addition to all major Italian cities, they cover the rest of Europe, Great Britain, Mexico, the Caribbean, and Hawaii. All arrangements can be made through their California office. As with any foreign rental, it is wise to take out cancellation insurance.

TELEPHONE
415-499-9490, 800-221-2260
FAX
415 499 9491
INTERNET
www.villasintl.com
CREDIT CARDS
None, cash only
RATES
Vary by location, but prices generally start around $700 a week for two in a small studio

WINDOWS ON TUSCANY (129)
Via dei Serragli, 6r (Pitti Palace)

TELEPHONE
055 26 85 10
FAX
055 23 81 524
INTERNET
www.windowsontuscany.com
CREDIT CARDS
AE, MC, V
RATES
From around 170€ per day, minimum 3-night stay; lower rates for weekly and monthly stays; inclusion of utilities, maid service, and final cleaning charges vary by location
ENGLISH
Yes

Windows on Tuscany consists of 120 near-perfect units, from studios to four-bedroom apartments, which are all owned, elegantly restored, and decorated by the well-known Ferragamo family. As Maria Beatrice Ferragamo says, "We are eager to share our experience with all of you who search for atmosphere, comfort, and beauty, and who want to spend an unforgettable holiday."

From start to finish, these apartments put the F in fabulous. The apartments are centrally located with no detail overlooked; each provides maximum comfort and convenience for guests. They are beautifully appointed with rich fabrics, magnificent furnishings, the latest in fitted kitchens and marble baths, and more than enough closet space for a yearly wardrobe. Some are in eighteenth-century buildings with restored frescoes; some feature massive beams in huge rooms with floor-to-ceiling windows and polished hardwood floors; and others have tranquil garden settings, terraces with breathtaking views of Florence, skylit loggias, and living rooms with working fireplaces. Any one is absolutely guaranteed to make your stay in Florence more than you ever expected or dreamed it would be.

Also available are equally lovely apartments in Venice (see Views on Venice, page 326), Rome, and the Florentine countryside. Reservations can be made directly through the Florence office (hours are Monday to Friday 9 A.M. to 1 P.M., 2:30 to 6:30 P.M.).

FACILITIES AND SERVICES: Air-conditioning in most, direct-dial phone, elevator in most, hair dryer, fully fitted kitchen with dishwasher, clothes washer and dryer, satellite TV in most, DVD and CD players in some, maid service extra (request when booking)

NEAREST TOURIST ATTRACTIONS: Central Florence

Camping

For the rough and ready, camping in Florence can provide some great cheap sleeps. Some of the campgrounds are open year-round, all are at least a thirty-minute trip from Florence proper, and all are jam-packed in summer. It is possible to rent almost everything you will need to set up rural housekeeping. Prices quoted here include a per-person fee plus a separate site fee (which includes water and electricity hookups). There is often a small convenience store on the premises, but due to the captive audience, prices will be high.

The Federazione Italiana del Campeggio, also called Federcampeggio, issues a free list of campgrounds in Italy along with a map. Write to them at Calenzano, Florence 50041, or call 055 88 23 91.

CAMPING

CAMPING MICHELANGELO
Viale Michelangiolo, 80 (outside Florence)

This campground has beautiful views and is loaded with things to do, but it is very crowded and hot in summer. You must arrive early to get a good spot. The office is open 7 A.M. to midnight. From Santa Maria Novella train station in Florence, take Bus 12 to the stop called "Camping." The campground is next to the gardens near the Piazzale Michelangelo.

FACILITIES AND SERVICES: Bar, restaurant and pizzeria, Internet cafe, minimarket, playground, tennis court, coin laundry, ATM, free showers

NEAREST TOURIST ATTRACTIONS: Piazzale Michelangelo

TELEPHONE
055 68 11 977
FAX
055 68 93 48
EMAIL
michelangelo@itvacanza.it
CREDIT CARDS
MC, V
RATES
Per person 9€, children 5–11 years 4.60€, under 5 free; tent 15€; camper 9€ plus 11.70€ parking
ENGLISH
Limited

CAMPING PANORAMICO/CAMPING DI FIESOLE
Via Peramonda, 1 (7 km. outside Florence)

This is a close campsite to Florence proper, and as a result it is usually packed to capacity. In addition to sleeping under the stars (you must bring your own tent), you can rent a bungalow that has private facilities and a kitchen (no utensils), or a caravan that comes with or without private facilities (but no kitchen). Reservations are required to rent a bungalow or caravan. From the Santa Maria Novella train station in Florence, take Bus 7 to Fiesole and get off at the main square; the campground is 300 meters uphill from the square.

FACILITIES AND SERVICES: Bar, convenience store, restaurant, free showers, coin-operated washer and dryer, ironing room, communal kitchen with fridge and freezer, swimming pool (summer only)

NEAREST TOURIST ATTRACTIONS: Fiesole, a beautiful town overlooking Florence; otherwise, about 30 minutes to Florence by car or bus

TELEPHONE
055 59 90 69
FAX
055 59 186
INTERNET
www.florencecamping.com
CREDIT CARDS
AE, MC, V
RATES
Per person 10€, children 3–12 years 7€, under 3 free; in own caravan 15€; bungalow (2–4 people) 65–100€, rental caravan (2–4 people) 45–75€
ENGLISH
Yes

VILLA CAMERATA
Viale Augusto Righi, 2-4 (outside Florence)

TELEPHONE
055 60 14 51
FAX
055 61 03 00
INTERNET
www.eufed.org
CREDIT CARDS
MC, V
RATES
Per person 6€, children
3–12 years 3.50€; tent 5€,
camper or large tent 11€
ENGLISH
Yes

The country setting of this campground beside a villa is not only pretty, it is cooler than most. The campsite is on the property of Ostello per la Giovent (see page 137). Reservations are not accepted. To get here, take Bus 17 from the Santa Maria Novella train station.

FACILITIES AND SERVICES: Affiliated with EUFED hostels, showers included, bar

NEAREST TOURIST ATTRACTIONS: None; at least 30 minutes from Florence by bus

Holy Hotels

Holy hotels are convents, monasteries, or other religious-run accommodations that appeal to Great Sleepers who want to get away from mainstream hotels. They tend to be quiet places where guests are joined by like-minded, conservative, budget travelers. While that basically defines most holy hotels, there are always exceptions, and in Florence, Suore di Santa Elizabetta is certainly unique.

SUORE DI SANTA ELIZABETTA
Viale Michelangiolo, 46

TELEPHONE & FAX
055 68 11 884
EMAIL
mabigus@tin.it
CREDIT CARDS
None, cash only
RATES
Single 42€, double 76€, triple
38€ per person, quad 35€ per
person
BREAKFAST
Continental breakfast included
ENGLISH
Usually Mon–Sat 8:30 A.M.–
2:30 P.M.; otherwise limited, but
enough

30 rooms, 18 with shower and toilet

All you need to know about Suore di Santa Elizabetta can be summed up in a single word—*wonderful!* No, make that two words—*absolutely wonderful.* Please read on.

I will admit I found this holy hotel by mistake. I was evaluating a three-star hotel next door, which had been recommended as an alternative to mid-city living in Florence. After touring the reception, dining room, and two or three rooms, I knew this was never going to make the cut for a Great Sleep. Before going back to Florence, I decided to walk by some of the lovely villas that line the tree-shaded streets in the neighborhood. To my surprise, right next door to the hotel was this holy hotel—which is, without question, one of the Greatest Sleeps in Florence, period. It costs three times less than the overpriced three-star next door and is ten times better!

When I walked in, a Ray Charles CD was playing, and the sister at the desk welcomed me with smiles. What a start! After apologizing that the breakfast service had just ended and they were out of coffee and fresh rolls, she took me on a guided tour of the comfortably furnished, old-fashioned bedrooms, a few of which had their own terrace, but all of which were antiseptically clean and pleasing. Over half have a private shower and toilet, one has its own bathtub, and the rest share pristine hall bathrooms. She pointed out the stained-glass window at the top of the stairs and showed me the chapel and the dining room with etched glass windows on the garden side. Then we went out to see the garden. Who would think an order of sisters would be fans of Snow White and the Seven Dwarfs? Well, they are, and throughout the well-tended gardens that wrap around the villa are brightly colored, plaster-of-paris dwarfs (including the famous seven) and assorted animals nestled among the very pretty plantings. There is also a cactus garden and a plot where kitchen herbs thrive. In one corner is a pond filled with turtles basking under a waterfall, and toward the back is an aviary with singing birds and a covered sitting area. Of course, guests are welcome to enjoy all of these gardens.

True, it is not a particularly central location, but if you have a car, there is free parking on the grounds. If you must rely on public transportation, there are three buses that take you directly into Florence. Taxis are not expensive in Florence and are, considering the price of the rooms, a viable option. If you are feeling really fit, the walk down the Viale Michelangiolo and along the Arno to the Pitti Palace or across to the Uffizi would be twenty to thirty minutes.

FACILITIES AND SERVICES: No elevator (2 floors), garden, TV in sitting room, free parking, nonsmoking hotel

NEAREST TOURIST ATTRACTIONS: None; must use car or public transportation; a pleasant 30-minute walk to Il Duomo and central Florence

Hostels

Hostels are Great Sleeps for travelers with youth on their side, wanderlust in their hearts, and not much cash in their pockets. These budget sleeps can vary widely, from rooms for two or three to dormitories housing up to twenty sleepers a night. Most of the sites impose a lockout during the day (that is, you cannot stay in your room during the morning and afternoon) and a curfew at night. There is nothing elaborate about any of them; they are strictly places to lay a weary head. Another point to remember is that often these accommodations are far from the center of Florence, entailing long bus commutes. It could be cheaper in the long run to find a small hotel closer in and apply the bus fares to the room rates. Depending on what you are hoping to see and do in Florence, these logistics may complicate your bargain Great Sleep to the point where ultimately it is not one.

Note that only Ostello per la Giovent is part of the International Youth Hostel Federation; you do not have to belong to a hostel organization to stay at any of the others.

HOSTELS

OSTELLO ARCHI ROSSI (12)
Via Faenza, 94 (Train Station)
96 beds, 14 rooms with shower and toilet

TELEPHONE
055 29 08 04

FAX
055 23 02 601

EMAIL
ostelloarchirossi@hotmail.com

INTERNET
www.hostelarchirossi.com

CREDIT CARDS
MC, V

RATES
Per person 17–28€, depending on size and type of room; towels 1€; lunch or dinner 11€

BREAKFAST
Continental breakfast included

ENGLISH
Yes

This strictly youth-oriented Great Sleep benefits from its location near the train station. There are ninety-six beds in unisex rooms set up for one to nine (no doubles). Many of these rooms have their own bathrooms. Sheets, blankets, and pillows are included; towels cost an additional 1€. The rooms have lockers, and hot showers are free. Breakfast and dinner are served in a university-style dining room with a huge television at one end and windows facing a garden, which is badly in need of a caretaker. There is also a bank of vending machines. The walls of the hostel are covered with an international tapestry of graffiti drawn by the guests. There was a time when chalk would have been available for you to add your own touches, but no longer—the walls are full. Reservations for individuals are not accepted in the high season, and there is no age limit. Hostel hours are as follows: at 6:30 A.M., it opens; at 9:30 A.M., guests must leave their rooms but can stay in common areas; at 11 A.M., the entire hostel closes for cleaning; at 2:30 P.M., it reopens, and guests may return to their rooms. The curfew is 12:30 A.M.

FACILITIES AND SERVICES: Elevator, coin laundry, luggage storage, restaurant for breakfast and dinner, office safe and room lockers, communal satellite TV and video, no smoking allowed, guest Internet terminal, one handicapped-accessible room, self-service coin laundry, 2 microwaves (but no use of kitchen)

NEAREST TOURIST ATTRACTIONS: Train station, Mercato Centrale, Medici Chapel, San Lorenzo Market

OSTELLO PER LA GIOVENT
Viale Augusto Righi, 2/4

320 beds, none with shower or toilet

The beauty of this hostel is its countryside setting; in addition you can make reservations by telephone, email, or fax several weeks ahead. The hostel is part of the EUFED network, and you can reserve at any other member hostel while you are here. The hostel is not close to Florence, requiring train, bus, and foot to get to it. The 320 beds are divided into rooms that sleep four to twelve. There is also a campsite here (see page 134). Breakfast is included in the price, but dinner is extra (10€). The office is open for check-in from 2 P.M. in the summer and 3 P.M. in the winter. Room lockout is 10 A.M. to 2 P.M.; curfew is at midnight.

FACILITIES AND SERVICES: Bar, TV room with English videos, office safe, dinner served (10€)

NEAREST TOURIST ATTRACTIONS: None; at least 30 minutes to an hour to Florence by bus or car

TELEPHONE
055 60 14 51
FAX
055 61 03 00
INTERNET
www.hihostels.com
CREDIT CARDS
MC, V
RATES
Per person 17.50€; dinner 10€
BREAKFAST
Continental breakfast included
ENGLISH
Yes

OSTELLO SANTA MONACA (130)
Via Santa Monaca, 6 (Piazza Santa Spirito)

114 beds, no private facilities

The Santa Monaca Hostel, once a convent for Santa Monaca nuns, is across the Arno River from Piazza Goldoni. It is popular, spacious, and clean, and offers kitchen privileges, a safe for valuables, laundry facilities, lockers (BYO lock), luggage storage, and a list of rules set in concrete. You must be out of your room for the day from 9:30 A.M. to 2 P.M. Lights are turned out at midnight, and the door is locked at 1 A.M. At no time is eating, drinking, or smoking allowed in the rooms. The hostel office is open from 6 A.M., and for reservations from 9:30 A.M. to 1 P.M. The office is completely closed from 1 to 2 P.M. Advance reservations may be made by fax or email, not telephone, but you can also show up and hope. Three meals a day are served Monday to Saturday at a trattoria down the street and cost extra (10–11€). The maximum stay is seven days in high season; longer stays are allowed the rest of the year.

The rooms range in size from four to sixteen beds, are segregated into men's and women's sections, and never the twain shall meet, even if you are married, but families get to stay together. Sheets are provided, and you must use them, not yours. You pay for your entire stay in advance. The communal kitchen is open 7 to 9:15 A.M. and 2 P.M. to midnight, but you will have to BYO utensils and cooking pots. The hot shower is free, but a towel is 0.50€.

TELEPHONE
055 26 83 38
FAX
055 28 01 85
INTERNET
www.ostello.it
CREDIT CARDS
AE, DC, MC, V
RATES
Per person 18€; lunch or dinner 10–11€
BREAKFAST
Breakfast 2.50–3.50€
ENGLISH
Yes

FACILITIES AND SERVICES: No elevator (2 floors), Internet terminal, coin-operated laundry, lockers, kitchen (not equipped), low-cost restaurant meals, office safe, communal satellite TV

NEAREST TOURIST ATTRACTIONS: Santo Spirito, Pitti Palace, Boboli Gardens

YOUTH RESIDENCE FIRENZE
Viale Raffaelo Sanzio, 16

74 beds in 23 rooms, 16 rooms with shower and toilet

TELEPHONE
055 233 55 58
FAX
055 23 06 392
EMAIL
bed@dada.it
INTERNET
www.youthhostelfirenze.it
CREDIT CARDS
DC, MC, V
RATES
Single 35–40€, double
56–66€, triple 75–90€, quad
104–112€, five 120–125€
BREAKFAST
Continental breakfast included
ENGLISH
Yes

It's new, the rooms are air-conditioned, and the price includes sheets, blankets, and towels in the room rate. In addition, there is no lockout, no curfew, no kitchen privileges, no TV anywhere, and no smoking allowed on the premises. The location on the Oltrarno near Piazza Pier Vettori is not close to action central, so plan on commuting via public transportation by taking Bus 12 from the Santa Maria Novella train station. The bus stops in front of the hostel.

FACILITIES AND SERVICES: Office safe

NEAREST TOURIST ATTRACTIONS: None; must use public transportation (about 30 minutes)

Residence Hotels

If you plan to be in Florence for longer than a few days and don't want to rent an apartment, a good way to cut costs is to stay in a residence hotel. Residence hotels are generally of at least three-star quality and provide the services and amenities found in good hotels. Other advantages include more space, a kitchen in which you can cook a few meals and save on restaurant costs (a big factor with families), and finally, the feeling of being more at home in Florence than you would be in a hotel room.

PALAZZO MANNAIONI RESIDENCE (131)
Via Maffia, 9 (Piazza Santo Spirito)

19 studios, all with shower or bath and toilet

TELEPHONE
055 27 17 41
FAX
055 27 17 402
INTERNET
www.florenceresidence.it
CREDIT CARDS
AE, MC, MC, V

The Palazzo Mannaioni is a moderately priced residence hotel not far from the Santo Spirito Church. Weekly stays are preferred, and because the stripped-down studios are so basic and lack cushy comforts, they are best reserved for short stays when a kitchen is needed. The best bets are on the third, fourth, and fifth floors, facing the cloisters of the church and the bell tower. Of these, I like Nos. 33, 43, 51, and 53, which are the only four with terraces. All nineteen units have a cooking corner, bathroom (get one with a tub; they are better), telephone, satellite television, modern furniture, and elevator service to four of the five floors. Everything from dishes, pots and pans, linens, and twice-weekly maid service with linen change is provided. The maid won't do your laundry, but there is a laundromat within a five-minute walk. Utilities are included; telephone charges are not. The neighborhood is interesting, filled with narrow streets and many old artisans' shops. On the second Sunday of every month there is a flea market and an organic market on the Piazza Santo Spirito. Office hours are Mon–Sat 9 A.M.–1 P.M., 3–7 P.M., and Sun 9 A.M.–noon.

FACILITIES AND SERVICES: Air-conditioning (4€ per day, 25€ per week, 80€ per month), direct-dial phone with private number, elevator to all but the fifth floor, fitted kitchen, satellite TV, twice-weekly maid service included

NEAREST TOURIST ATTRACTIONS: Santo Spirito, Piazza del Carmine, Pitti Palace, Boboli Gardens, Ponte Vecchio

RATES
Rates are per night (weekly stays preferred): single studio 70€, double from 120€, one extra bed 22€, two extra beds 15€ per bed; lower weekly and monthly rates

BREAKFAST
No breakfast served

ENGLISH
Yes

Villas in Tuscany

If you have read Frances Maye's two best-selling books, *Under the Tuscan Sun* and *Bella Tuscany,* you've heard about the quiet charm and natural beauty of this very popular area. The following recommendations are for those visitors to Florence who have a car, the time, and the desire to venture into the surrounding countryside and discover for themselves its colorful villages and peaceful rolling landscapes.

VILLAS IN TUSCANY

CASTELSERRE
Piazza XX Settembre, 1
Terme di Rapolano (Serre di Rapolano)
26 rooms, all with private bath or shower and toilet

Some men dream…other men make their dreams come true.

Dynamic Salvator Gangale has huge dreams, along with the foresight, tenacity, bank loans, and true grit to do what it takes to make them all come true. After a successsful

TELEPHONE
0577 705049, 338 504 0811
EMAIL
salvatore.gangale@tin.it
INTERNET
www.castellodelleserre.com

CREDIT CARDS
AE, MC, V
RATES
Double 85€, suites 200–250€
BREAKFAST
Continental breakfast included
ENGLISH
Yes

career in the United States in the restaurant business, he decided to return to his native roots and open a hotel. After two years of looking, he found this fourteenth-century castle, near the famous spa town of Terme di Rapolano. The property is surrounded by six acres of forests, more than one hundred olive trees, and majestic views over the rolling Tuscan hills.

The castle suffered from centuries of neglect, and Salvator admits it will be a work in progress for some time. Everything has to be restored and rebuilt, but his dream is to create twenty-six palatial rooms—one with its own wine cellar, a gym, Finnish and Turkish saunas, a tennis court, and a jogging track. As of now, he has restored a medieval tower, in which he added several lovely rooms, including a three-level suite with unspoiled views from every window and a private rooftop terrace. The swimming pool is completed, as is the bar and a restaurant, which is open for dinner. Guests who have already stayed here are as enthusiastic about Castelserre as is Salvator, and they are eager to return to celebrate the completion of his dream come true.

NOTE: Castelserre is closed from January 8 to February 1.

FACILITIES AND SERVICES: Air-conditioning, poolside bar, minibar, restaurant (dinner only), in-room safe, TV, swimming pool

NEAREST TOURIST ATTRACTIONS: You are in one; otherwise Rapolano di Terme is world-famous for its health and beauty spas and hot mud baths

CHIANTI CASHMERE COMPANY
Azienda Agricola La Penisola
53017 Radda in Chianti (Siena)

TELEPHONE & FAX
0577 738 080
INTERNET
www.chianaticashmere.it
CREDIT CARDS
MC, V
RATES
Farmhouse (6 people) 650€ per week in low-season, 2,200€ per week in high season; apartment (2 people) 80€ per night year-round
BREAKFAST
Not served
ENGLISH
Yes

Thirty-two years ago, Nora Kravis left Long Island, New York, and followed her heart to the Chianti countryside. During that time she became a successful horse trainer, a noted veterinarian, and a shrewd businesswoman. In 1988 she bought two goats to eat the weeds around her remodeled stone house and barn on her property. A few years later she added more goats, and now has two hundred who produce the milk and wool for her world-reknowned Chianti Cashmere Company skincare products and one of a kind, handwoven cashmere articles (see page 339), which Nora truthfully advertises as "Simple. Natural. Wholesome. Beautiful."

La Piensola farm is located three kilometers from Radda in Chianti, which is midway between Florence and Siena. For a unique experience of rural Tuscany at its best, you can stay at her farm, enjoying its peace and calm while watching the goats and their offspring graze in the pasture, or enjoying the company of Nora's flock of Bolognese dogs, which were the companion dogs of the nobility during the Renaissance. It is the perfect place to come alone, as a couple, or as a family to relax and leave the stresses and strains of the modern world behind. The original eighteenth-century stone farmhouse and barn have been renovated and provide homespun comforts. The farmhouse is on two levels and sleeps up to six in three bedrooms; it also has two bathrooms, a fitted kitchen, a dining room, a glassed-in porch with fireplace, and a vine-covered, outdoor barbecue area to enjoy alfresco dining and majestic sunsets. The barn is now an apartment for two. Both are available year-round. As Nora says, "Our farmhouse has no noise, no traffic, no schedules to keep, no appointments to make. Time stands still... what are you waiting for?"

FACILITIES AND SERVICES: Swimming pool

NEAREST TOURIST ATTRACTIONS: Aside from La Piensola, lovely drives, charming villages, peaceful landscapes

MARIGNOLLE RELAIS & CHARME
Via di S. Quirichino a Marignolle, 16 (outside Florence)

9 rooms, 2 Junior Suites, all with large shower and toilet (no tubs)

In 2000, the Bullari family built Marignolle Relais & Charme on their property, which lies in a wooded valley overlooking the Florentine hills. From the main road, the approach to this quiet and reserved place is down a long driveway. In creating Marignolle, Sra. Bullari, an artist, did all the decorating, and her husband designed the interiors... both sparing no expense nor overlooking any detail. The result provides the feeling of a private home, and once guests settle in, they are soon planning their next visit.

The classic bedrooms are finely furnished with nineteenth-century antique pieces and tapestries. They have parquet floors, coordinating fabrics, and wonderful bathrooms with Carrara marble sinks. Several open onto a private terrace that flows into the well-tended garden, which is full of beautiful flowers year-round. The main living and dining room have a fireplace and a wall of large picture windows overlooking the garden. Beyond is a gazebo, where summer breakfasts and light lunches are served (on request), or guests can simply sit and read or enjoy the view. To further relax and unwind from a day in Florence, there is a swimming pool that is open from May to October. From the Relais, guests can walk

TELEPHONE
055 22 86 910

FAX
055 20 47 396

INTERNET
www.marignolle.com

CREDIT CARDS
AE, DC, MC, V

RATES
Double deluxe 225€, junior suite for two 255€, for four 345€; lower rates in off-season

BREAKFAST
Buffet breakfast served

ENGLISH
Yes

to a tennis court or go horseback riding. It is only a ten- or twenty-minute drive into Florence or to reach three golf courses. In addition, city and shopping tours, winery visits, and cooking lessons in Sra. Bullari's kitchen can be arranged.

FACILITIES AND SERVICES: Air-conditioned, bar, direct-dial phone, no elevator (2 floors), hair dryer, minibar, in-room safe, satellite TV, tea and coffeemakers, swimming pool, light lunches, cooking classes on request

NEAREST TOURIST ATTRACTIONS: Walking distance to tennis court, 10- or 20-minute drive to Florence, horseback riding, three golf courses

VILLA DI PIAZZANO
Località Piazzano (near Cortona)
06069 Tuoro sul Trasimeno (PG)
21 rooms, all with shower, bath, and toilet

For the stay of your dreams, please read about the Villa di Piazzano.

The peaceful rolling countryside around Cortona invites you to shift gears and leave behind the stresses of everyday modern life. Amid this beautiful landscape is the Villa di Piazzano, where you will be graciously welcomed by Alessandra Wimpole and her family: Damian, her father; Adriana, her mother; Lisa, her adorable young daughter; and Nuvola, a calico cat who had the good sense to adopt the villa as her home. The villa, which is considered to be the most important in the region, was originally built in the early 1500s by Cardinal Passerini and used as his hunting lodge. Over time it has also been a convent and a private estate. During World War II, it served as the area headquarters for the Nazis, who shot holes in the wine casks to prevent the wine from falling into the hands of the approaching Allied forces. The cellar was completely flooded with wine, and when the owners returned and saw what had happened, they invited the local farmers and their families to come with their buckets to remove it. The response was enormous, and there are still elderly people in the surrounding villages who have fond memories of that day.

Afterward, the villa deteriorated, and it was in virtual ruins when Alessandra had the foresight and immense courage to buy it a few years ago. She and her family deserve enormous admiration for never losing sight of their dream and restoring the villa, returning it to its rightful place in the history of this area. The task was an undertaking of the greatest magnitude, a total restoration of everything

TELEPHONE
075 826 226
FAX
075 826 336
INTERNET
www.villadipiazzano.com
CREDIT CARDS
AE, DC, MC, V
RATES
Rates are quoted from low season (Mar, Apr, and Nov excluding Easter) to high season (May–Oct): Single 110–155€, double classic 130–175€, double superior 160–200€, double deluxe 180–235€, junior suite 200–250€; extra bed 60€; children 2–12 years 30€, free baby cot; 3-course dinner with wine (on request) 40€
BREAKFAST
Buffet breakfast included
ENGLISH
Yes

from the roof to the cellar, including removing colonies of bats who occupied every room. The result is nothing short of spectacular. The villa is now a finely tuned blend of luxury, comfort, and warm hospitality that could easily become a way of life. The family truly cares for their guests, and I hope you will become one of them. I know I can't wait to return.

The approach, along an avenue of cypress trees, is actually in Tuscany, but the villa itself is in Umbria. The grounds have been completely relandscaped and include a swimming pool, fruit trees, and masses of blooming flowers and plants. The interior is elegant but not at all conspicious. Most of the furnishings belong to the family, and this adds an informal yet high-quality tone reminiscent of a lovely country home. Many of the old stone floors and fireplaces are still in place, as are date markings over the doors into the dining room and the bar. The furniture in the seventeen bedrooms and four junior suites was custom-made for each individually decorated room, where from every window views stretch across the Val di Chiana, with its fields, olive groves, and softly rolling hills. La Limonaia was the original master bedroom. Today it has a king-size wrought-iron canopy bed and two double windows. Il Lecceto, a junior suite, is named after a protected tree that has been in this area for three hundred years, and La Colombaia, the tower room, is named after doves who occupied pigeon holes where the window now is. In the Studio Passerini, honoring the cardinal who built the villa, you see his family crest of moons symbolizing the crusades, and his name engraved inside the window casing. The original ceiling and floors are still in Stanza del Cardinale, and the stunning chandelier came from Arezzo. On the top floor, Alessandra has created several beamed, skylighted rooms that have terra-cotta floors and romantic canopy beds.

Dinner, accompanied by merlot from the Piazzano vineyard, is served from Monday to Saturday. The Villa di Piazzano is an ideal base for many cultural and historical sites around Cortona, which is known for its Etruscan origins. It is only a short drive to Perugia, Assisi, Gubbio, Florence, Siena, and Montepulciano. Cooking lessons (arranged in advance) are taught by Adriana, who believes that "the flavor is the way you cook the dish, not how many ingredients you add." You can also schedule private visits to the vineyards and cellars in the area (include tasting two famous reds: Nobile de Montepulciano and Brunello de Montalcino), tasting the pecorino cheese of Pienza, and listening to the daily gregorian chants of the monks at San Antimo Abbey. If this is not enough, there are golf courses close by and a lake less than thirty minutes away. Regular trains stop at Cortona, but to really capture the magic of this beautiful part of Italy, you do need a car. If you don't want to drive, a car and driver can be at your disposal.

NOTE: The Villa Piazzano is closed from December 1 to February 28.

FACILITIES AND SERVICES: Air-conditioning, bar, cooking lessons by request, elevator, hair dryer, guest laptop available, laundry service, minibar, satellite TV, office safe, swimming pool, dinner by request, private guide with or without a car

NEAREST TOURIST ATTRACTIONS: Cortona and its colorful Saturday morning market, surrounding towns including Perugia, Assisi, and Gubbio

VILLA IL POGGIALE
Via Empolese, 69
San Casciano Val di Pesa

19 rooms, 2 suites, 3 apartments with small kitchen, all with bath or shower and toilet

TELEPHONE
055 828 3111
FAX
055 829 42 96
INTERNET
www.villailpoggiale.it
CREDIT CARDS
MC, V
RATES
Double 150–200€, junior suite 225€, suite 250€, apartment with kitchen 285€; lower off-season rates
BREAKFAST
Buffet breakfast included
ENGLISH
Yes

The Villa il Poggiale is a Renaissance villa with a wide, arched loggia dating back to the sixteenth century. The interior decorations, frescoes, and hand-painted doors date back to the early nineteenth century. It is located seventeen kilometers from Florence in the heart of the Tuscan countryside. The gardens surrounding the villa are landscaped with towering cypress trees and fragrant rosebushes. The long swimming pool is framed by olive trees and has a panoramic view of the Val de Pesa. The villa seems to go on forever over three floors and countless steps. All the very large rooms are individually decorated with antiques and coordinating fabrics befitting their surroundings. The owners' extensive collection of botanical prints hangs throughout the common areas and in the bedrooms; bathrooms are exceptional. Guests can choose to be as busy or as relaxed and pampered as they wish: massages, manicures, and pedicures can be reserved for their rooms, and cooking lessons by well-known local chefs can be arranged for groups of four to eight persons. The villa is available for weddings and receptions, provided the entire villa is reserved by the wedding party.

Also under the same ownership are Residenza Johanna (page 70), Residenza Johlea I & II (page 92), and Antica Dimora Firenze (page 88).

NOTE: The villa is closed in February.

FACILITIES AND SERVICES: Air-conditioning, bar, no elevator (3 floors), hair dryer, in-room safe, tea and coffee-makers, satellite TV, swimming pool, light lunches, cooking classes, masseuse and manicurist on call, some nonsmoking rooms, reception open 8:30 A.M.–8 P.M. daily

NEAREST TOURIST ATTRACTIONS: Chianti countryside, 40-minute drive into Florence

VILLA ROSA
Via S. Leolino, 59
Panzano in Chianti

15 rooms, all with shower or bath and toilet

Villa Rosa is located about forty kilometers from Florence on the way to Radda in Chianti. This nineteenth-century private villa has fifteen comfortable rooms and a swimming pool and serves both breakfast and dinner. The rooms are furnished in a casual country style that lends itself to kicking back and taking a few days off from the hustle and bustle of everyday life. The surroundings villages are interesting places to stop, browse, eat a leisurely lunch, and take in the peaceful landscapes. If you want to eat dinner at the villa, please tell them so in the morning.

Also under the same ownership in Florence are the Hotel Torre Guelfa (page 107) and Palazzo Castiglioni (page 100).

NOTE: The villa is closed from November 1 till one week before Easter.

FACILITIES AND SERVICES: No elevator (3 floors), fans on request, TV in rooms, office safe, swimming pool, lunch or dinner on request

NEAREST TOURIST ATTRACTIONS: Villages and surrounding Tuscan countryside

TELEPHONE
055 852 577

FAX
055 856 0835

EMAIL
villa.rosa@flashnet.it

INTERNET
www.resortvillarosa.it

CREDIT CARDS
AE, MC, V

RATES
Single 60–90€, double 70–130€; extra bed 20€; 4-course dinner 23€

BREAKFAST
Continental breakfast included

ENGLISH
Yes

ROME

Everyone sooner or later comes by Rome.
—Robert Browning, 1868

The history of the whole world is linked to this city and I think of the day I arrived in Rome as a second birthday, a true rebirth.
—Goethe

The Romans take their city for granted, nonchalantly sipping espressos or cool drinks in a sidewalk *caffè* next to a piazza used by gladiators centuries ago. Ruined temples, triumphal arches, and Baroque fountains are everywhere, yet this vibrant city of over three million people refuses to be just a museum of history, art, and legend. The historic center includes the seven hills of the ancient walled city and contains 300 palaces, 280 churches, the ruins of Imperial Rome, numerous parks and gardens, the residence of the Italian president, the houses of parliament, and government offices, as well as banks, businesses, hotels, shops, and restaurants. Yes, it is crowded, and the traffic jams are legion, with progress gauged by centimeters, not kilometers. Julius Caesar banned traffic during daylight, and in parts of Rome today, cars are banned both night and day. It is often faster, and always more interesting, to walk.

History proves that Rome invented the tourist industry. Once Christianity was declared the Empire's official religion in the fourth century, Rome became the center for massive groups of religious pilgrims, who when they arrived had to be housed, fed, impressed, and amused. Developed at the same time as tourism was the other industry Rome has become renowned for: bureaucracy. Both are still going strong and show no signs of slowing down.

Rome was not built in a day, nor should it be visited in one. Rome can be like a good pizzeria: hot, noisy, smoke filled, overflowing with people, and offering more choices than you can handle. When you go, take your time and allow it to seep in gradually.

The year 2000 was designated the Grand Jubilee by the Roman Catholic Church. During the celebration, fifteen million Catholics were expected to make pilgrimages to Rome to renew their faith, and the Rome tourist industry anticipated a hotel shortage of tremendous proportions. To meet the need, low-cost loans were made, allowing many hotels to expand and upgrade facilities. However, two unexpected things happened: the tidal wave of visitors was less than expected, and the religious pilgrims stayed away from these redone hotels in droves, instead checking into chains and religious institutions on the outskirts of Rome, where the package deals were too cheap to ignore. The result of this economic double whammy: *La dolce vita* still exists, but it will cost you plenty. There are few inexpensive and acceptable hotels in the center of Rome. Unless you are willing to live very, very simply, plan on spending at least $100 a night—and more realistically about $140 to $160—for a decent double in a well-located hotel that may or may not have an elevator.

Hotel prices depend first on the season, then on the type of hotel, the location of the room, and its size. Government star ratings do not reflect decor, the grandeur of the building, how clean it is, or the attitude of the owner; they depend only on the facilities offered. Thus, it is important never to judge a hotel by its stars. Many one-star hotels in Rome offer more value for money than big three-stars, which can be cold, ugly, and impersonal, never mind terribly expensive.

The best-priced hotels always fill up fast, therefore it is essential to reserve your room in advance. While prices vary with the time of year, it always pays to try to bargain down the rate. The willingness of management to bargain increases with the length of your stay, the number of vacancies, and the size of your party. Cash is also the hallmark when you care enough to spend the very least.

If you are not looking for a wild time in Rome and are strapped for cash, institutional accommodations may be the way to go. Religious institutions, convents, and monasteries welcome boarders of all faiths throughout the year, but their strict curfews and set-in-stone rules will put a damper on frivolity. Many lock up tight and turn off the lights at the main switch at 11 P.M., just when Rome's nightlife is warming up. With a few exceptions, most are located just far enough away from public transportation to make them inconvenient, especially at night. On the other hand, many serve meals, which can be a bonus for women traveling alone. If this sort of accommodation interests you, see "Holy Hotels," page 226.

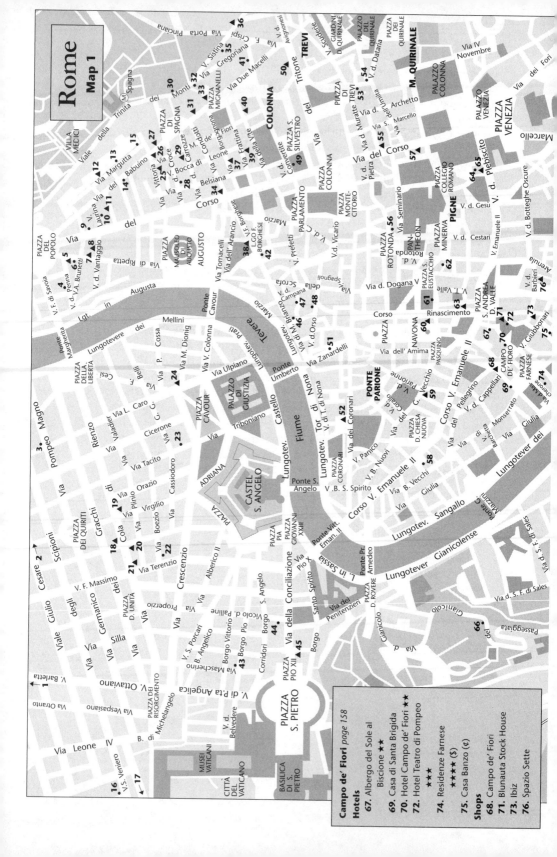

Rome
Map 1

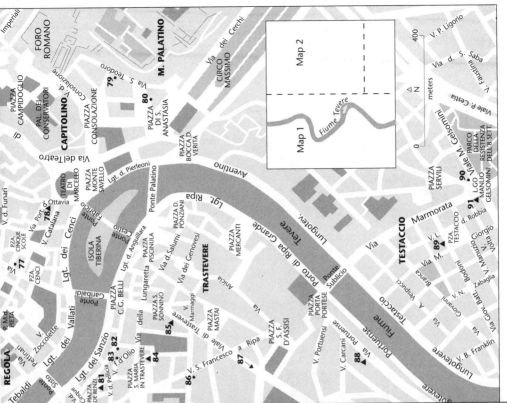

Colosseum and Forum
page 162
Hotels
79. Hotel Casa Kolbe ★★ (¢)
80. Residence Palazzo al Velabro

Jewish Quarter page 167
Hotels
77. Hotel Arenula ★★
Shops
78. Leone Limentani

Piazza del Popolo page 168
Hotels
4. Hotel Locarno ★★★ ($)
6. Residenza di Ripetta
9. Residenza al Corso
10. Hotel Margutta ★★ (¢)
14. Hotel Piranesi ★★★ ($)
Shops
5. The English Bookshop
7. Buccone
8. Dress Agency
11. Il Discount Dell'Alta Mode

Piazza di Spagna page 172
Hotels
13. Bed & Breakfast–Episcopo Lipinsky
15. Hotel Manfredi ★★★ ($)
28. Hotel Panda ★★ (¢)
30. Bed & Breakfast di Anna Manieri
32. Hotel Scalinata di Spagna ★★★ ($)
35. Albergo Internazionale ★★★
41. Casa Howard I
42. Hotel Fontanella Borghese ★★★ ($)
49. Hotel Pensione Parlamento ★★
Shops
12. Via Margutta

25. FFI–Fatta Fabbrica Italiana
26. Il Baco da Seta
27. Via del Babuino
29. Lara
31. Furla
33. Blunauta
34. Via Condotti
36. Via Sistina
37. Via Borgognona
38. Piazza Fontanella Borghese
39. Via Frattina
40. Anglo American Bookshop

Piazza Navona and the Pantheon page 180
Hotels
46. Fraterna Domus
47. Hotel Due Torri ★★★ ($)
48. Hotel Portoghesi ★★★
51. Residenza Zanardelli
56. Albergo del Sole al Pantheon ★★★★ ($)
58. Bed & Breakfast Italia
61. Hotel Navona ★★
62. Albergo Santa Chiara ★★★ ($)
Shops
52. Via dei Coronari
59. Via del Governo Vecchio
60. Officina Profumo Farmaceutica di Santa Maria Novella
63. Ai Monasteri

Piazza Venezia page 185
Hotels
64. Hotel Coronet ★★
Shops
57. Via del Corso
65. House and Kitchen

Testaccio page 186
Hotels
90. Hotel Santa Prisca ★★

Shops
89. Piazza Testaccio
91. Volpetti

Trastevere page 196
Hotels
82. Hotel Santa Maria ★★★ ($)
83. Villa della Fonte ★★★
86. Hotel Trastevere ★★ (¢)
87. Locanda Carmel ★ (¢)
Shops
81. Almost Corner Bookshop
84. Elleffe—LF
85. Standa/Oviesse
88. Mercato di Porta Portese–Trastevere

Trevi Fountain page 198
Hotels
53. Fontana Hotel ★★★ ($)
54. Hotel Trevi ★★★ ($)
Shops
50. Upim
55. La Rinascente

The Vatican page 203
Hotels
1. Hotel San Pietrino ★★ (¢)
2. Pension Paradise ★★ (¢)
3. Casa Valdese ★★ (¢)
16. Hotel Alimandi ★★★
17. Casa Bonus Pastor
22. Colors Hostel
23. Marta Guesthouse ★ (¢)
43. Hotel Sant' Anna ★★★
44. Hotel Bramante ★★★
66. Suore Dorotee
Shops
18. Coin
19. Via Cola di Rienzo
20. Franchi
21. Castroni
24. Enoteca Costantini
45. Ancora Bookshop

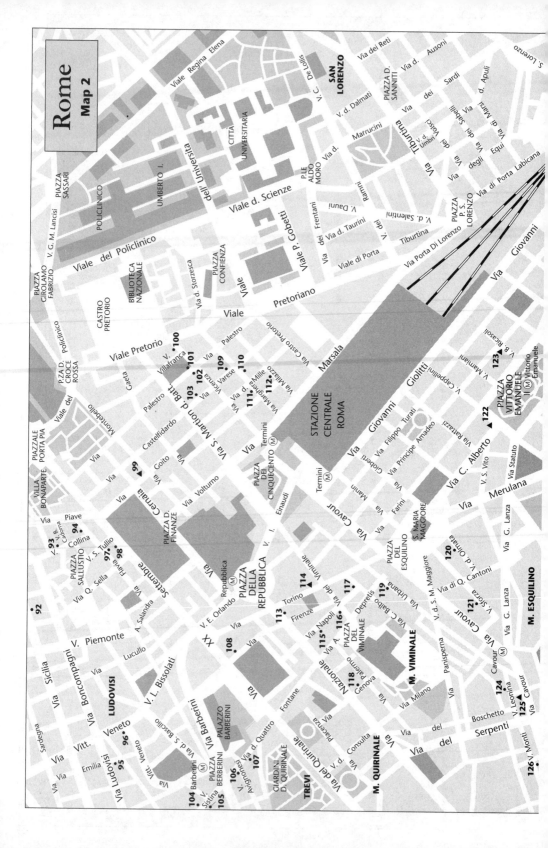

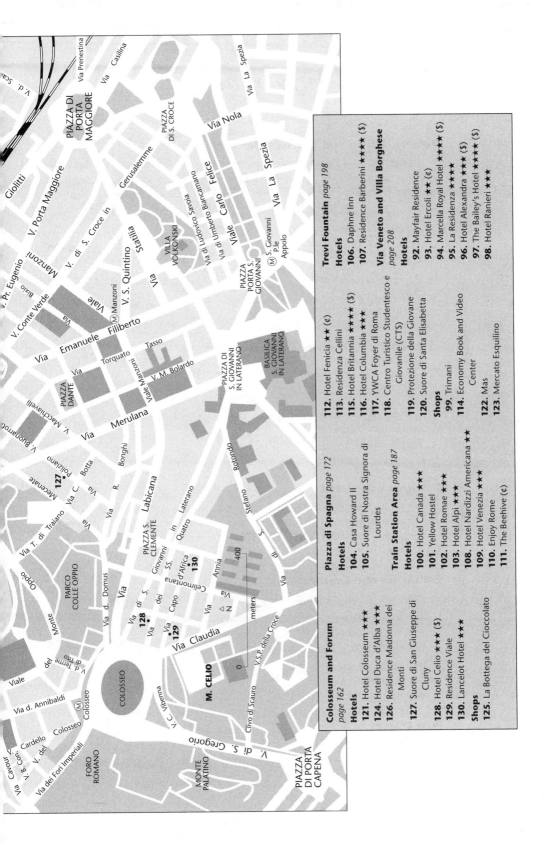

Colosseum and Forum
page 162

Hotels
121. Hotel Colosseum ★★★
124. Hotel Duca d'Alba ★★★
126. Residence Madonna dei Monti
127. Suore di San Giuseppe di Cluny
128. Hotel Celio ★★★ ($)
129. Residence Viale
130. Lancelot Hotel ★★★

Shops
125. La Bottega del Cioccolato

Piazza di Spagna *page 172*

Hotels
104. Casa Howard II
105. Suore di Nostra Signora di Lourdes

Train Station Area *page 187*

Hotels
100. Hotel Canada ★★★
101. Yellow Hostel
102. Hotel Romae ★★★
103. Hotel Alpi ★★★
108. Hotel Nardizzi Americana ★★
109. Hotel Venezia ★★★
110. Enjoy Rome
111. The Beehive (¢)

112. Hotel Fenicia ★★ (¢)
113. Residenza Cellini
115. Hotel Britannia ★★★★ ($)
116. Hotel Columbia ★★★
117. YWCA Foyer di Roma
118. Centro Turistico Studentesco e Giovanile (CTS)
119. Protezione della Giovane
120. Suore di Santa Elisabetta

Shops
99. Trimani
114. Economy Book and Video Center
122. Mas
123. Mercato Esquilino

Trevi Fountain *page 198*

Hotels
106. Daphne Inn
107. Residence Barberini ★★★★ ($)

Via Veneto and Villa Borghese
page 208

Hotels
92. Mayfair Residence
93. Hotel Ercoli ★★ (¢)
94. Marcella Royal Hotel ★★★★ ($)
95. La Residenza ★★★★
96. Hotel Alexandra ★★★ ($)
97. The Bailey's Hotel ★★★★ ($)
98. Hotel Ranieri ★★★

General Information

Tourist Offices and Tourist Information

Rome has a number of offices dispensing tourist information. You can also get information by visiting the city of Rome's Website (www.comune.roma.it) and the Website of the Rome Tourism Board (www.romaturismo.com).

City Information Kiosks
Termini Station (in front of platform 2)
Tel: 06 4890 6300
Open: Daily 8 A.M.–9 P.M.

Piazza Navona
Piazza Cinque Lune
Tel: 06 6880 9240
Open: Daily 9:30 A.M.–7 P.M.

Azienda di Promozione Turistica di Roma
Via Parigi, 5
Tel: 06 36 00 43 99
Open: Daily 9 A.M.–7 P.M.

Ufficio Informazioni Pellegrini e Turisti (Vatican Tourist Office)
Piazza San Pietro
Tel: 06 6880 9707, 06 698 81662
Open: Daily 9:30 A.M.–7:15 P.M.

Disabled Travelers

For information about handicapped-accessible facilities, transportation, and museum access in Rome and throughout Italy, contact Consorzio Cooperative Integrate (COIN; 06 712 90 11; www.coinsociale.it; Mon–Fri 9 A.M.–5 P.M.).

Embassies and Customs

For customs information, call either 06 659 56647 or 06 6501 0348.

American Embassy
Via Vittorio Veneto, 119
Tel: 06 467 41

British Embassy
Via Venti Settembre, 80/A, Esquilino
Tel: 06 4220 0001

Post Office

Stamps are sold at post offices and *tabacchis,* which are open longer hours and have no lines.

Main Post Office
Piazza S. Silvestro, 18/20
Tel: 06 679 5044
Internet: www.poste.it
Open: Mon–Fri 9 A.M.–6:30 P.M., Sat 8:30 A.M.–2 P.M., and Sun 9 A.M.–2 P.M.

The fastest way to send mail from Rome is to use the Vatican post office at Piazza San Pietro (06 6988 3406; open Mon–Sat 8:30 A.M.–6:30 P.M.). It costs the same as the Italian mail, but you must buy Vatican City stamps and send your letters, cards, or packages (two kilo weight limit) from the post office located within Vatican City.

Telephone

The city code for Rome is 06, and this must be included when dialing any land-line number in Rome. However, when dialing a cell phone, the city code is omitted. Coin-operated public telephones are being phased out. Most public phones now accept only *scheda telefonica,* plastic cards sold in denominations of 2.50 to 10€. These are sold in *tabacchis,* post offices, newsstands, and some bars. For more information about Italian telephones, see "Staying in Touch," page 34.

Emergency Numbers

For information on where to go to seek medical treatment in a nonemergency situation, see "Medical Treatment," below.

Police	112, 113
Fire	115
Ambulance	118

Medical Treatment

In a medical emergency, dial 118 for an ambulance. For emergency treatment, you can go to the *pronto soccorso* section of a public hospital.

The American Citizen Services at the American Embassy (Via Veneto, 121; 06 4674 2401) can provide a list of English-speaking dentists and physicians. Ospedale Bambino Gesù, or Children's Hospital (Piazza Sant'Onofrio, 4; 06 68 592 351), has twenty-four-hour emergency services, as does Ospedale San Giacomo (via Canova 29, off Via del Corso near Piazza del Popolo; 06 362 61, 06 322 7069).

The George Eastman Clinic (Viale Regina Elena, 287/B; office, 06 844 831; 24-hour emergencies 06 491 949) is an American-run dental clinic.

Pharmacies

Pharmacies are usually open Mon–Fri 9 A.M.–12:30 P.M., and 3:30–7:30 P.M., Sat 9 A.M.–12:30 P.M. They are open otherwise on a rotational system, and this information is posted on the pharmacy door.

The Farmacia del Vaticano, or Vatican Pharmacy, has an English-speaking staff and is the best stocked in Rome. It also fills prescriptions from other countries, which Italian pharmacies do not do. It is at Porta Sant' Ana entrance, Vatican City (06 698 83 422; open Mon–Fri 8:30 A.M.– 6 P.M., Sat 8:30 A.M. –1 P.M.).

The following are late-night or twenty-four-hour pharmacies:

Farmacia della Stazione (Train Station)
Piazza dei Cinquecento, 51(corner of Via Cavour)
Tel: 06 488 0019
Located within the station on the lower ground floor

Farmacia Senato
Corso Rinascimento, 46, 48, 50 (near Piazza Navona)
Tel: 06 688 037 60

Piram
Via Nazionale, 228
Tel: 06 488 0754

Money Matters

Normal banking hours are Mon–Fri 8:45 A.M.–1:30 P.M. and 2:45–4 P.M. ATMs are everywhere; Cirrus is the most common. Check www.oanda.com for current exchange rates.

The American Express office (Piazza di Spagna, 38; 06 67 641, 06 6764 2413; open Mon–Fri 9 A.M.–5:30 P.M., Sat 9 A.M.–12:30 P.M.) doesn't charge a commission for changing their traveler's checks. This office is also a full-service travel agency.

You can also convert to euros at three Thomas Cook-Travelex locations: Piazza Barberini, 21 (06 4202 0150); Via della Conciliazione, 23 (06 6830 0435); and Via del Corso, 23 (06 320 0224). All are open Mon–Sat, 9 A.M.–7 P.M., Sun 9:30 A.M.–5 P.M. A 2.5 percent commission is charged on any transaction other than Thomas Cook MasterCard or traveler's checks.

The post office at Piazza S. Silvestro has a currency exchange; they charge a 1 percent commission (see "Post Office," page 152). The Vatican post office at Via di Porta Angelica, 23 (near Piazza Risorgimento; no telephone), also has currency exchange; it's open Mon–Fri 8:30 A.M.–6:30 P.M., Sat 8:30 A.M.–1 P.M.

For money transfers, head for Western Union (Agenzia Tartaglia, Piazza di Spagna, 12; 800 464 464, 800 220 055).

For lost or stolen credit cards, call American Express, 06 7228 0371, 06 7228 0848, 800 874 333; Diners Club, 800 864 064; MasterCard, 800 870 866; or Visa, 800 877 232.

For lost or stolen traveler's checks, call American Express, 800 872 000; Thomas Cook and MasterCard, 800 872 050; or Visa, 800 874 155.

Vatican Visits with the Pope

For a very special experience, reserve a free ticket for a group audience with the pope at the Vatican. These are usually held every Wednesday (when the pope is in town) and last about an hour; the pope addresses the throng of ten- to fifteen-thousand pilgrims standing in St. Peter's Square in several languages and blesses them. You, however, will have a special ticket that allows you to be seated on a stage and have a much closer view of the pontif and all the proceedings. Though tickets are free, you must reserve in advance.

There are many ways to obtain a ticket; the main Vatican Website is www.vatican.va. However, the easiest way I have found is through the Bishops' Office for United States Visitors to the Vatican. The office in Rome is the Pontifical North American College–Casa Santa Maria (Via dell' Umiltà, 30; 06 690 011, fax 06 679 14 48; nacvisoffrome@pnac.org; www.pnac.org). Requests are handled for newlyweds, groups, and individuals for any papal event. Fax or email your request at least one month before you wish to attend. After reserving your ticket, you must go to this office on Tuesday afternoon (between 3 and 7 P.M.) to pick up them up. You will probably have to wait while those ahead of you attend a brief orientation, but the wait will be in the tranquil courtyard, or in the building of the four-hundred-year-old former convent, which is now occupied by sixty North American seminary students studying to be priests and working on their doctoral theses. While you are here, ask for the ten- to fifteen-minute tour of the Chapel of Our Lady of Humility, which is on the grounds and open only on Tuesday afternoon.

Tours and Services

Enjoy Rome (110)
Via Marghera, 8A (Train Station Area)

Enjoy Rome offers help with budget accommodations, air travel, and booking guided tours of Rome. Their walking tours of Rome last three hours, and go rain or shine. They are led by knowledgeable, native-English-speaking guides who hold univeristy degrees and are Rome residents. The informative tours cover the Vatican, Catacombs and the Appian Way, Trastevere and the Jewish Ghetto, Ancient Rome, a Night Tour, and Pompeii. For the very brave, they offer a Bike Tour.

Enjoy Rome also operates Colors Hostel (see page 230), which is near the Vatican. From April to November, office hours are Mon–Fri 8:30 A.M.–7 P.M., Sat 8:30 A.M.–2 P.M.; the rest of the year they are Mon–Fri 9 A.M.–6:30 P.M., Sat 9 A.M.–2 P.M.

Telephone: 06 445 1843, 06 493 827 24

Fax: 06 445 0734

Internet: www.enjoyrome.com

Credit Cards: MC, V

Rates: 16–32€ per person under 26 years; 22–37€ per person over 26 years; reduced rates for 12 years and younger; Vatican tour 7–10€ extra

English: Yes

Scala Reale and Context Rome

Via Baccina, 40

For enlightened walking tours and excursions in and around Rome, look no further than Scala Reale, which is a network of architects, historians, and archeologists, mostly American graduate students and English-speaking scholars based in Rome. These qualified experts lead small private or semi-private full- and half-day walking tours in Rome, as well as excursions by car or minivan outside Rome. These tours are both fascinating and fun and enable you to see Rome as you never would on your own. They are the antithesis of a big commercial city tour. After your Scala Reale experience, Rome will never again seem the chaotic metropolis it might appear at first glance.

Context Rome, which provides highly select travel services, has merged with Scala Reale. The merger enables independent visitors to customize not only their activities but their entire stay in Rome, as well as in Florence and Tuscany.

Telephone: 06 48 20 911 (Italy), 888-467-1986 (toll-free in the U.S.)

Fax: 06 45 43 9055 (Italy); 617-249-0186 (U.S.)

Internet: www.scalareale.com, www.contextrome.com

Credit Cards: MC, V

Rates: 25€ per person for 2-hour orientation walk; 50€ per person for 3-hour Renaissance and Baroque walk; 60€ per person for a 4-hour Vatican or Roman Antiquities walk. Fees for customized travel services and arrangements available on request.

English: Yes

Transportation

Airport: Fiumicino Airport (Leonardo da Vinci) has three twenty-four-hour information lines: 06 65 951, 06 659 53640, 06 659 55 571. You can also visit them online at www.adr.it. For items lost at the airport, call 06 659 53 343. The airport is connected by a direct train to Termini Station (5 A.M.–11:30 P.M.). Tickets can be purchased at vending machines in both the train station and airport; cost is 10€. The airport shuttle (06 420 14 507; www.airportshuttle.it) offers transfers to and from the airport in a minivan. Rates start at 30€ for one or two passengers.

Train: For train information at Termini Station (Stazione Termini), call 89 2021 (Italian only), or go to the ticket window, where someone will speak English. The office is open from 7 A.M.–9:45 P.M., and there is always a queue. Online, visit www.trenitalia.it or www.fs-on-line.com. For items lost on the train, contact the office at Via Giovanni Giolitti, 24 (06 4730 6682); it's open daily 7 A.M.–11 P.M.

Bus: For bus information, contact the City Transport Authority (ATAC; Via Volturno, 65; 800 43 17 84; www.atac.roma.it; Mon–Fri 8 A.M.–6 P.M.). This is Rome's public transport company operating the bus, metro, and trams. The same ticket is valid on all three. Tickets are valid for seventy-five minutes and cost about 0.80€. Daily, weekly, and monthly tickets are available. If you're caught without a ticket, it will cost you 55€. For items lost on a city bus or tram, contact ATAC.

Metro: For metro information, the main office is at Via Ostiense, 131-L; however, they have no English-speaking clerks. It's open Mon–Fri 8 A.M.–1:30 P.M., 2–4:30 P.M., Sat 8 A.M.–1:30 P.M. For lost items on metro Line A, call 06 487 4309; for Line B, call 06 575 32 264.

Taxi: As in Florence, never get into a private taxi in Rome. You can identify a car driven by a legitimate company because the company name and telephone number will be written on the side of the taxi. Before you get in the taxi, determine the rate, and make sure the starting rate is showing on the meter when you get in, or you may find yourself paying for someone else's ride. If possible, keep your bags, or at least your most important pieces of luggage, with you in the cab. In case of fare confrontation, you won't be at the further mercy of a dishonest cabdriver.

To order a taxi, call any of the following company numbers: 06 3570, 06 4994, 06 5551, 06 4157, 06 6645, 06 8822, 06 88177.

Private Car and Driver: Sometimes it pays to get where you are going with the least amount of stress and hassle. If you subscribe to this theory, as I do, please call Nicolas Dágostino's Prestige Cars (347 013 9873; email: prestigecars@tiscali.it). Nick is a jovial fellow, speaks English, and can provide you with a Mercedes and a driver to chauffeur you from the airport to your hotel, or throughout your Roman holiday. There is no extra charge for luggage or night service and the drivers are multilingual. Payment is in cash only, and prices are very fair.

Hotels in Rome

Campo de' Fiori

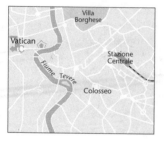

The Campo de' Fiori, which means "field of flowers," has been considered a central point of Roman life for centuries. Today the cobblestone streets are lined with many trattorias, shops, houses, and hotels with ancient, ochre-colored walls, tiny rooms, and innate charm. Monday through Saturday mornings, the *campo* is filled with the colorful stalls of market vendors; in the evening the scene and players change into roving partygoers.

HOTELS

OTHER OPTIONS
Bed-and-Breakfasts
Holy Hotels

($) indicates a Big Splurge; (¢) indicates a Cheap Sleep

ALBERGO DEL SOLE AL BISCIONE ★★ (67)
Via del Biscione, 76
58 rooms, 53 with shower and toilet

TELEPHONE
06 6880 6873, 06 6880 5258

FAX
06 6893 787

INTERNET
www.solealbiscione.it

CREDIT CARDS
None, cash or traveler's checks only

RATES
Single 65–85€, double 95–150€, triple 175–190€, quad 190–250€; lower off-season rates

BREAKFAST
Not served

ENGLISH
Yes

Albergo del Sole al Biscione sits on the remains of the ancient Roman Pompeius Theater, which dates back to 55 B.C., and it is considered the oldest working hotel in Rome. Presently, the well-located hotel, which has been in the same family for the past eighty years, appeals to travelers looking to keep their accommodation costs to a minimum, though the hotel doesn't accept credit cards, so you must be prepared to pay cash. Neither does the hotel serve breakfast, unless you count the packaged items sold in a vending machine. However, this is a plus because guests not only save the cost of a hotel breakfast but are forced to go to one of the many nearby neighborhood *caffès* and mingle with the locals over a steaming cappuccino and *cornetto*.

The family's collection of interesting black-and-white photos of Rome and other Italian cities adds interest to the long, white-washed corridors. The spotless, tiled-floor rooms are simply fitted with an antique piece of furniture and azure blue bedspreads. Some have views, others have terraces and beams, and a few overlook a lovely inside umbrella-shaded terrace. Air-conditioning is not standard in all rooms; if your room doesn't already include it, you can still get it, but it will cost you extra. The hotel also provides parking in its garage for an extra charge, and this must be reserved when booking a room.

FACILITIES AND SERVICES: Air-conditioning included in some room rates (otherwise 5€ per day), direct-dial phone, elevator, hair dryer available, parking by reservation only (15–24€ per day), office safe, satellite TV, nonsmoking rooms on request

NEAREST TOURIST ATTRACTIONS: Campo de' Fiori, Piazza Navona

HOTEL CAMPO DE' FIORI ★★ (70)
Via del Biscione, 6
27 rooms, 9 with shower and toilet, 4 with shower only, plus 10 apartments

Young-at-heart romantics with good backs and strong legs continue to keep the Campo de' Fiori booked solid year-round. They are willing to scale the six flights of steep and winding stairs necessary to reach their room and the fabulous two-tiered roof terraces, where the expansive views of Rome are thrilling and romantic both night and day.

The rooms offer a grab bag of comforts and not much in terms of amenities . . . but never mind. Adoring guests love them and are willing to overlook not only the stairs but the lines for the sparse hall facilities. If queuing for your turn in the bathroom is not your idea of vacation, then ask for a room on the first floor, all of which have private bathrooms. Three first-floor rooms (Nos. 104, 105, and 106) have exposed brick walls covered by huge arched mirrors facing the bed. Room No. 102 is a minuscule nest, with clouds painted on the ceiling and mirrors flanking two sides of the bed. Don't look for a table, chair, bedside tables, or lamps, but you do get a black-tile bathroom with blue accents.

The rooms on the second through sixth floors are similar in decor and amenities. They are characterized by a combination of blue, white, or yellow textured walls, hand-painted ceilings, wood beams, and a balcony or two.

TELEPHONE
06 6830 9036, 06 6880 6865, 06 687 4886
FAX
06 687 6003
EMAIL
campofiori@inwind.it
INTERNET
www.hotelcampodefiori.com
CREDIT CARDS
MC, V
RATES
Hotel: single 50–90€, double 80–140€, triple 120–170€, excellent off-season rates; apartments (2–5 people): 140–220€ per night, no minimum stay, discounts for stays over 5 nights
BREAKFAST
Continental breakfast included
ENGLISH
Yes

Some have a basin only, others a shower. On the second floor, five rooms share one toilet and four share the lone bath. Higher up, in No. 503, the space is larger, with frescoes, windows on the front of the hotel, and Art Deco furniture; there is a dresser and two stools, but no chair or private facilities. Avoid No. 601, a mini-room that has the benefit of opening on the hotel terrace, but the drawbacks are no space for luggage, a faded bedspread, and peeling wallpaper. The most requested room is the top-floor perch, No. 602, otherwise known as the "Honeymoon Room," maybe because you can lie in the canopy bed under a ceiling of fluffy clouds and look out over Rome and the dome of St. Peter's, or perhaps it is the statues of naked lovers—or perhaps the fact that there is no place to sit other than on the bed.

The ten fully equipped apartments, which are scattered in the Campo de' Fiori and Piazza Navona areas of Rome, are quite something, running the gamut from modern to funky. The biggest, G-4, which sleeps up to seven, is a sleek choice, with enough space to entertain thirty of your closest friends. The large corner kitchen has an eating bar, good counter room, and a full refrigerator and freezer. In the living room is a huge worktable and one entire wall of shelves and cupboards. The bedroom has more closets behind mirrored doors, ample drawer space, and a black-tile bathroom with a map of Rome on one wall and mirrors on the other. For apartment G-1, you had better be athletic enough to tackle fourteen stairs. It is small, consisting basically of a bedroom and a nice kitchen with a narrow bathroom. Apartment B-1 is across from the hotel. It has fifteen marble steps to climb, a nice kitchen with a four-burner stove and oven, a comfortable bedroom and living room, and a nice view to the corner of Campo de' Fiori.

Facilities and services in the apartments vary. There are no phones, but messages may be left for residents at the hotel. Daily maid service and breakfast at the hotel are included.

FACILITIES AND SERVICES: Hotel: direct-dial phone, no elevator (6 floors), fans, hair dryer available, office safe; apartments: no telephone or elevator, 3 with Italian TV, fitted kitchen, daily maid service included

NEAREST TOURIST ATTRACTIONS: Campo de' Fiori, Piazza Navona

HOTEL TEATRO DI POMPEO ★★★ (72)
Largo del Pallaro, 8
16 rooms, all with shower or bath and toilet

This attractive hotel was built around the ruins of the Roman Pompeius Theater, where Julius Caesar was assassinated. Breakfast is served in the excavated cavelike ruins of this ancient arena, and a sitting room is carved out of the cellars of the former theater. Some of the original stone walls are still intact. The Pompeo's bright and pleasant rooms rate high for charm, efficiency, and comfort. There are thirteen in the hotel itself, and three equally as nice in an annex across the street. In the hotel, the rooms are basically the same and have rustic decor, authentic beams, polished terra-cotta floors, luggage racks, a cushioned armchair, desk space, and a nice armoire with drawers and a mirror. In the annex, there is no elevator, but the rooms are on the first and second floors. These rooms display the same welcoming decorating touches, with the added extras of a Jacuzzi in one and fabulous closet space in another. The management is courteous, and the location near the Campo de' Fiori, the Pantheon, and Piazza Navona, along with good transportation to the train station and the Vatican, make this hotel hard to top.

FACILITIES AND SERVICES: Air-conditioning, bar, direct-dial phone, hair dryer, elevator (in the hotel, not in the 2-floor annex), laundry service, minibar, satellite TV, in-room safe

NEAREST TOURIST ATTRACTIONS: Campo de' Fiori, Piazza Navona, Pantheon

TELEPHONE
06 6830 0170, 06 687 2566
FAX
06 6880 5531
EMAIL
hotel.teatrodipompeo@tiscali.it
INTERNET
www.teatrodipompeo.it
CREDIT CARDS
AE, DC, MC, V
RATES
Single 150€, double 190€, triple 190–220€; lower off-season rates
BREAKFAST
Buffet breakfast included
ENGLISH
Yes

RESIDENZE FARNESE ★★★★ ($, 74)
Via del Mascherone, 59, off Piazza Farnese
31 rooms, all with shower or bath and toilet

The Residenze Farnese, which was built in the 1400s as a monastery, has been beautifully transformed into a classic hotel with twenty-nine rooms and two suites. Everything is done with excellent taste and attention to detail. The entrance is defined by a beautiful crystal chandelier, assorted paintings, and comfortably grouped seating arrangements. To keep up with the times, there is also an Internet terminal here for guests. To one side is a beautiful breakfast room displaying a collection of china and silver. In another *palazzo*-size room is a regulation billiard table, large television, and more welcoming sofas and chairs. A stainless-steel elevator takes guests to the aqua-colored hallways lined with a collection of contemporary art that is a nice contrast with the antiquity of the space.

TELEPHONE
06 6889 1388
FAX
06 6821 0980
EMAIL
residenzafarnese@libero.it
INTERNET
residenzafarnese.it
CREDIT CARDS
MC, V
RATES
Single 220–250€, double 300€, deluxe room 400€; lower off-season rates subject to availability
BREAKFAST
Buffet breakfast included
ENGLISH
Yes

Each room is individually done. Some are admittedly quite small but not lacking in amenities or traditional decor. Number 405, done in royal blue with two windows, would be better for one person than for two. Number 406 is a better double, also in blue, with a king-size wrought-iron bed, polished wood floors, mirrored armoir, a working desk, and a window in a long bathroom. I like No. 309, a deluxe room with frescoes on the ceiling and an arched sitting room. But it is the bathroom that really sells the room, thanks to the hydromassage shower. Number 306, another large double suite, has two windows and delicately hand-painted floral details on the closet and bathroom doors.

FACILITIES AND SERVICES: Air-conditioning, bar, direct-dial phone, elevator, hair dryer, Internet in lobby, laundry service, meeting room, minibar, room safe, room service, satellite TV

NEAREST TOURIST ATTRACTIONS: Piazza Farnese (French Embassy), Campo de' Fiori, Piazza Navona, Jewish Ghetto

Colosseum and Forum

The main archaeological ruins are concentrated in the area from the Campidoglio down Via dei Fori Imperiali to the Forum, and around the Colosseum to the Circus Maximus. The Colosseum, built between A.D. 72 and 80 for animal and gladiatorial contests and public entertainments, is the vivid and enduring symbol of Rome. The Forum was the heart of ancient Rome and a place where people gathered, justice was handed out, and religious ceremonies, banquets, and dances were held.

HOTELS

OTHER OPTIONS

($) indicates a Big Splurge; (¢) indicates a Cheap Sleep

HOTEL CASA KOLBE ★★ (¢, 79)
Via di S. Teodoro, 44
63 rooms, all with shower or bath and toilet

The Kolbe has been a hotel for more than two decades, but it is easy to see the former convent it once was. In fact, you are likely to catch a glimpse of monks during your stay, since the hotel's fourth floor is reserved exclusively for them. The quiet, serviceable rooms have all the ingredients one needs for a restful stay, but though well-mopped, they are institutional in spirit and offer the minimum of amenities. Several open directly onto the huge garden, which has a fountain, four rose beds, and palm trees, and these would be ideal choices for anyone with children. A large bar and sitting room with sofas and chairs also opens onto the garden. The dining room serves lunch and dinner, but like the rooms, the food is institutionally inspired. The Kolbe is located between Circus Massimo, the Capitoline, and the Palatino Hills. Bus service is two blocks away.

FACILITIES AND SERVICES: Bar, direct-dial phone, hair dryers available, elevator, office safe, TV in lounge, lunch and dinner served

NEAREST TOURIST ATTRACTIONS: Colosseum, Forum, Circus Massimo

TELEPHONE
06 679 4974/5, 06 679 8866
FAX
06 699 41550
CREDIT CARDS
AE, MC, V
RATES
Single 65€, double 85€, triple 105€; half-board lunch or dinner 15€ per person
BREAKFAST
Continental breakfast 6€
ENGLISH
Yes

HOTEL CELIO ★★★ ($, 128)
Via dei Santi Quatro, 35/C
20 rooms, all with shower or bath and toilet

Owned by Roberto Quatrini and his brother, Marcello, the Hotel Celio is highly recommended for readers looking for an elegant, small hotel in the heart of nineteenth-century Rome, near the Colosseum and all of Rome's most important ancient monuments and treasures. Rich, bold textiles and colors harmoniously blend to create a handsome, dramatic atmosphere, which prevails throughout the hotel. Even though a few of the individually decorated bedrooms in the first part of the hotel are basically small, they are well conceived and offer the warmth and comforts one would expect in a lovely Roman home. Each beautifully maintained room is named after an Italian master artist and has a large fresco on the wall behind the bed, which has a gold-and-blue striped cover. The Michelangelo has two comfortable armchairs and a view over the garden entrance, and in the bathroom, a soothing Jacuzzi. In the Donatello, a mirror reflects the high ceiling, giving the illusion of more space. The Tintoretto is a room for three, with gold fabric on the walls and a private terrace. Bathrooms have welcome extras such as magnifying mirrors, a radio, and a scale.

TELEPHONE
06 7049 5333
FAX
06 709 6377
INTERNET
www.hotelcelio.com
CREDIT CARDS
AE, DC, MC, V
RATES
Single 198€, double 255€, suites 260–620€; excellent lower off-season rates
BREAKFAST
Buffet breakfast included, served in the room or in dining room
ENGLISH
Yes

A magnificent new wing has been added with eight superior rooms, two stunning suites, and a beautiful tented breakfast room with hand-painted tables from one of the most important and famous ceramic works in Positano. Each room in this part is named after a Roman emperor and reflects Roberto's commitment to quality materials and his attention to the smallest detail. Joining the two sections of the hotel is a magnificent mosaic-tiled hallway lined with columns interspersed with frescoes and rich damask fabrics. This area alone took eight people working full time for two and a half months to finish to Roberto's specifications. The rooms display the best in composition and taste with built-in Sony televisions, lovely paintings, marble baths with Jacuzzis, work space with data ports, and enough closet space to inspire long stays.

While these eight rooms are absolutely wonderful, the two suites will take your breath away. The Ambassador Suite is done in green and gold with a leather sofa bed and comfortable easy chairs in a sitting area. Its walls are lined with an impressive collection of antique, leather-bound English books, including the complete works of Shakespeare. Two pillars frame the bed, which is covered in a fluffy duvet. Lighted, mirrored double closets, excellent work space, and a state-of-the-art bath round out this truly wonderful suite. If you like the Ambassador, you will be head over heels in love with the Pompeian Suite, a lavish penthouse, on its own private floor, with two of everything, including two flower- and plant-filled terraces with spectacular views of the dome of St. Peter's and the Colosseum. In addition to every comfort you can think of, you will have two minibars, two cable TVs, two telephones, two safes, and two big, well-lighted bathrooms, but only one Jacuzzi. Without question, it is absolutely wonderful, and the perfect choice to share with someone very special whenever your travels take you to the Eternal City.

If you like the style of the Hotel Celio and have Venice on your itinerary, you will enjoy their lovely boutique hotel, the Hotel Santo Stefano (see page 293).

FACILITIES AND SERVICES: Air-conditioning, bar, data ports, direct-dial phone, no elevator (3 floors), hair dryer, minibar, parking (16€ in hotel driveway, 30€ in garage), in-room safe, satellite TV with VCR, plasma TV in lobby, some trouser presses, magnifying mirror, radio, bathroom scale, many with Jacuzzis

NEAREST TOURIST ATTRACTIONS: Colosseum, Forum

HOTEL COLOSSEUM ★★★ (121)
Via Sforza, 10
50 rooms, all with shower and toilet

I am always happy to return to the Hotel Colosseum because it is such a well-run family-owned hotel. The impressive entryway, with its arched wooden ceiling, leads to a baronial sitting room furnished in dark, rustic reproductions that look as though they came from an old hunting lodge. Upstairs is a little bar where you can relax after your sightseeing in Rome. You will have a pleasant start to your day in the large, medieval-style dining room, with its original hand-painted ceiling, carved wooden armchairs, and long communal table. When you check in, please be sure to notice the original telephone the Ricci family used when they began this hotel over a quarter-century ago; it is on display to the right of the reception desk.

Heavy wooden furniture, wrought-iron sconces, electronic window shades, and parquet or marble floors distinguish the rooms. Some of the twin-bed chambers are small, but if you are traveling light and in search of a room with a view, Nos. 72, 73, 74, and 75 (a single) also offer terraces or a balcony overlooking the Colosseum and Santa Maria Maggiore Church. These rooms also connect, making them ideal for a family stay. Number 63, a large, bright twin, also has a wonderful view of the Colosseum and an old church tower, and in No. 71, a triple, the view is of Rome and the dome of St. Peter's. Several new rooms have been added on the fourth floor. These make a good use of space by utilizing built-ins and ample closets. No matter what view your room has, no one should miss the magnificent panorama from the beautiful rooftop terrace, which is shaded in the daytime and lighted at night.

FACILITIES AND SERVICES: Air-conditioning (12€ per day), bar, 2 conference rooms, direct-dial phone, elevator, hair dryer, parking by arrangement, satellite TV, in-room safe (2.50€ per stay), office safe (free), porter

NEAREST TOURIST ATTRACTIONS: Colosseum, Forum, Santa Maria Maggiore Church

TELEPHONE
06 482 7228
FAX
06 482 7285
INTERNET
www.hotelcolosseum.com
CREDIT CARDS
AE, DC, MC, V
RATES
Single 121€, double 161€, triple 212€; lower off-season rates
BREAKFAST
Buffet breakfast included
ENGLISH
Yes

HOTEL DUCA D'ALBA ★★★ (124)
Via Leonina, 14
27 rooms, all with shower or bath and toilet

For an impeccable stay in the Imperial section of Rome near the Forum and Colosseum, the Duca d'Alba continues to be one of my favorite choices. The old Roman neighborhood is dotted with crafts workshops, stores, and interesting

TELEPHONE
06 484 471
FAX
06 488 4840
INTERNET
www.hotelducadalba.com

CREDIT CARDS
AE, DC, MC, V

RATES
Single 100–160€, double 140–
200€, triple 170–230€, suite
310€; lower off-season rates

BREAKFAST
Buffet breakfast included

ENGLISH
Yes

restaurants (see *Great Eats Italy*), and public transportation is within easy reach.

This outstanding small hotel is owned by the same family that runs the four-star Hotel Britannia, near the train station (see page 189). Good taste in furnishings, high-quality materials, and constant attention and ongoing improvements extend throughout the hotel. Busts and bas-reliefs adorn the well-lit hallways, echoing the classic style that characterizes the rooms. Paneled doors lead to the rooms, which have been designed to appeal to both business travelers and tourists. All are soundproofed and have private safes, electronic door locks, air-conditioning, and of course, lovely baths. Those on the third and fourth floors do not have carpets (which may be preferred if allergies are an issue). Two singles and two doubles on this floor have terraces, another has a balcony. Unless dramatic changes have occurred in No. 110, an inside single with a weird closet, it is the only room I would positively avoid. Number 109, on the other hand, is a nice suite with a large walk-in closet and enough space to sleep four comfortably. Tricolored marble floors line the downstairs, which has a large sitting room with a bar and a mirrored breakfast room with black glass-topped tables. A buffet breakfast is served here every morning. The location is a block off the raceway known as Via Cavour, so while it's close to the action, it is relatively peaceful.

FACILITIES AND SERVICES: Air-conditioning, bar, direct-dial phone, elevator, hair dryer, laundry service, minibar, satellite TV, in-room safe

NEAREST TOURIST ATTRACTIONS: Colosseum, Forum, Piazza Venezia, Santa Maria Maggiore Church

LANCELOT HOTEL ★★★ (130)
Via Capo d'Africa, 47
60 rooms, all with shower or bath and toilet

TELEPHONE
06 7045 0615

FAX
06 7045 0640

INTERNET
www.lancelothotel.com

CREDIT CARDS
AE, DC, MC, V

Two thumbs up for the Lancelot, a three-star pick just a short sprint from the Colosseum and Forum. It was started as a pension in 1953 by a Sicilian countess and her husband, a member of the British navy. Since 1971 it has been owned and run by a mother and her attractive daughter and son, who welcome their guests as old friends, and indeed, after a stay here, many consider themselves just that. One of the real advantages of the hotel, especially for solo voyagers to Rome, is the dining room, which serves dinner; guests can book rooms with half-board or enjoy dinner "à la carte." Seating is at round tables for six or eight, which encourages conversation and a more pleasant experience than dining alone. Judging from the photos taken during the Christmas holidays, friendships blossom and a good time is had by all.

The recently renovated rooms are large and comfortable, especially those that open onto a terrace. Number 62, a double, shares a terrace with the room next door, but a bank of roses divides it into two sections. Number 60 (with a pair of Chinese glass doors from the 1930s) makes a nice family suite in which you have not only a terrace but a view that includes everything from Domus Auria and Santa Maria Maggiore to the Colosseum, Piazza Venezia, and St. Peter's. The marble bathroom has a window, a combination tub and shower, and heated towel racks. Single travelers should request No. 66, which has a seven-drawer chest, glass-topped desk with reading light, an enclosed stall shower, and a view of the Colosseum and St. Peter's. Other good choices are No. 6, an especially nice twin with a white-and-beige-tiled floor and an umbrella-shaded terrace; No. 7, a double with its own balcony; and No. 53, with a small balcony and view of the Colosseum.

NOTE: The half-board rates quoted are only applicable if dinner is taken for a minimum of three days. If taken for fewer days, the rate is considered à la carte and jumps to 25€ per meal. Only set meals are served, but special dietary needs can be accommodated with advance notice.

FACILITIES AND SERVICES: Air-conditioning, bar, direct-dial phone, hair dryer, elevator, laundry service, parking (10€ per day), satellite TV, in-room safe, half-board for dinner

NEAREST TOURIST ATTRACTIONS: Colosseum, Forum

RATES
All rates include breakfast: Single 95€, with half-board 110€; double 152€, with half-board 175€; triple 172€, with half-board 206€; quad 190€, with half-board 236€; suite 225€, with half-board 248€; rooms with a private balcony or patio 10–15€ daily supplement; half-board is a 3-course dinner and half-board rates require a 3-day minimum; otherwise dinner is 25€ per person

BREAKFAST
Buffet breakfast included

ENGLISH
Yes

Jewish Quarter

The Roman Jews have had an important place in Rome for more than two thousand years, making theirs the oldest Jewish community in Europe. Today the central focus of life in the quarter is along the Via del Portico d'Ottavia.

HOTEL ARENULA ★★ (77)
Via Santa Maria de' Calderari, 47
50 rooms, all with shower and toilet

For Great Sleepers who want a reasonably priced hotel near the heart of old Rome and the Jewish Quarter, the Arenula, just across the Ponte Garibaldi from Trastevere, is a consideration . . . so long as you can cope with stairs and

TELEPHONE
06 687 9454
FAX
06 689 6188
EMAIL
hotel.arenula@flashnet.it

INTERNET
www.hotelarenula.com
CREDIT CARDS
AE, DC, MC, V
RATES
Single 101€, double 133€, extra
bed 25€; lower off-season rates
BREAKFAST
Buffet breakfast included
ENGLISH
Usually

you can land the right room. One flight of stairs leads to the first-floor lobby, and the hotel continues another three flights up—meaning that those unlucky enough to get a room on the fourth floor must scale 123 steps from the entrance to reach their bed. The no-nonsense, uniformly austere bedrooms have easy-wipe blond wood furnishings, white walls, tiled floors, and canvas bedspreads. While all of the rooms have private facilities, you will want to make sure that in yours the bidet, shower, and sink are not sitting in the room as pieces of furniture, thus affording absolutely no privacy. You won't have this problem in Room 104, which has an enclosed bathroom with lights over the sink and room for a small seat. The bathroom situation is also okay in Nos. 106, 203, 402, and 409, which have enclosed stall showers.

The combination reception and lobby area is furnished in Art Deco–style red leatherette. A sign on the right warns guests: Beware of owner, never mind the dog.

FACILITIES AND SERVICES: Air-conditioning, bar, direct-dial phone, no elevator, hair dryer, satellite TV, office safe

NEAREST TOURIST ATTRACTIONS: Tiber River, Trastevere, Jewish Quarter, Campo de' Fiori

Piazza del Popolo

This large square was the first part of Rome pilgrims saw when they arrived through the northern gate, Porta del Popolo. The obelisk in the center was brought from Egypt by Augustus and stood in the Circus Maximus until 1589, when Pope Sixtus V moved it here. The very upmarket neighborhood has many good restaurants, interesting boutiques, and small hotels.

HOTELS

OTHER OPTIONS
Residence Hotels

($) indicates a Big Splurge; (¢) indicates a Cheap Sleep

HOTEL LOCARNO ★★★ ($, 4)
Via della Penna, 22

85 rooms, all with shower or bath and toilet

Since 1925, the family-owned Hotel Locarno, neatly tucked between Piazza del Popolo and the Tiber River, has been drawing a faithful clientele of international guests. This customer loyalty is due in no small part to the uniformly polite and welcoming attitude of the entire staff. The magnificent Belle Epoque lobby and sitting room, with wood-burning fireplace and a bar to one side, contains beveled-glass doors, dark wood paneling, and an impressive collection of Tiffany lamps.

The rooms in the main section of the hotel, all of which face out, vary in size and are nicely appointed with antiques, coordinated fabrics, cable television, and a data port. Several have balconies. Even the smallest single has enough space to unpack and stay in comfort. The bathrooms have been revamped in marble and offer soft towels, a telephone, and a selection of toiletries. Twelve new rooms and suites are linked to the hotel via an umbrella-shaded streetside terrace that is the perfect place for warm-weather breakfasts, cool afternoon drinks, or alfresco dinners. In this deluxe section, wide halls tiled in gray-and-white marble lead to huge rooms furnished in antiques and the latest in bathrooms. Number 602, with its faux-finished red walls, hand-detailed twenty-foot ceiling, and massive carved bed looks like a room in an ornate castle. Two Victorian armchairs rest at the end of the bed, and in the corner is a round pedestal table. The bathroom has a great clawfoot tub. Number 603, with its twelve-by-twelve, gold-trimmed sitting room, large green marble bathroom fit for a queen, and original mosaic-tiled floors is a similar ornate choice. In No. 506, there is another tub on legs, with the added benefit of a Frisbee-size shower head. The long bedroom has fabric-covered walls, a big wardrobe, and a wrought-iron bed. Unfortunately, there is no comfortable seating or work space here.

Quite frankly, the new, nonsmoking annex across the street does not have the same appeal for me as the main building. Here the depressing rooms are done in combinations of dull brown and green with gray accents. The views are on the street or facing a blank wall; seating is reduced to a backless stool or a hard, uncomfortable chair; luggage space is sparce; and room service from the hotel does not extend to these rooms. On the other hand, the mosaic-tiled baths are state-of-the-art with deep tubs, heated towel racks, and huge shower heads.

TELEPHONE
06 361 0841

FAX
06 321 5249

INTERNET
www.hotellocarno.com

CREDIT CARDS
AE, DC, MC, V

RATES
Single 120–160€, double 190–310€, triple 250–360€, suite 510€

BREAKFAST
Buffet breakfast included

ENGLISH
Yes

A summer roof garden and restaurant serving lunch and dinner adds to the hotel's charm and allure. Subway and bus stops, good restaurants (see *Great Eats Italy*), and tempting shopping opportunities are all within easy walking distance. For athletically inclined and very brave souls who are willing to risk life and limb by venturing into Rome traffic, the hotel provides free bicycles for guests to use during their stay.

FACILITIES AND SERVICES: Air-conditioning, bar, direct-dial phone, elevator, hair dryer, laundry service, meeting facilities, minibar, data ports, in-room safe, 24-hour room service (main building only), satellite TV, free bicycles, 23 nonsmoking rooms, 2 handicapped-accessible rooms, parking arrangements on request

NEAREST TOURIST ATTRACTIONS: Piazza del Popolo, Piazza di Spagna, Tiber River, shopping

HOTEL MARGUTTA ★★ (¢, 10)
Via Laurina, 34
24 rooms, all with shower or bath and toilet

TELEPHONE
06 322 3674

FAX
06 320 0395

EMAIL
htlmargutta@hotmail.com

CREDIT CARDS
AE, DC, MC, V

RATES
For 1–2 persons 90–104€, triple 130–150€

BREAKFAST
Continental breakfast included

ENGLISH
Yes

Nothing is frilly, fancy, or fantastic at the Rosati family–run Hotel Margutta, which is on a quiet street in a good location near the Piazza del Popolo. There is no way I can describe the small lobby other than to call it serviceable. The breakfast area is equally uninteresting. So are the dimly lit halls. The good news, however, is that the rooms are much better than the dark halls and uninspired lobby would suggest, and the prices are budget Great Sleeps for this rich patch of Rome. The rooms, with soundproofed windows, improved furnishings, and good lighting, can be recommended. Even though the elevator does not reach them, the best rooms are the three on the top floor because they have terraces. Number 52 is one of these, with a scrolled metal bed, a tiled bath, and terrace shared with No. 50 next door. Room 54, which has good light, is big enough to accommodate a writing desk and a sofa bed and has its own terrace. If you want to avoid stairs, check into No. 38, with whitewashed walls, a chair, small desk, and shower. Avoid Nos. 10 and 22, which have inside, depressing views. All the rooms have private bathrooms, which are not large, nor do they sport the latest designs, but they are private. You won't have to shuffle down the hall in search of the shower and toilet, or stand in line to wait your turn once you get there.

FACILITIES AND SERVICES: Air-conditioning, direct-dial phone, elevator, hair dryer, office safe, satellite TV

NEAREST TOURIST ATTRACTIONS: Piazza del Popolo, Tiber River, Piazza di Spagna, shopping

HOTEL PIRANESI ★★★★ ($, 14)
Via del Babuino, 196
32 rooms and suites, all with shower or bath and toilet

It would be hard to imagine a more gracious hotel than the Hotel Piranesi, which occupies the Palazzo Nanier, a regal building designed and built between 1819 and 1821 by Guiseppe Valadier. The prime location on one of Rome's most fashionable streets makes this the ideal setting for those wanting to be in walking distance for the best designer shopping Rome has to offer. Guests enter into a skylit sitting area with creamy leather funishings accented with Roman prints and masses of green plants. Glass kiosks near reception display a tempting assortment of the magnificent linens and lingerie sold next door at Cesari, which is world-renowned for its luxurious products. The original brick-arched dining room, which has a hand-painted mural of Rome, has soft yellow leather chairs around tables set with monogrammed china. Afternoon drinks are served on the terrace, which has views of Villa Borghese. The luxurious rooms combine classic Italian design with antique-style furnishings and rich fabrics that look as though they have belonged to the palace for generations. Several rooms have lovely Roman views from their private terraces. All guests are invited to use the gym and sauna or reserve time with the hotel masseuse.

FACILITIES AND SERVICES: Air-conditioning, bar, bathrobes, conference room, direct-dial phone, elevator, gym, sauna and masseuse, hair dryer, laundry, minibar, room service for breakfast and afternoon drinks, in-room safe, satellite TV, some nonsmoking rooms

NEAREST TOURIST ATTRACTIONS: Piazza del Popolo, Piazza di Spagna, Tiber River, shopping

TELEPHONE
06 328 041
FAX
06 361 0597
INTERNET
www.hotelpiranesi.com
CREDIT CARDS
AE, DC, MC, V
RATES
Single 240–270€, double 320–360€, junior suite 420–440€, Piranesi Suite 520€, extra bed 70€; lower rates in the off-season and on weekends
BREAKFAST
Buffet breakfast included
ENGLISH
Yes

RESIDENZA AL CORSO (9)
Via del Corso, 18
6 rooms, all with shower and toilet

The Residenza al Corso combines a central location with a warm, personalized atmosphere and friendly staff. It is the pride and joy of Riccardo Peroni, a professor of architecture, who had the vision and expertise to create six beautifully crafted rooms in this eighteenth-century building, known as the Bracci Palace. It was also the home of Goethe, who occupied quarters on the first floor during a two-month sojourn in Rome. Space is never an issue in

TELEPHONE
06 324 4482
FAX
06 361 2788
EMAIL
residenzalcorso@email.it
INTERNET
www.residenzalcorso.com
CREDIT CARDS
AE, DC, MC, V

RATES
Single 120€, double 155€,
triple 180€, suite 180–220€;
lower off-season rates
BREAKFAST
Buffet breakfast included
ENGLISH
Yes

the rooms, which beautifully integrate their elegant past with the comforts of today. In No. 1, bleached hardwood floors and the original ceiling (shown through a lighted glass cutout) mix well with the crystal teardrop lamps and the Roman red-and-white-striped bedspreads. The ceiling in the suite is a copy of one Sr. Peroni found here during the restoration. In this large, well-lit room, the king-size bed is draped as a tent, and a grand chaise worthy of Cleopatra can double as a bed. The bath is small by comparison, but still workable, with a stall shower and a five-tiered shelf.

There is no formal sitting room in this *affitta camere*, but guests can socialize each morning over a buffet breakfast, which is laid out on a marble-top table just outside the small dining area. Breakfast can also be served in your room at no additional charge. The location is one of the best in Rome, close to all the finest shopping and excellent restaurants (see *Great Eats Italy*), as well as to easy bus and metro connections.

FACILITIES AND SERVICES: Air-conditioning, direct-dial phone, elevator, hair dryer, minibar, parking (20€ per day), in-room safe, Italian TV

NEAREST TOURIST ATTRACTIONS: Piazza del Popolo, Piazza di Spagna, Tiber River, shopping

Piazza di Spagna (Spanish Steps)

Keats, Mendelssohn, Baudelaire, and Wagner were only a few of the visitors to Rome who stayed near this famous piazza named after the Spanish Embassy, which was located here for hundreds of years. It is better known, however, for the sweeping Spanish Steps that lead up to the Trinità dei Monti Church and for the many famous-name boutiques lining the streets that lead to the piazza. The steps are always massed with tourists, pickup artists, regular artists, and anyone else looking for some action. At Christmas there is a nativity scene halfway up, and in May, brilliant pink azaleas frame the steps. The piazza is home to one of the better places on the planet to consume a Big Mac, plus an American Express office, the famous Babington's Tea Room, and horse-drawn carriages ready to take you anywhere you want to go.

HOTELS

OTHER OPTIONS

Bed & Breakfasts

Holy Hotels

($) indicates a Big Splurge; (¢) indicates a Cheap Sleep

ALBERGO INTERNAZIONALE ★★★ (35)
Via Sistina, 79

42 rooms, all with shower or bath and toilet

Occupying a prime patch of real estate near the Spanish Steps, the Internazionale is one of Rome's best-located hotels. The modern reception and street-level sitting area give no hint of the real spirit of the hotel, which is truly captured in the upstairs eating and sitting spaces. When you are in the reception area, please be sure to look at the glass display case of hotel memorabilia and pieces of old Roman artifacts found here during various renovations. The dining room, with glass chandeliers and an inlaid terra-cotta floor, adjoins a massive sitting room with an impressive carved-wood ceiling, groupings of tufted leather chairs and couches, a glass-topped coffeetable with a display of silver, magnificent Murano chandeliers, and a huge wood-burning fireplace. The third-floor lounge resembles an old hunting lodge, with its collections of armor, spears, and other antique paraphernalia. The rooftop terrace has wonderful views over Rome and St. Peter's.

The rooms have double-glazed windows to buffer the traffic noise, color televisions with CNN, air-conditioning, and private safes. Almost all have turn-of-the-century furnishings, fabric-covered walls, double wardrobes, and luggage space. The tiled baths have terry towels, magnifying mirrors, assorted toiletries, and a drying line for quick laundry needs. Some have Jacuzzis. The rooms on the fourth

TELEPHONE
06 678 4686, 06 6994 1823, 06 6994 1827

FAX
06 678 4764

INTERNET
www.hotelinternazionale.com

CREDIT CARDS
AE, MC, V

RATES
Single 130€, double 190–217€, triple 235€, family room 300€, suite 350€; lower off-season rates

BREAKFAST
Buffet breakfast included

ENGLISH
Yes

floor come with their own private terrace. The management, under the expert direction of Andrea Gnecco, whose family has owned the hotel since 1935, is crisply professional and to the point. Vincent, the congenial concierge, along with the rest of the staff, is friendly and ready to ensure that your stay in Rome is smooth.

FACILITIES AND SERVICES: Air-conditioning, direct-dial phone, elevator, hair dryer, Internet services for guests, some Jacuzzis, minibar, parking (price depends on size of vehicle; reserve in advance), in-room safe, satellite TV

NEAREST TOURIST ATTRACTIONS: Piazza di Spagna, Via Veneto, Trevi Fountain, shopping

CASA HOWARD I & II (I, 41; II, 104)
Casa Howard I, 18, via Capo le Case; Casa Howard II, 149, via Sistina

Both with 5 rooms, all with shower or bath and toilet

A new trend in Italian hotels is the small, boutique-style guest house or bed-and-breakfast accommodation consisting of a few rooms that appeal to independent guests wanting a private homelike atmosphere. Nothing could underscore this phenomena more than Casa Howard I (and now II), which started as a place for the owner's friends to stay when they visited Rome but soon mushroomed into a full-time business. The well-met goal of the owners is to insure that their guests feel completely at home and are well looked after by their English-speaking staff, who live on site.

In Casa Howard I, the five rooms are defined by colors: blue, green, pink, white, and a vibrant Chinese red. The blue, white, and red rooms have bathrooms outside the room, but they are private to those rooms. Each room is unique and offers a different decorating experience. The pink room features a pink satin spread with fuscia highlights, built-in work space, and a feminine pink-tile bathroom with both shower and tub. The green room is highlighted by a hand-painted headboard over the bed, an antique desk, and a pretty upholstered windowseat; the white room has a four-poster canopy spool bed. I would book the red Chinese Room with its four-poster bed framed on each side by antique brass globe lights. It also has the benefit of a fabulous Turkish bath down the hall that is all yours; bathrobes (Japanese *yukatas*) and slippers are provided for hall transport.

TELEPHONE
06 6992 4555

FAX
06 6794 644

INTERNET
www.casahoward.com

CREDIT CARDS
AE, MC, V

RATES
Casa Howard I:
Single 160–170€, double 180–200€, triple 220–250€

Casa Howard II:
Single 150–180€, double 180–220€, Turkish bath 50€ per person

BREAKFAST
Continental breakfast 10€

ENGLISH
Yes

The success of Casa Howard I led to the opening in 2003 of Casa Howard II. All the rooms here have en suite bathrooms and display the same fanciful decorating spirit, starting with the red floors that lead to the dynamic rooms. There is the black-and-white Zebra Room with its Roman balcony; the frankly feminine Flower Room; and the American Cousin's Room, featuring a flat-screen television and king-size bed. The Indian Room has an intricately tiled bathroom done by the owner's sister and a framed painting of an elephant in the jungle, which was painted when her son was seven years old. Finally, there is Tommy's Room, a modern space done in soft mauve and green with a flat-screen television and a special mattress that molds to the shape of your body. The Turkish bath at this location is for the use of all guests. If you choose to have breakfast here, you can look forward to fresh orange juice, homemade pastries, fresh fruit, and honey from the owner's farm in Tuscany.

NOTE: If you will be in Florence, watch their Website for the opening of their latest venture on via della Scala, 18, a twelve-room site that includes an apartment, Turkish bath, and rooms devoted to children, dogs, lovers, and smokers.

FACILITIES AND SERVICES: Casa Howard I & II: Air-conditioning, hair dryer, Internet terminal for guests, office safe, satellite TV, electric tea kettles, driver services for airport transfers (rates on request); Casa Howard II: Courtesy cell phone, elevator, laundry service, Turkish bath

NEAREST TOURIST ATTRACTIONS: Piazza di Spagna, Trevi Fountain, shopping

HOTEL FONTANELLA BORGHESE ★★★ ($, 42)
Largo Fontanella Borghese, 84

29 rooms, all with shower or tub and toilet

The elegant Hotel Fontanella Borghese is situated inside a sixteenth-century noble building that once was home to the Borghese princes. Many of the rooms look onto the Borghese Palace and the charming Borghese Square, where a small antique and old print market is in operation Monday to Saturday. The entrance is through a graceful courtyard with a circular stairway. The hotel is on two floors, the first of which is accessible by elevator. The well-proportioned rooms are traditionally decorated with green and gold fabrics and watercolor paintings of Rome. The comfortable spaces have sunshine, work and luggage

TELEPHONE
06 6880 9504, 06 6880 9624
FAX
06 686 1295
EMAIL
fontanellaborghese@libero.it
INTERNET
www.fontanellaborghese.com
CREDIT CARDS
AE, DC, MC, V
RATES
Single 135€, double 205€, triple 250€, quad 270€

BREAKFAST
Buffet breakfast included
ENGLISH
Yes

space, and sky views from the top floor. All the perks are in place, including a minibar, in-room safe, satellite TV, and heated towel racks in the bathroom. Breakfast is served in a cheerful room with a mosaic marble floor. The location is super for upscale shopping, the Spanish Steps, Piazza Navona, the Pantheon, and many good restaurants covered in *Great Eats Italy*. Under the same ownership is Hotel Due Torri (see page 182).

FACILITIES AND SERVICES: Air-conditioning, bar, direct-dial phone, elevator to first floor, hair dryer, laundry service, minibar, in-room safe, satellite TV

NEAREST TOURIST ATTRACTIONS: Piazza di Spagna, Piazza Navona, Pantheon, shopping

HOTEL MANFREDI ★★★ ($, 15)
Via Margutta, 61

TELEPHONE
06 320 7676
FAX
06 320 7736
INTERNET
www.hotelmanfredi.it
CREDIT CARDS
AE, DC, MC, V
RATES
Single 140–200€, double 170–290€, triple 200–330€, junior suite 250–380€; rate ranges span low to high season; check for special Website offers
BREAKFAST
Buffet breakfast included
ENGLISH
Yes

18 rooms, all with shower or bath and toilet

If you are looking for contemporary efficiency in a classy location close to fine shops, interesting art galleries, and good restaurants (see *Great Eats Italy*), the Manfredi should suit you perfectly. The three brothers who own and operate the hotel are constantly upgrading it, and they provide hands-on management. On one visit, I found a smart new entry with a green marble reception desk and new wood-paneled room doors with brass number plaques. This time there were more Jacuzzis and a larger breakfast room. Previous improvements include computer data ports in all the rooms and the best air-conditioning system on the market. As one brother said, "Don't worry about being in our hotel in August. You will be in Alaska in three minutes after turning on the cool air."

The rooms upstairs are well turned out with coordinating colors on the beds, curtains, walls, and chairs. The floors are either carpeted or wood, an important consideration for those with allergies. The tiled and marble bathrooms have good lighting and space for more than just a razor and a toothbrush. In No. 101, the imaginative bathroom has its tub up a few steps; in No. 103, a single, there is a big shower; and in No. 106, a double, gold accessories and a marble sink highlight the bathroom. In the suite, guests can relax in the hydro-massage tub. For the area, the rooms are quiet. Discounts are given in the winter and summer seasons, airport transfers can be arranged, and management is always very helpful.

FACILITIES AND SERVICES: Air-conditioning, bar, direct-dial phone, elevator, hair dryer, minibar, data port and guest Internet access, in-room safe, satellite TV

NEAREST TOURIST ATTRACTIONS: Piazza di Spagna, Piazza del Popolo, shopping

HOTEL PANDA ★★ (¢, 28)
Via della Croce, 35

20 rooms, 12 with shower and toilet

The Panda keeps pace with its tony surroundings and yet remains a stand-out budget Great Sleep, providing well-scrubbed, whitewashed accommodations at sensible, economical prices. Its location, a colorful shopping street in one of Rome's most desirable neighborhoods—where you can browse through countless boutiques displaying the latest in fashion and dine in many excellent restaurants—is a stone's throw away from the Spanish Steps. The Panda does not try to be more than it is, so don't look for fancy furnishings, air-conditioning, or your own television with CNN. Twelve rooms have private bathrooms that include a stall shower, wrought-iron towel rails, and two shelves. Three of the rooms have original, eighteenth-century hand-painted ceilings. Back views are not appealing, especially in No. 14, a bunk-bedded roost that overlooks an air-conditioning system on the opposite building. The arched, brick hallway ceilings were discovered during a recent renovation project. Breakfast is not part of the package, but not to worry: lots of *caffès* and tempting bakeries are scattered throughout this part of Rome. Your problem will not be finding a place to eat but selecting one from all the choices. Also under the same family ownership is the Pension Paradise (page 208) and Hotel San Pietrino (page 206), both near the Vatican.

FACILITIES AND SERVICES: Air-conditioning (5€ per day), no elevator (hotel on first floor), hair dryer available

NEAREST TOURIST ATTRACTIONS: Piazza di Spagna, Piazza del Popolo, shopping, Tiber River

TELEPHONE
06 678 0179
FAX
06 699 42151
INTERNET
www.hotelpanda.it
CREDIT CARDS
AE, MC, V
RATES
Single 48–68€, double 68–98€, triple 130€, quad 170€; lower off-season rates
BREAKFAST
No breakfast served
ENGLISH
Yes, and French

HOTEL PENSIONE PARLAMENTO ★★ (49)
Via delle Convertite, 5

23 rooms, all with shower or bath and toilet

TELEPHONE
06 679 2082, 06 699 41697, 06 678 7880
FAX
06 699 21000
EMAIL
hotelparlamento@libero.it
INTERNET
www.hotelparlamento.it
CREDIT CARDS
AE, DC, MC, V
RATES
Single 115€, double 135€, triple 165€, quad 210€; lower off-season rates
BREAKFAST
Continental breakfast included
ENGLISH
Yes

A private apartment occupies the first floor of this building, which is owned by INA, the largest insurance company in Italy. The second floor houses parliament offices, and the third through fifth floors are home to the Hotel Pensione Parlamento, which is, for my Great Sleeping euro, an excellent value in this area of Rome. To reach the hotel, guests must walk up twenty-two steps to the first-floor lift, which takes them to a landing where there are more steps to the reception area. Inside the hotel, there will be more stair climbing if you are on a higher floor or want to enjoy the roof garden view.

Are the hikes worth the aerobic effort? Yes, because the hotel continues to offer many improvements, starting with the rooms and extending throughout the public areas. For maximum pleasure, request one of the bedrooms outfitted in a salmon color scheme and furnished with attractive reproduction pieces mixed with 1800 Imperial antiques—perhaps a matching marble-topped dresser, armoire, and side tables. New beds, tiled floors, double windows, and three-star bathrooms, some with Jacuzzis or hydro-massage showers, finish the picture. Several rooms, including No. 108, a junior suite, have a private terrace with a view of the San Silvester Church bell tower or overlooking the flowering roof garden. Number 82 is a large family room with black marble-topped furniture and a mauve-marble bathroom with heated towel racks and a three-way mirror. Number 76, with a tile floor and matching cherry armoire, desk, and dresser, sleeps two nicely but is too tight for three or four. Numbers 84 and 92 are quiet courtyard choices. The affable owner, Mr. Chini (pronounced KEE-ney), declares the bathroom in No. 94 to be his favorite. You will understand why when you see its green-marble sink, stall shower, and window that opens for light and ventilation. On warm mornings, breakfast is served on the terrace at umbrella-shaded tables.

FACILITIES AND SERVICES: Air-conditioning (12€ per day), direct-dial phone, elevator (to 3rd-floor lobby), hair dryer, some hydro-massage showers and Jacuzzis, in-room safe, satellite TV

NEAREST TOURIST ATTRACTIONS: Piazza di Spagna, Trevi Fountain, shopping

HOTEL SCALINATA DI SPAGNA ★★★ ($, 32)
Piazza Trinità dei Monti, 17
16 rooms, all with shower or bath and toilet

The Scalinata di Spagna used to be on everyone's list of small, charming, inexpensive hotels in Rome. It is still small and charming, but it is not inexpensive—not after its transformation from a modest pensione to a three-star hotel. I include it here for those with bigger budgets who are seeking a hotel that maintains high standards and provides personalized service. Guests enjoy a spectacular view from the flower-filled roof garden, where breakfast is served on warm days. The top-drawer location at the top of the Spanish Steps is directly across from the Hassler Hotel (where rates *start* at $600 for the plainest room and go to more than $2,200 for a suite per night—before taxes and breakfast), and it's within easy access to big-name shopping, good restaurants (see *Great Eats Italy*), and strolling in the Villa Borghese Gardens.

The rooms are on the small side and no two are alike, but all are nicely color coordinated in combinations of green, gold, and blue, and have a print of Rome on the entry door. The decor includes antiques, Murano glass light fixtures, and black-and-white pictures of old Rome. The bathrooms come with both a tub and shower. Numbers 15, 16, and 18 open onto private terraces and are good selections; if you need more space, Nos. 16 and 18 can connect. If you are alone, reserve No. 2, with a view of the Spanish Steps. Guests are served breakfast year-round on one of the most beautiful glass-enclosed open-roof gardens in Rome. Even though prices are no longer low, demand far exceeds supply because of the hotel's loyal following, with many guests plotting their return visit long before checking out.

FACILITIES AND SERVICES: Air-conditioning, direct-dial phone, no elevator (2 floors), hair dryer, laundry service, minibar, in-room computer access through TV, in-room safe, satellite TV

NEAREST TOURIST ATTRACTIONS: Piazza di Spagna, shopping, Villa Borghese Gardens

TELEPHONE
06 6994 0896

FAX
06 6994 0598

INTERNET
www.hotelscalinata.com

CREDIT CARDS
AE, DC, MC, V

RATES
Single 290€, double 320–350€, triple 370€, quad 390€, suite 410€; lower off-season rates

BREAKFAST
Buffet breakfast included

ENGLISH
Yes

Piazza Navona and the Pantheon

Piazza Navona has the exact shape of the original, built by Emperor Domitian in A.D. 86. In the center is Bernini's Fontana dei Quattro Fiumi, which represents four rivers: the Ganges, Nile, Plata, and Danube. Today, the piazza serves as a popular Baroque stage for the theater of Roman life. Any of the sidewalk *caffès* that surround the square provide a perfect front-row seat for unsurpassed people-watching any hour of the day or night. The neighborhood around the square is also known as one of the most expensive patches of real estate in Rome.

Dating from 119 to 128, when Emperor Hadrian built it as a temple, the Pantheon is considered the best preserved remains of ancient Rome, and it has been in perpetual use since it was built. Inside, the radius of its dome is equal to its height. While officially a church, it also contains the tombs of many important Italians, including Raphael.

HOTELS

OTHER OPTIONS

($) indicates a Big Splurge

ALBERGO DEL SOLE AL PANTHEON ★★★★ ($, 56)
Piazza della Rotonda, 63

25 rooms, all with shower or bath and toilet

The Albergo del Sole al Pantheon has remained true to its calling, that of a gracious inn as old as the famous piazza it overlooks. Its exclusive and intimate rooms and suites have served as welcome retreats for royalty, literary legends, political figures, and discerning travelers who value the hotel's rich ambience, which reflects both its pride in the past and its commitment to the present. Absolutely no detail has been overlooked; every creature comfort and

TELEPHONE
06 678 0441

FAX
06 6994 0689

EMAIL
info@hotelsolealpantheon.com;
hotsole@flashnet.it

INTERNET
www.hotelsolealpantheon.com

CREDIT CARDS
AE, DC, MC, V

service is provided. The stunning entry leads guests by a stone desk to a lush atrium garden with a waterfall along the back. To one side there is a beautiful bar and sitting room dominated by a large marble fireplace and leather settees. Breakfast is served on the first-floor terrace, but if you don't want to leave your room in the morning, room service will be happy to bring breakfast to you.

All the rooms are beautifully appointed with quality antique and reproduction furnishings and soothing, light earth-tone fabrics, and they are equipped with everything from thick terry towels and robes to free in-room movies, abundant closet space, and Jacuzzis in all of the modern bathrooms. Many of the rooms overlook the Pantheon and the Piazza della Rotunda, which is one of the most beautiful and busiest squares in Rome. It also can be one of the noisiest. If calm is what you crave, ask for a room on the back, where the view won't inspire, but the quiet will.

FACILITIES AND SERVICES: Air-conditioning, bar, direct-dial phone, elevator, hair dryer, Jacuzzis in all bathrooms, laundry service, minibar, in-room safe, satellite TV with free movies, double-glazed windows, free Internet terminal

NEAREST TOURIST ATTRACTIONS: Pantheon, Piazza Navona, central Rome

RATES
Single 227–268€, double 335€, suite 418–470€; lower off-season rates

BREAKFAST
Buffet breakfast included

ENGLISH
Yes

ALBERGO SANTA CHIARA ★★★ ($, 62)
Via di Santa Chiara, 21

100 rooms, all with bath or shower and toilet

It may take a minute or two, but soon after arriving at the Albergo Santa Chiara, guests realize they are in a special Great Sleep in Rome. All the furnishings, art work, and statuary you see are original and owned by the Corteggiani family, who have been overseeing their hotel for more than three centuries. Notice the marble pillars in the bar, the oil painting dating from 1700 over the fireplace, and the intricately inlaid clock. A study of the framed prints of Rome hanging downstairs is a quick review of ancient history. Naturally, the hotel has changed and improved over time, but wherever possible, original beams, terra-cotta floors, and stone steps have been left in place as reminders of the past.

The very comfortable accommodations are spread out in three buildings and vary from standard hotel rooms to junior suites and apartments. Everything matches, the furniture is attractive, and the bathrooms are up-to-date. Many of the rooms face a lovely interior courtyard, thus ensuring a good night's rest and peace and quiet during

TELEPHONE
06 687 2979

FAX
06 687 3144

EMAIL
stchiara@tin.it

INTERNET
www.albergosantachiara.com

CREDIT CARDS
AE, DC, MC, V

RATES
Single 143€, double 214€, suite 246€, apartment (2–5 people) 335–415€; lower off-season and weekend rates

BREAKFAST
Buffet breakfast included

ENGLISH
Yes

the day. Several rooms and suites have terraces, one large enough to have a tented section complete with chaises for sunbathing and a table and chairs for al fresco snacking. Closet space is never a problem, especially in the walk-ins, which have multiple shelf and drawer space, plus loads of hanging racks. If you are staying a month or more, consider one of the three spacious apartments, which include use of the kitchen if you are staying at least a month. They are also available for short-term stays, but without the use of the kitchen.

FACILITIES AND SERVICES: Air-conditioning, bar, conference room, direct-dial phone, 4 elevators, hair dryer, room safe, room service for light snacks and drinks, satellite TV, some Jacuzzis, kitchens in 3 apartments

NEAREST TOURIST ATTRACTIONS: Piazza Navona, Pantheon

HOTEL DUE TORRI ★★★ ($, 47)
Vicolo del Leonetto, 23
26 rooms, all with shower or bath and toilet

TELEPHONE
06 687 6983, 06 687 5765, 06 688 06956

FAX
06 686 5442

EMAIL
hotelduetorri@interfree.it

INTERNET
hotelduetorriroma.com

CREDIT CARDS
AE, DC, MC, V

RATES
Single 165€, double 245€, suite/family room 325€; lower off-season rates

BREAKFAST
Buffet breakfast included

ENGLISH
Yes

On top of being attractively decorated, the Due Torri is well positioned between the Piazza del Popolo and Piazza Navona in a neighborhood with winding streets and ancient buildings. Good shopping and restaurants are within an easy walk (see *Great Eats Italy*).

Past the entrance is a small sitting room with velvet sofas, an unusual hand-painted black chest, and a massive floor-to-ceiling mirror. To one side is the breakfast room, done in green with lattice wallpaper and yellow tablecloths, which gives the illusion of being in a garden. The blackboard greeting wishes you a "good morning" in four languages. The hallways are well lit and hung throughout with nicely framed prints. All rooms are carpet-free, and half are nonsmoking. Rooms on the fifth floor cost the same as the others but have the advantage of nice views, though you will sacrifice some space. Those on the fourth floor have small balconies. If you are not on the fifth floor, No. 202 is a large double with its own entry, a desk, and two armchairs. If you want room to spread out, No. 407/8 is a two-room suite. In the larger room is a king-size bed (or twins if you wish), two comfortable chairs, and a small balcony with a view of neighboring roof gardens. The second room is nice if you want some quiet work space, or a place to watch television while another person is resting.

Also under the same ownership is the Hotel Fontanella Borghese, near the Spanish Steps (see page 175).

FACILITIES AND SERVICES: Air-conditioning, 2 direct-dial phones, elevator, hair dryer, minibar, in-room safe, satellite TV, porter, half of rooms nonsmoking

NEAREST TOURIST ATTRACTIONS: Piazza Navona, Pantheon, shopping, Tiber River,

HOTEL NAVONA ★★ (61)
Via dei Sediari, 8
31 rooms, all with shower or bath and toilet

Historians will be interested to note that this hotel was built on the ruins of the Baths of Agrippa in the first century. The building was redone in the fifteenth century by Borromini and is now owned and run by an affable Australian, Corry Natale, a graduate of Notre Dame University. Corry came to Rome more than thirty years ago to study architecture and never left. Now he and his family own and operate this popular Great Sleep in Rome.

Over time, their improvements have been impressive and resulted in turning what was once a student hotel into a solid two star with many three-star amenities. Recent projects included restoring the handsome stairway leading from the street to the hotel, redoing the dining room, adding five new rooms on the second floor, each with its fourteenth-century ceiling restored, installing tiled baths with stall showers in all rooms, and exposing some of the walls to show the original bricks. Still in place are double-glazed windows to help keep out the incessant noise, which one contends with throughout the city. Ten rooms have balconies, all have custom-designed Murano glass lights, terra-cotta tile floors, and prints of old Rome warming the soft green walls. If you are with a group that values togetherness, reserve the apartment with four double bedrooms that open onto a communal sitting room. Also available are a few apartments that are separate from the hotel. If the Hotel Navona is fully booked, which is most of the time, consider the family's other hotel venture, the Residenza Zanardelli (see page 184).

FACILITIES AND SERVICES: Air-conditioning, direct-dial phone, no elevator (3 floors), hair dryer, satellite TV, office safe

NEAREST TOURIST ATTRACTIONS: Piazza Navona, Pantheon, Campo de' Fiori

TELEPHONE
06 686 4203, 06 6821 1392

FAX
06 6880 3802

INTERNET
www.hotelnavona.com

CREDIT CARDS
MC, V

RATES
Single 90€, double 125€, triple 180€, quad 200€, apartment (2 people) from 150€; lower off-season rates and special Internet deals

BREAKFAST
Continental breakfast included

ENGLISH
Yes

HOTEL PORTOGHESI ★★★ (48)
Via dei Portoghesi, 1

TELEPHONE
06 686 4231
FAX
06 687 6976
INTERNET
www.hotelportoghesiroma.com
CREDIT CARDS
MC, V
RATES
Single 150€, double 190€, junior suite 215€, suite 245–315€
BREAKFAST
Buffet breakfast included
ENGLISH
Yes

27 rooms, all with shower or bath and toilet

The setting is marvelous, right in the heart of historic old Rome near Piazza Navona and the Pantheon. The hotel and the street it is on take their name from the neighboring fifteenth-century National Portuguese Church of St. Anthony, which has a beautiful marble interior. Opposite the hotel stands the Torre dei Frangipane (Tower of the Monkey), which has a lamp on top given by a grateful family who believed their child was saved by a monkey.

No two rooms in this 160-year-old hotel are alike. The best choice, unquestionably, is La Torre, which has a tiled floor, a small sitting area, a walk-in closet, and a light beige marble bathroom with a stall shower and window. Its crowning glory is a beautiful private terrace where you can almost reach out and touch the sculpture on the church next door. Number 44 is a junior suite. I like the two-tone pink and Roman red colors, the view from both windows, and the ample sink space in the bathroom. Great wardrobes await guests who check into No. 20, a suite with hardwood floors, a sitting room with a sofa bed, and a bathroom with a tub and shower. Rooms 46 and 28 are standard doubles with views of the street; No. 6 is a compact double with a train-style bathroom that is saved by its corner view of the Torre dei Frangipane. In Nos. 14, 32, and 50, the bathrooms are good and the rooms have built-ins, desk space, a wicker armchair, and an inside view. The beautiful enclosed rooftop terrace, with wonderful vistas, is a romantic place to have breakfast or sip a glass of wine while watching the sun set over this part of ancient Rome.

FACILITIES AND SERVICES: Air-conditioning, direct-dial phone, elevator, hair dryer, some in-room safes, private safe in office, satellite TV

NEAREST TOURIST ATTRACTIONS: Piazza Navona, Pantheon, Campo de' Fiori, Tiber River

RESIDENZA ZANARDELLI (51)
Via G. Zanardelli, 7

TELEPHONE
06 6821 1392, 06 6880 9760
FAX
06 6880 3802
INTERNET
www.hotelnavona.com
CREDIT CARDS
AE, DC, MC, V

7 rooms, all with shower and toilet

The Residenza Zanardelli owes its renovation to architect Corry Natale, who also owns the nearby Hotel Navona (see page 183). The seven rooms are part of a noble Baroque palace whose style is considered to be one of the most characteristic of the late nineteenth century. While the rooms are not regal, they do have air-conditioning, coordinated colors, brass-tipped wrought-iron beds, tile floors, and private bathrooms. Several have views of the Palazzo Altemps, which has an important collection of ancient sculpture. As with most of these small guest houses, there is not a lobby or sitting area, but guests have an opportunity to get acquainted over breakfast, which is served at a big table in the dining area that is watched over by angels on the ceiling.

FACILITIES AND SERVICES: Air-conditioning, direct-dial phone, elevator, hair dryer on request, office safe, satellite TV

NEAREST TOURIST ATTRACTIONS: Piazza Navona, Pantheon, Tiber River, 20-minute walk to the Vatican

RATES
Single 125€, double 165€, triple 240€, quad 165.27€; discounts for *Great Sleeps Italy* readers
BREAKFAST
Continental breakfast included
ENGLISH
Yes

Piazza Venezia

The monolithic white Vittoriale honors the first king of Italy, Vittorio Emanuele of Savoy. Until the Allied troops liberated Rome in 1944, it was Mussolini's official residence and remained closed to the public. Now the west wing, Palazzo Venezia, serves as a museum for Byzantine and early Renaissance tapestries, ceramics, silver, and sculpture. This is also the site of the eternal flame that lights the tomb of Italy's unknown soldier. The square in front is a crossroads for Rome traffic, with a mad rush hour that goes at breakneck speed twenty-four hours a day.

HOTEL CORONET ★★ (64)
Piazza Grazioli, 5
13 rooms, 10 with shower or bath and toilet

Big, old-fashioned rooms with high beamed ceilings, a few exposed pipes, and a red-carpeted entry characterize this budget pick on the third floor of a seventeenth-century *palazzo*, which belongs to the aristocratic Doria Pamphili family. Seven of the rooms overlook the palazzo's lovely courtyard, as does the breakfast room. Since the three bathless rooms each have their own assigned bathroom outside the room with its own private key, the only real inconvenience to guests is a short walk in the hall, not shared facilities, and the savings, especially in the low season, is dramatic. Overall, this is not a place for uptight types, but for a young-at-heart group of three or four traveling together, it is a good bet in a safe, central location with prices that shouldn't max out a credit card. The rates listed range from prices for rooms without baths in low season to those with private facilities in the high season.

TELEPHONE
06 679 2341
FAX
06 699 22705
INTERNET
www.hotelcoronet.com
CREDIT CARDS
AE, MC, V
RATES
Single 70–150€, double 80–170€, triple 95–190€, quad 135–253€, five people 150–275€
BREAKFAST
Continental breakfast included
ENGLISH
Yes

FACILITIES AND SERVICES: Air-conditioning (10€ per day), direct-dial phone, elevator to reception, fans, hair dryer, office safe

NEAREST TOURIST ATTRACTIONS: Piazza Venezia, half-way between Piazza Navona and Trevi Fountain

Testaccio

Testaccio is a very Roman working-class district. Until 1970 the slaughterhouse was here, but now Testaccio is considered a with-it area with popular restaurants and a wild nightclub scene. At the Protestant cemetery, you can visit the tombs of John Keats, Shelley, and Richard Henry Dana, who wrote *Two Years Before the Mast*.

HOTEL SANTA PRISCA ★★ (90)
Largo Manlio Gelsomini, 35

TELEPHONE
06 574 1917, 06 575 0469, 06 575 0009

FAX
06 574 6658

INTERNET
www.hotelsantaprisca.it

CREDIT CARDS
AE, DC, MC, V

RATES
Single 102€, double 127€, triple 150€; 4-course lunch or dinner 20€

BREAKFAST
Continental breakfast included

ENGLISH
Yes

50 rooms, all with shower or bath and toilet

The quiet and dignified Hotel Santa Prisca is in the Testaccio district, which is definitely not a hub location, but many Rome veterans enjoy getting out of the noisy, traffic-clogged city center and staying, instead, in an area where they can experience more of the city's day-to-day life. This 1960s-style hotel is run by an order of Argentine and Italian nuns, the Sisters of Immaculate Conception. The hotel offers fifty rooms, all with private bath, direct-dial telephone, and air-conditioning. Other drawing cards are free parking and a pleasant restaurant that serves three meals a day and has a daily-changing menu. The restaurant is open Monday to Friday for lunch and dinner and Saturday for lunch.

The rooms are plain but immaculate. I like the reading lights over the beds, the spacious closets, the pull-down desks, and the showers with curtains. For lazy afternoons spent soaking up the sun, there is a pretty garden. On gray days you can settle into one of the sitting room's comfortable armchairs. If you are not into hotel dining, the Testaccio district is now a trendy area that's known for its earthy restaurants (see *Great Eats Italy*).

NOTE: The Hotel Santa Prisca can be reached by taking Tram 3, Bus 716 from Piazza Venezia, or the metro Blue Line B–Pyramide.

FACILITIES AND SERVICES: Air-conditioning (6€ per day), bar, direct-dial phone, elevator, free parking, office safe, satellite TV, porter

NEAREST TOURIST ATTRACTIONS: Aventine, Testaccio, Baths of Caracalla

Train Station Area

The neighborhood surrounding Termini Stazione, the train station, isn't on anyone's top-ten list of tourist must-dos in Rome, but many hotels in all price categories are dotted around the area. The train station underwent a massive renewal prior to the 2000 Jubilee Year, and it is now a chrome-and-glass, multilevel minicity with shops, cafés, bars, a supermarket, a pharmacy, and fast-food outlets (including two McDonalds and a Dunkin' Donuts). It is also the hub of Rome's bus, underground, and taxi transportation, including a special, direct train to the airport that leaves every thirty minutes between 6:50 A.M. and 9:50 P.M.

HOTELS

The Beehive (¢)	187
Hotel Alpi ★★★	188
Hotel Britannia ★★★★ ($)	189
Hotel Canada ★★★	190
Hotel Columbia ★★★	191
Hotel Fenicia ★★ (¢)	192
Hotel Nardizzi Americana ★★	192
Hotel Romae ★★★	193
Hotel Venezia ★★★	194
Residenza Cellini	195

OTHER OPTIONS

Holy Hotels	
Suore di Santa Elisabetta	229
Hostels	
Protezione della Giovane	231
Yellow Hostel	231
Student Accommodations	
Centro Turistico Studentesco e Giovanile (CTS)	235
YWCAs	
YWCA Foyer di Roma	236

($) indicates a Big Splurge; (¢) indicates a Cheap Sleep

THE BEEHIVE (¢, 111)
Via Marghera, 8

9 rooms, 3 with shower and toilet

For a cheap and cheerful Great Sleep in Rome, buzz into the Beehive, a nine-room hive of activity and fun. It is owned by a young couple who were tired of the yuppie rat race in the States and decided to chuck it all, follow

TELEPHONE & FAX
06 4470 4553
INTERNET
www.the-beehive.com
CREDIT CARDS
Cash only; can guarantee online reservation with MC, V

Rates are per person: room with
private bath 40€, shared bath
35€, dorm bed 20€

their dream, and move to Rome. Their Beehive is a cross-pollination of a hostel and a hotel, with nonsmoking room options ranging from a dorm housing up to eight in bunk beds to private rooms for one to three people with or without private bathrooms. Everyone can share the common kitchen, enjoy the changing art exhibits, pet the house cat, Ingmar, plug into the free wireless Internet, or shmooze in the reception area with the plugged-in, jovial staff. In warm weather there are chairs and tables in the raised garden in front of the hotel. Only a few rooms have air-conditioning, but all have window screens (a rarity in Rome) and fans. No smoking is allowed and no curfew is imposed.

NOTE: The Beehive has three sister properties: Millefiori, Clover, and Acacia. Unfortunately these are located in a dicey area that is considered unsafe, especially at night and for women traveling alone.

FACILITIES AND SERVICES: Some air-conditioners, free phone calls within Italy, no elevator (2 floors), fans, Internet access, laundry room, office safe, nonsmoking hotel

NEAREST TOURIST ATTRACTIONS: Santa Maria Maggiore Church, train station

HOTEL ALPI ★★★ (103)
Via Castelfidardo, 84/A
48 rooms, all with shower or bath and toilet

RATES
Single 140€, double 200€,
junior suite 218€; significantly
lower off-season rates

Walk through the door at 84/A Via Castelfidardo and you enter a special, private world of well-preserved nineteenth-century Liberty-style architecture. Quality and style, fine fabrics, and period furnishings are the hallmarks of the forty-eight individually decorated rooms and suites. Spacious marble-tiled bathrooms are equipped with the latest in fixtures, soft towels, and lighting. All of the rooms have oversized satellite television sets with direct Internet access; all of the superior rooms have Jacuzzis and balconies. Most have adequate space with the exception of No. 285, a mini-single with a bad view and no space for a chair. No. 281, on the other hand, is a large, sunny double with a balcony, four-poster bed, and walk-in mirrored closet. An exceptional buffet breakfast is served in a comfortable dining room decorated in soft yellow, rose, and gray. Or, if you prefer, a Continental breakfast can be brought to your room. The location is within walking distance to the train station, reasonably close to Via Veneto, and within striking distance of the Villa Borghese Gardens.

FACILITIES AND SERVICES: Air-conditioning, bar, direct-dial phone, cell-phone rental, elevator, hair dryer, Jacuzzis in superior rooms, laundry service, minibar, room service, in-room safe, satellite TV with Internet access, 10 non-smoking rooms

NEAREST TOURIST ATTRACTIONS: Via Veneto, train station, 30-minute walk to Villa Borghese Gardens

HOTEL BRITANNIA ★★★★ ($, 115)
Via Napoli, 64
33 rooms, all with shower or bath and toilet

The warmth of the welcome, the careful attention to details, and the personalized service at the Hotel Britannia add up to a winning combination. I like the fact that management recognizes the work of its staff, and that the employees repay with years of dedicated service: Mario and Enrico, the two concierges, have totaled more than fifty years at the hotel.

Located just off busy Via Nazionale and within walking distance to the train station, the hotel has been done in an attractive modern style. Mirrored walls give the downstairs public areas an open and spacious feeling, while soft built-in sofas, masses of pillows, and a breakfast room with a skylight, parquet floors, and wall murals depicting views from a Roman villa create an overall sense of style and comfort. The faux-finished marble lobby bathroom is without equal. The American-style bar is a nice place for a quiet rendezvous with other guests, comfortably seated in tufted leather armchairs.

Upstairs, each floor is done in a different muted color: gold and burgundy on the first, yellow and green on the second, and cream, gold, and green on the third and fourth. Each room has a fish bowl with a colorful fish swimming in it. The purpose, the owner told me, is to make your stay more pleasant, and it really does. While all the rooms are excellent, my favorites are the four rooms with private, plant-filled balconies. Room 403, a junior suite, is one of these. It is a beautiful, light room with a separate sitting area that has big windows looking onto the balcony. The soft brown and gray marble bathroom has a Jacuzzi and a heated towel rack in addition to all the other extras, which include a digital clock radio, mirrored ceiling, scale, clothes drying line, plenty of toiletries and towels, hair dryer, and sunlamp. Even though it does not have a balcony, No. 205, a standard twin, is appealing; highlights are the two cherubs painted above the bed, the lighted work space, and the pleasantly quiet view onto a side street. The singles tend to run small, but each has a double bed, all

TELEPHONE
06 488 3153

FAX
06 4889 6316

INTERNET
www.hotelbritannia.it

CREDIT CARDS
AE, DC, MC, V

RATES
Single 120–220€, double 180–260€, triple 200–310€, junior suite 220–380€; rates range from low to high season

BREAKFAST
Buffet breakfast included

ENGLISH
Yes

the amenities of larger rooms, and wonderful bathrooms. Only a few rooms have interior views, but if you are at all claustrophobic, it is best to avoid these.

In the morning, complimentary newspapers of your choice and a Rome weather report are placed by your door. The breakfast, which is included in the room price, is above average in quality and quantity; in addition to the usual coffee, tea, hot chocolate, and roll, it includes a choice of three or four cakes, cheese, and fruit juice.

Also under the same ownership is the Hotel Duca d'Alba near the Colosseum (see page 165).

FACILITIES AND SERVICES: Air-conditioning, bar, direct-dial phone, elevator, hair dryer, Internet access in lobby, some Jacuzzis, laundry service, minibar, free parking for 5 or 6 cars (first-come, first-served), in-room safe, tea and coffeemakers, satellite TV

NEAREST TOURIST ATTRACTIONS: Opera, Via Veneto, train station

HOTEL CANADA ★★★ (100)
Via Vicenza, 58

70 rooms, all with shower, bath, and toilet

TELEPHONE
06 445 7770
FAX
06 445 0749
INTERNET
www.hotelcanadaroma.com
CREDIT CARDS
AE, DC, MC, V
RATES
Single 155€, double 188€, triple 191€, quad 227€, junior suite 188–260€; lower off-season rates
BREAKFAST
Large hot and cold buffet breakfast included
ENGLISH
Yes

The Hotel Canada is a marvelous three-star hotel with five-star personnel and services. "The more you give, the more you get," states Sr. Pucci, the distinguished owner. A graduate of the Cornell School of Hotel Management, he has been at the helm since 1965, although he now shares the responsibilities with his son, who is an architect and the person responsible for the stylish appeal and arrangement of the entire operation.

The downstairs areas are exceptional, from the piano lounge and bar with inviting sofas and overstuffed chairs to the well-outfitted meeting rooms and large breakfast room—with tables big enough for a full place setting and a morning paper. The perfectly maintained bedrooms reflect not only good taste but care and concern for the comfort of guests. Room 104 is a double with a beautiful antique desk, a hand-painted wardrobe, and brass accent lamps. Number 108 has a sitting area with comfortable chairs and a large bath. Both Nos. 114 and 134 (with a balcony) are junior suites and especially suitable for long stays or for parties of three. Number 214 is a grand room in every way, from the armchairs and desk in the entry to the canopy over the bed, the spacious armoire, the three-drawer chest, and the rich fabrics. The rooms and baths have all the usual three-star amenities, including double-paned windows, automatic locking doors, and telephones and drying lines in the bathrooms. The generous breakfast includes cheese, three types of meat, a hot dish, fresh fruit, and cereals, along with bread, rolls, and hot or cold drinks.

If there is any drawback to this hotel, it might be the location, which is not tourist central. There are, however, many buses and two metro stops within easy walking distance.

FACILITIES AND SERVICES: Air-conditioning, bar, 2 direct-dial phones, elevator, hair dryer, free Internet access in lobby, fax and data port lines in rooms, laundry service, parking on request, porter, in-room safe, tea and coffeemakers, satellite TV, room service, two floors of nonsmoking rooms

NEAREST TOURIST ATTRACTIONS: Train station, excellent public transportation

HOTEL COLUMBIA ★★★ (116)
Via del Viminale, 15
45 rooms, all with shower or bath and toilet

Here are some of the enthusiastic accolades written by guests about the Hotel Columbia: "A small hotel with a big heart," "A flower of a hotel blooms in Rome," "A lovely hotel with excellent staff," "What a wonderful place to spend our last night in Rome. I don't want to go home!" and finally, "Bella . . . grazie!"

Patrizia Diletti, whose family also owns the popular Hotel Venezia (see page 194), dedicated one year of unbelievably hard work to the ambitious reconstruction project that resulted in the Hotel Columbia, now a beautiful modern property with an air of cosmopolitan dignity. Everything this well-connected family touches seems to turn out well. The forty-five bedrooms provide copacetic comforts with white walls, creamy quilted bed coverings, country-style furniture, and white-tile baths with marble sink tops, magnifying mirrors, and monogrammed towels. Thoughtful extras guests appreciate include "Pillows à la carte," which allows guests to select their choice of sleeping pillow: relaxing organic millet, hypoallergenic latex foam, tension-free neck roll, or dust-mite-free goose down. Several rooms have wood-beam or brick-arched ceilings and grillwork by a Perugian artist. On the fifth floor, guests are treated to a dazzling glassed-in breakfast room that opens onto a lovely roof terrace ringed with flowering plant boxes. The yellow marble tables team well with the upholstered chairs and gold sconces to create a garden setting that carries through to the sitting room, where modern paintings

TELEPHONE
06 488 3509
FAX
06 474 0209
INTERNET
www.hotelcolumbia.com
CREDIT CARDS
AE, DC, MC, V
RATES
Single 118–145€, double 160€, triple 216€; discounts for readers of *Great Sleeps Italy*
BREAKFAST
Buffet breakfast included
ENGLISH
Yes

by a friend of the family add bright splashes of color and light. The enthusiastic, multilingual staff works hard to please, but no one is more ambitious or single-minded in her determination to create a marvelous hotel than owner Patrizia Diletti.

NOTE: For a different Roman holiday, please see Villa Delros on page 222, the exclusive bed-and-breakfast Patrizia's mother has opened in her beautiful country estate on the edge of the city.

FACILITIES AND SERVICES: Air-conditioning, bar, 2 direct-dial phones, elevator, hair dryer, laundry service, minibar, data port, room service, in-room safe, satellite TV, pay-for-view TV

NEAREST TOURIST ATTRACTIONS: Opera, train station, 20-minute walk to Piazza di Spagna or Trevi Fountain

HOTEL FENICIA ★★ (¢, 112)
Via Milazzo, 20
14 rooms, all with shower and toilet

TELEPHONE & FAX
06 490 342
INTERNET
www.hotelfenicia.it
CREDIT CARDS
AE, DC, MC, V
RATES
Single 70–80€, double 100€, triple 110€, quad 130€; 5% discount for cash
BREAKFAST
Continental breakfast 4€
ENGLISH
Yes

For a decent bed in an area filled with bottom-of-the-barrel budget digs, the family owned Hotel Fenicia is a good cheap sleeping choice. True, you won't find luxury here, but the spiffy rooms and price, especially for *Great Sleep Italy* readers who pay cash, will make up for that. The entrance is admittedly uninspiring, but at least there is an elevator and, at the first-floor reception desk, a member of the friendly Brancadoro family to greet you. The quiet rooms are simple, clean, and well-maintained. Three have small balconies. All have tile or hardwood floors and more space than usual in this price range. Colors match; furniture is ding-free. The hairdresser next to the hotel gives hotel guests a 10 percent discount. From Monday to Saturday there is a typical neighborhood morning market just up the street from the hotel.

FACILITIES AND SERVICES: Air-conditioning (5€ per day), direct-dial phone, elevator, hair dryer, minibar, TV

NEAREST TOURIST ATTRACTIONS: Train station and good public transportation

HOTEL NARDIZZI AMERICANA ★★ (108)
Via Firenze, 38
28 rooms, all with shower and toilet

TELEPHONE
06 4890 3916, 06 488 0035
FAX
06 488 0368
INTERNET
www.hotelnardizzi.it
CREDIT CARDS
AE, DC, MC, V

A stay at the Nardizzi Americana guarantees guests twenty-four-hour security: right across the street, surrounded by armed guards, is the Ministry of Defense. You are also only a block or so away from a metro stop, or if you're trying to keep fit, you can either walk to the Trevi Fountain or keep up your jogging routine in the Villa Borghese. The hotel's owners, Fabrizio and Stephano, and their manager, Mario, are friendly guys who like Americans.

To make matters even better, the entire hotel has been restyled with excellent results. The reception area opens onto a year-around heated and covered roof garden where breakfast and drinks are served. Pieces of antique furniture are scattered throughout the corridors. Now all rooms have parquet flooring, new beds with matching blue-and-gold spreads, a place to sit, and tiled baths with enclosed stall showers and nice towels hanging on heated racks. Significant discounts are given to readers of *Great Sleeps Italy* who pay cash.

FACILITIES AND SERVICES: Air-conditioning, bar, direct-dial phone, elevator, hair dryer, parking on request, radio, in-room safe, satellite TV

NEAREST TOURIST ATTRACTIONS: Trevi Fountain, Via Veneto, train station

RATES
Single 100€, double 135€, triple 175€, quad 230€; discounts for *Great Sleeps Italy* readers (show book at check-in): pay cash to get 10% discount in high season, 20% in low season

BREAKFAST
Buffet breakfast included

ENGLISH
Yes

HOTEL ROMAE ★★★ (102)
Via Palestro, 49
22 rooms, all with shower or bath and toilet

"Some of the nicest guests we have come from your book," Lucy Boccaforno, who owns the hotel with her husband, Francesco, said to me. The young and attractive pair take great pride in their establishment and are on board every day to see that everything runs as it should. In addition, they will book tours for you, obtain tickets, and make sightseeing suggestions. Their English is perfect, and they make everyone feel at home.

Every time I return to the Romae, there are changes for the better. Last time, it was the reception area and hallways that had new treatments, and in the dining area, two Internet terminals for guests were added. As a result, the Romae added a third star. This time, they have added a restaurant, Mama Angela, named after Francesco's mother. It is open for lunch and dinner and serves a basic repertoire of trattoria favorites. It is also where hotel guests are served a buffet breakfast. The functional, well-manicured bedrooms have tiled floors, lacy white window curtains, pastel-colored walls, and flowers on the balcony rails. In addition to air-conditioning, firm mattresses, CNN television, and simple yet sweet decor, the best feature for many is that almost all rooms are exclusively nonsmoking. Also, Lucy has compiled an information booklet on Rome and places a copy in each room.

TELEPHONE
06 446 3554

FAX
06 446 3914

INTERNET
www.hotelromae.com

CREDIT CARDS
AE, MC, V

RATES
Single or double 135€; extra person 35% of double rate; discount for *Great Sleeps Italy* readers; children under 12 free

BREAKFAST
Buffet breakfast included

ENGLISH
Yes

FACILITIES AND SERVICES: Air-conditioning, bar, direct-dial phone, elevator, fan, hair dryer, minibar, in-room safe, satellite TV, free Internet access in lobby, many nonsmoking rooms, 10% guest discount at Mama Angela restaurant

NEAREST TOURIST ATTRACTIONS: Museo Nazionale in the Diocletian Bath, train station

HOTEL VENEZIA ★★★ (109)
Via Varese, 18

61 rooms, all with shower or bath and toilet

TELEPHONE
06 445 7101
FAX
06 495 7687; toll-free from the United States, 800-526-5497
INTERNET
www.hotelvenezia.com
CREDIT CARDS
AE, DC, MC, V
RATES
Single 118–145€, double 160€, triple 216€; discounts for *Great Sleeps Italy* readers
BREAKFAST
Large buffet breakfast included
ENGLISH
Yes

On a scale of one to ten, the Hotel Venezia is a ten-plus and climbing. I cannot say enough good things about it: it is a beautiful selection in a business and residential neighborhood a few minutes from the train station. Owner Rosmarie Diletti has turned over the reins to her capable daughter and son, Patrizia and Francesco, who continue the Venezia's tradition of caring for each guest and showing a personal interest in everyone's well-being. This kindness extends to the loyal staff, some of whom have been with the hotel since 1964. This multilingual staff is also one of the most competent and hospitable I have found in Rome.

The hotel is gracious and beautiful throughout, with a museum-worthy collection of fifteenth-, sixteenth-, and seventeenth-century antiques. Most of the paintings are by local artists and are part of the family's own collection. Everywhere you look something interesting catches your eye, including the beautiful fresh-flower arrangements that Sra. Diletti brings in weekly from her country garden. When checking in, notice the picture of the bride and groom hanging over the desk. This is a painting of Sra. Diletti's in-laws from the turn of the twentieth century.

A breakfast buffet is laid out on a fifteenth-century altar. Some of the doors leading from the lounge area are from the sixteenth century, and the glass-topped table base in the sitting room was used to carry saints into villages during the same era. The rooms are done in lovely reproduction and antique furnishings befitting the style and feel of the rest of the hotel. Each room has a Murano chandelier, heavy white curtains, crocheted covers over the bedside tables, and interesting framed prints hanging on the walls. In addition, the closet space is ample, and the bathrooms have pretty floral-tile inserts to give them interest. The rooms on the higher floors are flooded with light, and many have balconies that are perfect observation stations for watching the neighborhood life below. Special rates are available if you mention *Great Sleeps Italy* when reserving and show the book when checking in.

NOTE: Rosmarie Diletti has opened her magnificent home on the edge of Rome for visitors; see Villa Delros, page 222. In addition, Patrizia and Francesco also own the Hotel Columbia, which is close to and equal in its own way to the Venezia; see page 191.

FACILITIES AND SERVICES: Air-conditioning, bar, direct-dial phone, elevator, hair dryer, laundry service, magnifying mirror in the bathroom, minibar, in-room safe, satellite TV

NEAREST TOURIST ATTRACTIONS: Train station, excellent public transportation

RESIDENZA CELLINI (113)
Via Modena, 5

6 rooms, all with bath, shower, and toilet

Residenza Cellini is near Piazza della Repubblica, Via Veneto, and Piazza di Spagna, and just down the street from the Ministry of Defense. The former noble's residence is small, with only six rooms, but what spectacular rooms they are. Recently redone, the rooms and junior suites in this nonsmoking residence are a symphony of soft yellow, green, and blue floral fabrics, polished hardwood floors, traditional furniture, and comfortable beds with anti-allergic orthopedic mattresses. All the bathrooms have handmade marble sinks, heated towel racks, excellent light, and hydromassage showers with seats; in junior suites there are Jacuzzis. Creature comforts include a stereo system, remote controls by the beds, free wireless Internet hookup, and a large buffet breakfast, served either in a light blue room or in your own room. The staff, headed by two brothers and a sister, is exceptional in their commitment to guest comfort and enjoyment.

FACILITIES AND SERVICES: Air-conditioning, direct-dial phone, elevator, hair dryer, free wireless Internet in rooms, hydromassage showers, Jacuzzis, laundry service, minibar, room service, in-room stereo system, satellite TV, in-room safe, nonsmoking hotel

NEAREST TOURIST ATTRACTIONS: Opera, 20-minute walk to Piazza di Spagna and Trevi Fountain

TELEPHONE
06 4782 5204

FAX
06 4788 1806

EMAIL
residenzacellini@tin.it

INTERNET
www.residenzacellini.it

CREDIT CARDS
AE, DC, MC, V

RATES
Single 130€, double 145–185€, junior suite 170–210€, extra bed 30€

BREAKFAST
Buffet breakfast included

ENGLISH
Yes

Trastevere

Trastevere, which means "across the Tiber," is just that...across the Tiber River from the Jewish Quarter. If there is a picturesque bohemian section of Rome, this is it. The heart is around the Piazza di Santa Maria, which contains one of the oldest churches in Rome, Santa Maria in Trastevere. For a local slice of life, Piazza San Cosimato offers a morning open food market. Throughout, the narrow streets are full of flapping laundry lines stretched between windows of ancient pink-stuccoed buildings, elderly black-garbed widows gossiping on corners, funky boutiques displaying the latest trends in art and fashion, and one pizzeria after another. In the evening, a lively nightlife keeps the action in full force until the wee hours.

HOTELS

($) indicates a Big Splurge; (¢) indicates a Cheap Sleep

HOTEL SANTA MARIA ★★★ ($, 82)
Vicolo del Piede, 2

20 rooms, all with shower or bath and toilet

Originally, the seventeenth-century Hotel Santa Maria was a cloister for nuns of the Santa Maria in Trastevere Church. In 2000, it underwent a total renovation and now resembles a rambling hacienda with rooms opening onto an interior garden that has tables, chairs, and umbrellas and is framed by blooming orange trees and camelias. All the tiled-floor rooms are basically the same, done in a simple Romanesque style with bright colors, wrought-iron beds, light oak furniture, built-in closets, a desk and chair, and a well-lit bathroom. The hotel is completely nonsmoking; nineteen rooms are on the ground floor, and only one, with a mansard roofline, requires a few steps. Breakfast is served in a beautiful beamed room with a massive stone fireplace. The friendly staff is exceptional.

FACILITIES AND SERVICES: Air-conditioning, bar, direct-dial phone, no elevator (mainly ground level), laundry services, minibar, in-room safe, 2 parking spaces (10€ per day), satellite TV

NEAREST TOURIST ATTRACTIONS: Trastevere

TELEPHONE
06 589 4626

FAX
06 589 4815

EMAIL
hotelsantamaria@libero.it

INTERNET
www.htlsantamaria.com

CREDIT CARDS
AE, DC, MC, V

RATES
Single 163€, double 207€, triple 233–259€, suites 300–400€; lower off-season rates

BREAKFAST
American breakfast included

ENGLISH
Yes

HOTEL TRASTEVERE ★★ (¢, 86)
Via Luciano Manara, 24a/25
23 rooms, all with shower and toilet

Hotel Trastevere, formerly known as Antico Albergo Manara, is a plain-Jane address next to a motorcycle repair shop and across the street from the Vatican ministries. The spotless rooms are priced to sell...and with an enviable 96 percent occupancy rate, they are popular budget picks in this part of Rome. Each one has a bit of hand-painted detail work, tiled floors, Motel 6–inspired furniture, and a functional bathroom. Those needing more space have the option of three apartments in the same building that can accommodate up to five. These have kitchenettes equipped for light cooking and similar Motel 6–style furnishings. Daily maid service is included. The owner also includes, in both the hotel and the apartments, "taxes, service, buffet breakfast, and welcoming smiles."

FACILITIES AND SERVICES: Air-conditioning in 20 rooms, direct-dial phone, elevator, hair dryer available, office safe, TV, airport transfer service on request

NEAREST TOURIST ATTRACTIONS: Trastevere

TELEPHONE
06 581 4713

FAX
06 588 1016

INTERNET
www.hoteltrastevere.com

CREDIT CARDS
AE, DC, MC, V

RATES
Single 80€, double 105€, triple 130€, quad 154€, apartments (2 people) from 150€; lower rates, subject to availability, for stays over 5 days

BREAKFAST
Buffet breakfast included

ENGLISH
Yes

LOCANDA CARMEL ★ (¢, 87)
Via Goffredo Mameli, 11
10 rooms, 8 with shower or bath and toilet

The Locanda Carmel bills itself as a kosher board-inghouse near the main synagogue in Trastevere. While Trastevere is a great place to visit, not everyone wants to actually stay here. If you do and are in need of a cheap sleep, Locanda Carmel is on a tree-lined street about a five- or ten-minute walk from "action central."

David Bahbout took over the ten-room pensione from his mother, who had it for twenty years and strictly adhered to a philosophy of deferred maintenance. Fortunately, some necessary improvements have been made, including new doors on the rooms, some enclosed showers, and fresh paint here and there. Rooms 5, 6 (the only single), 10, and 11 open onto the hotel terrace. Several rooms reserved for students on long-term stays include kosher-only kitchen privileges. The pièce de résistance will one day be the glassed-in sunroom and vine-covered summer terrace, which is a welcoming place to curl up and write postcards to friends back home or to meet other guests, but first Signor Bahbout will need to keep his long-running commitment to *someday* replacing the seriously delapidated furniture that mars this special part of his hotel. Breakfast is included in the

TELEPHONE
06 580 9921

FAX
06 581 8853

INTERNET
www.hotelcarmel.it

CREDIT CARDS
AE, MC, V

RATES
Single 80€, double 90–100€, triple 130€, quad 160€; lower long-term and off-season rates

BREAKFAST
Continental breakfast at bar next door included Mon–Sat

ENGLISH
Yes

deal, and it's served from Monday to Saturday with the locals in the bar next door.

NOTE: To reach Locanda Carmel, take Bus 75 or H from Termini Station, or if you are already in Trastevere, catch Tram 3 or 8.

FACILITIES AND SERVICES: Air-conditioning, direct-dial phone, no elevator, hair dryer, minibar, office safe, TV, kosher kitchen privileges for long-term student rooms

NEAREST TOURIST ATTRACTIONS: Trastevere

VILLA DELLA FONTE (83)
Villa della Fonte d'Olio, 8

TELEPHONE
06 580 3797
FAX
06 580 3796
INTERNET
www.villafonte.com
CREDIT CARDS
AE, DC, MC, V
RATES
Single 110€, double 155€, extra bed 30€; lower off-season rates
BREAKFAST
Continental breakfast included
ENGLISH
Yes

5 rooms, all with showers and toilets

The mother/daughter team of Marisa and Simona run this jewel box–size hotel in the center of Trastevere. The heart of the appealing hotel is the high-walled terrace flooded in the spring and summer with geraniums, azaleas, and fragrant gardenias and roses. Tables with umbrellas and chairs are set out for al fresco breakfasts or quiet afternoon drinks. All five spotless rooms are color coordinated in easy-care fabrics and plain furnishings. White-walled No. 1, a king or twin-bedded room, has a tile floor, luggage and desk space, and an enclosed corner shower in the bathroom. I also like No. 2, with walnut built-ins, the same nice bathroom, and a side view of the neighborhood. Hanging throughout the hotel is an interesting collection of 1950-vintage black-and-white photos of people and places in Trastevere. In the glass case on the main floor is a photo of Simona and her father with the priest who blessed their hotel.

FACILITIES AND SERVICES: Air-conditioning, direct-dial phone, no elevator (2 floors), hair dryer, minibar, no safe, satellite TV, nonsmoking hotel

NEAREST TOURIST ATTRACTIONS: Trastevere

Trevi Fountain

The movie *Three Coins in the Fountain* and the Frank Sinatra song by the same name ensured that no traveler to Rome would leave without tossing a coin into the Trevi Fountain, the Eternal City's largest and most famous fountain. It is clear that every tourist comes here, and when you visit, you will probably think every one of them is standing in front of you trying to toss a coin. The massive white marble Rococo fountain, designed by Nicolò Salvi for Pope Clement XII, is magnificent. Don't miss it.

HOTELS

DAPHNE INN (106)
Via degli Avignonesi, 20 & Via San Basilio, 55

14 rooms, 12 with shower and toilet

The minimalist fourteen rooms in the Daphne Inn are spread out over two buildings located about halfway between Piazza di Spagna and the Trevi Fountain. The hotel is a perfect example of the new trend in small guest houses now popping up throughout major Italian cities. Their appeal lies in many different areas: some have oh-so-in-vogue decor; others are quaintly antique. In the case of the Daphne Inn, no one is checking into any of the rooms for the views because they don't have them. What the Daphne Inn does offer are three types of sleek rooms and hand-holding customer care by a young, enthusiastic staff.

The type and cost of the room depends on its plumbing: shared, private but outside the room, or private inside the room. The rooms have tile or wood floors, a glass-door wardrobe, woven chair seating, American-made mattresses, fluffy comforters, and a free cell phone. Internet access is available in the lobby. The owners are passionate about the well-being of their guests, even to the point of suggesting they call the hotel when they are hungry, and the hotel will suggest restaurants in whatever neighborhood guests happen to be in. Of course, this only happens with guests who did not pack a copy of *Great Eats Italy*. In addition to restaurant advice, the staff is well-versed in Rome's tourist sites, and will help create the best itinerary to suit the needs of each guest.

FACILITIES AND SERVICES: Air-conditioning, free cell-phone, elevator in one building (38 steps in the other), hair dryer, in-room safe, Internet access in lobby, nonsmoking hotel

NEAREST TOURIST ATTRACTIONS: 15- to 20-minute walk to Trevi Fountain, Piazza di Spagna, and lower end of Villa Borghese

TELEPHONE
06 4782 3529
FAX
06 2332 40967
INTERNET
www.daphne-rome.com
CREDIT CARDS
AE, DC, MC, V
RATES
Single 100–120€, double 120–176€, triple 145–220€, quad 180–264€; lower off- and mid-season rates
BREAKFAST
Continental breakfast included
ENGLISH
Yes

FONTANA HOTEL ★★★ ($, 53)
Piazza di Trevi, 96

25 rooms, all with shower or bath and toilet

TELEPHONE
06 678 6113, 06 679 1056
FAX
06 679 0024
INTERNET
www.hotelfontana-trevi.com
CREDIT CARDS
AE, DC, MC, V
RATES
Single 190–235€, double
255–275€, triple 340€; lower
off-season rates
BREAKFAST
Buffet breakfast included
ENGLISH
Yes

If you want to toss your three coins into the Trevi Fountain from the comfort of your own room, check into the top floor at the Fontana. Elena Daneo, the stylish owner, has transformed the rooms in this fourteenth-century former monastery into imaginative and unusual choices that will have definite appeal for those who don't want to forget for a minute that they are in Rome. For those who demand quiet in uniformly predictable surroundings, however, this hotel may not be the best choice.

There wasn't much Sra. Daneo could do about the size of the rooms, but she has certainly created a charming atmosphere in each one. No two rooms match (aside from their black enamel doors), and therein lies their character. Even though it is on the back, people clamor for No. 303—and no wonder. Its two double beds with white covers can sleep up to four, and it has heavy wood beams, bleached pine floors, a mirrored armoire, and a step-down bathroom with a skylight. I think you will like the sunny and romantic No. 302, which has the same great bathroom, a king-size bed, and a wall of windows looking at a tiled roof so close you could almost reach out and touch it. The BBC has used Room 105, facing the Trevi Fountain, as the setting for several shows . . . need I say more? Number 208, a small room done in pale orange sorbet, has a wonderful armoire and full view of the fountain. From both Nos. 101, a triple, and 109, a twin, you won't see the famous fountain in action, but you will definitely hear it, and pay the same price as the guests in the rooms facing it.

The rooftop breakfast and sitting room with a grand piano and terrace has universal appeal, especially if you get there early enough in the morning to nab a windowside table overlooking the fountain. If you select this hotel, bear in mind that it can be very noisy—not only does the fountain spout day and night, but every tourist in Rome has to come and toss a coin into the magical waters to ensure their return to the Eternal City. To be sure her guests will return, Sra. Daneo gives them all a special coin to toss in as well.

FACILITIES AND SERVICES: Air-conditioning in the back rooms, fans in the other rooms, direct-dial phone, elevator, hair dryer, laundry service, porter, room service for drinks, office safe, satellite TV

NEAREST TOURIST ATTRACTIONS: Trevi Fountain, Quirinale Palace

HOTEL TREVI ★★★ ($, 54)
Vicolo del Babuccio, 20/21
29 rooms, all with shower and toilet

The value is high, and so is the recommendation, at this Big Splurge choice in the heart of Rome, close to the Trevi Fountain. If you like to walk, you can find something interesting or a photo opportunity in almost any direction. Restaurants and shops are close, as are taxis and buses for farther destinations.

The user-friendly rooms have the works: space, mirrors, in-room safes, minibars, air-conditioning, good bathrooms, showers with doors, light, and color-coordinated decor. A few have balconies; others have beamed ceilings. Room 109 is a romantic double in soft rose with burgundy carpets and a terrace. The white-tile bathroom is accented with green and has shelf space and big towels. The top-floor garden offers sketchbook views of Rome. In summer, the buffet breakfast is served here, while in cooler months, it's served in an underground grotto with stone ceilings. The service is always polite, and year-round discounts are extended to *Great Sleeps Italy* readers—two more good reasons to select this exceptionally nice hotel.

FACILITIES AND SERVICES: Air-conditioning, direct-dial phone, elevator (but not to roof garden), hair dryer, laundry service, minibar, in-room safe, satellite TV

NEAREST TOURIST ATTRACTIONS: Trevi Fountain, Quirinale Palace

TELEPHONE
06 678 9563, 06 678 5894, 06 699 41406
FAX
06 699 41407
INTERNET
www.gruppotrevi.it
CREDIT CARDS
AE, DC, MC, V
RATES
Single 155€, double 216€, triple 268€, quad 295€; discounts for *Great Sleeps Italy* readers, subject to season and availability
BREAKFAST
Buffet breakfast included
ENGLISH
Yes

RESIDENCE BARBERINI ★★★★ ($, 107)
Via delle Quattro Fontane, 171/172
11 suites and 1 penthouse, all with shower, bath, and toilet

There is just one word to describe the Residence Barberini: stunning.

The twelve-suite residence hotel is located in a completely restored three-hundred-year-old building in front of the Barberini Palace, which is between Piazza di Spagna and Via Veneto. Contemporary artwork is part of the hotel's overall design, especially in the public areas, which serve as de facto galleries for owner Raffaella Frascarelli and her husband's remarkable twenty-year collection of cutting-edge modern art. This type of art, which can sometimes appear obscure and confusing, often inspires debate. Here it attracts an enlightened clientele who appreciate viewing and discussing both the art and the artists. The couple is very involved with the artists, many of whom they have discovered, and are willing to take time to explain the

TELEPHONE
06 420 3341
FAX
06 4203 3417
INTERNET
www.residencebarberini.com
CREDIT CARDS
AE, DC, MC, V
RATES
Suite (1–4 people) 319–465€; penthouse (1–2 people) 340–555€; special rates for weekly or longer stays
BREAKFAST
No breakfast is served
ENGLISH
Yes

works. For instance, in the reception is "The Day After," in which a statue of Yoda wears a papal hat (depicting wisdom) and holds a set of scales (signifying equality and justice). An enormous photo by American photographer Spencer Tunic shows piles of naked people fanned out on the Piazza Navona. To get his models, Tunic places ads in newspapers for people to show up at dawn, undress, pose, and receive a copy of the finished photo as their payment.

The owners are equally passionate about providing every possible comfort to their guests, and this is reflected in the simple yet elegant suites and the breathtaking penthouse, with its hundred meters of private terrace. In this entirely nonsmoking residence, each suite has a separate bedroom with excellent closet space, living room, beautiful marble bathroom, and fully equipped kitchen. Bang & Olufsen flat-screen satellite televisions with direct Internet access, telephone, fax, duck-down duvets, and pieces of contemporary art are standard amenities. The romantic, all-white penthouse is a very special experience. Not only does it have tented and open candlelit terraces with panoramic views of St. Peter's Cathedral and all of Rome, but there's a wall of windows from the bedroom where guests can lie in bed and enjoy much of the same view. A stay at the Residence Barberini will exceed Sra. Frascarelli's promise: "We want our guests to feel at home and enjoy their stay in luxurious comfort, whether travelling for business or pleasure."

FACILITIES AND SERVICES: Air-conditioning, babysitter, 24-hour business center, direct-dial phone, elevator, hair dryer, fax and data port lines, laptop with ADSL connection available on loan, fully equipped kitchen, laundry service, twice-daily maid service, private car service and car rental, flat-screen satellite TV, nonsmoking hotel

NEAREST TOURIST ATTRACTIONS: Piazza di Spagna, Via Veneto, Trevi Fountain

The Vatican

No visitor to Rome can leave without a pilgrimage to the most holy place in Christendom, the Vatican and Vatican City. The tiny city-state covers about 108 acres, which is the size of most golf courses, but it is full of glorious treasures: the Vatican Museums and Gardens, the Sistine Chapel, and St. Peter's Basilica, all of which deserve as much time as you can afford to give them. If you are mailing things, the Vatican post office sells its own stamps and has faster service than the Rome post offices.

HOTELS

Casa Valdese ★★ (¢)	**203**
Hotel Alimandi ★★★	**204**
Hotel Bramante ★★★	**205**
Hotel San Pietrino ★★ (¢)	**206**
Hotel Sant' Anna ★★★	**206**
Marta Guesthouse ★ (¢)	**207**
Pension Paradise ★★ (¢)	**208**

OTHER OPTIONS

Holy Hotels

Casa Bonus Pastor	**226**
Suore Dorotee	**229**

Hostels

Colors Hostel	**230**

(¢) indicates a Cheap Sleep

CASA VALDESE ★★ (¢, 3)
Via Alessandro Farnese, 18

35 rooms, all with shower and toilet

Whether you are traveling alone, with your significant other, or as a family, one of the best two-star Great Sleeping values in Rome is the Casa Valdese. Located in Prati, one of Rome's more exclusive neighborhoods, the hotel gives guests the advantage of being about a thirty-minute walk from St. Peter's Square on this side of the Tiber River, or crossing one of the bridges and being at the Spanish Steps in the same length of time. For trips farther afield, take Buses 81 or 78 or head for the Lepanto metro station, where in ten minutes you can get to Termini Station and the shuttle to Fiumicino Airport.

The hotel is part of a group run by a Christian Protestant organization that has similar properties throughout Italy

TELEPHONE
06 321 8222, 06 321 5362
FAX
06 321 1843
EMAIL
casavaldese@tiscalinet.it
INTERNET
www.valdese.roma.vch.de
CREDIT CARDS
AE, MC, V
RATES
Single 83€, double 110€, triple 150€, quad 180€; children under 3 stay free, children 4 to 10 get a 50% discount; lower and group rates for stays of 3 nights or more; set-price 3-course dinner 20€

BREAKFAST
Buffet breakfast included
ENGLISH
Yes

(in Florence, see Istituto Gould, page 120, and in Venice, see Foresteria Valdese, page 328). The Casa Valdese, a former hostel, opened in 1989 after a complete refurbishing and upgrading. The color-coordinated rooms are simple yet ample, all with air-conditioning, wintertime duvets, good showers, and decent towels; three have private terraces. Plus, there are two wonderful rooftop gardens and a restaurant that serves a fixed-priced dinner. The daily menu is posted at the reception desk, where you can reserve your table. Smoking is only permitted in the television room or on the terrace.

FACILITIES AND SERVICES: Air-conditioning, bar, direct-dial phone, elevator, hair dryer available, Internet in lobby, TV, all rooms nonsmoking

NEAREST TOURIST ATTRACTIONS: Castel Sant'Angelo, Vatican, Spanish Steps, and Piazza Navona within a 20- to 30-minute walk

HOTEL ALIMANDI ★★★ (16)
Via Tunisi, 8

TELEPHONE
06 397 239 48, 06 397 239 41
FAX
06 397 23 943
EMAIL
alimandi@tin.it
INTERNET
www.alimandi.org
CREDIT CARDS
AE, DC, MC, V
RATES
Single 95–130€, double 155€, triple 185€, quad 195€; lower off-season rates
BREAKFAST
Buffet breakfast included
ENGLISH
Yes

35 rooms, all with shower or bath and toilet

The Alimandi continues to improve, and as a result is better than ever. To say it has come a long way from its humble beginnings is a vast understatement! It all began in 1963, when Sra. Alimandi opened three rooms on the first floor to guests. Her daughter, Grazia, and sons, Paolo, Enrico, and Luigi, now own not only the thirty-five room hotel but the entire building. This means that—provided they can cut through the Roman red tape that unfurls the minute a building change is suggested—they are free to do what they want to improve their hotel and not have to heel to the demands of a euro-pinching owner.

Guests are welcomed into an attractive reception area that has a bas-relief done by the brothers' nephew (who is also responsible for the thirty-five other bas-reliefs in the hotel). Also noteworthy is the Spanish-style bar that has windows made of colored glass, a bust of Sra. Alimandi, and a fanciful baby grand player piano. There is also a TV and game room displaying a picture of the three brothers taken in Greece in 1968 when they drove from Rome to Istanbul. On the fourth floor is an inviting garden, and on the roof, depending on the weather, a shaded or heated terrace with a view to the Vatican, its gardens, and the Sistine Chapel. Finally, downstairs is a full gym with a glass floor showing holy water fron the Vatican bubbling over original stones.

Indeed, the public parts of the hotel are far grander than the rooms. Of course they have three-star comforts and come with a built-in wardrobe, a desk and chair, some luggage space, and a tile floor. The showers have curtains, a simple feature missing in all too many Italian hotels. One room is suitable for handicapped visitors, and to further assist those with disabilities, there is a wheelchair lift by the front entrance. Most of the rooms are designated nonsmoking.

The brothers are committed to offering the best service possible to their guests. To make sure of this, they are on the job daily, checking up on the maids, answering guests' questions, and providing helpful advice. There is a minivan available to provide free airport transfers, which must be booked when reserving. Never content to rest on their laurels, they are opening Alimandi Hotel al Vaticano, a four-star residence hotel across the street, which will have fully equipped kitchens in every unit and secure garage parking.

FACILITIES AND SERVICES: Air-conditioning, bar, direct-dial phone, 2 elevators (one glass-enclosed), full gym, hair dryer, Internet access in rooms, magnifying mirror, in-room safe, satellite TV, one handicapped-accessible room, parking on request, coin-operated self-service laundry, free Fiumicino airport transfers

NEAREST TOURIST ATTRACTIONS: Vatican, Vatican Museums

HOTEL BRAMANTE ★★★ (44)
Vicolo delle Palline, 24/25
16 rooms, all with shower or bath and toilet

The Hotel Bramante was the home of noted architect Domenico Fontana in the sixteenth century and is now a charming family-owned hotel in the Borgo Pio neighborhood less than a ten-minute stroll from the Vatican. The sixteen rooms are attractively furnished with coordinating colors and fabrics in Roman red and soft gray-green. Except for No. 20, the largest rooms are on the second floor. Number 22, a double that can stretch to a quad, is one of the biggest rooms, with a sloping beamed ceiling, two windows, and a bathroom with a tub and shower and two more windows. I also like No. 26, an executive double with a sofa and the same large bathroom. Singles will be very comfortable in No. 11, a quiet, interior gold-and-green room that features a hand-painted Florentine chest. Breakfast is served in a stone-floor dining room with oak gate-leg tables and leather chairs. A lovely silver tea set

TELEPHONE
06 6880 6426, 06 687 9881

FAX
06 6813 3330

EMAIL
hotelbramante@libero.it

INTERNET
www.hotelbramante.com

CREDIT CARDS
AE, DC, MC, V

RATES
Single 140€, double 195€, triple 220€, quad 240€; lower off-season rates

BREAKFAST
Buffet breakfast included

ENGLISH
Yes

and triple candleholders add elegant touches. There is also a small roof garden with tables and chairs. Guest satisfaction is a top priority, beginning with the head housekeeper who has been here for twenty years to the friendly desk staff and the husband-and-wife team who are the owners.

FACILITIES AND SERVICES: Air-conditioning, direct-dial phone, no elevator (2 floors), hair dryer, Internet access in lobby, laundry service, minibar, in-room safe, satellite TV, tea and coffeemakers

NEAREST TOURIST ATTRACTIONS: Vatican, Vatican Museums

HOTEL SAN PIETRINO ★★ (¢, 1)
Via Giovanni Bettolo, 43
12 rooms, 8 with shower and toilet

TELEPHONE
06 370 0132
FAX
06 370 1809
INTERNET
www.sanpietrino.it
CREDIT CARDS
AE, DC, MC, V
RATES
Single 40–55€, double 75–103€, triple 95–110€, quad 115–160€; lower off-season rates; also in low season, 10% discount for *Great Sleeps Italy* readers
BREAKFAST
Not served
ENGLISH
Yes

If you are a fan of the Hotel Panda (see page 177), you will also like its newest sister location near the Vatican. Opened in 2003 after extensive refurbishing, it is a Great Sleep budget entry that is loaded with extras seldom found in this price range: air-conditioning in rooms with private facilities, Internet access in the room, satellite TV, bicycles for rent, and airport transfers. The plain, spotless rooms have cozy duvets and terra-cotta floors, but not much in the way of seating or table space. The tiled baths have heated towel racks, a shelf, and good lighting. Your room cost is reduced because breakfast is not served. That is not only a money-saver for you but provides you a chance to mingle with the neighborhood regulars over a foamy latte or cappuccino at the corner bar.

NOTE: Also under the same family's ownership is the Hotel Panda near Piazza di Spagna (page 177) and Pension Paradise (page 208).

FACILITIES AND SERVICES: Air-conditioning in rooms with en suite facilities, direct-dial phone, elevator, fans, hair dryer available, in-room Internet access, office safe, satellite TV, bicycles for rent, airport transfers on request

NEAREST TOURIST ATTRACTIONS: Vatican, Vatican Museums

HOTEL SANT' ANNA ★★★ (43)
Borgo Pio, 133
20 rooms, all with shower or bath and toilet

TELEPHONE
06 6880 1602
FAX
06 6830 8717
EMAIL
santanna@travel.it

The Hotel Sant' Anna scores high for location, only a few blocks from St. Peter's, and remains one of the best choices in this area. No matter where you look, there is something of interest: perhaps a stained-glass window echoing the vibrant colors of a basket of seasonal flowers sitting nearby, an exposed section of an ancient stone wall uncovered during remodeling, or a garden with an old marble fountain and two blossoming citrus trees. The hard-working owner has a definite maintenance plan, thus keeping the hotel in tip-top condition at all times. The rooms have either wallpaper or hand-painted murals depicting various Roman scenes. All are nonsmoking. Those on the top floors have their own private terraces. On the third floor, the hand-detailed rooms have slanting roofs and built-in furniture, which allows for more living space. Many of them have frescoes, cross beams, or a small sitting area. In all, the use of mirrors is effective in adding not only light but a feeling of space. The lovely marble baths continue to pamper guests with marble showers, magnifying mirrors, terry towels, slippers, and up-to-date fixtures. The frescoed lobby with a small sitting room leading to a garden and the two basement breakfast rooms, where the buffet is served, are always delightful places to begin your Roman day.

FACILITIES AND SERVICES: Air-conditioning, 2 direct-dial phones, elevator, hair dryer, laundry service, magnifying mirrors, minibar, in-room safe, satellite TV, parking (24€ per day), 2 handicapped-accessible rooms, all rooms nonsmoking

NEAREST TOURIST ATTRACTIONS: Vatican, Vatican Museums

INTERNET
www.hotelsantanna.com
CREDIT CARDS
AE, DC, MC, V
RATES
Single 145€, double 195€, extra bed 20€; lower off-season rates
BREAKFAST
Buffet breakfast included
ENGLISH
Yes

MARTA GUESTHOUSE ★ (¢, 23)
Via Tacito, 41
14 roooms, all with shower or bath and toilet

Marta Guesthouse offers cozy rooms done up in the current, popular decorating trend . . . shabby-chic. The fourteen rooms are individually furnished in flea market finds that have been dusted, polished, and positioned for best effect. In one room, a blue washstand is the focal point; in several others antique doors serve as headboards. On the third floor, I like No. 1, a triple with a marble-top desk and a petit point chair. In No. 6, guests sleep in a wrought-iron bed and hide their valuables in a safe tucked behind a picture. For a quiet twin, request No. 5 with brass beds and sheer curtains with pockets filled with dried wild flowers. From the front door, guests are close to Piazza Cavour and about a twenty-minute walk from the Vatican. Breakfast is not served, but coffee and tea are.

TELEPHONE
06 324 0428, 06 6889 2992
FAX
06 6821 7574
EMAIL
martaguesthouse@iol.it
INTERNET
www.martaguesthouse.com
CREDIT CARDS
AE, DC, MC, V
RATES
Single 45€, double 98€, triple 120€; lower off-season rates
BREAKFAST
Not served
ENGLISH
Depends on receptionist

FACILITIES AND SERVICES: Air-conditioning in some rooms, elevator, fans, hair dryer, communal minibar, in-room safe, satellite TV, airport transfers (1–4 people, 45€)

NEAREST TOURIST ATTRACTIONS: Vatican, Vatian Museums

PENSION PARADISE ★★ (¢, 2)
Viale Giulio Cesare, 47 (third floor, stair A)
10 rooms, 8 with shower and toilet

The clean, neat, frill-free rooms at Pension Paradise have identical green quilt bedspreads, built-in headboards, one chair, noise in those facing front, and televisions firmly anchored to the ceiling. Bunk beds fold down in some to accommodate four cheap sleepers. The white-tile bathrooms are above average because they have enclosed showers and heated towel racks. The pension is part of the recommended family-owned trio that includes Hotel Panda (see page 177) and Hotel San Pietrino (see page 206).

FACILITIES AND SERVICES: Elevator, fans, communal minibar, office safe, satellite television

NEAREST TOURIST ATTRACTIONS: Vatican, Vatican Museums

TELEPHONE
06 3600 4331

FAX
06 3609 2563

INTERNET
pensionparadise.com

CREDIT CARDS
AE, DC, MC, V

RATES
Single 40–50€, double 60–85€, triple 100–110€, quad 125–135€; lower off-season rates

BREAKFAST
Not served

ENGLISH
Yes

Via Veneto and Villa Borghese

What was once the famed center of *la dolce vita,* Via Veneto is now a wide boulevard where you will find the American Embassy, big hotels, expensive restaurants and impersonal cafés patronized by the cell-phone glitterati, who hide behind dark glasses day and night. The area around Via Veneto is where many offices, stores, ministries, banks, and airlines have offices.

The Villa Borghese is Rome's premier park with long avenues of trees, jogging trails, three important art museums, an amazing children's hands-on museum, a lake with rowboats for hire, and a zoo.

HOTELS

OTHER OPTIONS
Residence Hotels

($) indicates a Big Splurge; (¢) indicates a Cheap Sleep

THE BAILEY'S HOTEL ★★★★ ($, 97)
Via Flavia, 39
29 rooms, all with shower, bath, and toilet

The twenty-nine deluxe rooms in Bailey's Hotel are designed for the business guest who needs all the electronic bells and whistles to stay connected to his or her sphere on a twenty-four-hour a day basis. This means that you can check in, have a porter bring up your bags, take a relaxing bath, don the fluffy terry robe provided, order room service, send a fax, and hook up to high-speed Internet, on either your laptop or one on loan from the hotel. Having a problem with your computer? Not to worry—it can be solved by the in-house tech. If you want some company, but don't feel like going far, drop into the comfortable Art Deco wine bar downstairs, which stocks over three hundred wines and is also open to the public. At the end of the day, enjoy a piece of fresh fruit from the welcome basket, flip on the television, and select a movie from the pay-per-view selections. The color-coordinated, carpeted rooms are as impressive as the hotel amenities: king or twin beds, well-lit desks with a comfortable chair, and mirrored, marble bathrooms.

FACILITIES AND SERVICES: Air-conditioning, bar, direct-dial phone, elevator, in-room fax, hair dryer, in-room and lobby Internet access, laptops for guests, laundry service, minibar, room service for drinks and meals, in-room safe, satellite TV and pay-per-view movies, robes, porter

NEAREST TOURIST ATTRACTIONS: Via Veneto, Villa Borghese, 20 minutes to Piazza di Spagna and Trevi Fountain

TELEPHONE
06 4202 0486
FAX
06 4202 0170
INTERNET
www.hotelbailey.com
CREDIT CARDS
AE, DV, MC, V
RATES
Single 181€, double 242–284€, triple 352€, family room 517€; lower off-season rates; special weekend rates online
BREAKFAST
Buffet breakfast included
ENGLISH
Yes

HOTEL ALEXANDRA ★★★ ($, 96)
Via Vittorio Veneto, 18
60 rooms, all with shower or bath and toilet

The Alexandra has managed to retain some style while yielding to the demand for color television, air-conditioned rooms, and minibars. It is on the busy Via Veneto, just down from the American Embassy. Ear-shattering automobile and motor-scooter traffic and partyers in search of the lost *la dolce vita* surge along this famous street twenty-four hours a day. If undisturbed sleep is a priority, request a room

TELEPHONE
06 488 1943/4/5
FAX
06 487 1804
INTERNET
www.hotelalexandraroma.com
CREDIT CARDS
AE, DC, MC, V

RATES
Single 180–205€, double
230–260€, suites 300–350€,
penthouse 800€; lower
off-season and promotional rates
BREAKFAST
Buffet breakfast included
ENGLISH
Yes

away from the constant noise, or plan to keep the windows closed and the air-conditioning running at all times.

To permanently impress the love of your life, request the penthouse, which feels more like an elegant home than a hotel suite. It has a fabulous view terrace that is large enough to have four orange trees and multiple bird of paradise plants in addition to outdoor furniture. Inside there is a spacious sitting room, a dining area with architectural prints on three walls, a gray-green bedroom furnished in antiques, and a marble bath with a Jacuzzi.

The rest of the hotel rooms have enough space for guests to spread out and stay a while. The six suites, some with Liberty-style furnishings, have nice bathrooms and separate sitting areas. A good choice for one of these is Suite 444, with wainscoting detailing the walls. The brass bed is down two steps in a space large enough to accommodate a desk, armchair, triple-mirrored armoire, and a three-drawer dresser. Room 160 is a deluxe Art Deco–style double with a fabulous Parisian wardrobe with secret side panels. In the marble bathroom, there is a Jacuzzi. Room 219, a standard double on the front of the hotel, is in feminine pinks and perfect for a single traveler. There is an armoire for your clothes and a bathroom with a shower, but remember, noise will prevail unless you keep your window shut tight. Room 220 is the same story. Number 442 is also a single but with the advantage of a higher location. I like the view of the tree and the original inlaid furniture. The bathroom has one mirrored wall, a corner sink, and a shower.

A glass-enclosed garden dining room on Via Veneto is an interesting place to start the day or to enjoy an afternoon drink and watch the passing parade.

FACILITIES AND SERVICES: Air-conditioning, bar, direct-dial phone, elevator, hair dryer, minibar, parking by arrangement (26–36€ per day, depending on size of car), in-room safe, satellite TV, 10 nonsmoking rooms

NEAREST TOURIST ATTRACTIONS: Via Veneto, Villa Borghese, 10- to 15-minute walk to Piazza di Spagna and fine shopping

HOTEL ERCOLI ★★ (¢, 93)
Via Collina, 48

TELEPHONE
06 474 5454
FAX
06 474 4063
INTERNET
www.hotelercoli.com

14 rooms, all with shower and toilet

For Great Sleepers in search of the good life for less, the Hotel Ercoli offers fourteen snappy bedchambers. The color scheme is yellow and blue; the fabric matches on the curtains, headboards, and beds; the mattresses are orthopedic; and the all-new baths have stall showers, a small sink, a shelf, plus a hook. Three or four cheap sleepers can check into viewless No. 11, but one or two of you should have backs strong enough to withstand sleeping on a foldout chair/bed. Better sleeping can be had in No. 7, a small two-room suite with a proper double bed in one room and a single in the other. Breakfast is served in a formal room with round tables and white tablecloths.

FACILITIES AND SERVICES: Air-conditioning, direct-dial phone, elevator, hair dryer, office safe, TV

NEAREST TOURIST ATTRACTIONS: Via Veneto, Villa Borghese

CREDIT CARDS
MC, V

RATES
Single 80€, double 105€, triple 140€, quad 155€; lower off-season rates

BREAKFAST
Continental breakfast included

ENGLISH
Yes

HOTEL RANIERI ★★★ (98)
Via Venti Settembre, 43

50 rooms, all with shower or bath and toilet

I like the Ranieri, located on the second through the fifth floors of a building facing the Ministry of Defense, because it consistently offers exceptional value for money and delivers a high standard of personalized service to its contented guests. It is the type of place that, once found, eliminates the need to shop for any other hotel in Rome.

Luana, the hospitable Italian-Australian manager, provides an enthusiastic and warm welcome from the moment you get off the elevator, and she is loaded with tips and suggestions on what to see and do, places to shop, and good local restaurants (see *Great Eats Italy*). Carrying the welcome further are the two bellmen, brothers Carlo and Silverio, who have been with the hotel for over a quarter of a century. They are eager to help with luggage, mix a drink, or do whatever you need to smooth out your visit to Rome. Housekeeping is constantly on its toes to ensure that all is running well, and that the spotless and well-groomed rooms never fall below the hotel's high standards of cleanliness and maintenance.

The owner of this outstanding three-star hotel, Mr. Ranieri, must lie awake nights thinking of ways to improve his up-to-the-minute quarters. Absolutely no detail escapes his notice, and he is not afraid to spend lavishly to provide his guests with every amenity possible. To prove this, he has added a new floor with seven beautiful rooms, all with light wood built-ins, excellent reading lights, customized closets, marble bathrooms, and, of course, all the other amenities and features found in the other rooms. Slippers are placed next to the beds, which have fine orthopedic mattresses to ensure a good night's rest. Double-glazed

TELEPHONE
06 4201 4531

FAX
06 4201 4543

INTERNET
www.hotelranieri.com

CREDIT CARDS
AE, DC, MC, V

RATES
Single 145€, double 185€, triple 218€; lower off-season and weekend rates (subject to availability)

BREAKFAST
Continental breakfast included

ENGLISH
Yes

windows, acoustic ceilings, and hall insulation buffer traffic and other noises, and hall air-conditioning keeps you cool and refreshed during the sizzling summers. The large-screen television sets are the best brand money can buy. Guests arriving with PCs will be able to hook up directly to the Internet through a separate international plug (which means you can leave the adapter at home). If you didn't bring a computer, there is free Internet access in the lobby. Rooms have abundant closet space, a private safe, and trouser presses. The polished granite bathrooms are equal matches for the rooms and provide plenty of shelf space for toiletries. They even have the latest word in Swedish bidets.

There is more. If you do not want to venture out for lunch or dinner, tell the desk ahead of time and they will reserve you a place in the dining room for a delicious, freshly prepared three- to four-course meal. In addition, hot snacks are always available in the cheerful bar, or they can be brought to your room if you prefer.

Mr. Ranieri told me he feels he has to offer more for his guests because his hotel is on the second floor. I can't imagine what he is going to do for encores next time around, but I know he will think of something.

NOTE: If your travels will take you to Tuscany outside Florence, consider staying at the magnificent Villa di Piazzano (see page 142), which is owned by Sr. Ranieri's niece and her family.

FACILITIES AND SERVICES: Air-conditioning, bar, direct-dial phone, elevator, hair dryer, laundry service, minibar, international PC plugs and data ports, Internet access in lobby, radio, in-room safe, satellite TV, trouser press, room service for light snacks, dining room for lunch or dinner

NEAREST TOURIST ATTRACTIONS: Via Veneto, Villa Borghese, opera, Termini Station

LA RESIDENZA ★★★★ (95)
Via Emilia, 22/24
29 rooms, all with shower or bath and toilet

La Residenza is a polished, relaxed, and quiet converted villa in the high-rent district near Via Veneto and the Villa Borghese. Its intimate atmosphere combines the amenities of a luxury hotel with the comforts of a private home, making this an agreeable stopover in the Eternal City.

The public rooms are comfortably outfitted with Oriental carpets, oil paintings, and overstuffed chairs and sofas. The breakfast room is enormous, with a large center buffet

TELEPHONE
06 488 0789

FAX
06 485 721

EMAIL
la.residenza@
thegiannettihotelsgroup.com

INTERNET
www.thegiannettihotelsgroup
.com

and a grill where two chefs are busy cooking whatever you want to eat, from pancakes with maple syrup to bacon and eggs or a veggie pizza. When you return from a day of sightseeing and are too tired to partake of *la dolce vita* on the nearby Via Veneto, then you can cocoon in your room and watch an in-house film. However, if you want to paint the town red, plenty of nocturnal pleasures and nightclubs await.

Most of the rooms feature comfort, space, and good light, but some need to have a fabric facelift. Many have balconies or covered terraces, a real bonus when the temperature hits three digits. The suites have the added advantage of a separate sitting room. The bathrooms provide phones and terry robes. The only ones to avoid are the gloomy singles with opaque windows.

FACILITIES AND SERVICES: Air-conditioning, bar, 2 direct-dial phones, hair dryer, elevator, laundry service, parking for 4 cars (7€ per day) porter, in-room safe, satellite TV, in-house movies

NEAREST TOURIST ATTRACTIONS: Via Veneto, Villa Borghese, 15- to 20-minute walk to Piazza di Spagna and great shopping

CREDIT CARDS
MC, V
RATES
Single 93€, double 195€, junior suite 223€, extra bed 47€, baby cot 20€; lower off-season, weekend, and honeymoon rates
BREAKFAST
Large American-style cooked breakfast included
ENGLISH
Yes

MARCELLA ROYAL HOTEL ★★★★ ($, 94)
Via Flavia, 106

85 rooms, all with shower or bath and toilet

Guests enter the Marcella Royal through a contemporary Roman red lobby with piano bar to one side and a lounge with cushy sofas and armchairs on the other. Breakfast is served either on a dazzling glass-enclosed seventh-floor terrace with picture-postcard views of Rome, or at shaded tables on the wraparound enclosed terrace filled with attractive plantings.

The entire look of the hotel is well coordinated, with smart touches such as Napoleonic draped beds, recessed lighting, and fabric-covered walls. Room 626 is a super top-floor twin with a floral theme carried out on the headboards, the bedspreads, and along an archway above. Big windows open onto a panoramic view of Rome. You have the same view in No. 618, in addition to a newer-style bathroom. Number 428 is a red-walled junior suite with a large executive desk, two armchairs, and a Jacuzzi in the bathroom. The immediate neighborhood is interesting for its market stalls, which sell everything from meat, cheese, fruits, and vegetables to bread and household items. Good restaurants (see *Great Eats Italy*) are within easy reach. If you need to go to the American Embassy, it is a short

TELEPHONE
06 4201 4591
FAX
06 481 5832
INTERNET
www.marcellaroyalhotel.com
CREDIT CARDS
AE, DC, MC, V
RATES
Single 135€, double 230€, junior suite 350€; lower off-season rates
BREAKFAST
Buffet breakfast included
ENGLISH
Yes

walk from the hotel door. This factor alone was one of the reasons former President Clinton's bodyguards and staff stayed here during his official 1994 visit to Rome.

FACILITIES AND SERVICES: Air-conditioning, piano bar, direct-dial phone, elevator, hair dryer, Internet facilities for guests, laundry service, minibar, room service for light snacks, in-room safe, satellite TV, porter, 4th floor is nonsmoking

NEAREST TOURIST ATTRACTIONS: Close to American Embassy; walking distance to Villa Borghese, Via Veneto

Edge of Rome

The following hotel is on the northeastern edge of the city, a location that will appeal to those who are driving and do not want to fight the crazy Rome traffic, or to those who don't mind a commute of at least thirty or forty minutes to most of Rome's main tourist attractions. Of interest to many, however, is Santa Agnese, a circular church with catacombs, and the nearby Villa Torlonia, Mussolini's home, which is now a museum famous for its gothic stained-glass windows and summer classical concerts.

HOTEL VILLA DEL PARCO ★★★
Via Nomentana, 110

29 rooms, all with shower or bath and toilet

If you are looking for something out of the ordinary or have a car, this beautifully tranquil retreat at the edge of Rome proper is a marvelous choice. The Bernardini family villa and gardens date from 1910, and since 1958, they have been operating their home as a gracious hotel.

The hotel is lovingly appointed with tasteful, coordinated fabrics that enhance the mixture of family antiques and comfortable furniture. The sitting room has an heirloom grandfather clock and old-style sofas and inviting wing chairs set in cozy conversational clusters. From June through September, breakfast is served on a shaded terrace that wraps around the front and side of the hotel. In winter months, breakfast is served in a room with polished hardwood floors, a collection of colorful fruit prints, and five nicely set tables.

A winding staircase with a burnished handrail leads to the individually decorated bedrooms, which have been done in a style that will please followers of Martha Stewart. Those on the second and fourth floors have been redecorated.

TELEPHONE
06 4423 7773
FAX
06 4423 7572
INTERNET
www.villadelparco.it
CREDIT CARDS
AE, DC, MC, V
RATES
Single 116–131€, double 151–180€, triple 185–225€, family room 200–250€; lower rates on weekends and in Aug; discounts for senior citizens and honeymooners
BREAKFAST
Buffet breakfast included
ENGLISH
Yes

Those on the second now have hydromassage showers, as does No. 25 on the ground floor and several on the third floor. Six rooms on the fourth floor have mansard roofs with skylights that open automatically. On the fourth floor, No. 28, in a soothing green-and-beige color scheme, has a white beamed ceiling, white iron bed, comfortable chair and desk, and bathroom with two windows; it can combine with No. 29 to make a comfortable suite. On the second floor, No. 10, a double with a balcony, has an inlaid wooden floor complementing a handmade armoire. Number 11, another double, has pink wallpaper and a small entryway lined with prints. The rooms on the first and third are recommended, with the exception of No. 20, which does have the advantage of a small balcony, but unappealing pea green walls and a vintage bathroom.

NOTE: Buses to the center of Rome stop by the hotel: it's thirty minutes to Piazza Venezia on Bus 84, or faster on Bus 60, the express line. Bus 36 takes you to Termini Station. Metro line B, Bologna, is a ten-minute walk. For motorists there is off-street parking in front of the hotel. Airport transfers can also be arranged.

FACILITIES AND SERVICES: Air-conditioning, bar, direct-dial phone, elevator, hair dryer, minibars, parking (8€ per day), porter, in-room safe, satellite TV, 24-hour room service for light snacks, dogs accepted

NEAREST TOURIST ATTRACTIONS: Villa Torlonia (Mussolini's home), Santa Agnese Church, Afghan and Russian Embassies; otherwise must have car or use public transportation

Other Options

In addition to hotels, there are many other reasonable and quite often less-expensive options that make Great Sleeping sense in Rome. For the cheapest sleep, it is possible to pitch a tent in a campground on the outskirts of Rome. A more central cheap sleeping choice is a Holy Hotel run by nuns, or if you are a student, a bunk in a multibedded hostel. For a closer look at Roman life, plan to stay with an Italian family in a B&B. Other cost-saving tactics include residence hotels or your own apartment, both of which allow more space and the possibility of interacting with merchants and neighbors while experiencing *la dolce vita* in your own corner of Rome.

Apartment Rentals

Some lucky travelers require a home base for several weeks, a month, or more, but hotel rooms can grow very small and impersonal over a long stay. Apartment living gives you more space than a hotel, and often for less money, but more importantly, makes you feel more a part of your neighborhood as you get to know your favorite *caffè*, butcher, fruit and vegetable seller, bakery, and friendly restaurants. Before reserving any apartment, please refer to "Tips for Renting an Italian Apartment," page 15.

NOTE: The following B&B organizations also have a selection of apartment rentals, both in the city center and in the suburbs: Bed & Breakfast Association of Rome, page 218, and Bed & Breakfast Italia, page 219.

APARTMENT RENTALS

ITALIAN HOLIDAY APARTMENTS
Via Rutilio Namaziano, 50

Stefania Leonetti deals in forty top-drawer Italian holiday apartments in Rome, and I can assure you there are no horrors awaiting her clients. She started her company ten years ago and still personally inspects every apartment she handles, and then keeps tabs on them to make sure they continue to meet her high standards. While she does cover the entire city, she has an excellent selection in the center, especially around Campo de' Fiori, Piazza Navona, and the Vatican. Each apartment is different and so are the features, such as air-conditioning, elevators, clothes washing machines, cable television, terraces, and more. Maid service is always optional, cell phones are provided, airport transfers can be arranged, and lower rates are available for stays of two weeks or more and in the off-season. When you contact Stefania, state your needs in detail, and she will undoubtedly be able to meet them all.

TELEPHONE
06 561 1746, 06 4080 0700;
cell phone 333 613 1331
FAX
06 561 1746, 06 4080 0701
INTERNET
www.ulysseholidays.com
CREDIT CARDS
Accepted only to hold a booking; otherwise, cash in euros only, payable upon arrival
RATES
Two people from 110€ per day
ENGLISH
Yes

Bed-and-Breakfasts

A few of the B&B listings below are organizations dealing in a wide range of properties, not just B&Bs.

BED-AND-BREAKFASTS

($) indicates a Big Splurge; (¢) indicates a Cheap Sleep

BED & BREAKFAST ASSOCIATION OF ROME
Via A. Pacinotti, 73

TELEPHONE
06 5530 2248

FAX
06 5530 2259

INTERNET
www.b-b.rm.it

CREDIT CARDS
MC, V accepted for reservation advance; balance is cash only, paid to host family

RATES
B&Bs (2-night minimum): single 48–60€, double 64–150€; apartments (3-night minimum): 90–120€ for 2 people

BREAKFAST
Breakfast included in B&Bs, not included in apartments

ENGLISH
Yes, in booking office; not always in the host home

The Bed & Breakfast Association of Rome has earned a reputation as one of the best in the city. Why? Because owner/director Francesca Alatri takes a personal interest in her guests and her hosts, and she always stresses cleanliness and hospitality in the homes she represents, most of which are centrally located. While elevators and English-speaking hosts are not the norm, they do exist, and fluent English is spoken in the booking office. Other amenities and services vary with each rental. When reserving, there is a two-night minimum stay, and a 25 percent advance payment is required. The balance is paid in cash to the host family. They also have a roster of very nice apartment rentals that have three-night minimum stays and discounts offered after seven nights.

BED & BREAKFAST DI ANNA MANIERI (30)
Piazza Trinità dei Monti, 16 (Piazza di Spagna)
3 rooms, all with shower or bath and toilet

TELEPHONE & FAX
06 679 4266

EMAIL
bedbreakfast16@hotmail.com

INTERNET
tiscalinet.it/bedbreakfast16

CREDIT CARDS
None, cash only

RATES
150€ per room

BREAKFAST
Continental breakfast included

ENGLISH
Yes

Once they find it, guests become devotees and spread the word to their friends about this very special bed-and-breakfast in one of the most famous parts of Rome... at the top of the Piazza di Spagna and across from the famed Hassler Villa Medici. Charming Anna Manieri, a transplanted Italian-American born in Philadelphia, has opened her lovely home to visitors eleven months of the year (it is closed in August). Entrance from the street is via a magnificent curved wrought-iron and marble stairway, which leads to three well-furnished rooms all done in a style befitting the palatial building. Each morning, guests are served breakfast in her private dining room, and they are encouraged to meet in her large, modern sitting area during the day. Personally conducted tours of Rome can be arranged with her daughter.

FACILITIES AND SERVICES: Air-conditioning, fans, office safe, satellite TV

NEAREST TOURIST ATTRACTIONS: Piazza di Spagna, shopping

BED & BREAKFAST—EPISCOPO LIPINSKY (13)
Via Margutta, 33 (Piazza di Spagna)
2 suites, both with shower, bath, and toilet

Sigmund Lipinsky, a noted painter, lived and worked in this home from 1901 to 1945. In 2003, his grandson, Miguel, who grew up in the house, and Miguel's wife, Viviana, decided to convert two large rooms into nonsmoking suites for guests. One is a two-room red suite with a wisteria-covered balcony railing and televisions in both rooms; it can sleep up to six people. The other suite, with a similar balcony, is a large double with either a king bed or two twins, tiled floor, and bathroom with an enclosed shower. The art work hanging in the public and private rooms of the home are by Lipinsky. Guests are served breakfast in a small dining room off the terrace. In the afternoon, tea and apéritifs are served.

NOTE: There is no sign outside.

FACILITIES AND SERVICES: Air-conditioning, direct-dial phone, elevator, on-call hairdresser, hair dryer, laundry service, room service for drinks, in-room safe, satellite TV, car and driver or car rental can be provided, nearby garage with valet parking, nearby fitness and beauty center

NEAREST TOURIST ATTRACTIONS: Piazza di Spagna, excellent shopping for clothes and antiques

TELEPHONE & FAX
06 369 994; cell phone 3335 708 879

INTERNET
www.bbepiscopolipinsky.it

CREDIT CARDS
None, cash only

RATES
Single 150–170€, double 180–200€, triple 230€, quad 260€, extra bed 20€

BREAKFAST
Continental breakfast included

ENGLISH
Yes, ask for Vivianna

BED & BREAKFAST ITALIA (58)
Palazzo Sforza Cesarini, Corso Vittorio Emanuele II, 282 (Piazza Navona)

Bed & Breakfast Italia has jumped onto the rapidly growing bandwagon of bed-and-breakfast accommodations. With more than a thousand different apartments or houses in Italy offering fifteen hundred room options—ranging from simple rooms with shared bathrooms to your own castle—chances are excellent they will have something for you, whatever your budget or desires. In Rome, their offerings run the gamut from a big room in a suburban apartment to a great loft in Trastevere or a modern Scandinavian penthouse flat with a wraparound terrace and views that never end. All the accommodations are graded from two to four crowns. A two-crown site will be a room and shared bath with your host; three crowns means you will have your own bathroom; and four means luxury. The host has to meet certain standards laid out in a Hospitality Charter that ensures each guest will receive the best service possible. The charter includes, among other things, being treated as a friend of the host and having a cup of coffee or tea offered upon arrival. To be assured

TELEPHONE
06 687 8618

FAX
06 687 8619

INTERNET
www.bbitalia.it

CREDIT CARDS
MC, V

RATES
All rates per person: single 33–58€, double 27–50€, triple 26–45€; 2-night minimum

BREAKFAST
Breakfast included

ENGLISH
Yes, in booking office; not always in host home

of the best experience in this type of Great Sleep, before booking be sure to state your needs and requirements very clearly—such as your level of tolerance for smoking, cats, children, stairs, shared bathrooms, and so on. Also ask for a map with the B&B or apartment well marked on it. The minimum stay is two days, but you can stretch that to forever if you wish.

CASA BANZO (¢, 75)
Piazza Monte di Pietà, 30 (Campo de' Fiori)
3 rooms, all with shower or bath and toilet

TELEPHONE
06 683 3909;
cell phone 338 338 7284
FAX
06 686 4575
EMAIL
elptomas@tin.it
INTERNET
www.mariamilani.com
CREDIT CARDS
MC, V (3€ surcharge)
RATES
Single 100€, double 120€, triple 145€
BREAKFAST
Continental breakfast included
ENGLISH
Somewhat limited

Casa Banzo is a magnificent palace in the heart of Rome. The minute I arrived, I realized that this was a very special home that had been lovingly tended over the years. High frescoed ceilings and walls complement the huge stained-glass windows and marble floors. Family furnishings and antiques create a warm and welcoming atmosphere that guests find irresistible. In the dining room is a huge breakfront displaying family silver, crystal, and china. Six windows let in morning light and the almost walk-in fireplace adds just the right baronial touch.

The attractively furnished rooms keep pace with their surroundings. One room for three, which has a small working kitchen, can be combined with the room across the hall to create a comfortable two-bedroom apartment. The second bedroom has a flower-lined balcony with a courtyard view and a light green mosaic-tile bathroom. Another room (also sleeping three) has a feminine dressing table with a three-way mirror and a tan marble bathroom. Unfortunately there is not much of a view from the small window, but when compared against everything else in the palace, you will hardly notice.

FACILITIES AND SERVICES: Air-conditioning, no elevator (2 floors), TV, reception open Mon–Sat 9 A.M.– 1 P.M., 4–8 P.M., Sun 9 A.M.–1 P.M.

NEAREST TOURIST ATTRACTIONS: Campo de' Fiori, Piazza Navona

CASA STEFAZIO ($)
Via della Marcigliana, 553 (outside Rome)
4 rooms, 1 suite, all with shower or bath and toilet

TELEPHONE
06 8712 0042
FAX
06 8712 0012
EMAIL
casastefazio@hotmail.com
INTERNET
www.casastefazio.com

"We've traveled all over the world, and our best trips have always been those we've stayed with friends. It was wonderful to go sightseeing during the day and then in the evening to come 'home.' It is that 'coming home' feeling we try to create for our guests at Casa Stefazio," Stefania

Azzola says in her brochure. I think she certainly succeeds, and at least one *Great Sleeps Italy* reader enthusiastically agrees: "The minute we walked into the house we felt we were visiting family (except that they won't let you do any work), and I will always consider this to be my home in Italy. Stefania was wonderful regarding ideas for sightseeing, and Orazio's cooking was magnificent. Leaving to come home was very difficult indeed."

Casa Stefazio is not only absolutely wonderful, but it ranks as the best B&B I have seen anywhere. Even if this sort of accommodation has never appealed to you before, Casa Stefazio will change your mind, since a stay here is truly a special experience you will always treasure. Not just the reader above, but every guest who walks in feels immediately at home and leaves as a friend.

Several years ago when the last of their children left the nest, Orazio and Stefania Azzola decided to sell their beautiful Tuscan-style home. But when it came time to do it, they realized they loved it too much to follow through. With the encouragement of their many American friends, they opened their home as a bed-and-breakfast, but the Casa Stefazio bears as much resemblance to a normal bed-and-breakfast as a Rolls Royce does to a bicycle. Come once and you will not consider vacationing anywhere else in Italy.

The home is located about thirty minutes from central Rome in a quiet compound of private residences surrounded by rolling countryside and beautiful gardens. Tennis courts and a swimming pool at a private club are within walking distance. A horseback-riding stable is across the road, and an eighteen-hole golf course is nearby. If you do not have your own car (and you should seriously consider renting one if you stay here), there is local bus service, and taxis can be called.

The spacious guest rooms are as attractively furnished and appointed as the rest of the house. Each has a private bathroom and is air-conditioned. One is a two-room suite with a private living room, its own sauna, and a separate entrance. If you do not like steps, ask for the Pink Room on the ground floor. The Blue Room is just right for one, and if you want a television set, ask Stefania and she will bring one for you.

Both Orazio and Stefania speak perfect English and love people. They have traveled extensively and spend part of each year in the United States. Orazio is a Cordon Bleu chef, and Stefania, a native Roman, is a virtual encyclopedia of

CREDIT CARDS
None, cash only

RATES
No singles; double 220€, suite 275€; half required as deposit, balance due upon arrival

BREAKFAST
Breakfast included

ENGLISH
Yes

knowledge about her city. They both do everything possible to make their guests feel at home by serving breakfast either in your own room or in their kitchen. At sunset, you will be invited to join them on the terrace or beside the roaring fire for a glass of wine and Orazio's delicious appetizers. If you want him to prepare dinner, just say so the night before and they will set a place for you at their table. Orazio will conduct cooking classes if there are enough requests.

They go even further by personally conducting deluxe eleven- and sixteen-day guided tours. The eleven-day trip starts in Rome and continues along the Amalfi Coast to Positano, Capri, Pompei, and Tuscany, including Florence and Siena. The sixteen-day trip starts along the Appian Way, goes on to Florence, Venice, Lake Como, San Gimigiano, Siena, and Orvieto, then heads back to Villa d'Este and Tivoli. These tours are absolute knockouts and so popular that reservations are required at least four months in advance. The tours are for a maximum of seven or eight persons, and everything but airfare to Italy, hotel extras, and a few lunches is included. They can also customize their tours. Even if you have been to these places before, with Orazio and Stefania as your guides, you will see them anew.

NOTE: Casa Stefazio is closed from mid-November through mid-March.

PRIVATE TOURS: Rates are per person and range from 2 to 8 people (getting progressively lower): The 11-day tour runs 7,100–4,100€; the 16-day tour runs 10,900–6,500€. All tours include accommodations, all meals with wine, admission fees, tips, and ground transportation. Not included are airfare, lunches on leisure days, and hotel extras.

FACILITIES AND SERVICES: Air-conditioning, bar, minibar, free parking, satellite TV, sauna in the suite, dinner available (45€ per person, including wine), airport transfers (120€), no smoking allowed, no pets

NEAREST TOURIST ATTRACTIONS: None within walking distance, but plenty of activities, such as swimming, tennis, horseback riding, and golf

VILLA DELROS

TELEPHONE
06 3367 9837;
cell phone 340 929 5488
FAX
06 3367 8402
EMAIL
villadelros@tiscalinet.it

3 suites, fully equipped

Welcome to Villa Delros, *un mondo di sogni* (a world of dreams).

Readers of *Great Sleeps Italy* who have stayed at Rosmarie Diletti's lovely Hotel Venezia (see page 194) will be pleased to know that after turning over the reins of the hotel to her son and daughter, she found retirement did not suit her.

Always the consummate businesswoman and experienced hostess eager for a new challenge, she decided to turn part of her magnificent country estate on the edge of Rome into a very exclusive bed-and-breakfast. The beauty of Villa Delros lies not only in its peaceful setting but most of all in Rosmarie herself, who welcomes her guests with a warm friendliness and gracious charm we seldom encounter in this busy, impersonal world.

Discerning guests who appreciate the beauty of staying in a tranquil country villa not far from the center of Rome (it's about thirty minutes by car or train) will never forget their sojourn at Villa Delros and will probably spend a good portion of their stay plotting their return. Set among the rolling hills surrounding Rome, the magnificent villa provides guests with a rare look inside the art-filled home Sra. Diletti built a quarter of a century ago. Over the years she has collected priceless pieces of museum-quality furniture, paintings, and artifacts. The expansive grounds serve as the perfect backdrop for her beautiful plants and flowers. Guests are invited to enjoy the terraces, the swimming pool, or a stroll through the grounds.

The three suites are all lavishly furnished with Rosmarie's beautiful antiques and paintings. Each has a bedroom with one large bed that can be divided into twins, a sitting room with a comfortable sofa, chairs, and worktable, and a nice kitchen. One has a fireplace. The beautiful baths have hand-painted ceramic tiles, both a tub and shower, and are fully stocked with toiletries. Their private terraces have chairs, tables, and shade coverings. A wonderful breakfast is, of course, included, and upon request, Rosmarie will prepare dinner for her guests, usually using herbs and vegetables from her gardens. For motorists, there is free parking. The train to Rome is about a ten-minute drive away, and a shuttle can be provided for guests without their own cars. The train takes about fifteen minutes to Piazza del Popolo.

NOTE: Villa Delros is closed from November through February. Reservations can be made directly or through Rentvillas.com (page 129).

FACILITIES AND SERVICES: Air-conditioning, direct-dial phone, dishwashers in 2 suites, hair dryer, fitted kitchen, free parking, in-room safe, no lift, satellite TV, swimming pool, free transport from the villa to public transportation, dinner by advance request only

NEAREST TOURIST ATTRACTIONS: The Roman Villa Livia & Arco di Costant; otherwise, must use public transportation or drive

INTERNET
www.villadelros.com
CREDIT CARDS
None, cash only
RATES
Double 170€, extra bed 60€; lower weekly rates for Saturday–Saturday stays; discount for *Great Sleeps Italy* readers (bring the book); dinner by advance reservation only, 15€ per person for a light meal (wine included), 50€ per person for a romantic dinner (wine included)
BREAKFAST
Breakfast included
ENGLISH
Yes

Camping

Yes, you can camp in Rome. You can rent tents or cabins, but in tents, you will have to bring your own camp stove. The locations require long bus rides with transfers to get into central Rome, but the prices for tents are extremely cheap, so for some, the savings may be worth the trek back and forth to civilization. Campsite rates are calculated by adding the per-day rate for the type of site and the per-day rate per person.

CAMPING

Flaminio	**224**
Seven Hills	**224**
Tiber	**225**

FLAMINIO
Via Flaminio Nuova, 821 (outside Rome)

TELEPHONE
06 333 2604

FAX
06 333 0653

INTERNET
www.villageflaminio.com

CREDIT CARDS
AE, DC, MC, V

RATES
Camping: 11€ per person, 8€ for children 3–12, plus automobile 5€, camper 12€, minivan 9€, motorbike 4€, tent 7€; cabin 22€ per person; bungalow: for 2 people 61€, for 3 people 100€, for 4 people 112€; Continental breakfast 3€, buffet breakfast 7€; lower off-season rates

ENGLISH
Generally, yes

This campground has cabins with private showers and a swimming pool, plus a market, restaurant, pizzeria, disco, bar, free showers, and coin-operated washers. The air-conditioned bungalows can accommodate two to six persons with bath and bed linens provided. They also have verandas, kitchens, private facilities, in-room safe, satellite television, and free parking. No matter where you sleep in the campground, the swimming pool is free.

The campground is open from March to the end of October (and closed November through February). Office hours are 6 A.M. to 12:30 A.M. To get here (it is about eight kilometers from Rome), take Bus 910 from the train station to Piazza Mancini, then transfer to Bus 200. Get off on Via Flaminio Nuova when you see the Philips building.

FACILITIES AND SERVICES: Swimming pool, market, restaurants, disco, bar, coin-operated laundries

SEVEN HILLS
Via Cassia, 1216 (outside Rome)

TELEPHONE
06 303 62751, 06 3031 0826

FAX
06 3031 0039

EMAIL
sevenhills@info.it

INTERNET
www.sevenhills.it

This campsite has lots going for it: beautiful grounds with peacocks, swans, goats, deer, and rabbits, and creature comfort extras that include a swimming pool, disco, bar, market, and pizzeria. A daily shuttle bus transports happy campers the two kilometers to a nearby train station, which has a direct train that takes twenty minutes to the city center, with a stop at St Peter's. After a five-day stay, there is a 10 percent discount for *Great Sleeps Italy* readers; showers are free, and so are children up to age three. If your idea of camping is a hotel *without* room service, they have bungalows with kitchens, and you can provide your own room service. The campground is open from mid-March to November.

FACILITIES AND SERVICES: Bar, supermarket, pizzeria, pool, laundry, disco, money exchange, Internet access

CREDIT CARDS
AE, MC, V

RATES
Camping: 9€ per person, children under 3 free, tent 6€, motorcycle 3€, automobile 4€, caravan 8€, camper 10€, mobile home for 2 without toilet, shower, or kitchen 35€, with shower, toilet, and kitchen 60–65€, bungalow for 1–2 people 60€, 3 people 90€, 4 people 120€; lower off-season rates; shuttle service to train to Rome 1€ each way; sheets, blankets, hot showers, and electricity are free

ENGLISH
Yes

TIBER
Via Tiberina (outside Rome)

The Tiber is open for campers from March until the end of October. Here you can drink at the bar, shop at their market, swim in the pool, and eat in the restaurant/ pizzeria. A free shuttle to the metro (1.5 kilometers away) runs every ten minutes between 8 A.M. and 10 P.M.; the metro will take you the rest of the way to Rome (another fifteen kilometers).

FACILITIES AND SERVICES: Bar, market, pool, restaurants

TELEPHONE
06 336 10733

FAX
06 336 12314

EMAIL
info@campingtiber.com

INTERNET
www.campingtiber.com

CREDIT CARDS
MC, V

RATES
All rates are per person, per day: adult 10€, children 3–12 years 7€, tent 5€, car 5€, caravan 8€, camper 11€, 2-room mobile home without shower and toilet 30€, with shower and toilet 45€

ENGLISH
Yes

Holy Hotels

Convents, monasteries, and religious institutions provide spartan accommodations to travelers who do not mind austere surroundings (with a few exceptions), out-of-the-way locations, and lockouts by 11 P.M. (again, with exceptions). Prices are not always as low as the surroundings suggest, but these are very safe places to stay, and many provide meals at nominal cost. As a result, holy hotels are very much in demand. It is therefore essential that you telephone, email, or fax your reservations as far in advance as possible, and don't think for a minute that a year ahead is too soon to start planning. Some English is usually spoken, but of course Italian will get you much further. Mentioning your priest or bishop will not hurt either.

The following selection is by no means exhaustive, but it should get you started.

HOLY HOTELS

CASA BONUS PASTOR (17)
Via Aurelia, 208 (Vatican)

89 rooms, all with shower and toilet

TELEPHONE
06 6987 1282

FAX
06 6987 1435

EMAIL
bonuspastor@glauco.it

CREDIT CARDS
AE, MC, V

RATES
Single 77€, double 108€, triple 131€, quad 165€; half-pension 15€; lower off-season rates

BREAKFAST
Continental breakfast included

ENGLISH
Yes

Casa Bonus Pastor opened in 2000 to house pilgrims coming to Rome for the Jubilee year. How fortunate for all subsequent visitors to Rome who appreciate a quiet stay in comfortable surroundings with high standards. The Casa is located in a beautiful palace, surrounded by a park and very close to the Vatican walls. From the fifth-floor terrace, the views of Rome are picture perfect. It is basically geared to groups, but individuals are certainly welcome. The air-conditioned rooms are done simply, with light wood built-ins, tile floors, and satellite television. No smoking is allowed. Buses 46 and 49 take guests directly into the Vatican and the center of Rome.

FACILITIES AND SERVICES: Air-conditioning, direct-dial phone, elevator, hair dryer, free parking, in-room safe, satellite TV, half-pension

NEAREST TOURIST ATTRACTIONS: Vatican, Vatican Museums

CASA DI SANTA BRIGIDA (69)
Piazza Farnese, 96 (Campo de' Fiori)

22 rooms, all with shower or bath and toilet

Definitely one of the most central and most expensive of the holy hotels, Santa Brigida is just next to Campo de' Fiori, which puts you in the center of tourist Rome. Inside, it has the atmosphere of an elegant and aristocratic home filled with lovely furniture. Santa Brigida takes guests of every age, nationality, and creed. There is a small church for those who wish to attend the sisters' liturgical worships. On the first floor are the three rooms in which St. Bridget lived, including the one where she died in 1373. Full-board, half-board, or just bed-and-breakfast plans are available. Each room has a bath or shower, toilet, air-conditioning, and a direct-dial telephone. This is an extremely popular place and reservations are required as far in advance as possible; fax or email them the minute you know your Rome dates. If you do not get an answer within two to three days, it means you are on the waiting list. Singles pay more than two people sharing a room, there are no double beds, and no one-night reservations are accepted.

NOTE: Rome has two other residential guest homes run by the same order of nuns. Both are far from the center; I've included them here just in case that does not matter to you: Suore di S. Brigida, Via delle Isole, 34; Tel: 06 841 4393, 06 841 7251; Fax: 06 854 0845; Suore di S. Brigida, Via Cassia, 2040; Tel: 06 378 0272; Fax: 06 3088 0272.

FACILITIES AND SERVICES: Air-conditioning, direct-dial phone, elevator, hair dryer available, office safe, TV in lounge, full- and half-board available

NEAREST TOURIST ATTRACTIONS: Campo de' Fiori, Piazza Navona, Pantheon, Piazza Venezia

TELEPHONE
06 6889 2596, 06 6889 2497

FAX
06 6889 1573, 06 6889 2497

EMAIL
brigida@mclinik.it

INTERNET
www.brigidine.org

CREDIT CARDS
V

RATES
Single 100€, double 175€; half-pension: single 120€, double 220€; full-pension: single 140€, double 275€

BREAKFAST
Continental breakfast included

ENGLISH
Yes

FRATERNA DOMUS (46)
Via dell' Cancello, 6 (at Via di Monte Brianzo, 62) (Piazza Navona)

18 rooms, all with shower or bath and toilet

If the holy hotel route appeals to you, this is a great choice—and it is, in fact, my favorite. The smoke-free, absolutely spotless rooms are simple, fitted with a table, an armoire, a religious picture, and twin (no double) beds. Lockout is at 11 P.M. The food is wonderful, and the sisters are warm-spirited, friendly, and welcoming. It is located close to the Tiber River, near Piazza Nicosia, Piazza Navona, and the Spanish Steps. The small ninth-century church, Santa Lucia della Tinta, is beautiful, inspired by St. Francis of Assisi, with original mosaic floors that date

TELEPHONE
06 6880 2727, 06 6880 5475

FAX
06 683 2691

EMAIL
domusrm@tin.it

CREDIT CARDS
MC, V

RATES
Single 50€, double 80€; lunch or dinner 15€

BREAKFAST
Continental breakfast included

ENGLISH
Yes

from the Middle Ages. The ceiling was done in the 1800s by a Polish painter, and the original stained-glass backdrop by the altar dates from the 1400s. Mass is held on Sundays at 11 A.M. and is open to the public.

Even though the sisters received church funds to expand and improve their bed-and-breakfast and dining operations for the Jubilee 2000, no money has been forthcoming for the badly needed restoration of this magnificent thousand-year-old chapel. The sisters are very worried about its condition and told me they are praying daily for a miracle . . . maybe you can help.

Even if you do not want to stay at Fraterna Domus, please consider coming for lunch or dinner (see *Great Eats Italy*). Lunch is served at 1 P.M. and dinner is at 7:30 P.M.; both cost the same, around 15€ per person, wine extra. The food is served family style, and there is no choice of dishes. They are closed on Thursday. Reservations are required.

FACILITIES AND SERVICES: Air-conditioning (10€ per day), office safe, communal satellite TV

NEAREST TOURIST ATTRACTIONS: Tiber River, Piazza Navona, Spanish Steps, excellent shopping

SUORE DI NOSTRA SIGNORA DI LOURDES (105)
Via Sistina, 113 (Piazza di Spagna)

17 rooms, 11 with shower and toilet

There is very limited English spoken at this holy hotel in the shadow of the Spanish Steps. The curfew is 10:30 P.M. In theory, office hours are from about 9 A.M. to 6 P.M., but the office is often shut tightly between 12:30 and 1:30 P.M. or 2 and 2:30 P.M. while the sisters have lunch, and at other times it is difficult to get anyone's attention.

FACILITIES AND SERVICES: None

NEAREST TOURIST ATTRACTIONS: Spanish Steps, Via Veneto, shopping

TELEPHONE
06 474 5324
FAX
06 474 1422
CREDIT CARDS
None, cash only
RATES
Single 35€, double 75€, triple 100€
BREAKFAST
Continental breakfast included
ENGLISH
Limited

SUORE DI SAN GIUSEPPE DI CLUNY (127)
Via Angelo Poliziano, 38 (Colosseum and Forum)

20 rooms, 9 with shower and toilet

If you want to brush up on your French during your stay in Rome, here is a good place to do it, as most of the Sisters of Saint Joseph of Cluny speak French but virtually no English. The holy hotel is well located on the Esquiline Hill, not far from the Termini Station, Colosseum, and Forum. On the grounds there is a pretty chapel and a garden. No single men are allowed, but women, couples, and families are welcome. It is a popular holy hotel, especially

TELEPHONE
06 487 2837/8
FAX
06 4890 4132
CREDIT CARDS
None, cash only
RATES
Rates are per person: single 50€, double 44€; lunch 15€; children under 8 are half price

from April through December, so get your reservation in at least three to four months in advance. There is a three-night minimum. Breakfast is included (served Monday to Saturday, never on Sunday or holidays), and lunch is served daily (except in August).

FACILITIES AND SERVICES: Chapel, elevator

NEAREST TOURIST ATTRACTIONS: Colosseum, Forum

BREAKFAST
Continental breakfast included

ENGLISH
Limited, but the sisters speak French

SUORE DI SANTA ELISABETTA (120)
Via dell'Olmata, 9 (Train Station Area)
38 rooms, 28 with shower and toilet

Polish sisters have been running this lovely holy hotel for more than a hundred years. Rooms are spartan, but several have balconies, most have private facilities, and children under three are free. There is a modern chapel where daily mass is held, a huge garden with an arbor, and a stunning third-floor roof garden with a view of the Colosseum and St. Peter's. English is spoken, and smoking is forbidden.

FACILITIES AND SERVICES: Direct-dial phone, elevator, hair dryer available, office safe, nonsmoking hotel

NEAREST TOURIST ATTRACTIONS: Opera, train station, Colosseum, Forum

TELEPHONE
06 488 8271

FAX
06 488 4066

EMAIL
s.elisabetta@libero.it

CREDIT CARDS
MC, V

RATES
Single 39–46€, double 63–78€, triple 100€, quad 120€, five 130€; children under 3 years free, 3–6 years half price, 7–12 years 30% discount

BREAKFAST
Continental breakfast included

ENGLISH
Yes

SUORE DOROTEE (66)
Via del Gianicolo, 4 (Vatican)
30 rooms, all with shower and toilet

Halfway up Janiculum Hill above Vatican City, the Suore Dorotee is in a quiet spot with a pretty garden near the North American College, where many Americans study for the priesthood. Climbing up and down some hills is required, but if you have a car and feel up to braving Rome traffic, parking is free. Guests must take half-board, curfew is at 11 P.M., and a few of the sisters speak English. This holy hotel is closed in August.

FACILITIES AND SERVICES: Elevator, free parking, office safe

NEAREST TOURIST ATTRACTIONS: Vatican, Vatican Museums (quite a walk)

TELEPHONE
06 6880 3349

FAX
06 6880 3311

CREDIT CARDS
None, cash only

RATES
65€ per person, including breakfast and obligitory half-board

BREAKFAST
Breakfast included

ENGLISH
Limited

Hostels

Hostels are definitely the way to go for Great Sleepers of all ages who don't mind sharing dorm-style accommodations, communal bathrooms, and a spirit of camaraderie with like-minded budget-conscious travelers.

A membership in the International Youth Hostel Federation (IYHF) opens the door to many inexpensive dormitory accommodations in youth hostels and other student lodgings, as well as to a host of travel-related savings. It is possible to buy the card on-site at some places, but it is much more convenient to buy it before you go. For more, see "Students" under "Discounts," page 28.

HOSTELS

COLORS HOSTEL (22)
Via Boezio, 31 (The Vatican)

14 rooms, one with shower or toilet

TELEPHONE
06 687 4030

FAX
06 686 7947

EMAIL
info@enjoyrome.com

INTERNET
www.colorshotel.com

CREDIT CARDS
None, cash only

RATES
Dorm (5-beds) 22–25€, single 45–60€, double 75–85€; lower off-season rates

BREAKFAST
Not served

ENGLISH
Yes

Colors Hostel is under the umbrella of Enjoy Rome, a local company dedicated to helping budget conscious visitors to Rome get the most for their money (see Enjoy Rome, page 155). The Colors Hostel, as the name implies, is a bright place with primary colors decorating the doors of the boldly painted rooms. Both dormitory and private rooms are available. Advantages include no curfew or midday lock-out, coin-operated laundry, communal kitchen, Internet access in lobby, terrace, no-smoking policy, and a friendly international staff who will arrange for walking and bicycle tours. Sheets and towels are provided; breakfast is not.

FACILITIES AND SERVICES: Hair dryer available, no elevator (4 floors), communal kitchen, coin-laundry, office safe, walking and bicycle tours, nonsmoking hostel

NEAREST TOURIST ATTRACTIONS: Vatican, Vatican Museums

PROTEZIONE DELLA GIOVANE (119)
Via Urbana, 158 (Train Station Area)
40 beds, none with shower or toilet

This Catholic-run organization offers bottom-of-the-budget accommodations to women under twenty-five years old. In addition to the price, the good news includes no-smoking rooms, optional lunch and dinner from Monday to Saturday, and a good location. The bad news is the weeknight 10 P.M. curfew (midnight on Saturday) and the rooms—which, even though clean, are reminiscent of a prison cell. Showers are only allowed between 6:30 and 8 A.M. and 5 and 9 P.M., and room laundries are forbidden.

FACILITIES AND SERVICES: Elevator, office safe, TV in lounge, garden

NEAREST TOURIST ATTRACTIONS: Termini Station, Colosseum, Forum

TELEPHONE
06 488 0056

FAX
06 482 7989

EMAIL
acisjf@virgilio.it

CREDIT CARDS
None, cash only

RATES
Single 24€, double 19€ per person, dorm (5–8 people) 16€ per person

BREAKFAST
No breakfast served

ENGLISH
Limited

YELLOW HOSTEL (101)
Via Palestro, 44 (Train Station Area)
115 beds

The Yellow Hostel is a winner in several categories. First, it won an award for being one of the world's top ten hostels according to Hostel World, an association that has 5,500 affiliated hostels worldwide. Next, there are no single rooms, but the nonsmoking rooms (which sleep from two to six people) are clean, and so are the communal bathrooms, which are swabbed three times a day. Sheets and towels are provided, but BYO lock (or buy one here for 2€). There is free Internet access in lobby, coin-operated laundry, kitchen privileges, and a TV with loads of DVDs. Finally, there is no lockout during the day and no curfew at night.

FACILITIES AND SERVICES: Air-conditioning in some rooms, bar, elevator, fans in all rooms, hair dryer available, free Internet access, communal kitchen, coin-operated laundry, lockers, nonsmoking rooms

NEAREST TOURIST ATTRACTIONS: Train station, Museo Nazionale in the Diocletian Bath

TELEPHONE
06 4938 2682

FAX
06 4470 2874

INTERNET
www.yellowhostel.com

CREDIT CARDS
Prefers cash, but MC, V okay over 50€ or to guarantee reservation

RATES
22–25€ per person, depending on number of beds in the room

BREAKFAST
Not served

ENGLISH
Yes

Residence Hotels

At first glance these accommodations might seem expensive, but when you consider that you have the space and comfort of an apartment, plus maid and linen service, a kitchen, often parking, and other perks, it is worth the extra outlay, especially if a family or a group of three or four are involved. In addition, if you stay a while, you will soon be living like a local, shopping with your neighbors and having your morning cappuccino at the same bar with the other regulars. All in all, it gives one a real feel for the city, one you never experience from the vantage of a hotel room.

MAYFAIR RESIDENCE (92)
Via Sicilia, 183 (Via Veneto)

41 apartments, all with shower or bath and toilet

TELEPHONE
06 4282 0481

FAX
06 4281 5753

EMAIL
mayfair@italyhotel.com

INTERNET
www.italyhotel.com/roma/mayfair

CREDIT CARDS
AE, DC, MC, V

RATES
Studio (1 person) from 168€, apartments for 2–4 people from 210–280€; all taxes included; discounts for longer stays

BREAKFAST
Continental breakfast included

ENGLISH
Yes

Via Veneto is one of Rome's most expensive addresses, and the Mayfair Residence is about a twenty-minute walk from this tree-lined boulevard. Unless you know what to look for, you will pass right by the Mayfair, as it is in a very nondescript building with only a brass plaque noting its name. Once inside, all that changes. This apartment hotel offers attractive, large studios and one-bedroom units for those who are staying longer in Rome and need more space than normal hotel rooms provide. The quarters on the first two floors have their own terraces, but I think the best choices are on the upper floors because they have better light. All are fully fitted and have maid service, nice furnishings, hardwood or carpeted floors, good bathrooms, and more closet space than many of us have in our own homes. If you are not inspired to get busy early in the morning in the well-stocked kitchen, a Continental breakfast is included. As with other residence hotels, the longer the stay, the better the rates.

FACILITIES AND SERVICES: Air-conditioning, conference rooms, direct-dial phone, elevator, hair dryer, in-room safe, satellite TV, fully equipped kitchen, maid service (Mon–Sat)

NEAREST TOURIST ATTRACTIONS: Via Veneto, Villa Borghese Gardens

RESIDENCE MADONNA DEI MONTI (126)
Via della Madonna dei Monti, 84
(Colosseum and Forum)

10 apartments, all with shower or bath and toilet

The advantage of these ten apartments lies in their size: they are almost barnlike, and just about as cozy. They are probably best for families with boisterous children, because goodness knows, there will be plenty of space to play and run around, especially in No. 5, which has cathedral ceilings and two living rooms. The rustic furnishings and leather-like, tufted sofas are attractive, yet look indestructible. The floors are bare, which means no worries about spills. Claustrophobics should avoid the completely viewless No. 1 on the ground floor, which feels like a cave dwelling. Dishwashers and washing machines are provided in most units, as is maid service, which swoops through twice a week and changes the linens. Storage space is good, and so are the marble bathrooms. There is a one-week minimum stay.

FACILITIES AND SERVICES: Air-conditioning, direct-dial phone with dedicated number, elevator, hair dryer available, laundry service, in-room safe, TV, dishwasher and washing machine in most units, twice weekly maid service

NEAREST TOURIST ATTRACTIONS: Colosseum, Forum

TELEPHONE
06 697 6161

FAX
06 6992 4918

INTERNET
www.romeresidence.com

CREDIT CARDS
AE, DC, MC, V

RATES
All rates per week: smallest units (2 people) 1,000€, largest units (6 people) 1,700€; lower rates for longer stays; all rates add 10% VAT

BREAKFAST
No breakfast served

ENGLISH
Yes

RESIDENCE PALAZZO AL VELABRO (80)
Via del Velabro, 16 (Colosseum and Forum)

35 apartments, all with shower or bath and toilet

For first-timers it may be difficult to find, but once there, you will agree that the accommodations are exceptional. The Residence Palazzo al Velabro sits on the Piazza Bocca della Verità, facing the Palatino Hill, the Arch of Giano, and the Temple of Vesta.

The spacious, comfortable studios and apartments have modern furnishings, kitchens large enough for some serious cooking, excellent closet space, and enviable bathrooms with sink space, enclosed showers and tubs, and plenty of towels. Daily maid service is included. The drawback is that the studios on the first three floors face a wall that in some instances is so high you cannot see the sky. Be sure to ask for something on the fourth or fifth floors if you want a view. Number 35, for instance, looks out at the Palatino Hill.

The residence is quite a walk from shops, an important point if you are setting up housekeeping for any length of time. However, if you have a car, this will not be a problem—except for the hairy Rome traffic. There also

TELEPHONE
06 679 2758, 06 679 2985, 06 679 3450

FAX
06 679 3790

INTERNET
www.velabro.it

CREDIT CARDS
AE, DC, MC, V

RATES
All rates are per day: studios (1–2 persons) 170–210€, doubles (2–4 persons) 280€; extra bed 30€; extra cot 20.66€; all taxes included; minimum 7-night stay; discounts for month stays or longer

BREAKFAST
Continental breakfast 10€ extra

ENGLISH
Yes

is good bus service across the Tiber River to Trastevere, where there are many shopping possibilities. The minimum stay is seven days.

FACILITIES AND SERVICES: Air-conditioning, bar, direct-dial phone, elevator, hair dryer, iron and ironing board available, laundry service, office safe, satellite TV, fully equipped kitchen, free parking, daily maid service

NEAREST TOURIST ATTRACTIONS: Colosseum, Forum, Trastevere

RESIDENCE VIALE (129)
Via Capo d'Africa, 7 (Colosseum and Forum)
6 apartments, fully equipped

TELEPHONE
06 7045 2089
FAX
06 700 5897
EMAIL
residence.viale@virtgilio.it
CREDIT CARDS
AE, MC, V
RATES
All rates are per week and vary by apartment size: 1-bedroom 1,100€, larger 1-bedroom with terrace 1,298€; all taxes included; lower rates for longer stays
BREAKFAST
No breakfast served
ENGLISH
Yes

The six apartments are modern in tone. The largest two come with their own terrace, but all six have white walls, hardwood floors, glass-topped tables, excellent closets, and tiled bathrooms with a shower, or shower and tub. The apartments also have a separate fully equipped kitchen and a proper bedroom—a real bonus if you have children and need to put them to bed early. Down the street is a morning vegetable market, and for all your other housekeeping needs, small shops are close by. If you are not cooking, there are neighborhood restaurants (see *Great Eats Italy*). The underground stop is less than fifteen minutes away, and bus connections are even closer. There is a one-week minimum stay. Office hours are Monday to Friday 9:30 A.M. to 1:30 P.M., 2:30 to 5:30 P.M.

FACILITIES AND SERVICES: Air-conditioning, direct-dial phone with dedicated number, elevator, hair dryer, laundry service, satellite TV, VCR in largest apartment, maid service Mon–Fri, twice-weekly linen changes

NEAREST TOURIST ATTRACTIONS: Colosseum, Forum

RESIDENZA DI RIPETTA (6)
Via di Ripetta, 231 (Piazza del Popolo)
69 studios and apartments, all with shower or bath and toilet

TELEPHONE
06 323 1144
FAX
06 320 3959
INTERNET
www.ripetta.it
CREDIT CARDS
AE, DC, MC, V

The Residenza di Ripetta has always been my home away from home during my Rome visits, and every time, from beginning to end, my stays are wonderful. I like returning year after year to greet the same reception and office staff and say hello to the hardworking maids. Everyone always goes out of their way to be helpful, not only to me but to every other guest, some of whom came to stay for a short time and have never left.

The Residenza is housed in a seventeenth-century former convent a block or so down from the Piazza del Popolo. The exceptional apartments vary in size from studios with no kitchen facilities to studios, apartments, and two-level units with kitchen facilities. Every extra imaginable is offered, including a coffee and cocktail bar, twenty-four-hour concierge, roof garden, garage, and meeting rooms. The furnishings are modern, the closets tremendous, the kitchens fully equipped, and the marble, mirrored bathrooms well-lit, with shelf space and good towels. Taxis are a whistle away, there is a metro stop at the Piazza del Popolo, and excellent bus service zips right by the front door. You will be a short walk away from the best shopping in Rome and many outstanding restaurants (see *Great Eats Italy*). There is a one-week minimum stay.

FACILITIES AND SERVICES: Air-conditioning, bar, direct-dial phone, elevator, hair dryer, fully equipped kitchen in most, laundry service, meeting rooms, locked garage parking, in-room safe, satellite TV, VCR on request, roof garden, Mon–Fri maid service

NEAREST TOURIST ATTRACTIONS: Piazza del Popolo, shopping, Piazza di Spagna, Tiber River

RATES
All rates are per week: studio without kitchen (1–2 people) from 930€, studio with kitchen 1,025€, 2-room apartment (2 people) 1,465€, 3-room apartment (4 people) 1,648€; all add 10% tax; lower rates for longer stays

BREAKFAST
Breakfast served, not included in rates (call for price)

ENGLISH
Yes

Student Accommodations

Low-cost short-term (e.g., tourist) student housing does exist in theory in Rome, but nailing it down may take some doing. It is important to know that these facilities are open to visiting students only when the regular Italian students are away on summer vacation or during other vacation periods of the year. The accommodations are far from luxurious. Most are beds in dorms that sleep anywhere from two to ten people. Plan on bringing your own soap and towels, although sheets and blankets are usually available at a nominal cost. Many sites are far from the action in Rome, but the prices are right. Always call ahead to see if you qualify and if there is space before making the long trek. Bring cash; credit cards are never accepted. Breakfast is almost never served, but English is not a problem—someone always knows enough to help you.

CENTRO TURISTICO STUDENTESCO E GIOVANILE (CTS) (118)
Via Genova, 16 (Train Station Area)
This Italian student organization helps visiting students and teachers find dorm lodgings (not hostels), book transportation by air or rail, hook up with inexpensive tours, and generally get plugged into the student Great Sleeping and traveling groove. They issue ISIC, ITIC, and Euro<26

TELEPHONE
06 462 0431, 06 687 26 72
FAX
06 4620 4326
INTERNET
www.cts.it

CREDIT CARDS
MC, V
RATES
Vary according to the establishment
ENGLISH
Yes

Cards (see "Discounts," page 28). Office hours are Monday to Friday 9:30 A.M. to 1 P.M., 2:30 to 6:30 P.M., and Saturday 9:30 A.M. to 1 P.M.

YWCAs

There is one central YWCA in Rome that provides some Great Sleeps for bargain hunters who don't mind institutional surroundings.

YWCA FOYER DI ROMA (117)
Via Cesare Balbo, 4 (Train Station Area)
45 rooms, 15 with shower and toilet

TELEPHONE
06 488 0460, 06 488 83917
FAX
06 487 1028
CREDIT CARDS
None, cash only
RATES
From 26–62€ per person, depending on number of roommates and plumbing; lunch 11€
BREAKFAST
Continental breakfast is included Mon–Sat, but never Sun, holidays, or in Aug
ENGLISH
Yes, usually

The YWCA, off Via Torino, is open to women, couples, and families, but not single men. Guests sleep in seventy-four single beds, spread out in forty-five rooms with either a private shower and toilet, or with neither. The shower in the hall is included in the price. Lunch is the only meal besides breakfast that is served. There is a lockout at midnight, no refunds, no showers between 10 P.M. and 7 A.M., no smoking (except in the garden), and of course, no credit cards. But you have all-day access to the rooms and the opportunity of eating lunch here. The welcome can range from pleasant to frozen stiff, and in all of my visits, I have gotten the picture that this is hardly "fun city."

FACILITIES AND SERVICES: Elevator, office safe, TV/video lounge, coin-operated washer, refrigerator, and hot plate on fifth floor

NEAREST TOURIST ATTRACTIONS: Termini Station

VENICE

A wonderful piece of world. Rather itself a world.
—*John Ruskin*

I loved her from my boyhood; she to me was a fairy city of the heart, rising like water-columns from the sea.
—*Lord Byron*

Visitors are caught by the spell of Venice for many reasons: Few cities have produced so much literature and art, so many photos, so much history, or so many proposals of marriage. Venice reflects life and love with an intensity and magnificence that has never been duplicated. The same grandeur that inspired Byron, Goethe, Shelley, and Wagner is on display to the millions of people who visit Venice each year. The Doge's Palace, Piazza San Marco, the Basilica, the Bridge of Sighs, and the huge Arsenale shipyards recall the golden age of Venice, when Marco Polo sailed from the harbor to open trade routes to the East. Venice then rose to become Europe's main trading post between East and West. At its height, more than two hundred thousand people lived in Venice, more than three times its present population of 63,000. Today, tourism is the biggest industry, and ten million visitors routinely spend more than $100 million a year to gaze at her beauty.

Venice was officially founded on March 25, A.D. 421. The city is made up of a hundred islands separated by more than 150 canals and joined by 428 bridges, 50 of them private. The largest canal, appropriately called the Grand Canal, makes a sinuous S-curve that bisects the city in half, which is divided into six districts, or *sestieri:* Cannaregio, Castello, and San Marco on the east side of the Grand Canal, and Dorsoduro, Santa Croce, and San Polo on the west side. This is also how the Venice listings in this guide are organized, followed by the islands. Only three bridges cross the Grand Canal: the Ponte degli Scalzi at the train station, the Rialto, and the Accademia. There are three thousand *calli* (narrow alleyways and streets), the same number as there are wooden stakes under each of the two bridgeheads at Rialto Bridge. To begin to know and understand Venice, it is essential that you arm yourself with the best street map money can buy. This will not help much, other than to give an overall picture, because as those who love the city will tell you, Venice cannot be learned by rote; it is absorbed through the pores. Part of being in Venice is to become hopelessly lost in the magical beauty of this fairy-tale city of gondolas and crumbling ornate palaces. See "Addresses," page 245, for advice on how to find an actual address in Venice. (If you want to have the best all-around view of Venice, take the vaporetto from Riva degli Schiavoni across the lagoon to San Giorgio and go to the top of the San Giorgio Maggiore Church. The spectacular vista is better than that from the Basilica of San Marco.)

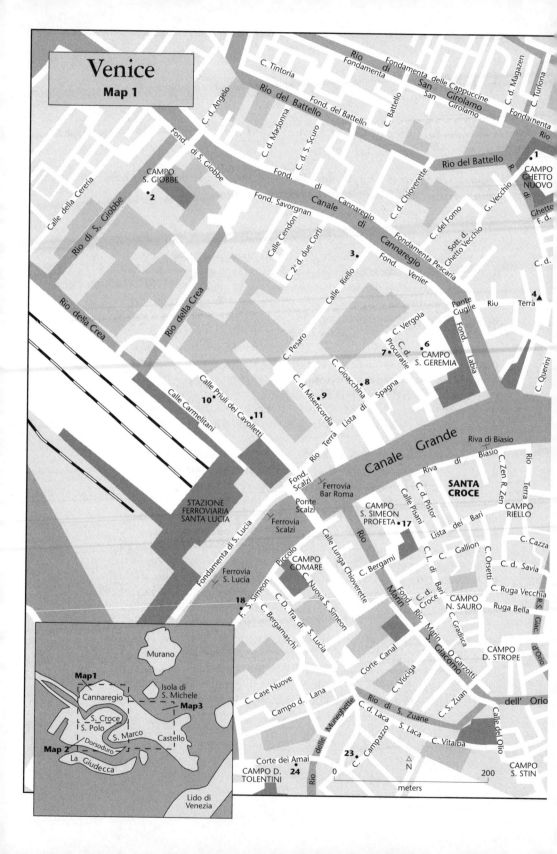

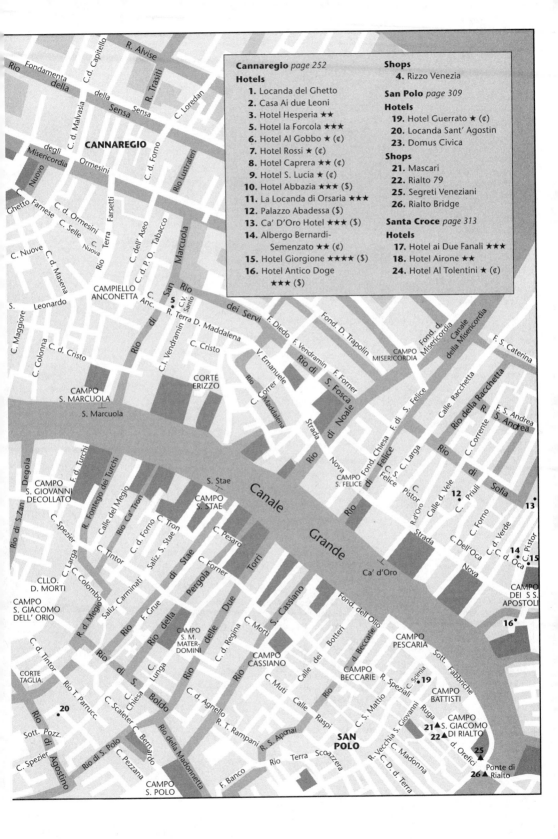

Cannaregio *page 252*
Hotels
1. Locanda del Ghetto
2. Casa Ai due Leoni
3. Hotel Hesperia ★★
5. Hotel la Forcola ★★★
6. Hotel Al Gobbo ★ (¢)
7. Hotel Rossi ★ (¢)
8. Hotel Caprera ★★ (¢)
9. Hotel S. Lucia ★ (¢)
10. Hotel Abbazia ★★★ ($)
11. La Locanda di Orsaria ★★★
12. Palazzo Abadessa ($)
13. Ca' D'Oro Hotel ★★★ ($)
14. Albergo Bernardi-
     Semenzato ★★ (¢)
15. Hotel Giorgione ★★★★ ($)
16. Hotel Antico Doge
     ★★★ ($)

Shops
4. Rizzo Venezia

San Polo *page 309*
Hotels
19. Hotel Guerrato ★ (¢)
20. Locanda Sant' Agostin
23. Domus Civica

Shops
21. Mascari
22. Rialto 79
25. Segreti Veneziani
26. Rialto Bridge

Santa Croce *page 313*
Hotels
17. Hotel ai Due Fanali ★★★
18. Hotel Airone ★★
24. Hotel Al Tolentini ★ (¢)

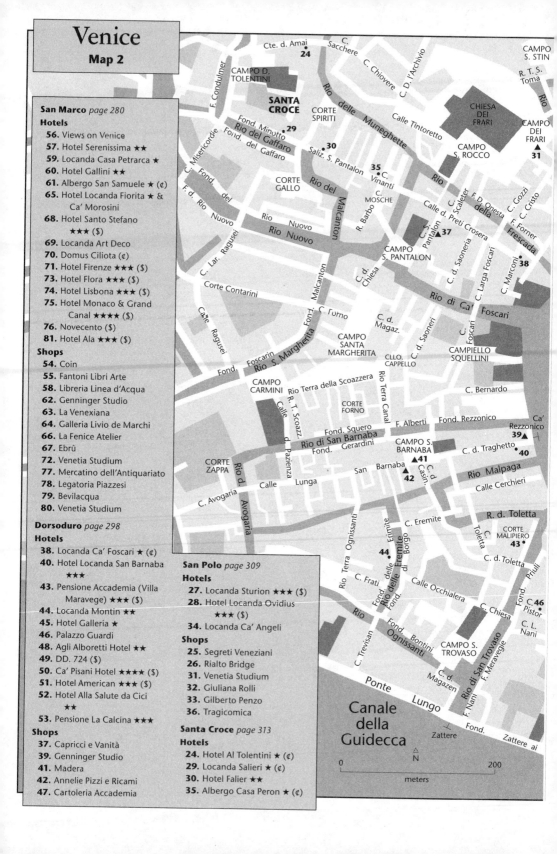

Venice
Map 2

San Marco page 280
Hotels
56. Views on Venice
57. Hotel Serenissima ★★
59. Locanda Casa Petrarca ★
60. Hotel Gallini ★★
61. Albergo San Samuele ★ (¢)
65. Hotel Locanda Fiorita ★ & Ca' Morosini
68. Hotel Santo Stefano ★★★ ($)
69. Locanda Art Deco
70. Domus Ciliota (¢)
71. Hotel Firenze ★★★ ($)
73. Hotel Flora ★★★ ($)
74. Hotel Lisbona ★★★ ($)
75. Hotel Monaco & Grand Canal ★★★★ ($)
76. Novecento ($)
81. Hotel Ala ★★★ ($)

Shops
54. Coin
55. Fantoni Libri Arte
58. Libreria Linea d'Acqua
62. Genninger Studio
63. La Venexiana
64. Galleria Livio de Marchi
66. La Fenice Atelier
67. Ebrû
72. Venetia Studium
77. Mercatino dell'Antiquariato
78. Legatoria Piazzesi
79. Bevilacqua
80. Venetia Studium

Dorsoduro page 298
Hotels
38. Locanda Ca' Foscari ★ (¢)
40. Hotel Locanda San Barnaba ★★★
43. Pensione Accademia (Villa Maravege) ★★★ ($)
44. Locanda Montin ★★
45. Hotel Galleria ★
46. Palazzo Guardi
48. Agli Alboretti Hotel ★★
49. DD. 724 ($)
50. Ca' Pisani Hotel ★★★★ ($)
51. Hotel American ★★★ ($)
52. Hotel Alla Salute da Cici ★★
53. Pensione La Calcina ★★★

Shops
37. Capricci e Vanità
39. Genninger Studio
41. Madera
42. Annelie Pizzi e Ricami
47. Cartoleria Accademia

San Polo page 309
Hotels
27. Locanda Sturion ★★★ ($)
28. Hotel Locanda Ovidius ★★★ ($)
34. Locanda Ca' Angeli

Shops
25. Segreti Veneziani
26. Rialto Bridge
31. Venetia Studium
32. Giuliana Rolli
33. Gilberto Penzo
36. Tragicomica

Santa Croce page 313
Hotels
24. Hotel Al Tolentini ★ (¢)
29. Locanda Salieri ★ (¢)
30. Hotel Falier ★★
35. Albergo Casa Peron ★ (¢)

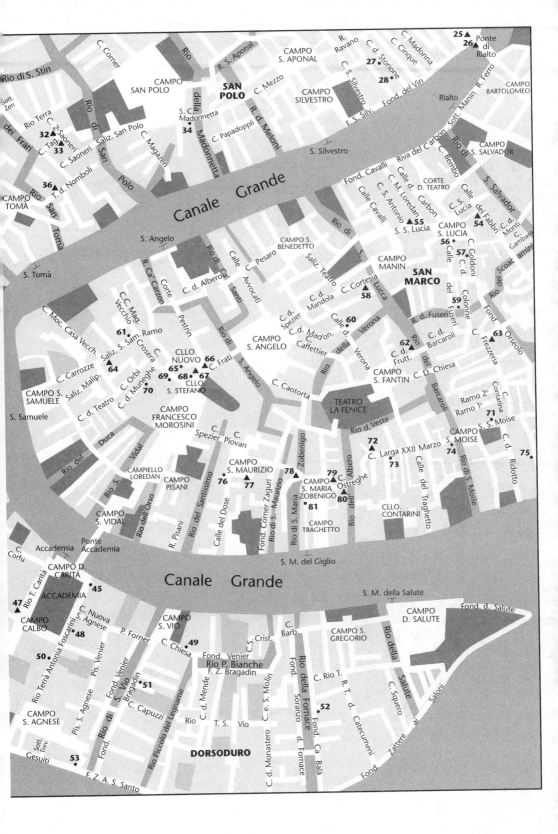

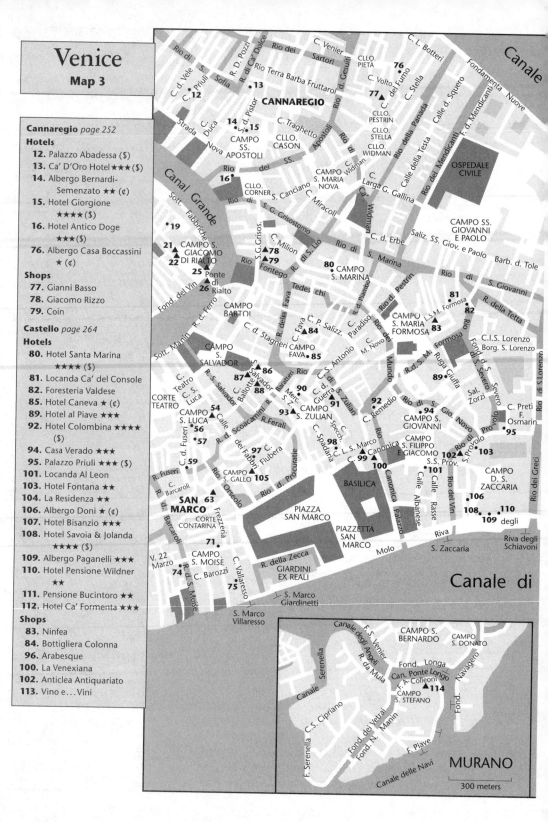

Venice
Map 3

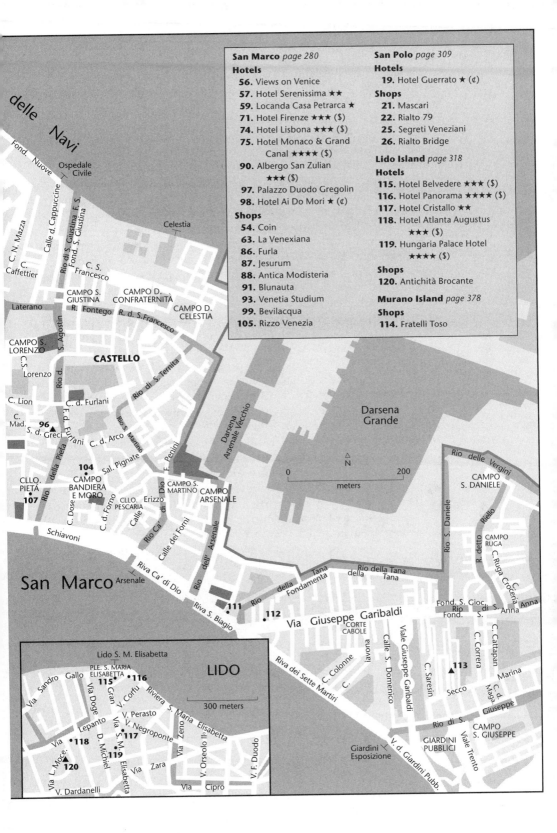

San Marco *page 280*
Hotels
  56. Views on Venice
  57. Hotel Serenissima ★★
  59. Locanda Casa Petrarca ★
  71. Hotel Firenze ★★★ ($)
  74. Hotel Lisbona ★★★ ($)
  75. Hotel Monaco & Grand
      Canal ★★★★ ($)
  90. Albergo San Zulian
      ★★★ ($)
  97. Palazzo Duodo Gregolin
  98. Hotel Ai Do Mori ★ (¢)

Shops
  54. Coin
  63. La Venexiana
  86. Furla
  87. Jesurum
  88. Antica Modisteria
  91. Blunauta
  93. Venetia Studium
  99. Bevilacqua
 105. Rizzo Venezia

San Polo *page 309*
Hotels
  19. Hotel Guerrato ★ (¢)
Shops
  21. Mascari
  22. Rialto 79
  25. Segreti Veneziani
  26. Rialto Bridge

Lido Island *page 318*
Hotels
 115. Hotel Belvedere ★★★ ($)
 116. Hotel Panorama ★★★★ ($)
 117. Hotel Cristallo ★★
 118. Hotel Atlanta Augustus
     ★★★ ($)
 119. Hungaria Palace Hotel
     ★★★★ ($)

Shops
 120. Antichità Brocante

Murano Island *page 378*
Shops
 114. Fratelli Toso

There is no use pretending that one of the world's most romantic cities is anything but very expensive, especially during the weekends in high season and anytime at Carnivale. However, time spent here does not necessarily call for dipping into retirement funds or mortgaging the ranch, although you will have to use a degree of self-restraint and, at the same time, plan on spending more for everything here than you will elsewhere in Italy. Consider your trip to Venice a gift to yourself—you work hard and deserve it, and as the old saying goes, you can't take it with you. One way to trim costs is to reserve an apartment managed by a hotel. This opportunity is unique to Venice, and it will both save you money and increase your appreciation of the city. See "Hotels with Apartments," page 397.

The best times to go are from April through June, from September until November, and at Christmas, but these are also when most other people come. There are two off-seasons: one is approximately November to March, not including Christmas and Carnivale, and then again during all of July and August, when the heat and the mosquitoes drive even the natives away. During these times, the pace is slower, crowds thinner, and hotel prices can be less, though note that from the beginning of January until Carnivale, many hotels and shops close completely. And then there is Carnivale, which is roughly the two weeks before Lent. If you would like to attend this event, you must make your reservations far, far in advance, and then it doesn't hurt to pray to St. Christopher, the patron saint of travelers, and to St. Anthony, the patron saint of finding things—then cross your fingers, bow to Mecca, and rub a Buddha. You will need all the help you can get just to find a room, and it will take a true miracle to find one that is reasonably priced. For Carnivale, the price gouging is unbelievable, but then again, so are the "Great Tourist Hordes," who create positively the worst crush of humanity you will ever experience. The crowds are so thick you simply cannot move more than one centimeter every five minutes! Avoid this period at all costs unless you are passionate for claustrophobic crowds and ridiculously high prices for everything in sight.

It is important for visitors to adopt a philosophical attitude about Venetian hotels. First of all, you will not get the values you will in other places. Some hotels could earn a higher star rating, except that they are in a historic building that cannot be altered, preventing such improvements as an elevator, modern plumbing, air-conditioning, or simply more space. While you will probably sacrifice comfort in small quarters that will never be modernized, this will be compensated for by frescoed ceilings and the age-old beauty of the building surrounding you—and, perhaps, by the final payoff of a view onto the Grand Canal, inspiring you to fall in love all over again. Who could put a price on that?

General Information

Our Venice is Your Venice...handle with care.
—Sign posted by the Venetian tourist bureau

Addresses

You can't avoid it: some time during your stay, perhaps many times, you will become completely lost. Partly this is the nature of Venice. Partly this happens because there is very little consistency in the spelling of place and street names; don't expect street signs or business cards to match your city map (including the maps and spellings in this guide!). But mainly this happens because of Venice's language dialect and confusing address system, whereby each *sestiere* has only one long series of addresses, which are usually written only with the name of the *sestiere* and the number of the address (such as, San Marco, 2207). Unless you are a native *and* a postal official, chances are you will have no idea where that number is in the district of San Marco. To put this in perspective, San Polo, the smallest district, has 3,144 addresses; Castello, the largest, has 6,828. As you can imagine, this makes looking for places desperately frustrating and can make maps irrelevant. It is always important to ask for specific directions, including street names and landmarks, such as a *campo* or a church. Though you may be lost, there is no need to panic. Look for the yellow signs posted throughout the city to find the general direction you want and just follow the crowd. For example: If you are heading to the Rialto Bridge, look for the sign saying Rialto. If your destination is Piazza San Marco, look for signs pointing to San Marco. Accademia is your direction if you want to see the Peggy Guggenheim Collection. If you are going to the train station, go in the direction marked *Ferrovia,* train station.

Venetian Street Terms

Calle	main alleyway or street, often picturesque
Campiello	small square
Campo	square, usually with a church on it with the same name as the square
Corte, corti	courtyard
Fondamenta	street along a canal or lagoon
Piscina	former pool that has been filled in
Ponte	bridge
Ramo	small side street or alleyway linking two streets, often dead-end
Rio	small canal used by gondolas and cargo boats
Rio Terà	a canal filled in to make a street
Riva	major stretch of pavement along water

Ruga (and Rughetta)	main shopping street
Salizzada	sometimes spelled *salizada,* the main street of a district
Sestiere	district
Sottoportico	small alley or street running beneath a building

Tourist Offices

Azienda di Promozione Turistica (APT) is the Venetian tourist bureau. The main office is near Piazza San Marco, but there are branches at the Santa Lucia railroad station and Marco Polo Airport, in the arrivals hall. If you have a complaint, call 800 355 920.

Main APT office
Calle dell' Ascensione, 71-F, off Piazza San Marco
Tel: 041 529 8711
Fax: 041 523 0399
Internet: www.turismovenezia.it
Open: Daily 9:30 A.M.–3:30 P.M.

Disabled Travelers

Informahandicap, located on the mainland in Mestre, is an organization providing information on transport, hotels, restaurants, and museums with handicapped access. For disabled transport, call 041 523 9977, 041 524 5357.

Informahandicap
Via Catalani 9/a, Mestre
Tel: 041 976 435
Internet: www.comune.venezia.it/handicap
Open: Tues, Thur, Fri 3:30–6:30 P.M., Wed & Sat 9 A.M.–1 P.M.

Consulates

The closest U.S. representative is in Trieste: Via dei Pellegrini, 42; Tel: 041 191 780. The British Consulate is at Campo della Carità, 1051 (Dorsoduro); Tel: 041 522 7207; Open: Mon–Fri 10 A.M.–1 P.M.

Post Office

For postal information, dial 160.

Main Post Office
Salizada del Fontego dei Tedeschi, Campo San Bartolomeo, near Rialto Bridge
Tel: 041 271 7111
Open: Mon–Sat 8:30 A.M.–6:30 P.M.

Federal Express
San Marco, 71G, off Piazza San Marco
Tel: 041 277 0785, toll-free 800 123 800
Internet: www.fedex.com/it

Telephone

The city code for Venice is 041; this must be dialed before every land-line phone number. However, when dialing a cell phone, the city code is omitted. If you are having problems making an international call from Venice, you can dial 172 3535 from 7 A.M. to 9 P.M., or directory assistance by dialing 12. For more information on Italian telephones, see "Staying in Touch," page 34.

Emergency Numbers

First Aid/Ambulance	118
Police	112/113
Fire	115

Medical Treatment

In a medical emergency, dial 118 for an ambulance. There is also Emergency Services for Foreigners at Castello 4693/A; Tel: 041 520 4777; all should have English-speaking operators. For a hospital with an emergency room, or if you need dental care, go to Santi Giovanni & Paolo (Ospedale Civile), at Campo dei SS. Giovanni e Paolo in Castello; Tel: 041 529 4111.

Pharmacies are identified by a green cross above the door. Hours are Mon–Fri 9 A.M.–12:30 P.M., 3:45–7:30 P.M., Sat 9 A.M.–12:30 P.M. The pharmacists are qualified to give medical and homeopathic advice on common ailments. A few pharmacies are open twenty-four hours on a rotating basis. The names and locations are posted outside every pharmacy and in the local newspapers. For information on pharmacies, dial 192, or 041 531 1592.

Money Matters

Banks are usually open Mon–Fri from 8:30 A.M.–1 P.M., 3–4 P.M. Most have ATMs, which in theory operate twenty-four hours a day. Commission rates vary.

American Express is at Salizzada San Moisè, 1471 (San Marco), Tel: 041 520 0844. Hours for travel services and currency exchange are Mon–Fri 9:30 A.M.–5:30 P.M., Sat until 12:30 P.M.; American Express is also the fastest way to wire money.

For assistance with lost or stolen traveler's checks or credit cards, these toll-free numbers have English-speaking operators.

American Express	
credit cards	800 864 046
traveler's checks	800 872 000
Diners' Club	800 864 064
Mastercard	800 874 299
Visa	800 877 232

Discount Cards

Venice has three discount tourist cards that visitors might consider purchasing: the Museum Card, the VENICEcard, and the Rolling VENICEcard.

The Museum Card (Carta dei Musei di Venezia) costs 35€, is valid for one year, and allows access to forty major Venetian museums, *palazzos,* and churches. If you plan to be in Venice awhile and will return to your favorites several times, it is a good deal, but it won't save you money if you are only going to hit a few on the top ten list. The card is available at all participating museums and at the main APT tourist office (see page 246).

VENICEcard is a one-, three-, or seven-day card giving holders discounts and accesses to many services in Venice. Its main benefit is that it allows holders free access to public transport (i.e., the vaporettos) and reduced fare on the Alilaguna boat service from and to the airport. There are two types of cards: orange and blue. The orange card costs twice as much as the blue but offers much more, including free or reduced access to museums, churches, and cultural events, as well as discounts in the carparks near Piazzale Roma, and in bars, restaurants, and shops with the VENICEcard logo. You can reserve a VENICEcard online (www.venicecard.it) or by telephone (39 041 2424). If you reserve and pay in advance online by credit card, you get a discount. VENICEcards without advance reservations can be bought from Vela, APT, and Ava tourist offices, which have booths at Piazzale Roma. For one to seven days, the orange card costs 18 to 81€ for those 28 and younger, and 28 to 88€ for those 29 and older; the blue card costs 9 to 71€ for those 28 and younger, and 14 to 71€ for those 29 and older.

The Rolling VENICEcard is for visitors between 14 and 29 years old. Holders are entitled to discounts at selected hotels, restaurants, museums, and shops, as well as reduced-fare three-day vaporetto tickets and 50 percent off concerts at La Fenice. The card can be purchased at any Vela office. There is one at Piazzale Roma, Tel: 041 272 2249 (no credit cards accepted). A central one that accepts MasterCard and Visa is near Piazza San Marco at Calle dei Fuseri, 1810; Tel: 041 272 2310. For further information, consult the Website: www.velaspa.com.

Tours

Venetian Travel Advisory Service

Special Venetian travel tip: Whatever reason takes you to Venice, all I can say is—don't miss Samantha!

For a memorable private tour through the back streets of Venice and an inside peek into how Venetians live, work, play, and even die, please call Samantha Durell at her Venetian Travel Advisory Service. Samantha is from New York, but years ago she fell in love with Venice, and eventually followed her dream by moving there. Besides being delightful, she knows and understands Venice better than most natives, and she seems to know them all. You cannot walk more than a block without someone rushing up to her with everything from a "Ciao, Samantha" to a huge bear hug. It is clear that everyone adores Samantha, and after one day spent on a tour with her, you will too.

She offers four distinct walks; each lasts about four hours and is limited to four people. *The Art of Living Well* is a culture walk through the back streets of Venice that shows the hidden aspects of Venetian life. *The Art of Eating Well* is designed for those who love good food. With Samantha's guidance, you will shop in neighborhood markets, then prepare and eat your Venetian specialty meal in her beautiful home overlooking a picturesque lagoon. Believe me, this will be one *buon appetito* you will never forget. On *Through the Camera Lens* Samantha, a renowned photographer in her own right, will lead photo buffs to Venice's charming nooks and crannies as well as to some of her own secret spots. Finally there is her incomparable excursion, *Sailing Back in Time Through the Venetian Lagoons;* this lasts about six hours and is limited to three people. It starts with a neighborhood walk that leads to a gondola building boatyard, where guests visit a private workshop and learn about the process of building a gondola. Then you go sailing on a beautiful Venetian-crafted boat, winding your way through the waterways of Venice and the surrounding islands. The sail lasts about three hours and includes a gourmet picnic. Any of these tours will be your own unique Venetian adventure you will never forget.

NOTE: Samantha is in Venice from Carnivale to Thanksgiving.

Telephone & Fax: New York, 212-873-1964; Venice, 041 523 2379

Rates: From $325 for the first two people and $60 for each additional person; school-age children are $25; the sailing tour is $600.

Transportation

> **Venice is all about strolling around with your head in the clouds without having to worry about traffic.**
> —*Anonymous*

How true that is, since the best way to see and feel the beauty of Venice is on foot. However, there are times when other means of getting where you want to go make sense. There are several options to get you to and from the airport, but in Venice itself, all the options use the water.

Airport: For general inquiries at Marco Polo Airport, call 041 260 9260; www.veniceairport.it. To arrange a shuttle bus to and from the airport, call 041 541 5180; www.atvo.it. For a water taxi to and from the airport, call 041 541 5084 (no credit cards). To go by the Alilaguna boat service, call 041 523 5775; www.alilaguna.com. If you lose something while at the airport, call 041 260 6436.

Train: For general inquiries, call 041 1478 88 088 or 041 848 888 088. For lost and found at the Santa Lucia Train Station, call 041 785 238.

Bus: For general information, call 041 899 909 090. If you lose something on a bus, call 041 272 2838.

Car taxis: For a taxi on Lido Island, call 041 526 5974 or 041 526 5975. For a taxi from the Piazzale Roma to points outside of Venice, call 041 523 7774.

Gondola: Hiring a gondola to take you from points A to B in Venice is a unique but very expensive way to commute. A fifty-minute gondola ride for one to six people starts around 70€, and jumps to 95€ after 8 P.M., singing extra. There are four hundred *gondolieri* in Venice, but these are not just men who row boats...far from it. Theirs is a time-honored Venetian tradition that is handed down from father to son. Each gondola is custom made and is composed of more than 250 pieces of eight different types of wood. The six-pronged *fero* on the bow is said to represent the six *sestieri* of Venice and the Grand Canal. To arrange for your gondola trip, go to one of the main places where they originate: Hotel Danieli on Riva degli Schiavoni, by the Vallaresso vaporetto stop, by Santa Maria del Giglio vaporetto stop, Piazza San Marco, Campo Santa Sofa near the Ca'D'Oro Vaporetto stop, San Tomà vaporetto stop, Hotel Bauer Grunwald Hotel in Campo San Moisè, and the southern end of the Rialto Bridge. Or, call the head office in San Marco, 041 528 5075.

Water Taxis: Water taxis are also very expensive and not worth the money unless there are several in your party and you are coming or going to the train station with mounds of luggage. For general information, call 041 240 6711; to order a taxi twenty-four hours a day, call 041 522 2303; www.veneziamotoscafi.com.

However, there is another water-taxi service, largely unknown to visitors—the *traghetto*. Years ago there used to be hundreds of these gondolas crossing the Grand Canal, but now their number has been reduced to seven. The *traghetti* gondoliers go back and forth with five or six people, but forget about getting on with piles of luggage. The fare is around 0.40€, which you pay when you get in. The natives stand, but it's okay if you want to sit. It is an inexpensive way to ride in a gondola, and it can save you extra miles of walking from one bridge to another in an attempt to cross the Grand Canal. The *traghetto* crossing points are: San Marcuola–Fontego dei Turchi, Santa Sofia–Rialto, Riva del Carbon–Rive del Vin, Ca' Garzoni–San Tomà, San Samuele–Ca'Rezzonico, Santa Maria del Giglio–Santa Maria della Salute, and San Marco–Dogana. Hours vary, but they start between 7 and 9 A.M. and finish between 2 and 6 P.M.

Vaporetto: Using the *vaporetti*, or water buses, is the most economical and efficient way to go any distance in Venice. Tickets are available at all the main landing stages. If the booth is closed, tell the uniformed person on board, and you will be issued a ticket. If you travel without a valid ticket, you will be liable for a 35€ fine plus the cost of the ticket. Don't think, as I once did, that you won't get caught...the uniformed ticket checkers are vigilant. One-way tickets, at 5€ for 90-minutes, can add up in a hurry. If you are going to be in Venice for a while, consider a seventy-two-hour unlimited ticket for around 20€, or a weekly unlimited ticket for less than 40€. For everything you need to know about tickets and for the schedule of the various vaporetto routes, pick up a copy of the Italian/English Orario–Timetable, available at any ACTV vaporetto ticket booth. If you lose something on a vaporetto, call 041 272 2179.

Porters: If you need help getting your bags from one place to another, call these burley porters, who can be seen everywhere in Venice making deliveries and moving goods with their carts: Rialto, 041 520 3070; Piazzale Roma, 041 522 3590; and Ferrovia (train station) 041 715 272.

Parking

If you arrive in Venice by car, you could leave your car in one of the parking garages at Piazzale Roma. This could cost you an arm and a leg. If your hotel belongs to the Venetian Hoteliers Association (AVA), ask about the discount given at the Tronchetto car park. You should be able to get your discount voucher from the hotel and present it at the car park cashier when you pay to leave. The price per day is around 20€.

Hotels East of the Grand Canal

Cannaregio

In the strangeness of this city, full of myth and magic, we find ourselves in a world half real and half dream, a world each of us comes to love in his own special way.
—Braudel

This is the northwestern district of Venice, where you will find the train station leading to one of the most tourist-trod and tacky streets anywhere—Lista di Spagna. At the end of this street is the imposing Palazzo Labia, with frescoes by Tiepolo of the life of Cleopatra, set in the pomp of eighteenth-century Venice rather than in ancient Egypt. Venture a few streets away from all the commercial hustle and you will find the quiet Jewish Quarter, which is also known as the Jewish "Ghetto"(and was the first place in the world to use the term). The Venetian Jewish Ghetto is the world's oldest, dating from 1385 when the first Jews were allowed to settle here. At its height, in 1650, 4,000 Jews lived in a space equal to two and a half city blocks. By World War II, the Jewish population had dwindled to 1,300; 289 of these were deported and only 7 returned. There are relatively few tourist attractions here other than the Madonna dell' Orto, with its Tintoretto paintings, and the Ca' d'Oro, a magnificent Gothic palace on the Grand Canal with a collection of beautiful paintings and carvings.

HOTELS

($) indicates a Big Splurge; (¢) indicates a Cheap Sleep

ALBERGO BERNARDI-SEMENZATO ★★ (¢, 14)
Calle del Oca, Campo dei SS. Apostoli, 4363/66

30 rooms, 24 with shower or bath and toilet

Gregarious owner and English teacher Maria Teresa Pepoli and her husband, Leonardo, a pharmacist, owned this hotel for a few years before they finally bit the bullet, sinking a tremendous amount of money and two years of their time and labor into redoing the hotel and annex. Maria designed the Murano glass lights in the reception, as well as most of the renovation project itself; Leonardo painted the walls.

In the hotel, the rooms are almost all alike—simple, clear-cut, many with original beams and views. Number 7, a double with a nice bathroom featuring handmade decorative tiles, has two windows opening onto a very narrow street. Number 10, another double with roofline views, has fifth-century beams, and the Caterina de Medici Room has a canopy bed and a view. For a canal-side room, book No. 8—the furniture is modern and there is no toilet... but, oh, what a romantic sunset view!

The rooms in the annex feature more antiques and hand-painted beamed ceilings, and they overlook a garden or a canal. Number 301, a huge room for two or three overlooking the garden, has Venetian cream-colored furnishings and a green-tile bath. Number 302 has a canopy bed, quiet corner view, and more Venetian hand-decorated furniture. Even bigger than No. 301 is No. 303, with its private bathroom just outside the room.

NOTE: The hotel is closed the last half of January (dates vary).

FACILITIES AND SERVICES: Air-conditioning, direct-dial phone, hair dryer available, no elevator (3 floors), in-room safe, satellite TV, nonsmoking hotel, reception open from 7 A.M.–1 A.M.

NEAREST TOURIST ATTRACTIONS: Jewish Quarter, Grand Canal, Fondamenta Nuove for trips to Murano and Burano

TELEPHONE
041 522 7257

FAX
041 522 2424

INTERNET
www.hotelbernardi.com

CREDIT CARDS
AE, DC, MC, V

RATES
Single 33–60€, double 61–85€, triple 103€, quad 125€; discounts for *Great Sleeps Italy* readers who mention book when reserving (subject to availability)

BREAKFAST
Continental breakfast included

ENGLISH
Yes, and French, Russian, and German

ALBERGO CASA BOCCASSINI ★ (¢, 76)
Calle del Fumo, 5295

TELEPHONE
041 52 29 892
FAX
041 52 36 877
CREDIT CARDS
MC, V
RATES
Single 30–60€, double 45–
115€, triple 115–140€, quad
130–160€; rate range is for
rooms without and with
private bathrooms
BREAKFAST
Continental breakfast included
(can deduct 2.50€ per person
if not taken)
ENGLISH
Yes, and French

12 rooms, 6 with shower or bath and toilet

One damp March day I was walking from my flat to the Fondamenta Nuove to catch the No. 52 boat to go to Murano when I noticed the Albergo Casa Boccassini tucked along a narrow alley in this Venetian working-class neighborhood, one that most visitors barely notice, let alone explore. However, for more than twenty-five years, Fernanda Bortoluzzi has been running her artistically funky hideaway, which she has filled with family furniture that ranges from the good to the bad to the ugly. If you are a modernist, computer-dependent, or an exacting scientist or engineer, this is probably not your Venice dream hotel. If, on the other hand, you are a poet, a nostalgic romantic, or a pair of cash-strapped lovers . . . read on.

The rooms are not all created equal. The best is No. 6, a double with matching antiques, a garden view, and a manageable bathroom. Number 9 has a polished sea-green-tile floor, white walls, and modern furniture. There is no view or bathroom, but the hall facilities are just fine. The furniture is also modern in No. 11, and you will wake to the singing of birds from the sunny windows facing the narrow street. Number 8 is a large blue room with a garden view from all three windows. The purple-tile bath has a half-tub and shower. If you don't want to climb stairs, request No. 5, a half-knotty-pine-paneled double on the ground floor that has a gold metal bed and a big shower. The garden is as eclectic as Fernanda, but it's lit at night and large enough to accommodate several tables, where breakfast is served in summer.

NOTE: The hotel is closed from November 20 to one week before Carnivale.

FACILITIES AND SERVICES: Air-conditioning in 4 rooms, direct-dial phone, no elevator (2 floors), hair dryer available, TV on request, office safe

NEAREST TOURIST ATTRACTIONS: Fondamenta Nuove and boats to Murano and Burano; about a 20-minute walk to Rialto and the Grand Canal

CA' D'ORO HOTEL ★★★ ($, 13)
Corte Barbaro, 4604

TELEPHONE
041 241 1212
FAX
041 241 4385

24 rooms, all with shower or bath and toilet

Some of the best Great Sleeps I find by accident. While looking out of the window of a nearby hotel, I spotted the discreet courtyard entrance of the Ca' D'Oro Hotel but did not realize it was a hotel. When I saw the pretty flowers around an old well, and a dock where guests could arrive by boat, that was all I needed. What I found was a charming hotel with six of the rooms and two junior suites opening onto canal views, an elevator to all floors (a rarity in Venice), fabric-covered walls that complement attractive light-colored furnishings, coordinated bed linens and curtains, good closet space, nice bathrooms, and Jacuzzis in the suites. Plus, it's a ten-minute walk to Rialto Bridge and an easy fifteen to twenty minutes to Piazza San Marco.

FACILITIES AND SERVICES: Air-conditioning, direct-dial phone, elevator, hair dryer, guest Internet terminal, in-room safe, satellite TV, boat dock

NEAREST TOURIST ATTRACTIONS: Rialto, Grand Canal, Fondamenta Nuove and boats to Murano and Burano

INTERNET
www.venicehotelcadoro.it
CREDIT CARDS
AE, DC, MC, V
RATES
Single 170€, double 240€, junior suite 320€, extra bed 70€; excellent lower off-season rates
BREAKFAST
Buffet breakfast included
ENGLISH
Yes

CASA AI DUE LEONI (2)
Campiello Santa Marina de la Pazienza, 565
7 rooms all with shower or bath and toilet

The appealing Casa Ai due Leoni takes its name from the two stone lions guarding the entrance. The sixteenth-century building is located in a hidden yet picturesque little corner of Venice, with twisting and turning walkways and *campiellos* . . . but once found, it will not be forgotten by those looking for something off the beaten track. The seven quiet rooms are named after famous Venetian painters and have a print of one of their works hanging inside. Tiziano is a large ground-floor room with two windows on the hotel garden and one of his nudes hanging over the wrought-iron double bed. There is an alcove with a twin bed in it and a marble bath with a stall shower. Canaletto, a triple, also faces the garden. It has beams, a tiled floor, and a nice deep tub in the bathroom. Giorgione is a two-level double with an L-shaped entry leading to a small sitting room and full bathroom. The sleeping quarters and television are upstairs.

FACILITIES AND SERVICES: Air-conditioning, direct-dial phone, no elevator (2 floors), hair dryer, minibar, in-room safe, satellite TV

NEAREST TOURIST ATTRACTIONS: Grand Canal, Jewish Quarter, train station

TELEPHONE
041 524 4138
FAX
041 524 4155
EMAIL
ai2leoni@libero.it
INTERNET
www.aidueleoni.com
CREDIT CARDS
AE, DC, MC, V
RATES
Single 82–160€, double 95–190€, triple 145–245€, family room 170–300€
BREAKFAST
Continental breakfast included
ENGLISH
Yes

HOTEL ABBAZIA ★★★ ($, 10)
Calle Priuli dei Cavolletti, 68

50 rooms, all with shower or bath and toilet

TELEPHONE
041 717 333
FAX
041 717 949
INTERNET
www.abbaziahotel.it
CREDIT CARDS
AE, DC, MC, V
RATES
Single 180€, double 210€;
extra person 30% of room rate;
discounts for *Great Sleeps Italy*
readers, must mention the book
when reserving and show it
upon arrival
BREAKFAST
Buffet breakfast included
ENGLISH
Yes

In its golden age, the Abbazia was a monastery housing forty to fifty barefoot Carmelite Friars of Venice. Their work included producing a special medicinal water called Melissa Water. Now the main center for this production has been moved to Verona. Eventually, the friars relinquished part of their Venice property, and it has been converted into this tranquil hotel. Today, a few of the monks still live in quarters on the other side of the garden and run the church next to the train station.

The location, in a small alley next to a row of low-cost hotels behind the station, is not spectacular in itself. However, once inside the hotel, you will feel a million miles removed from all the activity surrounding the station. The rooms have been faithfully restored, maintaining the quiet atmosphere and spirit of the original abbey. Scattered throughout the hotel are pieces of furniture the monks used in their daily lives and church services. For example, the lobby, which was once the chapel, has wooden abbey benches around the perimeter and the pulpit along one side. The yellow breakfast room, with a huge skylight, was once the kitchen. Wide Venetian mosaic-tile hallways are graced with Oriental carpet runners and black-and-white prints of old Venice.

The largest rooms are upstairs and face the garden, which was the central courtyard of the monastery. All have plenty of closet and luggage space, ample light, nice bathrooms, and attractive reproduction furnishings. Favorites include No. 203, a double overlooking the garden and its gazebo. I also like No. 409, a beamed room with a hardwood floor and a large bathroom with a Jacuzzi. The view is over the glass roof of the convent, where the monks still live. The singles are very small, and a few are frankly depressing and must be avoided. To do this, ask for a small double for single use. The management is especially helpful and courteous, but best of all, they offer discounts (subject to season and availability) to *Great Sleeps Italy* readers; make sure to mention the book when reserving and show it upon arrival.

FACILITIES AND SERVICES: Air-conditioning, bar, direct-dial phone, no elevator (2 floors), hair dryer, minibar, parking by arrangement, satellite TV, in-room safe

NEAREST TOURIST ATTRACTIONS: Grand Canal, train station, Piazzale Roma

HOTEL AL GOBBO ★ (¢, 6)
Campo S. Geremia, 312
12 rooms, 8 with shower or bath and toilet

For 63 years, this one-star jewel was run by Maria di Vinco, who fits everyone's picture of the perfect Italian grandmother: regal yet genteel and with a heart of gold. She has now passed the day-to-day running of the hotel along to family members, and I am happy to report, none of her spirit has been lost on them.

The word *gobbo* means "hunchback." The Italians have a superstition that if you touch the back of someone with a hump, it will bring you good luck. If you stay here, you will feel lucky, for this is a wonderful budget choice. The neat, clean bedrooms have unadorned wash-and-wipe furniture. A few of the roosts overlook a lovely garden, while others open onto Campo S. Geremia. Number 1, always a favorite, faces the *campo* and has a bathroom with an enclosed stall shower. In No. 6, the view is of a garden, the beds are twins, and there is an enclosed stall shower. For those opting for bathless rooms, the communal bathroom is one of the best in Venice, with a stretch tub and separate stall shower. Breakfast is served on a round table in the sitting room, where you will feel as though you are in someone's nice Venetian home, not in a hotel near the train station.

NOTE: The hotel is closed from December 20 to January 17 (dates can vary).

FACILITIES AND SERVICES: Air-conditioning in some rooms, no elevator (2 floors), some fans, TV

NEAREST TOURIST ATTRACTIONS: Jewish Quarter, Grand Canal, train station

TELEPHONE
041 715 001
FAX
041 714 765
INTERNET
www.albergoalgobbo.it
CREDIT CARDS
MC, V
RATES
Single 70–80€, double 83–105€, triple 105–135€, quad 125–160€; some discounts for low-season and longer stays
BREAKFAST
Continental breakfast included
ENGLISH
Yes, and French and German

HOTEL ANTICO DOGE ★★★ ($, 16)
Campo SS. Apostoli, 5643
11 rooms, all with shower or bath and toilet

Mariella Bozzetto spent two years transforming a peeling, wilting eleven-room disaster in the Palazzo del Doge Marin Falier into a dynamic Great Sleep that faces the waters of a romantic canal. To capture the feeling of the beauty and importance of Venice when it was the center of commerce for the entire Orient, she used layers of silk, rich brocades, heavy damasks, gilt mirrors, and ornate Murano glass and mixed them with antiques, both real and reproduction. The elegant result pleases a discerning audience, one that appreciates the individuality of the rooms, which are each named after a famous Doge. The Falier Suite is a sensational romantic choice with a four-poster bed under a

TELEPHONE
041 241 1570
FAX
041 244 3660
INTERNET
www.anticodoge.com
CREDIT CARDS
AE, MC, V
RATES
No single rates; double 199–225€, suite with canal view 260–340€, suite with courtyard view 245–315€, extra bed 60€; excellent lower off-season rates

BREAKFAST
Buffet breakfast included
ENGLISH
Yes

massive ceiling. Lush gold-and-red fabric covers the walls and combines well with the modern mirrored entry and blend of old and new furnishings. A small terrace provides a good vantage point for the activity in the *campo* below, and the Jacuzzi in the marble bath is the perfect place to relax after a day in Venice. The Grimani is a pleasant, roomy double with a typical Venetian view of neighborhood life. In Orseolo, another double, gondolas are parked along the canal by your window and serve as vivid reminders of the remarkable beauty of this magical city.

FACILITIES AND SERVICES: Air-conditioning, bar, direct-dial phone, no elevator (2 floors), hair dryer, Jacuzzis in suites, minibar, in-room safe, satellite TV, nonsmoking hotel

NEAREST TOURIST ATTRACTIONS: Rialto Bridge, Grand Canal

HOTEL CAPRERA ★★ (¢, 8)
Calle Gioacchina, 219

TELEPHONE
041 715 271
FAX
041 715 927
INTERNET
www.hotelcaprera.it
CREDIT CARDS
AE, MC, V
RATES
Single 49€, double 72€, triple 92€, quad 155€; 20% lower off-season rates
BREAKFAST
Continental breakfast 6€
ENGLISH
Yes

20 rooms, 4 with shower or bath and toilet

Massimo Bico, his wife, their three young children, his mother, and a friendly black cocker spaniel named Matisse run the tidy Caprera, which is situated on a side street off the pulsating Lista di Spagna. In the lobby area, Massimo displays his unusual collection of hundred-year-old wooden Venetian boat miniatures. Be sure to take a few minutes to admire them, each a faithful reproduction of Venetian transport boats, a covered gondola, and a gondola regatta. The whitewashed rooms are pillbox modern and neat, with bright bedspreads and easy-wipe Formica furniture. Those with bathrooms have a shower spout on the wall—which will get not only you wet but the entire bathroom as well. Don't pay extra for a room with a shower like this when there is no extra charge for the excellent hall shower on each floor. On the third floor, five rooms have air-conditioning, five have a terrace, and one is a large family room (No. 31). On the ground floor is a room suitable for a handicapped visitor. In line with the basic approach here, you are not stuck for an expensive breakfast, but you will need to climb stairs, as there is no elevator.

NOTE: The hotel is closed from November 15 to January 15.

FACILITIES AND SERVICES: Air-conditioning in 5 rooms, direct-dial phone, no elevator (3 floors), fan, guest Internet terminal, office safe, TV in lounge, reception open 7 A.M.–midnight

NEAREST TOURIST ATTRACTIONS: Train station, Grand Canal, Piazzale Roma

HOTEL GIORGIONE ★★★★ ($, 15)
Campo SS. Apostoli, 4587
76 rooms, all with shower or bath and toilet

The century-old Hotel Giorgione is in a fifteenth-century palace not too far from the Rialto Bridge. The rooms and split-level suites with private terraces are fundamentally appealing and well-manicured with quality fabrics and furnishings. Room 132, sold as a double or triple, is painted in vibrant aqua and has a floral-tile bathroom. The bed is on a platform in No. 127, and in Suite 105, there is a sitting room and a double bedroom with a half-tester bed and antique dresser. Number 102, a suite with a private terrace, is the favorite of the Queen of Norway, who stayed here for one month. Number 309 is another favorite of many. The two-level choice has a king-size bed and a bathroom downstairs and a sofa bed upstairs, which leads to the private *altana*—a wooden terrace built over the tile rooftop. The public areas of the hotel are luxurious and alluring. I like the game room with a pool table, the tented brick patio, and the large dining room where breakfast and afternoon tea are served under a massive, floral Murano chandelier. As you would expect in a four-star hotel, all services are available from a very professional staff.

FACILITIES AND SERVICES: Air-conditioning, bar, concierge, direct-dial phone, 2 elevators, hair dryer, guest Internet terminal, laundry service, minibar, porter, in-room safe, satellite TV, all rooms nonsmoking

NEAREST TOURIST ATTRACTIONS: Rialto Bridge, Grand Canal

TELEPHONE
041 522 5810

FAX
041 523 9092

INTERNET
www.hotelgiorgione.com

CREDIT CARDS
AE, DC, MC, V

RATES
Single 173–200€, double 265–310€, junior suite 360€, suite 400€, extra bed 60€; children under 2 are free; children 2–12 half price; excellent off-season rates

BREAKFAST
Buffet breakfast included

ENGLISH
Yes

HOTEL HESPERIA ★★ (3)
Calle Riello, 459
20 rooms, 18 with shower or bath and toilet

The Hotel Hesperia is owned by two friendly sisters: Carolina and Martina Derai. Theirs is the perfect hideaway for romantics who do not like big, brassy hotels in busy areas. If you are willing to be around the corner from the well-worn tourist track near the train station, you will be rewarded by their two-star, which offers many three-star features. The tranquil haven on a quiet little canal includes a pretty rooftop terrace, as well as a terrace in front of the hotel. Many of the rooms are named after well-known artists, and copies of the artists' works hang inside. The bedrooms are not large, but they are nicely equipped and tastefully decorated with Murano glass chandeliers. Four of the rooms face the Cannaregio Canal. Number 301, dubbed the "honeymoon room," has gold-striped fabric on

TELEPHONE
041 715 251, 041 716 001

FAX
041 715 112

EMAIL
hesperia@shineline.it

CREDIT CARDS
AE, DC, MC, V

RATES
Single 160€, double 180€, triple 220€; lower off-season rates

BREAKFAST
Continental breakfast included

ENGLISH
Yes

the wall and an aqua-blue mosaic-tile bath with a glass-enclosed shower. In No. 208, a two-story duplex, there is a windowless downstairs sitting area and, upstairs, a bedroom with a double bed and a bath with a skylight.

FACILITIES AND SERVICES: Air-conditioning, bar, direct-dial phone, no elevator (3 floors), fans on request, hair dryer, minibar, in-room safe, satellite TV

NEAREST TOURIST ATTRACTIONS: Jewish Quarter, Grand Canal, train station, Piazzale Roma

HOTEL LA FORCOLA ★★★ (5)
Rio Terrà delle Maddalena 2353
23 rooms, all with shower and toilet

All twenty-three rooms in this new hotel have sunlight and are decorated with gold fabrics, hardwood floors, and dark wood furniture. Many have balconies with canal views. Thankfully, none face narrow alleys or dank walls. However, some of the rooms are singles masquerading as doubles. Good rooms to ask for are No. 105, with canal views from the room and the bathroom, and No. 206, a favorite corner double. You can safely avoid No. 102, a streetside room with a bad shower, and No. 307, which is just too small for comfort. Families will be happy in No. 205, a two-room suite with a terrace, Jacuzzi, and good light. Just in case you are wondering, a *forcola* is the walnut wood rest for the gondola's oar, and each one is custom made to the gondolier's exact specification.

NOTE: The hotel is often closed the last two weeks in January.

FACILITIES AND SERVICES: Air-conditioning, direct-dial phone, elevator, hair dryer, minibar, in-room safe, satellite TV

NEAREST TOURIST ATTRACTIONS: Grand Canal, train station

TELEPHONE
041 524 1484
FAX
041 524 5380
INTERNET
www.laforcolahotel.com
CREDIT CARDS
AE, DC, MC, V
RATES
Single 70–120€, double 100–180€, family room 150–240€; lower off-season rates and Internet specials
BREAKFAST
Buffet breakfast included
ENGLISH
Yes

HOTEL ROSSI ★ (¢, 7)
Calle delle Procuratie, 262
14 rooms, 10 with shower or bath and toilet

To find Hotel Rossi, look for the two camp chairs on each side of the lion statue at the end of Calle delle Procuratie. Just to the left is the hotel, which has been in the Rossi family for over half a century, ever since it was opened by the grandmother of the present owner, Francesco Rossi. The grandmother's portrait hangs on the right of the breakfast room entrance. The Rossi continues to be a terrific little Great Sleep, but staying here entails a few minor sacrifices. First of all, there is no elevator, but you

TELEPHONE
041 715 164
FAX
041 717 784
EMAIL
rossihotel@hotmail.com
INTERNET
www.hotelrossi.net
CREDIT CARDS
MC, V

could consider the climb up three flights of stone stairs a good way to work off all those pasta dishes. Also, charm and character are sacrificed for modern furniture and chenille bedspreads. But music to the ears of frugal Great Sleepers is the 10 percent discount during the off-season; the cheerful hotel staff; rooms that are quiet, clean, and kept up; and plumbing that works. Breakfast is served in a small, no-smoking room with benches, stools, and four tables with red-and-white cloths, or it can be served in your room at no additional charge. Another point in the Rossi's favor is the location, on a narrow alley off the busy Lista di Spagna, which means you can walk easily to the train station or to the Piazzale Roma parking garages.

NOTE: The hotel is closed from January to Carnivale.

FACILITIES AND SERVICES: Air-conditioning, direct-dial phone, office safe, reception open from 6 A.M.–1 A.M.

NEAREST TOURIST ATTRACTIONS: Jewish Quarter, Grand Canal, train station, Piazzale Roma

RATES
Single 53–69€, double 77–92€, triple 112€, quad 132€

BREAKFAST
Continental breakfast included

ENGLISH
Yes

HOTEL S. LUCIA ★ (¢, 9)
Calle della Misericordia, 358
15 rooms, 10 with shower and toilet

No carpets, but a pretty, sunny front patio, spotlessly clean rooms (thanks to the head maid, who has been here almost twenty-five years), and stall showers with doors more than make up for the lack of zing in the rooms. The half-century-old hotel, owned by the Parcianello family, is on a peaceful side street just off the "zoo" area along Lista de Spagna, which runs from the train station to Campo San Geremia. The plain, cream-colored rooms with blond wood furniture are all good-sized, light, and quiet, ensuring visitors a pleasant night's rest. Only four of the rooms are on the dull back; the rest either overlook the patio or open onto it. Breakfast can be served inside a tiny room with four tables or on the front patio, which is shielded from the street and pedestrians by an ivy-covered fence bordered by flower beds. The breakfast is mandatory during the high season, but in winter, the cost can be deducted from the room rate.

NOTE: The hotel is closed from December through January.

FACILITIES AND SERVICES: Air-conditioning, direct-dial phone, no elevator (hotel on the ground floor), hair dryer available, office safe, satellite TV

NEAREST TOURIST ATTRACTIONS: Train station, Piazzale Roma, Grand Canal, Jewish Quarter

TELEPHONE
041 715 180

FAX
041 710 610

INTERNET
www.hotelslucia.com

CREDIT CARDS
AE, MC, V

RATES
Single 50–70€, double 60–110€, triple 110–140€, quad 140–170€

BREAKFAST
Continental breakfast included (deduct 5€ per person in off-season if not taken)

ENGLISH
Yes, also Spanish and French

LA LOCANDA DI ORSARIA ★★★ (11)
Calle Priuli dei Cavolletti, 103

TELEPHONE
041 715 254
FAX
041 715 433
INTERNET
www.locandaorsaria.com
CREDIT CARDS
AE, DC, MC, V
RATES
Single 80–130€, double 80–190€, triple 100–240€, quad 120–260€; discounts for *Great Sleeps Italy* readers (mention book when reserving); children under 4 free
BREAKFAST
Continental buffet breakfast included
ENGLISH
Yes

18 rooms, all with shower and toilet

From June until September, Venice is full of tourists and mosquitoes— the man eating variety who show little mercy and are immune to the most repellent sprays and lotions money can buy. You would think windows with screens would be as common as a glass of vino with a plate of pasta, but they are not. The exception to this phenomenon is La Locanda di Orsaria. However, window screens are not the only plus offered in this well-run, family-owned and -managed hotel. Here you have air-conditioning, private safes, and attractive, clean rooms, which are furnished in dark wood and appointed with full-length mirrors, Murano light fixtures, and spacious wardrobes. All the tiled bathrooms have stall showers. Keeping up with emails is easy on the guest Internet terminal. In the morning, they serve a generous Continental breakfast, which includes cold cereals, yogurt, cheese, pastries, and fresh croissants.

FACILITIES AND SERVICES: Air-conditioning, direct-dial phone, no elevator (3 floors), hair dryer, guest Internet terminal, laundry service, minibar, in-room safe, satellite TV, 2 ground-floor rooms, and window screens (!)

NEAREST TOURIST ATTRACTIONS: Train station, Piazzale Roma, Grand Canal

LOCANDA DEL GHETTO (1)
Campo Ghetto Novo, 2892

TELEPHONE
041 275 9292
FAX
041 274 7987
INTERNET
www.veneziahotels.com
CREDIT CARDS
AE, DC, MC, V
RATES
Single 80–160€, double 90–220€, junior suite 130–240€; special rates on weekends and for *Great Sleeps* readers (subject to availability)
BREAKFAST
Kosher continental breakfast included
ENGLISH
Yes

6 rooms, all with shower and toilet

The Locanda del Ghetto occupies a prime location on the Campo Ghetto Nuovo in the Jewish Quarter. The building dates back to the 1400s and was a synagogue in the 1500s. The harmonious rooms have an understated Liberty-style theme, gold bedspreads, and hardwood floors. Several still have their original painted beam ceilings. Number 18 is sold as a triple and has an original beamed ceiling, but I would not suggest it unless you want to crawl over the extra bed to get to the gray marble-tile bathroom. A better choice is No. 19, a junior suite with a terrace and a small sitting room where an extra bed can be easily accommodated. I think No. 16 is the best room in the house: first, its two windows overlook a little canal and a Venetian apartment, which lets you see what life might be like living in Venice. But its large wardrobe and bathroom with good sink space and huge bathtub (inviting leisurely bubble baths) also makes it a good choice for longer stays.

The reception and sitting area are done in pale colors that create an uncluttered backdrop for the artwork of local Jewish Quarter artists. A certificate from a rabbinical authority guarantees that the breakfast you eat is 100 percent kosher.

NOTE: Also under the same ownership is the Hotel Pensione Wildner (see page 272) and the Hotel Cristallo (see page 322).

FACILITIES AND SERVICES: Air-conditioning, direct-dial phone, no elevator (2 floors), hair dryer, minibar, in-room safe, satellite TV, nonsmoking hotel

NEAREST TOURIST ATTRACTIONS: Jewish Quarter, Grand Canal

PALAZZO ABADESSA ($, 12)
Calle Pruili, 4011
12 rooms, all with shower or bath and toilet

If you want to be king or queen for a day, a week, or more, nowhere will you feel more royal than as a guest at the Palazzo Abadessa, which is owned by the friendly Maria Luisa, whose family has lived here for generations. Everywhere you look, there is something to remind you that you are living in a sixteenth-century palace: regal red draperies, a banquet-size dining room with gold damask table coverings and magnificent china and silver, beautiful Oriental rugs, museum-quality antiques, handmade silk wall coverings, inlaid and hand-painted Venetian furniture, ornate Murano chandeliers, ceiling frescoes, massive gilt-etched mirrors, and countless portraits and paintings from the Tintoretto School. Finally there is a large garden where weddings are often held.

The bedrooms are reached by double-wide stone stairs that wind up two floors, the first of which is called the *piano noble,* the floor where the family members lived. Each elaborate room is different, facing either the garden, a canal, or a quiet street. Each has its own marble bathroom and otherwise has space to spare, especially the eighty-square-meter President's Suite. To quote Maria Luisa: "We want you to be involved in an unexpected and unforgettable experience in Palazzo Abadessa...that is the spirit we would like to have our guests feel."

FACILITIES AND SERVICES: Air-conditioning, bar, direct-dial phones, no elevator (3 floors), hair dryer, minibar, in-room safe, satellite TV, boat dock (accessible by water taxi or gondola), banquets, balls, weddings, nonsmoking hotel

NEAREST TOURIST ATTRACTIONS: Ca'd'Oro, Grand Canal

TELEPHONE
041 241 3784
FAX
041 521 2236
INTERNET
www.abadessa.com
CREDIT CARDS
MC, V
RATES
No singles; double as single 190€, double 230–300€, junior suite 350€, suite 490€, extra bed 50€; excellent low-season rates, especially in July and August
BREAKFAST
American buffet breakfast included
ENGLISH
Yes

Castello

**Venice...is my head, or rather
my *heart*-quarters.**

*—Lord Byron, Letter to Thomas
Moore, 11 April 1817*

The largest district and the only one not touching at
some point on the Grand Canal, Castello is divided in
two by the Arsenale, the shipyards where Venice built her
shipping fleet, which once dominated the Mediterranean.
The focal point for this district is the Gothic church Santi
Giovanni e Paolo, the pantheon of Venice and considered
one of the most monumental squares in the city. One of
the prettiest squares is Campo Santa Maria Formosa. The
San Zaccaria Church in the south portion of the district
played an important if controversial role in the history of
Venice; in the sixteenth century, the nuns at San Zaccaria
revolted against the bishop and the Church. For a glimpse
of real Venetian life, stroll down Riva degli Schiavoni on
the southern waterfront to Via Garibaldi. In the morning
it is filled with housewives pushing strollers and shopping
at the small outdoor markets; in the early evening it serves
as a meetingplace and living room for the neighborhood,
coming alive with children, parents, grandmothers, work-
ers, bar flies, prostitutes, old men...just about everyone,
all out for their nightly shmooze.

HOTELS

OTHER OPTIONS
Hostels

($) indicates a Big Splurge; (¢) indicates a Cheap Sleep

ALBERGO DONI ★ (¢, 106)
Calle del Vin, 4656 (off Riva degli Schiavoni)
13 rooms, 4 with shower and toilet

In back of St. Mark's Square, as you head toward Campo San Zaccaria and just off Riva degli Schiavoni, is this old-fashioned cheap sleep, the sort that an injection of hard cash would do wonders to improve. The rooms either overlook the parked gondolas on the Rio del Vin or a garden with fruit trees. The majority of the large and airy bedrooms are outfitted with a bidet, a basin with hot and cold running water, vintage furniture, creaking wooden floors, and exposed pipes—all of which tells you they have not been blessed by renovation. Four have canal views and are always booked by an older group of thrift-seekers who know a bargain deal when they see one. The only room with air-conditioning is No. 8, which also has seventeenth-century frescoes and a beautiful pink-and-green antique Murano chandelier. To make your sleep here even cheaper, ask to have the 7€ cost of breakfast deducted and go instead to a neighborhood *caffè* and do as the Venetians do: have your cappuccino and *cornetto* while standing at the bar.

FACILITIES AND SERVICES: Air-conditioning in one room, no elevator (3 floors), office safe, nonsmoking hotel
NEAREST TOURIST ATTRACTIONS: Piazza San Marco

TELEPHONE & FAX
041 522 4267
EMAIL
albergodoni@libero.it
INTERNET
www.albergodoni.it
CREDIT CARDS
None, cash only
RATES
Single 52€, double 78–105€, triple 105–140€
BREAKFAST
Continental breakfast included (deduct 7€ per person if not taken)
ENGLISH
Yes

ALBERGO PAGANELLI ★★★ (109)
Riva degli Schiavoni, 4182
22 rooms, all with shower or bath and toilet

Most hotels along this premium stretch of water in Venice charge almost half again as much as the Paganelli. While the prices may seem high for some cost-conscious Great Sleepers, there is significant value in what you get. Francesco Paganelli, who was born at the hotel, continues his family's tradition of hotel-keeping, which began when his grandfather opened the Paganelli in 1874. Before that, the hotel was part of the San Zaccaria convent, whose

TELEPHONE
041 522 4324
FAX
041 523 9267
EMAIL
hotelpag@tin.it
INTERNET
www.hotelpaganelli.com
CREDIT CARDS
AE, MC, V

claim to fame is the infamous sixteenth-century revolt by its nuns.

The hotel now consists of two sections: the annex on the square (Campo San Zaccaria, 4687) and the older section facing the lagoon. While some may feel the annex rooms have the edge for their slightly more modern features and bathrooms, most of those in the older section have lagoon views. If you select the annex, ask for No. 222, a double on the square with a side view of the San Zaccaria Church and its bell tower. This room has its original pitched ceilings with exposed beams, lovely painted Venetian furniture, and Oriental rugs. The bathroom has a shower and a half-tub. Room 224, also with a corner view of the church, is the room in which Sr. Paganelli was born, but avoid this room until it receives some much-needed maintenance. Number 223, a small double with wood beams, has an excellent bathroom. Views over the lagoon in Rooms 206, 216, and 218 announce, "This is Venice!" If you are not in a view room, the *altana* (a wooden rooftop terrace particular to Venice) provides magestic views of the city for all guests. The hotel is booked months in advance, so please do not wait until the last minute to reserve.

FACILITIES AND SERVICES: Air-conditioning, bar, direct-dial phone, double windows for noise, no elevator (2 floors), hair dryer, guest Internet terminal, in-room safe, satellite TV, nonsmoking hotel

NEAREST TOURIST ATTRACTIONS: Piazza San Marco

CASA VERADO ★★★ (94)
Calle Castagna, 4765 (near Campo San Giacomo)
20 rooms, all with showers, bathtubs, and toilets

Sitting on a narrow canal just after you cross over the Ponte Storto, off Ruga Giuffa, the building is a fourteenth-century *palazzo* that was at one time a school for Jewish students not confined to the Ghetto. Today, after various incarnations, it is a magnificent twenty-room three-star deluxe hotel befitting its historical monument status.

With a sense of style and great imagination, Francesco and Danielea Mestre have created a truly outstanding hotel that is a celebration of their talents and skills. On the ground floor there is a breakfast room dotted with eighteenth-century antiques and an antique chandelier. In the walkway to the sunny rattan-furnished terrace is an original well and thirteenth-century column that is the same as those in the Palazzo Ducale (Doges Palace) on St Mark's Square. The rooms have luminous interiors, silk fabrics, and hand-done Venetian furnishings. Some rooms

RATES
Rates span low/high seasons: single 70–160€, double 100–230€; extra bed 30% of room rate
BREAKFAST
Buffet breakfast included
ENGLISH
Yes

TELEPHONE
041 528 6127, 041 528 61 38
FAX
041 52 32 765
EMAIL
casaverado@tin.it
INTERNET
www.casaverardo.it
CREDIT CARDS
AE, MC, V
RATES
Rates span low/high seasons: single 60–120€, double 90–220€, junior suite 130–275€, extra bed 20–40€; check for Internet specials
BREAKFAST
Continental breakfast included
ENGLISH
Yes

have exposed sections of ancient walls or cross beams; others have private terraces and double windows with views onto a canal. The marble bathrooms are wonderful; each one has a shower and tub and a different style mirror. I like room No. 305, especially in the spring and summer when the sunny terrace, with a view of the golden angel on the Santa Maria Bell Tower, adds a further dimension to the otherwise somewhat tight-fitting room. Another favorite is No. 301, a mansard twin room with a long work space and an Oriental rug on the polished wood floor. Number 101 is a large junior suite with a canal view, gold-and-green painted Venetian furnishings, and a great bathroom with loads of sink space.

FACILITIES AND SERVICES: Air-conditioning, bar, direct dial phone, elevator, hair dryer, guest Internet terminal, minibar, in-room safe, satellite TV

NEAREST TOURIST ATTRACTIONS: Piazza San Marco

HOTEL AL PIAVE ★★★ (89)
Ruga Giuffa, 4830

25 rooms and 2 apartments, all with shower and toilet

Paolo, his wife, Mirella, their daughter, Ilarla, and dog Molly are carrying on the tradition set by Paolo's father when he opened the doors of the Piave in 1945. If you look above the reception desk, you will see a photo of his mother and father proudly displayed. In the last few years, Paolo has slowly but surely renovated the hotel, replacing the bizarre color schemes in the rooms with soft, coordinated colors and serviceable reproduction furnishings. He has added six family suites, which provide enough extra space to make the difference, and he has replumbed the baths, putting in heated towel racks, marble tilework, and better lighting.

The two apartments are nicely organized and arranged, but in most, views are limited. Guests don't seem to mind, and they feel compensated by the well-equipped kitchens, four-star bathrooms, daily maid service, and interesting location, where they can get to know the merchants and quickly feel a part of day-to-day Venetian life. A Continental breakfast is included in both the hotel and apartment rates and is served in a breakfast room with cushioned banquette seating.

NOTE: The hotel is closed from January 6 to Carnivale.

FACILITIES AND SERVICES: Air-conditioning, direct-dial phone, no elevator (2 floors), hair dryer, in-room safe, satellite TV, office safe, all nonsmoking rooms

NEAREST TOURIST ATTRACTIONS: Piazza San Marco, interesting local neighborhood with great shopping

TELEPHONE
041 528 5174

FAX
041 523 8512

INTERNET
www.hotelalpiave.com

CREDIT CARDS
AE, DC, MC, V

RATES
Single 80–125€, double 100–180€, triple 150–210€; family rooms for 3 people 160–230€, 4 people 200–260€, 5 people 220–300€, 6 people 240–330€; apartments (2–3 people) 110–180€; lower off-season rates and for longer stays in the apartments

BREAKFAST
Continental breakfast included

ENGLISH
Yes

HOTEL BISANZIO ★★★ (107)
Calle della Pietà, 3651 (off Riva degli Schiavoni)

TELEPHONE
041 520 3100
FAX
041 520 4114
INTERNET
www.hotelbisanzio.it
CREDIT CARDS
AE, DC, MC, V
RATES
No singles; double 130–260€;
extra person 30–50€; lower
off-season rates and Internet
specials
BREAKFAST
Buffet breakfast included
ENGLISH
Yes

47 rooms and 3 apartments, all with shower or bath and toilet

The Bisanzio's brochure states, "Visiting Venice is like falling into an unforgettable atmosphere." That is certainly true, and to enhance the atmosphere of your stay in this romantic city, consider this choice in a redone sixteenth-century villa off Riva degli Schiavoni, only a few minutes from St. Mark's Square.

Even though you are close to it all, the rooms are quiet and coordinated in the antique Venetian style, featuring tiled baths, inlaid parquet floors, and eight rooms with private balconies. Room 408, overlooking a small *campiello,* is sold as a standard double, but I think it is best for one person, thanks to its narrow closet and corner shower. Better for two is No. 503, a wonderful twin with an ancient timbered ceiling and its own balcony with green plants and a view to the bell tower on St. Mark's Square. The bathroom is generous, with enough space to unpack your cosmetics and actually see what you have in front of you. There are three family rooms and two apartments in a separate annex next to the hotel. While not as luxuriously outfitted as the main hotel rooms, they are certainly comfortable and well-constructed for those needing more space or accommodations with a kitchen. For all guests, a buffet breakfast is served in a pleasant dining room with a bouquet of dried flowers on each gray tablecloth-covered table.

FACILITIES AND SERVICES: Air-conditioning, bar, direct-dial phone, elevator (in main hotel), hair dryer, minibar, porter, in-room safe, satellite TV, 3 apartments with kitchens (no elevator)

NEAREST TOURIST ATTRACTIONS: Piazza San Marco

HOTEL CA' FORMENTA ★★★ (112)
Via Garibaldi, 1650

TELEPHONE
041 528 5495
FAX
041 520 4633
INTERNET
www.hotelcaformenta.it
CREDIT CARDS
AE, DC, MC, V

21 rooms, all with shower or bath and toilet

Veteran cheap sleepers in Venice will no doubt remember this address as a spartan stop once known as the Locanda Toscana–Tofanelli, which was run for decades by sisters Nella and Nicole. Several years ago, I found their hotel boarded up and knew the sisters were gone. On my last trip, I wanted to see what had happened, and lo and behold, in its place is this beautiful three-star hotel that, unfortunately, is not for cheap sleepers any longer.

Completely restored, Hotel Ca' Formenta is located at the beginning of Via Garibaldi, a vibrant street alive with Venetian life. Although only a ten-minute walk from Piazza San Marco, the area has not been invaded by masses of tourists. Instead, the *caffès* and restaurants are crowded with local Venetians who want to escape the hustle and bustle of the touristy atmosphere of San Marco. The hotel, fresh from its renovation, gleams in the classic Venetian style, mixing sunny Mediterranean colors with deep azure blues and resplendent reds. Guests can enjoy front and side lagoon views from eight rooms, and from the roof terrace and the private front terrace. My favorite room is No. 203, the only one with a balcony overlooking the magnificent lagoon. It is done in yellow and blue, with three cupids in the clouds pointing arrows at the bed. The only drawback is the bathroom, which has a nice enclosed shower, but no shelf space. A better bathroom with more space and a bathtub, plus access to the interior hotel terrace, is No. 201.

NOTE: Also under the same ownership is the Hotel Panorama on Lido (see page 323).

FACILITIES AND SERVICES: Air-conditioning, bar, direct-dial phone, elevator, hair dryer, guest Internet terminal, data ports, minibar, in-room safe, satellite TV

NEAREST TOURIST ATTRACTIONS: Piazza San Marco, window on Venetian life along Via Garibaldi

RATES
Single 100–140€, double 170–260€, triple 220–340€; children under 3 are free; children 3–12 receive 20% discount; excellent mid- and low-season rates (two-night minimum on weekends)

BREAKFAST
Buffet breakfast included

ENGLISH
Yes

HOTEL CANEVA ★ (¢, 85)
Ramo Dietro la Fava, 5515

23 rooms, 14 with private shower and toilet

It is not a fancy Great Sleep, but you can't complain about the picture-postcard views. Five rooms have a balcony and a canal view, twelve have a canal view but no balcony, and the rest have no view at all—and you absolutely don't want one of these viewless numbers. What for? The view rooms are the same price, so why not get one?

Massimo Cagnato's family has been running the hotel since the midfifties, and they have certainly saved money by not upgrading the rooms, springing for better beds, or replacing the auditorium foldup chairs that provide the only seating in many of the rooms other than the two-inch mattress lying on a metal cot (ouch!). Even the kitchen floor is an original from when the building was built six hundred years ago! I can assure you, however, that cleanliness is taken seriously: the green linoleum hall floors are swabbed daily and the bathrooms don't need an extra dousing of Lysol. The setting, about halfway between San Marco and the Rialto Bridge, is another strong point, and so are some of the amenities, such as air-conditioning

TELEPHONE
041 522 8118

FAX
041 520 8676

INTERNET
www.hotelcaneva.com

CREDIT CARDS
AE, MC, V

RATES
Single 45–70€, double 77–100€, triple 95–120€, quad 155€; lower off-season rates

BREAKFAST
Continental breakfast included

ENGLISH
Yes

in ten rooms at no additional charge, plus hair dryers and televisions in all the rooms. So, if you don't mind a fifties-style room and a thin mattress and value a great Venetian view and location, this Great Sleep in Venice can be yours fifty weeks of the year.

NOTE: The hotel is closed for one week in November and one week in January (dates vary).

FACILITIES AND SERVICES: Air-conditioning in ten rooms, direct-dial phones, no elevator (2 floors), hair dryer, TV, office safe

NEAREST TOURIST ATTRACTIONS: St. Mark's Square, Rialto Bridge

HOTEL COLOMBINA ★★★★ ($, 92)
Calle del Remedio, 4416

32 rooms, 3 suites, all with shower or bath and toilet

TELEPHONE
041 277 0525
FAX
041 277 6044
INTERNET
www.hotelcolombina.com;
www.hotelcolombina.com/
remedio
CREDIT CARDS
AE, DC, MC, V
RATES
Rates span low/high seasons:
hotel: single 115–360€, double 180–410€, triple 210–495€, suite from 300€; annex: single 60–280€, double 95–300€, triple 110–350€
BREAKFAST
Buffet breakfast included for hotel and annex
ENGLISH
Yes

History rubs shoulders with beauty at the wonderful Hotel Colombina, where most rooms on this seventeenth-century *palazzo* overlook a canal with a splendid view of the famous Bridge of Sighs. This bridge linked the Palazzo Ducale to the prisons, and it was so named because it was the last look at the outside world for the condemned. When it comes to taste, everyone has their own, but for lovers of all things Venetian, I cannot imagine a better location . . . in this setting, the woes of everyday life seem to melt away. All the rooms display high standards of luxury and comfort with softly colored, hand-painted Venetian-style furnishings combined with beautiful fabrics; the marble bathrooms look and are expensive. For a total submersion into Venice, reserve No. 203, done in gray-blue damask with a massive Murano chandelier and two large windows. The view from the balcony is on a canal, across two bridges to the Bridge of Sighs in the distance. At dusk, when the gondolas are floating by and the sun setting, this puts the R in romance—it is sheer perfection. A dozen or so steps are required to reach Rooms 405 and 406, but the fabulous payoff is a panoramic view of Venice from their terraces, where breakfast or light snacks and drinks can be served. Guests do not have to climb stairs to savor almost the same view from the balconies in Rooms 203 and 303, but in Room 206, a triple, you don't have a view at all. The access to the hotel is either by foot through a picturesque Venetian maze of meandering alleyways or by private boat or water taxi at the hotel dock.

The hotel's twelve-room *dipendeza,* or annex, Locanda Remedio, is on a small walkway next to the hotel. These rooms don't have views, and there is no elevator for the two floors. However, all the very comfortable rooms are furnished in the colorful Venetian style. The best part is that they cost less than those in the main part of the hotel and offer all the same services and amenities hotel guests receive. Reservations are handled at the Colombina.

FACILITIES AND SERVICES: Hotel: air-conditioning, bar, direct-dial phone, elevator to most rooms, hair dryer, guest Internet terminal, laundry service, minibar, room service for light snacks, in-room safe, pay-for-view and satellite TV, 18 nonsmoking rooms; annex: all the same facilities except no elevator (2 floors), pay-per-view TV, 6 nonsmoking rooms

NEAREST TOURIST ATTRACTIONS: Piazza San Marco, shopping

HOTEL FONTANA ★★ (103)
Campo S. Provolo, 4701
16 rooms in hotel, 4 in annex, all with shower or bath and toilet

The Hotel Fontana has turned into a Great Sleeping jewel, where a family atmosphere prevails from the sitting room and bar to all four floors of the hotel. This is in large part thanks to the matriarch of the family, Lina Stainer, a warm and wonderful lady adored by her children, grandchildren, and all who meet her.

Since 1967, the Fontana has been owned by the Stainer family. For four hundred years before that, the building was a convent for Austrian nuns, and their influence is still apparent, especially in the breakfast room, which is more than just a room in which to enjoy a morning meal. The consecrated brick archway means that Mass can be celebrated here, and the stained-glass windows were probably installed long before the Stainers bought the place. Included in the sale were all the books and furnishings from the convent, many of which are on display. Before you leave the room, be sure to look for Mario and his brother Roberto's childhood photos by the door.

Speaking of photographs, when you walk into the hotel, you will notice a museum-quality display of Venetian photos. These stunning photographs, as well as the large posters hanging throughout the hotel, are the work of Mario Stainer. Sr. Stainer's magnificent photography is world renowned, especially his work detailing the intricate floors of the Basilica on St. Mark's Square (look for his book *Pavimenti* in Venetian bookshops) and his beautiful photographs of antique Venetian glass beads (in *Perle Veneziane*).

TELEPHONE
041 521 0533, 041 522 0579
FAX
041 523 1040
EMAIL
htlcasa@gpnet.it
INTERNET
www.hotelfontana.it
CREDIT CARDS
AE, DC, MC, V
RATES
Single 55–110€, double 85–170€, triple 120–210€, quad 140–240€
BREAKFAST
Buffet breakfast included
ENGLISH
Yes

The well-lit, well-furnished rooms have shiny bath-rooms, pleasing color schemes, and crisp cotton bed-spreads. Many have pieces from the family's collection of antiques. The majority have views over the garden or of San Zaccaria Church. I like Rooms 11 and 12 on the fourth floor because of their private terraces with views of the church, which are pleasant for a summer breakfast or an afternoon drink. Families should request No. 14, a two-room suite with a skylight and a charming church view. Other good choices include No. 4, a triple with a terrace and a view of the garden; No. 5, which is a double that can be expanded to a quad; No. 6, a double with two windows on the square; and No. 8, a light-filled double on the back with two armchairs and the hotel's usual spotless bathroom. The four rooms in an annex across the street are just as recommended. In particular, Room B consists of two rooms overlooking the square, and Room C is the convent's former laundry with its wooden floor and beams intact. Unless you are traveling solo with light luggage avoid Room A, which has its tiny closet behind a curtain and limited light. Many *Great Sleeps* readers have found the Fontana, making it one of the most requested hotels in this area of Venice...so plan accordingly!

FACILITIES AND SERVICES: Air-conditioning, bar, direct-dial phone, no elevator (4 floors), fan, hair dryer available, office safe, satellite TV, nonsmoking hotel

NEAREST TOURIST ATTRACTIONS: Piazza San Marco

HOTEL PENSIONE WILDNER ★★ (110)
Riva degli Schiavoni, 4161
16 rooms, all with showers and toilets

If you stay at the famed Hotel Danieli, a magnificent palace built in the fourteenth century by Doge Dandolo, you will be in the company of kings, princes, political lead-ers, artists, and the host of other famous persons who have stayed there. The prices range from 275€ for the littlest single and 629€ for a view double to more than 3,300€ for the Royal Suite. Breakfast, at 50€, is extra. However, just a minute or two down the way is the Hotel Pensione Wildner, with the same views from eight of its front rooms. In 1881, Henry James completed *Portrait of a Lady* while staying in one of these rooms on the fourth floor.

The Wildner is hardly a palace...call it a fifties-style pensione complete with leatherette sofas, orange and beige colors, Murphy beds in some rooms, and laminated furniture. Dated it is, but expensive (for the location) it is not. Even though some of the rooms are past their due

TELEPHONE
041 522 7463
FAX
041 241 4640
EMAIL
wildner@veneziahotels.com
INTERNET
www.veneziahotels.com
CREDIT CARDS
AE, DC, MC, V
RATES
1–2 people 180–230€ (low season 70–100€); extra person 36€; half-pension 15€; discount for *Great Sleeps Italy* readers (mention book when reserving)
BREAKFAST
Buffet breakfast included
ENGLISH
Yes

date from a decorator's standpoint, they are clean and livable for short or long stays, especially those on the third and fourth floors that have lagoon and rooftop views. If you stay here, and want a front-facing view room (even though they are more expensive), No. 16, all in blue, is a good choice, with three view windows, twin beds, a sofa bed, and two chairs. Otherwise, the back rooms, such as No. 48, have quiet views of the San Zaccaria Church and the tiled rooftops surrounding it.

The hotel operates a restaurant in front. It offers guests half-pension for lunch and/or dinner, which includes two courses, vegetables, cover, and service; or the hotel offers guests a 15 percent discount for à la carte (see *Great Eats Italy*).

NOTE: Also under the same ownership is Locanda del Ghetto (see page 262), and Hotel Cristallo on Lido (see page 322).

FACILITIES AND SERVICES: Air-conditioning, bar, direct-dial phone, no elevator (4 floors), in-room safe, satellite TV, restaurant for lunch or dinner

NEAREST TOURIST ATTRACTIONS: Piazza San Marco

HOTEL SANTA MARINA ★★★★ ($, 80)
Campo di Santa Marina, 6068
20 rooms, all with shower or bath and toilet

The Santa Marina is a smartly refurbished candidate on a neighborhood square in the heart of Venice. Guests are served breakfast on the hotel's private terrace, the ideal place to observe Venetian life as you relax and contemplate the day ahead. Otherwise, breakfast is served in the bar, which has moss-green velvet-covered booths. The management is not only accommodating but generous with its time, helping guests maximize their Venetian holiday.

The bedrooms, with floral-painted doors, are tastefully done with reproduction-style painted furniture, modern Murano glass lighting, and soft colors assigned to each floor. For the best views, be sure to request one of the rooms looking onto the square. On the first floor, the rooms are coordinated in blue; on the second, everything is in beige, and these are the lightest rooms; and pink rules on the third floor. I like No. 106, which has a tiny balcony, painted Venetian furniture, and a tub and shower in the bathroom. Number 107, sold as a triple, is another favorite because it is the biggest, with twin beds, a sofa bed, and two windows overlooking the square. One of the best restaurants in Venice, L'Osteria di Santa Marina, is across the square (see *Great Eats Italy*).

TELEPHONE
041 523 9202, 041 520 3994

FAX
041 520 0907

INTERNET
www.hotelsantamarina.it

CREDIT CARDS
AE, DC, MC, V

RATES
Rates span low/high seasons: single 100–250€, double 120–280€, triple 160–330€; check for Internet specials

BREAKFAST
Buffet breakfast included

ENGLISH
Yes

NOTE: On my last visit, extensive work was being done on the square resulting in dust, dirt, and noise. When reserving, please ask if the work has been completed.

FACILITIES AND SERVICES: Air-conditioning, bar, direct-dial phones, elevator, guest Internet terminal, hair dryer, minibar, in-room safe, satellite TV, some nonsmoking rooms

NEAREST TOURIST ATTRACTIONS: Rialto Bridge, Campo Santa Maria Formosa

HOTEL SAVOIA & JOLANDA ★★★★ ($, 108)
Riva degli Schiavoni, 4187
35 rooms, all with shower or bath and toilet

TELEPHONE
041 529 6644
FAX
041 520 7494
INTERNET
www.hotelsavoiajolanda.com
CREDIT CARDS
AE, DC, MC, V
RATES
Single 207€, double 289€, junior suite 400–500€ (depends on size); annex: single 155€, double 240€; lower off-season rates for both locations
BREAKFAST
American hot and cold buffet breakfast included
ENGLISH
Yes

The Hotel Savoia & Jolanda is infinitely blessed with location, location, and location . . . those three little words that mean so much, whether you are buying real estate or merely occupying it for a short time while on holiday. This grande dame of Venetian hotels stands on the Riva degli Schiavoni, with breathtaking views of the basin of St. Mark's and the island of San Giorgio from fifteen of its junior suites. The traditional wood-paneled lobby has groupings of tufted leather sofas and chairs and is lit by Murano wall sconces and chandeliers. Also on this level are two restaurants, one inside and another on the front terrace overlooking the lagoon.

The bedrooms and fabulous view suites are statements of well-padded comfort. From No. 307, a standard double, you have a direct view of the side of the famous Hotel Danieli, and in No. 201, a superior double done in a warm mixture of green and gold, space is yours not only in the beamed bedroom but in the large bathroom. It would be impossible to find fault with Suite 303, done in regal blue and gold, with a super bathroom complete with Jacuzzi, double sinks, and a wall of mirrors; the view from the terrace is captivating both day and night. The same raves are due No. 304, which can connect with the No. 306 next door to make up a huge suite, which would have two bedrooms, two bathrooms with Jacuzzis, and sliding picture windows on the Venetian panoramic view. There is a *dipendenza,* or annex, not far from the hotel, where the beautifully done rooms face the fifteenth-century Campo San Zaccaria and Church, where it is said that Cassanova came to "spend time with the nuns." True, these rooms are lovely and several have *altanas* (wooden terraces built over the rooftop), but quite frankly, if you decide on the Savoia & Jolanda as a Big Splurge in Venice, why not reserve a room with a view of Venice you will never forget?

FACILITIES AND SERVICES: Air-conditioning, bar, direct-dial phone, elevator, hair dryer, laundry service, minibar, full-service restaurant (25% discount for hotel guests), in-room safe, satellite TV, robe and slippers in junior suites
NEAREST TOURIST ATTRACTIONS: Piazza San Marco

LA RESIDENZA ★★ (104)
Campo Bandiera e Moro, 3608
15 rooms, all with shower and toilet

A two-star Great Sleep in a former Gritti Palace with affordable prices? No, you are not dreaming. The quiet neighborhood around La Residenza is a world away from the milling hordes near Piazza San Marco and the pedestrian-clogged Riva degli Schiavoni, but both are only a short walk from the hotel. When you reach the Campo Bandiera e Moro and see the red flag flying in front of the magnificent fifteenth-century Gothic building with five central windows outlined with fragments of Byzantine sculpture, and colorful flower boxes forming a border underneath, you will know you have found La Residenza. To enter, press the nose of the lion to the right of the large entrance doors and walk through the inner courtyard, with statues and a coat of arms, and up two flights of stairs to the reception desk.

This fifteenth-century Gothic *palazzo* was the former home of the Gritti family, one of the wealthiest, and certainly the most prestigious, in Venice. The ornate salon, with its magnificent sculpted plaster walls and ceilings, lovely paintings, marble floors, and massive furniture, complete with a grand piano, suggests the type of opulent life the former residents led.

For too long it was run by a grouchy old skinflint who refused to spend one euro to improve or update anything. People were forgiving and came anyway, enamored of the history of the hotel and its location. They don't have to look the other way anymore! I am happy to report that the hotel has a new owner, who had the foresight and wherewithal to revamp this drooping dowager, turning her into the well-dressed, elegant lady she should be. He kept the beautiful salon with its black lacquered piano, re-covered the furniture, cleaned the floor-to-ceiling frescoes, and gave all fifteen rooms new looks. For my Great Sleeping euros, these rooms are a quantum leap ahead of most of the two-star competition in all Venice. They are decorated in soft colors that serve as quiet backdrops for the painted Venetian furnishings, Murano lights, and good

TELEPHONE
041 528 5315
FAX
041 523 8859
INTERNET
www.venicelaresidenza.com
CREDIT CARDS
MC, V
RATES
Single 50–100€, double 80–160€, extra bed 35€
BREAKFAST
Continental breakfast included
ENGLISH
Yes

bathrooms with enclosed stall showers. While they do not have romantic canal and gondola outlooks, they do have quiet vistas over gardens, shops, and other apartments that remind us that people really do call Venice home.

FACILITIES AND SERVICES: Air-conditioning, direct-dial phone, no elevator, hair dryer available, minibar, in-room safe, TV

NEAREST TOURIST ATTRACTIONS: St. Mark's Square

LOCANDA AL LEON (101)
Campo SS. Filippo e Giacomo, 4270
11 rooms, all with shower and toilet

TELEPHONE
041 277 0393
FAX
041 521 0348
INTERNET
www.hotelalleon.com
CREDIT CARDS
MC, V
RATES
Single 130€, double 155€; 10% discount for cash, 20% discount in low-season
BREAKFAST
Continental breakfast included, served in room
ENGLISH
Yes

Small Italian hotels and *affitta camere* with fewer than a dozen rooms are becoming very popular alternatives to big, impersonal hotels with absentee owners, identi-kit rooms sold at soaring prices, and a bored staff with a care-less attitude. The Locanda Al Leon is one of this new breed of *piccolo* Great Sleeps in Venice. What is so special about the atmosphere of this ideally located eleven-room find, only a moment or two from Piazza San Marco? Topping the list for praise is the genuinely friendly attitude of owners Giuliano and Marcella, who are justifiably proud of their hotel. The charmingly recycled rooms have original touches, such as a two-hundred-year-old partition in Room 22, which separates a small sitting area from the rest of the room. The white-on-white fabric-covered walls are the perfect background for the soft salmon-and-cream-colored bedspread. This room can connect with No. 23, another bright double with corner windows on the *campo*. This is definitely the way to go if you need a third bed, because the extra bed in No. 22 is a real backbreaker. Bathrooms feature stall showers, plus all rooms have double-glazed windows, are nonsmoking, and if you pay cash, will cost you 10 percent less. What a Great Sleep in Venice!

FACILITIES AND SERVICES: Air-conditioning, direct-dial phone, no elevator (3 floors), hair dryer, minibar, office safe, satellite TV, email and guest Internet terminal, all rooms nonsmoking, pets accepted

NEAREST TOURIST ATTRACTIONS: Piazza San Marco

LOCANDA CA' DEL CONSOLE (81)
Calle Trevisana, 6217 & calle del Console, 6240
8 rooms, 3 apartments, all with shower or bath and toilet

TELEPHONE
041 523 3164;
cell 329 365 2315
FAX
041 244 3396

In 1850, this palace was the home of the Austrian Consul in Venice. After that it became the home of Marina Scarpa's family. Several years ago she followed the lead of many other

Venetians who had grand-scale properties and turned it into a revenue-generating business. The result of her efforts is this lavish *affitta camere,* where each room is individually decorated using an antique Murano floral mirror as one of its focal points. The walls have been returned to their original pastel colors, the furniture restored, and textiles reproduced as closely as possible to go with the rest of the *fin de siècle* style of the palace. The abundantly ornate noble floor of the palace faces a lovely Venetian canal.

If you require more space than a hotel room provides, Sra. Scarpa has two small apartments and a larger one near San Zaccaria to rent for short or long term. Quite honestly, I am not a fan of the two small apartments, both of which I find depressing, and since they are on the ground floor, lacking in security. They have all the perks on paper, but none in reality. This is certainly *not* the case with her sensational apartment near San Zaccaria, which for twenty-three years was the home where she and her husband raised their family. A bit of athletic ability is required to climb the eighty-three stone steps to the top floor apartment—remember, she did this for twenty-three years!—but when you get there, it will be worth twice the hike. The large, open apartment reminds me of a mountain chalet, all done in dark wood, with heavy beams and leather-covered furniture. The kitchen is large enough for serious cooking and of course has every size dish, pot, and pan you can imagine. There is even a separate laundry room. The three bedrooms are simple yet spacious and have plenty of closet and drawer space to unpack and settle in. Bathrooms are more than adequate. On warm days, you can sit on the roof terrace and enjoy an unparalled view of Venice to the Dolomite Mountains, and contemplate your return to this magical, mystical city.

FACILITIES AND SERVICES: Hotel: air-conditioning, no elevator (2 floors), minibar, in-room safe, TV; apartment: direct-dial phone, TV, fitted kitchen (no dishwasher), washer

NEAREST TOURIST ATTRACTIONS: Hotel: Santi Giovanni e Paolo Church; apartment: San Zaccaria Church, Piazza San Marco

INTERNET
www.locandacadelconsole.com

CREDIT CARDS
AE, DC, MC, V

RATES
Hotel: single 90€, double 120–200€; triple 225€; quad 250€; apartments: 1–2 people 100€, 3–4 people 150€, 6 people 300€; 10–15% lower off-season rates

BREAKFAST
Continental breakfast included

ENGLISH
Yes

PALAZZO PRIULI ★★★ ($, 95)
Fondamenta de l'Osmarin, 4979

TELEPHONE
041 277 0844
FAX
041 241 1215
INTERNET
www.hotelpriuli.com
CREDIT CARDS
AE, DC, MC, V
RATES
Rates span low/high seasons:
hotel: no singles; double
as single 80–250€, double
95–415€, triple 150–450€,
junior suite 135–450€; annex:
no singles; double 100–360€,
triple 115–405€
BREAKFAST
Buffet breakfast included
ENGLISH
Yes

19 rooms, all with shower, bathtub, and toilet

First, some background on this well-known palace. In the year 1000, an unknown Hungarian forefather of the noble Priuli family arrived in Venice on a diplomatic mission, was smitten by her beauty, and never returned to his homeland. His famous descendents became part of Venetian aristocracy at the beginning of the fourteenth century and included three doges, fourteen *procuratores* (attorneys), and five cardinals. The palace was built in the late fourteenth century by the Priuli family as a testament to their wealth and prominence, and its facade continues to inspire many artists.

Today, guests use one of the first marble staircases built in Venice and can admire the original well in the reception area. The rooms have seventeenth-century brick fireplaces, timbered ceilings, original mosaic-tile floors, and canal views from all but one. The late 1900s furnishings have been carefully selected to complement the spirit of the rooms, as have the paintings, which are copies of those in the Accademia. Number 102, a junior suite with three canal-side windows, has a massive armoire with matching bed and bedside tables. A gold-leaf mirror hangs over the dressing table. The marble bathroom is huge and has ten feet of shelf space (I measured!) and a deep bathtub that invites lazy bubble baths. Beams in both the bedroom and bathroom, a fireplace, two windows, and a walk-in closet are the standout features in No. 101. In No. 104, you will hear and see the gondolas floating by not only the bedroom window, but the bathroom window as well.

Following the lead of so many hotels in Venice, the owners have opened a nine-room *dipendenza*, or annex, with another eleven-room annex on the drawing board. Some of the stone-walled rooms are huge but rather dark; those on the ground floor have windows facing the canal, but because they are on the street, you probably would not open the curtains, and if you did, you would not see much through the iron security bars. All the annex rooms cost less, so it is up to you whether to trade history for price.

FACILITIES AND SERVICES: Air-conditioning, direct-dial phone, no elevator (2 floors in main hotel, 3 in annex), hair dryer, laundry service, minibar, guest Internet terminal, in-room safe (hotel), satellite TV, all nonsmoking rooms

NEAREST TOURIST ATTRACTIONS: Piazza San Marco, Campo Santa Maria Formosa

PENSIONE BUCINTORO ★★ (111)
Riva San Biagio, 2135

28 rooms, 23 with shower or bath and toilet

Welcome to one of the best Great Sleeping values in Venice.

The Pensione Bucintoro is a family-run hotel with a minimum of style and upgrades. The rooms are spotlessly clean, well maintained, and damage free, but they are also a bit boring and nondescript. They are, however, more than saved by the absolutely fabulous views from every one—over the San Marco basin with the Lido on one side and the Doge's Palace on the other. Considering these views, which no other hotel in Venice can match, and their amazingly low prices for the platinum location, it is no wonder that reservations are nigh unto impossible unless you plan way ahead. Primo people-watching is available from an outside terrace facing the walkway along Riva San Biagio. The hotel is an easy walk to Piazza San Marco, the center of all the action in Venice. For trips farther afield, you can walk along the Riva degli Schiavoni and catch one of the vaporettos that depart every few minutes. The sad news is that the family has sold the hotel, but they will continue to manage it for the next three or four years, so enjoy it now before it becomes a luxury five-star with starry-eyed prices.

NOTE: The hotel is closed from December to Carnivale.

FACILITIES AND SERVICES: Bar, direct-dial phone, no elevator (4 floors), fans, hair dryers, office safe, TV in lounge

NEAREST TOURIST ATTRACTIONS: Piazza San Marco

TELEPHONE
041 522 3240

FAX
041 523 5224

CREDIT CARDS
MC, V

RATES
Single 76–96€, double 140–170€, triple 222€; lower off-season rates

BREAKFAST
Continental breakfast included

ENGLISH
Yes

San Marco

The wildest visions of the Arabian Nights are nothing to the piazza of St. Mark, and the first impression of the inside of the church.
— *Charles Dickens, in a letter, 1844*

This district has always been the heart and soul of Venice. It was in the area we now know as Piazza San Marco (St. Mark's Square) that the early rulers built the Palazzo Ducale and established their most important church, Basilica di San Marco. The basilica became one of the richest churches in Christendom, and the Palazzo Ducale the seat of a government that lasted longer than any other Republican regime in Europe. The lofty one-hundred-meter-high Campanile di San Marco, with a golden Archangel Gabriel weathervane on the top, is the highest structure in the city. Two other prominent landmarks on the square are the formidable granite columns, which were brought here from Constantinople. One has a winged lion, the symbol of San Marco, on top, and the other has a statue of St. Theodore, a former patron saint of the city. The public space of San Marco is so revered that it is the only one in Venice granted the name *piazza*. All the other Venetian squares are either *campi* or *campielli*.

Piazza San Marco is important for another reason: almost every visitor to Venice passes through here and spends lots of money. Even if you just sit at one of the *caffès* and listen to the music while sipping an espresso and watching the multitudes of pigeons, you will spend a lot of money. Away from the piazza, along the Merceria and Calle de Fabbri, are some of the city's most expensive boutiques and shopping opportunities. In addition, San Marco is dense with hotels and restaurants of all categories and price ranges.

HOTELS

OTHER OPTIONS
Apartment Rentals

($) indicates a Big Splurge; (¢) indicates a Cheap Sleep

ALBERGO SAN SAMUELE ★ (¢, 61)
Salizzada San Samuele, 3358

10 rooms, 7 with shower and toilet

What can you expect at this San Marco cheap sleep run by the trio of Dominick, Bruno, and Roberto? The approach, through a courtyard and upstairs to the lobby, is much better than you would think, and so are the livable, coordinated rooms that never say "budget!" To begin, No. 1 is a big room with a sunny view of the street. The original tile floor has been revealed, the pedestal sink saved, and a wardrobe and modern desk added. Number 9, on the back, is a big double with an open closet, luggage space, and an enclosed shower in the bathroom. Bright and also sunny, No. 3 has two windows with colorful geranium flower boxes and pink-accented walls in a room that can sleep two or three with plenty of flat surface space for luggage. Number 6, the prettiest, is a smaller corner room with a view of the archway and street beyond. Nice curtains hang in the wood-frame windows, but the bathroom is down the hall. The hall facilities are fine; in fact, I recommend saving a few euros and opting for a bathless room. I would avoid the two rooms on the first floor, both of which have ghastly views. Breakfast is extra. Save this hotel expense, be Venetian, and start your day at a *caffè*.

NOTE: The hotel is sometimes closed in December or January if they are doing work on the hotel; otherwise it remains open. Please call to check.

FACILITIES AND SERVICES: No elevator (2 floors), office safe, nonsmoking hotel

NEAREST TOURIST ATTRACTIONS: Ca' Rezzonico, Accademia Gallery, Piazza San Marco

TELEPHONE & FAX
041 522 8045
CREDIT CARDS
None, cash only
RATES
Single 30–45€, double 50–100€, triple 70–130€
BREAKFAST
Continental breakfast 4.50€
ENGLISH
Yes

ALBERGO SAN ZULIAN ★★★ ($, 90)
Campo della Guerra, 527

22 rooms, 5 apartments, all with shower and toilet

TELEPHONE
Hotel: 041 522 5872; annex and
apartments: 041 241 1275

FAX
Hotel: 041 523 2265; annex and
apartments: 041 241 4490

INTERNET
www.hotelsanzulian.it;
www.palazzoschiavoni.com

CREDIT CARDS
AE, DC, MC, V

RATES
Hotel and annex: single 203€,
double 236€, triple 288€, quad
340€; apartments (2 people)
from 242€, lower rates for
longer stays; excellent lower
off-season rates and Internet
promotions

BREAKFAST
Continental breakfast included
in hotel, not in apartments

ENGLISH
Yes

Good management skills from a devoted owner have moved the Albergo San Zulian to a top slot in the ranks of three-star hotels near Piazza San Marco. A nice balance has been struck between new and old, which are harmonized by fabrics and furnishings that recall Italy's artistic heritage and at the same time offer a splash of contemporary sophistication.

The rooms are all good—not a poor choice in the bunch. They offer sound comforts and are intelligently outfitted with muted wall coverings, carpeted floors, ample closet space, luggage racks, and hand-painted furniture. Honeymooners will want to request No. 304, which has a beautiful wooden ceiling and a private terrace. Another special room is No. 203, which is done in shades of red with a carved settee, swag headboard, white watermarked wallpaper, gold-framed mirror, and a built-in closet. Room 104 is a large double with Oriental throw rugs, a sofa, two chairs, and a bathroom with a stall shower. Numbers 97 and 98 are ground-floor rooms suitable for handicapped guests. In addition to size both in the room and bathroom, they both have painted Venetian furnishings and tile floors. Because they are on street level, views, sunshine, and some solitude are sacrificed. The hotel is an ideal command post for excellent shopping and for walking to the Rialto Bridge or to Piazza San Marco. There is also a choice of good restaurants within a short stroll (see *Great Eats Italy*).

The hotel also has eight additional annex rooms and five outstanding apartments in the Palazzo Schiavoni, which is on a canal in Castello, a pleasant ten- or fifteen-minute stroll from Piazza San Marco. The annex rooms have all the amenities of those in the hotel proper. Two of the smaller rooms, Venezia and L'Altana, have terraces that provide welcome sitting space, and most of the others are large enough to invite longer stays. The attractive apartments, named after famous Venetian painters, vary in size from a large studio to two bedrooms. I like them because of their quality and livability—the result of nice furnishings, sunny views of neighboring rooftops and canals, daily maid service, air-conditioning, private safes, and equipped kitchens. The building has an elevator, and each apartment also has a direct-dial telephone, data port, and satellite TV. Everything except telephone calls is included in the price, plus an early morning delivery to your door of hot bread from a nearby bakery. The owners prefer a three-night-minimum stay in the apartments.

FACILITIES AND SERVICES: Hotel: air-conditioning, direct-dial phone, elevator, hair dryers, laundry service, minibar, in-room safe, satellite TV; annex rooms and apartments: all of the above plus guest Internet terminal, all rooms nonsmoking

NEAREST TOURIST ATTRACTIONS: Rialto Bridge, Piazza San Marco

DOMUS CILIOTA (¢, 70)
Calle delle Muneghe, 2976 (near San Stefano)
34 rooms, all with shower and toilet

The thirty-four-room Domus Ciliota has to qualify as one of the more astonishing Great Sleeping values in Venice, especially in the high-rent district of San Marco near Palazzo Grassi and Campo San Stefano. The Domus was part of an old Augustinian monastery founded by Cardinal Maffeo Girardi in 1488. Until just recently, it was primarily an accommodation geared to university students during the school year and to tourists only in the off-times. After its latest transformation, its first floor is now open for female university students from October to May, and the other two floors have been redone and are open year-round to anyone who is fortunate enough to secure a reservation. The ultra-hygenic rooms may smack of industrial design, but they have built-in furniture, air-conditioning (June–September), private bathrooms, satellite televisions, good closets, drawer and shelf space, and nice bathrooms. On each floor is a small sitting room for guests. There is a large formal breakfast room, but the only other food served is dispensed from a bank of vending machines in the hall.

FACILITIES AND SERVICES: Air-conditioning, direct-dial phone, elevator, hair dryer, luggage room, some minibars, office safe, satellite TV, reception open 6 A.M.–midnight

NEAREST TOURIST ATTRACTIONS: Palazzo Grassi, Piazza San Marco, Accademia

TELEPHONE
041 520 4888
FAX
041 521 2730
INTERNET
www.ciliota.it
CREDIT CARDS
MC, V
RATES
Single 85€, double 105€; lower off-season rates
BREAKFAST
Continental breakfast included
ENGLISH
Yes

HOTEL AI DO MORI ★ (¢, 98)
Calle Larga San Marco, 658
11 rooms, 10 with shower or bath and toilet; 4 apartments, all with shower and toilet

At one point, Antonella Bernardi's Hotel Ai Do Mori could charitably be described as a dump. Not anymore, thanks to her hard work and her dedication to making her dream of owning a hotel come true.

TELEPHONE
041 520 4817, 041 528 9293
FAX
041 520 5328
INTERNET
www.hotelaidomori.com
CREDIT CARDS
MC, V

RATES
Single 50–100€, double
70–135€, triple 90–150€, quad
100–180€; discounts for cash
BREAKFAST
No breakfast served
ENGLISH
Yes

Prices, unfortunately, are now at the tip-top of the one-star scale, but if you are talking location, this one ranks high—a minute from Piazza San Marco and the Grand Canal, and close to the Rialto Bridge and more shopping and restaurant possibilities than you could try in ten visits to Venice.

The hotel has eleven rooms on three floors, most with reach-out-and-touch-them views of San Marco and the Basilica. Please remember, this is a one-star, so there will be stairs to climb, very small rooms to live in once you get to them, no breakfast served, some noise, and probably not much closet space to accommodate your steamer trunks full of clothing. One of my favorites is No. 3, a beamed room done in yellow with a snazzy new bathroom. Rooms 4 and 5 can be combined into a suite for five that has a large tub and shower, but you will have to forego the view. If these two rooms are rented separately, only No. 5 gets the bathroom. In No. 6, three voyagers can look out the two windows at Piazza San Marco and the clock tower. For romantics willing to undergo a real workout climbing to the top floor, Room 11, called the Painter's Room, pays off its winded guests with an absolutely unbeatable view of the Basilica, San Marco bell tower, and more, not only from the room but from the bathroom and the private terrace. To get this panorama you must sacrifice space inside, so you should plan to do your living on the terrace. On rainy days or in winter, cabin fever could set in, since the room is furnished basically with only a king-sized bed and a closet—simply because there is not space for one other item, including the TV, which had to be mounted on the ceiling. There are, however, chairs on the terrace.

In keeping with the current annex trend, Antonella has added four compact apartments in a nearby building. These are ideal for families because they have small kitchenettes, but they have absolutely no views.

FACILITIES AND SERVICES: Hotel and annex: Air-conditioning, direct-dial phone, no elevator (3 floors in hotel, 2 in annex), hair dryer, in-room safe, satellite TV

NEAREST TOURIST ATTRACTIONS: Piazza San Marco, Grand Canal, shopping, Rialto Bridge

HOTEL ALA ★★★ ($, 81)
Campo Santa Maria dei Giglio, 2494

TELEPHONE
041 520 8333
FAX
041 520 6390

87 rooms, all with shower or bath and toilet

For those wanting to be in the historic center of Venice, only minutes by foot from Piazza San Marco, the Hotel Ala, under the competent ownership and direction of the

Salmazo family, is one outstanding answer. It is a neighbor of the famous Gritti Palace Hotel, where double rooms start at around $800 per night, so you know this is an exclusive area. If romance is on your agenda, plan to arrive at the hotel's private dock via gondola or water taxi. Otherwise, the vaporetto stop is Line 1, Santa Maria del Giglio.

While the hotel cannot be termed glamorous, it does have a pleasing Venetian air that has been discovered by loads of *Great Sleeps Italy* readers. The large club/lounge and the breakfast room are hung with local artwork. These rooms also display Murano glass chandeliers, a mixture of old and new furniture, and an interesting collection of firearms. On lazy summer afternoons, the shaded roof terrace is the ideal place to relax and remind yourself how lucky you are to be in this enchanting city. Most of the rooms have enough room for you and your belongings, and so they are inviting for long stays. All are individually decorated in various styles, ranging from Venetian Baroque to early 1900s. Many have original beams and frescoed ceilings. Four have balconies, three have terraces, half look onto the canal, ten are specifically nonsmoking, and one is nonallergic.

Every room seems to be somebody's favorite, with the possible exception of No. 101, a nice but dark room that faces a cement wall. Also viewless is No. 139. Many Great Sleepers like Nos. 240 and 241, which can be combined to form a large suite. The rooms are attractively outfitted with light furniture with floral accents, and the balcony view is of a canal. Number 108, also on a canal, is a standard double with wood beams, luggage space, and a nice bathroom with a tub, heated towel racks, and monogrammed towels. Room 460, on the top floor, has blue graphic wallpaper and a balcony view of the leaning tower at San Stefano. The ceiling alone could sell No. 243, a twin in blue and light gold with a tapestry in back of the bed. An unusual claw-foot king bed is the centerpiece of No. 272, which also has marble floors and a Jacuzzi and separate shower in the bathroom.

For special occasions, my unequivocal favorite is the Antonia junior suite, with sweeping views all the way to Lido. Trust me, once you check in, you will start thinking about becoming a permanent resident... just as Antonia was. Antonia was an old lady who lived in this part of the hotel for more than twenty years. When she died in her late nineties, the hotel redid her quarters and named them after her. I like the living room with its big desk and large-screen television, the bedroom with a reproduction Guardi

INTERNET
www.hotelala.com
CREDIT CARDS
AE, DC, MC, V
RATES
Single 190€, double 260–340€, triple 300€, Antonia 340€; excellent lower off-season rates
BREAKFAST
Hot and cold buffet breakfast included
ENGLISH
Yes

painting over the bed, the bathroom with an automatic skylight, and of course, that million-dollar view.

The hotel operates the Ristorante da' Raffaele and offers discounts to guests who eat there. The setting alongside a canal is picture perfect, and the food is generally equal to the setting.

NOTE: Under the same ownership is the Pensione Accademia (see page 306). The hotel is closed for two weeks in January after Epiphany.

FACILITIES AND SERVICES: Air-conditioning, American bar serving light snacks, conference room, cigar corner, direct-dial phone, elevator, hair dryer, some Jacuzzis, minibar, data port, restaurant, in-room safe, satellite and pay-per-view TVs, some nonsmoking rooms

NEAREST TOURIST ATTRACTIONS: Piazza San Marco, Grand Canal, Accademia, Santa Maria della Salute Church, Peggy Guggenheim Collection, shopping

HOTEL FIRENZE ★★★ ($, 71)
Salizzada San Moisè 1490

25 rooms, all with shower or bath and toilet

If a San Marco location is a priority and your pocket-book is flexible, the Hotel Firenze sits on a prime parcel of real estate only thirty meters from Piazza San Marco. The building was rebuilt at the end of the nineteenth century and has an Art Nouveau facade of marble and iron with paned glass and red accents, which is at its best at night. The exceptional pink-and-white breakfast room (no smoking, please) shows off the inside of these leaded stained-glass windows and has comfortable banquette and settee seating. In the 1800s, this room housed the Borsalino hat factory, which has moved but remains one of the most important hat factories in Venice.

A solid room choice is No. 301, a large double (or triple if you must) with soothing seafoam green furniture trimmed in gold, blue, and pink, colors that are carried out in the Murano chandelier. The bathroom has all the perks, including a telephone and ample light. Number 302 is another good room, with a streetside view, built-ins, and a luggage rack. The rooftop, flower-decked terrace has breathtaking views of Giudecca, the bell tower and dome of the Basilica San Marco, the reconstruction of La Fenice Theater, and beyond. If you want your own balcony, and are willing to climb some steps to get there, ask for Nos. 401, 402, or 403.

TELEPHONE
041 522 2858
FAX
041 520 2668
INTERNET
www.hotel-firenze.com
CREDIT CARDS
AE, DC, MC, V
RATES
Single 190€, double 270€; lower rates for *Great Sleeps Italy* readers (mention when reserving)
BREAKFAST
Continental breakfast included
ENGLISH
Yes

FACILITIES AND SERVICES: Air-conditioning, bar, 2 direct-dial phones in most rooms, elevator, hair dryer, minibar, in-room safe, satellite TV, 6 nonsmoking rooms

NEAREST TOURIST ATTRACTIONS: Piazza San Marco, Grand Canal, wonderful shopping

HOTEL FLORA ★★★ ($, 73)
Calle Larga XXII Marzo, 2283-A

44 rooms, all with shower or bath and toilet

There is absolutely no question about it, the Flora is one of the best three-star hotels in Venice. Its genuine warmth and hospitality are in evidence from the minute you arrive until you reluctantly must leave. "The most important thing we have to offer our guests is our service and our best hospitality," Ruggero Romanelli told me. You will find these important ingredients, and many more, during your memorable stay at the Hotel Flora—which for its many devotees is the perfect example of a romantic hotel, to which many others are compared but never quite measure up.

This small hotel is owned and operated by Ruggero Romanelli and his son, Gioele, who are carrying on the family tradition of hoteliers. Quality and impeccable taste show throughout. The entry is off Calle Larga XXII Marzo and down a narrow lane from which you can see the garden through the glass doors as you arrive. This garden oasis in the middle of Venice is dominated by an old well and several pieces of statuary. It is all bordered by twisting vines and beds of hydrangeas, pansies, and camellia bushes. Breakfast and afternoon drinks are served here in warm weather, and several of the rooms open onto it. During the cooler months, breakfast is served in the wood-paneled dining room, where pink-covered tables are laid with English floral-print china and pieces of family silver.

A beautiful hand-painted stairway leads to the bedrooms, all individually decorated but still respecting the atmosphere of the hotel. Number 47 is among the most popular, thanks to its enviable antiques and its postcard view of the Santa Maria della Salute Church. Number 34 is another well-loved choice, with two windows overlooking the garden, an ornate, velvet-covered headboard, and a matching armoire and side tables. Soft beige walls, Murano lights, a detailed ceiling, and a small green-and-white-tile bath round it out. Number 36, for two to four guests, overlooks the Palazzo Contarini, the historical palace of Desdemona and Othello. It has comfortable chairs and enough space to live in, and the bathroom is new. Even the smallest rooms are very well done, especially No. 38,

TELEPHONE
041 520 5844
FAX
041 522 8217
INTERNET
www.hotelflora.it
CREDIT CARDS
AE, DC, MC, V
RATES
Single 180€, double 230€, extra bed 50€; lower off-season rates and Internet specials
BREAKFAST
Large Continental breakfast included
ENGLISH
Yes

a ground-floor selection with two windows opening onto the garden. When reserving, please state your size requirements and remember that all the rooms are nice, but the very best overlook the gardens.

NOTE: Never content to rest on their laurels, the Romanellis have opened a nine-room *locanda* called the Novecento (see page 296).

FACILITIES AND SERVICES: Air-conditioning, bar, direct-dial phone, elevator, hair dryer, laundry service, in-room safe, satellite TV, room service for light snacks, screens on some windows, 2 handicapped-accessible rooms

NEAREST TOURIST ATTRACTIONS: Premier shopping, Piazza San Marco

HOTEL GALLINI ★★ (60)
Calle della Verona, 3673

50 rooms, 43 with shower or bath and toilet

The Hotel Gallini offers Great Sleepers not only excellent value for their money but a discount if they mention *Great Sleeps Italy* when reserving and show a copy when they arrive. Adriano Ceciliati and his brother, Gabrielle, have owned and personally managed the Gallini since 1953. Now Gabrielle has retired and in his place is Adriano's delightful daughter, Gabriella. Adriano's charming wife comes early every morning to oversee the breakfast service and make sure that everyone leaves satisfied. This committed, hospitable approach to the business has earned the family and their hotel an impressive roster of repeat international visitors, many of whom have been coming here since they opened.

The platinum location puts guests within easy walking distance of Piazza San Marco, La Fenice (the opera house), and marvelous shopping. The closest vaporetto stop is just a few minutes away on the Grand Canal, or guests can arrive directly at the hotel by gondola or water taxi. The building was once the site of the brothers' family home. When they converted the original seven-room flat into a hotel, they named it after their mother. The brothers personally rebuilt the hotel, putting it together piece by piece, even laying the intricate flooring. Every year the hotel is closed from November through February, which is when they paint and do repairs and remodeling projects.

The basic rooms do not sport fine antiques or expensive fabrics. They are, however, well coordinated and large enough to be comfortable. They are also the cleanest in Venice, thanks to Piera and Bruna, two sisters who have worked here as the cleaning staff for over three decades,

TELEPHONE
041 520 4515

FAX
041 520 9103

EMAIL
hgallini@tin.it

INTERNET
www.hotelgallini.it

CREDIT CARDS
AE, MC, V

RATES
Single from 103€, double from 154€, suite from 209€; for stays longer than 4 days: 10% discount from Apr–June and in Sept and Oct, 20% discount in Mar, July, and Aug; discounts for *Great Sleeps Italy* readers (subject to availability)

BREAKFAST
Continental breakfast included

ENGLISH
Yes

and Yolanda, who isn't far behind in loyal service. The pride they take in their job is certainly evident, and it also says a great deal about the Ceciliatis and how they treat their employees. All of the rooms are good, but I would have to give a slight edge to those on the third floor and those directly on the Verona Canal, where you can hang out and almost touch the hats of the gondoliers who ply by throughout the day, serenading their passengers—and you as well. One never tires of this wonderful scene, not even Adriano and his brother. I know because I was lucky enough to stay in the hotel during one of my trips to Venice. During the day when I would hear the gondoliers singing, I would rush to the window. Many times, standing on the bridge over the canal, were the two brothers, listening to the music along with the rest of us. It was a very tender picture.

Finally, when staying here, please be sure to say hello to the real manager and boss of this hotel, the handsome Mr. Pallino, a black cat who had the good sense to adopt the hotel, move in, and now takes his job of surveying the daily scene and generally keeping tabs on everyone very seriously. During the day he is often stretched out along his sunny front window perch. After his breakfast and morning walk, you will find him purring on the back of a chair or, more likely, in someone's lap.

NOTE: The hotel closes from around November 20 to Carnivale.

FACILITIES AND SERVICES: Air-conditioning in some rooms, direct-dial phone, no elevator (3 floors; they will help with luggage), hair dryer available, minibar, office safe, some TVs

NEAREST TOURIST ATTRACTIONS: Piazza San Marco, excellent shopping, La Fenice

HOTEL LISBONA ★★★ ($, 74)
Off Campo San Moisè, 2153 (along Calle Larga XXII Marzo at Corte Barozzi)

15 rooms, all with shower or bath and toilet

The Hotel Lisbona was the hotel I stayed in many years ago on my first visit to Venice. I was traveling with a school friend, and we requested a "room for two with a bath." What we wanted was a room with twin beds and a private bath. What we got was a room slightly bigger than a walk-in closet with one bed and a bathroom so tiny you could literally touch both sides of the walls at the same time. It was the middle of high season and we were stuck . . . the Lisbona, and everywhere else, was fully

TELEPHONE
041 528 6774

FAX
041 520 7061

INTERNET
www.hotellisbona.com

CREDIT CARDS
AE, DC, MC, V

RATES
Single 200€, double 290€, extra bed 70€; excellent lower off-season rates

BREAKFAST
Continental breakfast included
ENGLISH
Yes

booked. Despite the miniature quarters, we loved the location, and when I started writing my hotel guide to Italy, I wanted to include it, but nothing had changed. The rooms were still really drab and rundown, not to mention so small you almost had to go outside to change your mind. But I never gave up, always going back, hoping it would change. On my 1999 visit...bingo! With a new owner at the helm, the hotel had been improved 100 percent, and the rooms were slightly enlarged and entirely redone. Today, all remains well at the Lisbona, and I am happy to continue recommending it to you in this latest edition of *Great Sleeps Italy*.

Talk about a photo op! If this one doesn't inspire you to pick up your camera, nothing else in Venice will. Some of your neighbors will be the high rollers staying at the Bauer-Gruenwald across the little canal and paying five or six times your room rate. These people you probably won't get to know. You will get to know the cluster of handsome gondoliers who park their colorful vessels alongside the Lisbona, and use the walkway under the arch leading to the hotel as their gathering place for playing cards, kibitzing, and flirting between gondola rides.

I must admit, the rooms are still small, but they are now livable and large enough to think a new thought. They have been completely redecorated with coral or gold damask wall coverings, new carpeting, better furniture, and improved baths. You definitely want one of the twelve that have canal views. If space counts, the rooms with bathtubs are somewhat larger than those with just a shower. Twin-bedded No. 15, with a canal view, is a good example. Number 11 is a bigger perch for two, with double windows and a little balcony where you will use up plenty of film shooting the gondola activity below. I would avoid Nos. 14, 21, and 31. They are really too small unless you are a single with one very little piece of luggage, although they do have canal views and a tiny balcony. No. 12, also with a balcony, exhibits very clever use of minuscule space: the minibar is fastened onto the wall! From the hotel door you are minutes from Piazza San Marco, the best shopping in Venice, good restaurants (see *Great Eats Italy*), vaporetto stops, and all those gondolas.

FACILITIES AND SERVICES: Air-conditioning, bar, direct-dial phone, no elevator, hair dryer, laundry service, minibar, in-room safe, satellite TV

NEAREST TOURIST ATTRACTIONS: Piazza San Marco, excellent shopping, Grand Canal, the gondoliers around the hotel

HOTEL LOCANDA FIORITA ★ &
CA' MOROSINI (65)
Campiello Nuovo, 3457

10 rooms, 8 with shower and toilet; 9-room annex, all with shower and toilet

Great Sleepers will want to share this great find: an affordable hotel that is friendly and exceptionally well-located. The ten-room establishment is off Campo San Stefano on Campiello Nuovo, an inconspicuous square in the premier San Marco district between the Accademia Gallery and the Palazzo Grassi. The entrance is upstairs, through a reception area with a beamed ceiling. Breakfast is served here around four tables. In summer you can have your coffee and rolls served on the terrace below.

The thoughtfully planned rooms and baths are really amazing for a one-star, and for many two-stars for that matter. The rooms are carpeted or tiled and have some exposed beams, a framed black-and-white print of Venice, a small desk, and an adequate-size wardrobe. The bathrooms have stall showers and lighted mirrors over the sinks, so you can see what you are doing while dressing for the day. The towels are Italian cotton. A word of caution for the two bathless rooms: in theory, these rooms share two hall bathrooms, but since one of these is the staff bathroom to use while on duty, this effectively means that guests actually share only one bathroom. Two of my favorite rooms are still No. 1, a large green-and-gold double that opens onto a courtyard, and No. 9, fit for four, with two view windows onto the street. My least favorite is No. 7, thanks to its overwhelming mix of red, which is on the carpet and in checkerboard fashion on the bathroom tiles.

The nine room *dipendenza* or annex, Ca' Morosini, is definitely more upmarket, even though it's spread out on three floors without an elevator. Color and character reign. Minimalism is nowhere to be seen in the rooms, which have billowing cloud frescoes, colorful hand-painted furnishings, and Venetian brocades draping the beds and windows. Guests who want a stair-step workout getting to their room on the top floor will, from their balconies, be an arm's-length from the Santo Stefano Church. The seductive Casanova Suite is wrapped in red and gold fabrics and has three windows on a small square. The marble bathroom has a large stall shower. Number 27, however, is just too cramped for comfort. True, it has an awning-shaded and jasmine-scented terrace, but the bed in the room gets in the way of using the desk, and there is no light over the sink in the yellow-striped bathroom. As with all of these

TELEPHONE
041 523 4754

FAX
041 522 8043

INTERNET
www.locandafiorita.com

CREDIT CARDS
AE, MC, V

RATES
Hotel: single 85€, double 115–135€, lower rates in Aug and Jan; annex: single 130€, double 180€, extra bed 30% of double rate; 50€ less in Aug and Nov

BREAKFAST
Continental breakfast included

ENGLISH
Yes

types of accommodation, the reception hours at the annex are limited and to check in or out, you must do so at the Locanda Fiorita.

FACILITIES AND SERVICES: Hotel: air-conditioning, direct-dial phone, no elevator, hair dryer available, office safe, satellite TV; annex: all the same with the addition of a minibar and an in-room safe

NEAREST TOURIST ATTRACTIONS: Campo San Stefano, shopping, Grand Canal

HOTEL MONACO & GRAND CANAL ★★★★ ($, 75)
Calle Vallaresso, 1332

99 rooms in hotel, 36 rooms in annex, all with shower, bath, and toilet

TELEPHONE
041 520 0211
FAX
041 520 0501
INTERNET
www.hotelmonaco.it
CREDIT CARDS
AE, DC, MC, V
RATES
Rates span low/high seasons:
single 110–290€, double
170–560€, suites 260–725€;
half-board for lunch or dinner
50€ per person
BREAKFAST
Continental breakfast included
ENGLISH
Yes

The present and the past blend perfectly at the luxurious Hotel Monaco & Grand Canal, which is across the street from Harry's Bar, the historic watering hole for the rich and famous who flow through Venice as quickly as the Bellinis (fresh peach juice and sparkling wine) do from behind the bar.

The magnificent palace has an interesting Venetian history. It originally belonged to the noble Dandolo family, who ran it from 1638 to 1774 as a gathering place to gamble, enjoy the favors of courtesans, and engage in social and political meetings. Finally it was closed at the insistence of moralists, and in the nineteenth and twentieth centuries it was used for many things, including a dance hall and a theater. In 1992, it was purchased by the Benetton Group, who spent several years restoring it to its former grandeur and glory. Nowhere is this more evident than in the Sala del Ridotto, the main room of the palace that is now resplendent with its original frescoes, marbles, mirrors, balustrades, and stuccoes, which give the impression that nothing has changed. This room, and those surrounding it, are now used for conferences, banquets, and other important events.

One of the main focal points of the hotel proper is the lobby, which is a beautiful blend of Venetian and international contemporary art. In restoring the area, architects left the original columns, and installed twenty-first-century interpretations of mosaic-tiled floors and Carnivale figures, and added a glass atrium garden surrounded by sleek, sophisticated seating. Along the Grand Canal is a covered dining terrace that has become one of the "in" places to see and be seen.

The rooms and suites were created in two phases: the first has a traditional, restrained air, the second is modern in spirit. All, of course, have the benefits of impeccable service from the professional staff and all the luxurious whistles and bells befitting their stature and price, and that are expected by their occupants. Aside from fine fabrics and furnishings, even the simplest double will have comfortable armchairs, Bang & Olufsen televisions, double sink marble bathrooms, and Murano glass everywhere, including the door handles. The suites have sensational views from their private terraces or balconies overlooking the Grand Canal and St. Mark's Basin.

The thirty-six rooms in the residence-annex will appeal to a younger, design-conscious crowd who like a modern atmosphere that's tempered by accents of the past. This is achieved by the beamed ceilings, polished wood floors, and contemporary palate of colors, along with mirrored closets and well-lit, large bathrooms.

Yes, it can be very expensive to check in, but if you go when the rates are lower, it becomes more affordable. It is especially appealing for those who want to transform their hotel stay into a very special occasion.

FACILITIES AND SERVICES: Air-conditioning, bar, concierge, data ports, elevator, hair dryer, guest Internet terminal, laundry service, in-room safe, room service, restaurant with full or half-board available, tea and coffeemakers in residence-annex, satellite TV

NEAREST TOURIST ATTRACTIONS: Piazza San Marco, Grand Canal, shopping

HOTEL SANTO STEFANO ★★★ ($, 68)
Campo Santo Stefano, 2957
11 rooms, all with shower or bath and toilet

The Hotel Santo Stefano is located right on the colorful Campo Santo Stefano, which boasts a pretty church, several outdoor restaurants and *caffès,* and interesting local activity. The hotel is intimately charming, with views onto the *campo* from many of the rooms. A tiny garden patio along the front provides a place for warm-weather breakfasts or a calm oasis for reading or people-watching. The hotel is owned by Roberto Quatrini (who also owns the beautiful Hotel Celio in Rome, page 163). For Roberto, "the sky is the limit" when it comes to upgrading and client satisfaction, so he spent a mega-amount redoing the corridors with marble floors, improving bathrooms, sparking up the breakfast room and lobby area by adding painted beam ceilings, installing special armchairs, and putting in a new bar.

TELEPHONE
041 520 0166
FAX
041 522 4460
INTERNET
www.hotelsantostefanovenezia
.com
CREDIT CARDS
AE, MC, V
RATES
Single 130–195€, double 170–280€, triple 250–350€; discounts for *Great Sleeps Italy* readers
BREAKFAST
Continental breakfast included
ENGLISH
Yes

The compact rooms are thoughtfully done and attractively decorated with typical hand-painted Venetian furniture, subdued fabrics (including watered silk), and crystal lights. The marble bathrooms all have a Jacuzzi, either in the tub or in the steam shower. Over 100 DVDs are available for guests to watch on their large-screen televisions. My favorite room is No. 11, the only one on the top floor; it has a view of the square and the San Maurizio Tower and is large enough to fit a sofa with two chairs and a pretty Venetian-style painted wardrobe with two drawers. If you are a light sleeper, ask for a room away from the square, as it can get noisy at night, especially in summer. To keep in touch digitally, one of the best cybercafes in Venice is next door. During the off-season, good discounts are offered.

FACILITIES AND SERVICES: Air-conditioning, direct-dial phone, DVDs for rent, elevator, hair dryer, Jacuzzis in all bathrooms, laundry service, minibar, satellite TV, in-room safe, nonsmoking rooms

NEAREST TOURIST ATTRACTIONS: Piazza San Marco, Grand Canal, wonderful shopping

HOTEL SERENISSIMA ★★ (57)
Calle Goldoni, 4486

37 rooms, all with shower or bath and toilet

No groups are accepted at the Serenissima, which is a distinct difference, and advantage, over the tour-bus dinosaur hotel across the street, where management grinds them in and grinds them out and offers as little as possible along the way. The theme here is cordial service by the Dal Borgo family and rooms that are routinely dusted, polished, and maintained. The furniture in the white rooms is postmodern and the colors are coordinated. The bathroom showers have doors, along with a shelf for your toiletries. An added note is the owner's interesting modern art collection, which is hung in the hotel. A sketched portrait of her as a young girl marks the top of the second-floor landing. Prices in the off-season should appeal to most Great Sleepers looking for a deal.

NOTE: Watch the Website for the opening of their new three-star hotel next door.

FACILITIES AND SERVICES: Air-conditioning, bar, direct-dial phone, no elevator (3 floors), hair dryer, office safe, satellite TV

NEAREST TOURIST ATTRACTIONS: Piazza San Marco, excellent shopping

TELEPHONE
041 520 0011
FAX
041 522 3292
INTERNET
www.hotelserenissima.it
CREDIT CARDS
AE, MC, V
RATES
Single 105€, double 175€; lower off-season rates
BREAKFAST
Continental breakfast included
ENGLISH
Yes

LOCANDA ART DECO (69)
Calle delle Botteghe, 2966
6 rooms, all with shower and toilet

Don't assume that "affordable" translates into lack of style at this smart *affita camere* that lauds an Art Deco theme. In the reception area is a working Art Deco radio, a vintage Singer sewing machine, and a bright red leather sofa. Alphonse Mucha prints hang on the upstairs landing, where there is another period sofa and two footstools. The large, livable rooms are light and cleverly outfitted with wrought-iron furnishings. They also sport wooden floors, crisp white bed covers, and an interesting piece or two rescued from the 1920s. A massage therapist is on call to help you unwind after a day of sightseeing and meandering through Venice.

FACILITIES AND SERVICES: Air-conditioning, direct-dial phone, no elevator (3 floors), hair dryer available, office safe, TV, 24-hour desk

NEAREST TOURIST ATTRACTIONS: Accademia, shopping, Grand Canal

TELEPHONE
041 277 05

FAX
041 270 2891

INTERNET
www.locandaartdeco.com

CREDIT CARDS
AE, MC, V

RATES
Single 80–130€, double 90–160€, extra bed 25€; 5% discount for *Great Sleeps Italy* readers (mention book when reserving)

BREAKFAST
Continental breakfast included

ENGLISH
Yes

LOCANDA CASA PETRARCA ★ (59)
Calle degli Schiavine, 4386
8 rooms, 6 with shower or bath and toilet

Only those who already know it are ever able to find Locanda Casa Petrarca. When you book your room, Nellie, the hospitable English-speaking owner, will give you directions on how to get to her seven-room hideaway tucked at the end of Calle degli Schiavine. As you approach it, look for the flower boxes in the archway windows by the main entrance.

The rooms are clean and cheerful, with tile floors, bedside rugs, and simple furniture. They are often filled with guests on long stays, and the hotel can easily adopt a happy, houseparty atmosphere. A two- to three-month lead time is needed to book No. 8, a beautiful room with a great view onto a canal. Perks include the only TV/VCR in the house, stereo music, loads of living and closet space, and flowers brightening each window. The small reception area is done in wicker, and you can eat breakfast here, or Nellie will serve it in your room, which could add the perfect touch to your stay, depending on your roommate.

FACILITIES AND SERVICES: Air-conditioning, elevator, hair dryer, TV/VCR in one room, nonsmoking hotel

NEAREST TOURIST ATTRACTIONS: Piazza San Marco, shopping

TELEPHONE
041 520 0430

FAX
"Same as telephone, when it works," states Nellie

EMAIL
capetrarca@libero.it

CREDIT CARDS
None, cash only

RATES
Single 50–80€, double 70–130€, No. 8 150–200€; extra person 40% of room rate; discounts for long stays

BREAKFAST
Continental breakfast included

ENGLISH
Yes

NOVECENTO ($, 76)
Calle del Dose, 2683/84, off Campo San Maurizio
9 rooms, all with shower and toilet

TELEPHONE
041 241 3765
FAX
041 521 2145
INTERNET
www.novecento.biz
CREDIT CARDS
AE, DC, MC, V
RATES
No singles; doubles 230€, triple 260–280€
BREAKFAST
Buffet breakfast included
ENGLISH
Yes

The Novecento boutique hotel blends original 1900 exotic furnishings from Egypt, Morocco, and Thailand into a multiethnic environment that is captivating from the moment you enter. The mixture of old, new, and Eastern works, from the three-tiered brick heater with copper piping to a gold glass Buddah keeping watch over the small library and lounge area. Changing contemporary art exhibits and a shaded garden complete the ground-floor space.

Each room has its own style and personality, but they are alike in comforts, which include duvets instead of blankets, individually controlled piped-in music (which runs the gamut from jazz to Arabic and Italian pop), and large bathrooms with stainless-steel washstand sinks. On the second floor, a Moroccan sitting area has masses of giant pillows tossed on Oriental rugs, and guests are encouraged to nestle in. A favorite room on this floor is No. 6, which has, in addition to a tiny balcony and beamed ceiling, a teakwood king-size bed covered in a thick duvet and mounted on a platform. The backdrop is a piece of framed Thai fabric. Lighting is romantically limited to sparkling bedside lights. The bathroom has a decorative antique mirror and a shower with two types of spouts: large and huge. Number 9 is another interesting room. The entryway has a Chinese chest and a wrought-iron light that looks like a big spider. The four-poster bed is swagged on each side and framed by two cloth-covered bedside tables with Moroccan lights. Number 5 is the biggest room (and can stretch to sleep three), and it is the only one with a tub in addition to a shower. The street-facing room itself has twin canopy beds with a matching armoire and an Indian Dhury rug on the mosaic-tile floor. Number 3, with a garden outlook, is another twin choice. I like the marble-topped bedside tables, the Indian tapestry, and the little dressing room.

NOTE: Under the same ownership is the Hotel Flora, page 287.

FACILITIES AND SERVICES: Air-conditioning, bar, direct-dial phone, no elevator (2 floors), data ports, laundry service, minibar, piped-in room music, in-room safe, satellite TV, free baby cots, nonsmoking hotel

NEAREST TOURIST ATTRACTIONS: La Fenice Theater, Grand Canal, Accademia, Piazza San Marco

PALAZZO DUODO GREGOLIN (97)
Calle dei Fabbri, Ramo Duodo

3 suites, all with shower or bath and toilet

The stunning Palazzo Duodo Gregolin is a good example of the current popular trend whereby small hotels reinvent dilapidated structures by taking over sections of an old palace or a floor of an unused building and refashioning these spaces into something quite impressive. The Palazzo Duodo is owned and operated by the Hotel Centauro, which is currently completing a longterm redecorating project. Until this is completed, I cannot recommend the hotel itself as a Great Sleep, but I certainly can highly recommend Palazzo Duodo Gregolin, their *dipendenza* (or annex), which was the former home of the owner of the hotel.

There are now three suites that open onto a lovely salon decorated in muted shades of rose, burgandy, and blue. Also opening onto the salon is the breakfast room, with a marble fireplace and a communal table where everyone is invited to gather each morning. The advantage of the three suites is that they can be reserved independently or as a whole if three couples or a family want to be together. There is no staff on duty here, but there is daily maid service and a direct telephone line to the hotel.

Angels in back of the bed watch over guests who occupy the red suite, which can adequately sleep three and offers a canal view and a shower in the bathroom. The largest is the white suite, with a rooftop view, lovely Venetian furniture, huge closet space, and both a tub and shower in the bathroom. My favorite is the green suite, with a beautiful matching antique bed and side tables, dresser, and three-door armoire. The views from the two windows are onto neighboring rooftops and, if you lean out, a canal. The bathroom has five feet of shelf space and can still accommodate a large chest. Not to be overlooked is the hospitality of the Tomasutti family and the warmth and friendliness of their multilingual staff, especially Ninfa, who works at the front desk. If you are a collector of unusual, handcrafted jewelry, please take a minute to see Ninfa's unusual pieces, which are on display in the lobby of the hotel. Also, see the Madera art gallery in "Shopping: Great Chic," page 374.

FACILITIES AND SERVICES: Air-conditioning, direct-dial phone, elevator, hair dryer, minibar, in-room safe, satellite TV, nonsmoking hotel

NEAREST TOURIST ATTRACTIONS: Piazza San Marco, excellent shopping

TELEPHONE
041 522 5832

FAX
041 523 9151

INTERNET
www.palazzoduodo.com

CREDIT CARDS
AE, DC, MC, V

RATES
Single or double 130–200€; lower off-season rates

BREAKFAST
Buffet breakfast included

ENGLISH
Yes

Hotels West of the Grand Canal

Dorsoduro

Dorsoduro, a long finger of land between the center of the city and the lagoon, constitutes the southern part of Venice. Campo Santa Margherita is its largest open space, with a daily market and a life of its own almost twenty-four hours a day. Moored along Rio San Barnaba is a colorful barge selling fruits and vegetables that has become a photo-op destination for visitors from around the world. Standing on the Grand Canal is the seventeenth-century Baroque church of Santa Maria Della Salute, one of the most beautiful buildings in Venice. Inside are three Titians on the ceiling and Tintoretto's *Marriage at Cana* in the sacristy. Also in Dorsoduro is the Peggy Guggenheim home, which now holds her collection of contemporary art; the Accademia, the city's most important art museum; and Ca' Rezzonico, which is the museum of eighteenth-century Venetian art.

HOTELS

($) indicates a Big Splurge; (¢) indicates a Cheap Sleep

AGLI ALBORETTI HOTEL ★★ (48)
Rio Terrà Antonia Foscarini, 884

23 rooms, all with shower or bath and toilet

The Agli Alboretti, owned by Anna Linguerri, is close to the Accademia, which has the world's finest collection of Venetian art. For other sightseeing, the Accademia vaporetto stop is only a few steps away. The entrance off the

TELEPHONE
041 523 0058
FAX
041 521 0158
EMAIL
alboretti@gpnet.it

street leads to an intimate paneled lobby with a collection of concert posters on the walls. An interesting model of a seventeenth-century ship is permanently docked in the window. Beyond the lobby is a little lounge and a garden with a vine-covered arbor, where you can have breakfast on warm mornings or relax in the shade on hot summer afternoons. On the second floor is a comfortable sitting room. Sra. Linguerri operates a high-end restaurant next door to the hotel, and guests can take a half- or full-board. Sra. Linguerri is a wine connoisseur, and her wine list offers a nice variety of Italian selections.

The rooms are in good repair but are small, as are the bathrooms, many of which are new or have deep half-tubs with hand-held shower nozzles and no shower curtains. One must be philosophical: this is an old building, and you cannot expect spacious quarters. Single voyagers will check into No. 107, with a ship theme carried out by the ship-style lower bunk bed and three framed prints of old sailing vessels. The view is onto the side of the hotel's garden restaurant and small side street. Number 108 does duty as a double, triple, or quad and makes the grade no matter the number of guests, who each will be sleeping in a twin bed and using a new bathroom. Next door, No. 109 is a simple double with a Fortuny-style light and a small bath with an enclosed shower. Luggage space is at a premium. The only room you really don't want is No. 106, which has the main hotel air-conditioning unit by the window.

NOTE: The hotel is sometimes closed from January 6 to 30, and the restaurant is closed the first three weeks of August.

FACILITIES AND SERVICES: Air-conditioning, bar, direct-dial phone, no elevator (4 floors), hair dryer, minibar, office safe, satellite TV

NEAREST TOURIST ATTRACTIONS: Accademia, Peggy Guggenheim Collection

INTERNET
www.aglialboretti.com
CREDIT CARDS
AE, DC, MC, V
RATES
Single 105€, double 150–180€, triple 210€; half-board 50€ per person
BREAKFAST
Continental breakfast included
ENGLISH
Yes

CA' PISANI HOTEL ★★★★ ($, 50)
Rio Terrà Antonia Foscarini, 979/A
29 rooms, all with shower or bath and toilet

The hotel takes its name from a great admiral of the ancient republic of Venice, Vettor Pisani, whose family owned this fourteenth-century palace. The name, however, is all that remains of the past. This is now a hyper-trendy, twenty-nine-room boutique hotel that will knock the socks off anyone who values the latest word, in fashion or hotels. Everything about the hotel makes an architectural or

TELEPHONE
041 240 1411
FAX
041 277 1061
INTERNET
www.capisanihotel.it
CREDIT CARDS
AE, DC, MC, V

RATES
Single or double 297–342€,
suite 396€; excellent low-season
rates

BREAKFAST
Buffet breakfast included

ENGLISH
Yes

decorating statement, from the collection of original pieces of furniture from the thirties and forties to the cutting-edge modern art and sculpture.

Five different styles of inlaid doors lead to the state-of-the art guest rooms, which are coordinated and meticulously arranged, down to the matchbooks and special wardrobe hangers. Beige linen, white walls and bed coverings, and polished wood floors serve as the perfect backdrops for the vibrantly colored accent pieces that punctuate each room. Blackened steel and hot orange sorbet leather easy chairs and zebra-patterned bedside mats work well with stunning aubergine-tile bathrooms splashed with sparkling pumpkin paint. Deep-soaking Jacuzzis, piped-in music, and fluffy robes are standard issue.

For activities outside the rooms, a fireman's spiral staircase leads to a Turkish bath and rooftop solarium with views over the Santa Maria della Salute Church. Downstairs there is a wine bar serving sandwiches and seasonal specialties. The sleek staff has lots of ego and attitude, but that is part of the allure for the specially targeted, upscale clients who inhabit this stunning, artistic choice, which is the embodiment of hotel as theater.

NOTE: The hotel is closed for two weeks in January and two weeks in August. Call to check exact dates.

FACILITIES AND SERVICES: Air-conditioning, bar, direct-dial phone, elevator, guest fax and Internet terminal, hair dryers, Jacuzzis in all bathrooms, laundry services, parking by arrangement (price on request), in-room safe, satellite TV, nonsmoking rooms, solarium, Turkish bath, wine bar, restaurant

NEAREST TOURIST ATTRACTIONS: Accademia, Peggy Guggenheim Collection, Grand Canal, Giudecca Canal

DD. 724 ($, 49)
Ramo da Mula, 724, off Calle della Chiesa
7 rooms, 1 apartment, all with shower or bath and toilet

TELEPHONE
041 277 0262

FAX
041 296 0638

INTERNET
www.dd724.com

CREDIT CARDS
AE, DC, MC, V

RATES
1–2 people 200–350€;
apartment 200–500€ (apt. rates
depend on length of stay); lower
off-season rates

The ultra modern DD. 724 is as sleek and unadorned as its name. Since it opened, it has become a shrine to a contemporary Italian, neo-industrial look that attracts an arts crowd who, after enjoying the ornate beauty of Venice, want to return to contemporary surroundings. The pale, uncluttered rooms are models of understated colors and furnishings. In Room B, dark beams and a fireplace facade with candles on the mantle add a touch of needed warmth, as do the two off-white armchairs facing a square table with a large tic-tac-toe game laid out. One wall has a large flat-screen television. The three windows on this corner room look straight down onto the street and a canal. A little box beside each bed opens to display discreet lighting. Room C, with a bleached wood floor, is done in monochromatic black and brown with cream accents. The four-poster canopy bed lends just the right romantic air. Pulling the draperies on one wall does not reveal a window. Instead, guests see a large white geometrical design that lights up as the face of Michelangelo. Huge double closets with built-in drawers add practicality to the mix. In Room G, the incandescent pop art glows with the face of Toto, a famous Italian comedian. The bathroom here is similar to all the others, with a floating sink, wood bamboo shower and bath mat, monogrammed towels, and bars of Savon de Marseille soap.

For those needing more space, there is a two-bedroom, two-bathroom apartment on the second floor of a building not far from the hotel. The decor is not as hard-edge as the hotel but certainly provides high-quality style and harmonious comforts. It has a large living room with original Venetian mosaic floors, a watermarked satin sofa and two armchairs, and a flat-screen television. In one corner is a glass-topped wrought-iron dining table with four cushioned chairs and a rustic sideboard holding attractive pottery and glassware. The kitchen is big enough for another dining table and chairs, in addition to a regulation four-burner stove and oven, a refrigerator with a full freezer, and a dishwasher. Both of the attractive bedrooms are quiet and have nice bathrooms with plenty of move-in space.

FACILITIES AND SERVICES: Hotel: air-conditioning, direct-dial phone, elevator, hair dryer, in-room safe, satellite TV; apartment: same as hotel, plus clothes washer

NEAREST TOURIST ATTRACTIONS: Peggy Guggenheim Collection, Accademia, Santa Maria della Salute, Grand Canal, Giudecca Canal

BREAKFAST
Buffet breakfast included
ENGLISH
Yes

HOTEL ALLA SALUTE DA CICI ★★ (52)
Fondamenta Ca Balà, 222

50 rooms, 36 with shower, bath, and toilet

If you are looking for a serviceable family-type hotel with reasonable price tags that come in way under the cost of a wallet at Prada or Gucci, this is the place to go. For more than fifty years, it has been owned by the Cici family, and they have paid little heed to modern trends. Still, they have maintained their hotel well, keeping the sturdy furnishings in good order and the bathrooms—both private and public—in spotless condition. Recently five rooms with

TELEPHONE
041 235 404
FAX
041 522 2271
INTERNET
www.hotelsalute.com
CREDIT CARDS
MC, V

RATES
Single 80–120€, double 145€,
triple 180€, quad 160–220€,
family room (5 people) 260€;
rates 15€ less in Mar, July,
and Aug
BREAKFAST
Continental breakfast included
ENGLISH
Yes

garden views were redone in basic white furniture and simple fabrics; these have private baths, as do the doubles and triples. These new rooms cost the same as those on the front with canal views, including No. 15, a double with a balcony that was once Ezra Pound's room, and No. 16, which has the shower booth *in* the room. Number 18, a two-room suite, sleeps six and also faces the canal. Take your pick.

NOTE: The hotel is closed November and December until Christmas and from January 7 to Carnivale.

FACILITIES AND SERVICES: Air-conditioning in new rooms, no elevator (3 floors), fans and hair dryers on request, office safe

NEAREST TOURIST ATTRACTIONS: Peggy Guggenheim Collection, Santa Maria della Salute, Grand Canal

HOTEL AMERICAN ★★★ ($, 51)
Rio de San Vio, Fondamenta de Bragadin, 628
34 rooms, all with shower or bath and toilet

TELEPHONE
041 520 4733
FAX
041 520 4048
INTERNET
www.hotelamerican.com
CREDIT CARDS
AE, MC, V
RATES
Single 180€, double 250–300€,
extra bed 60€; lower off-season
and sometimes midweek rates,
5% discount for cash, Internet
specials
BREAKFAST
Buffet breakfast included
ENGLISH
Yes

An Old World Venetian formality reigns at the completely restored Hotel American on the San Vio Canal, which is away from the hustle and bustle and yet close enough for easy exploration of art galleries, shops, and good restaurants. A large, inviting lobby furnished with a leather tufted settee and chair, Oriental rugs, and the ever-popular Murano glassware sets the tone for the rest of the hotel. A first-floor, vine-covered terrace is a delightful place for summer breakfasts. In winter, you eat in a gold-colored dining room on red-velvet chairs placed around linen-covered tables.

Be sure to request one of the twelve rooms that face the canal or any room with a terrace. Fourth-floor rooms require some extra stair climbing, but occupants are rewarded with views of the canal and of gondolas drifting by. I also like No. 301, with canal views. Green-and-yellow diamond-print carpeting complements yellow hand-painted Venetian furniture. I like the small balcony view from No. 302, as well as its long marble sink in a nice bathroom with a window. The reception staff is exceptional. The hotel is owned and managed by Salvatore Sutera Sardo, who also owns the two-star Hotel Falier in Santa Croce (see page 316).

FACILITIES AND SERVICES: Air-conditioning, bar, direct-dial phone, no elevator (3 floors), hair dryer, guest Internet terminal, data port, minibar, porter, in-room safe, satellite TV, some nonsmoking rooms

NEAREST TOURIST ATTRACTIONS: Accademia, Peggy Guggenheim Collection

HOTEL GALLERIA ★ (45)
Rio Terrà Antonia Foscarini, 878-A (at the Accademia Bridge)

10 rooms, 6 with shower or bath and toilet

The Galleria is amazing, especially for a one-star. Years ago, this seventeenth-century *palazzo* at the foot of Accademia Bridge was cut and pasted into a hotel. The furniture no one bought at your last garage sale, along with those rolls of red flocked wallpaper, were alive and well in the rooms, which were a potpourri of colors, patterns, and styles that blended into an appealingly faded Venetian charm.

But new owners can mean many things in the hotel business, especially so with Stefano, the debonair new owner of the Galleria. His stiff broom swept the place clean of dusty clutter, replacing it with better furniture and some antiques. He polished the floors and accented them with Oriental rugs, added Art Deco–style lights to the inventory of chandeliers, put in a new hall bathroom, plus six others in the rooms, and made sure the flowers in the window boxes were in full bloom from May to October. At least six of the rooms have commanding views of the Accademia Bridge and/or the Grand Canal. Everyone's favorite is No. 8, with a raised platform and two bamboo chairs, from which you can almost reach out and touch the canal below. Other top picks are Nos. 3 and 5, with views of both the bridge and the canal, and No. 10, which, in addition to the luxury of space and private facilities, has a seventeenth-century frescoed ceiling and a twenty-first-century Venetian view from both windows. The hotel is small, and there is no dining room, so breakfast is served in your room. For Great Sleepers on a budget who opt for bathless abodes, hall showers are just fine.

FACILITIES AND SERVICES: Direct-dial phone, no elevator (2 floors), fans, hair dryer available, TV

NEAREST TOURIST ATTRACTIONS: Accademia, Peggy Guggenheim Collection, Grand Canal

TELEPHONE
041 523 2489
FAX
041 520 4172
EMAIL
galleria@tin.it
INTERNET
www.hotelgalleria.it
CREDIT CARDS
AE, MC, V, but cash preferred
RATES
Single without bath 75€, with bath 115€; double without bath 100–105€, with bath 115–150€; triple 145–190€; extra bed 30% of room rate
BREAKFAST
Continental breakfast included
ENGLISH
Yes

HOTEL LOCANDA SAN BARNABA ★★★ (40)
Calle del Traghetto, 2785-86

13 rooms, all with shower or bath and toilet

The Locanda San Barnaba is in an interesting neighborhood close to the lively Campo Santa Margherita, within easy reach of the Accademia, the Peggy Guggenheim Collection, and a pleasant vaporetto ride from the Ca' Rezzonico stop to San Marco. The hotel, which was once a grand, noble palace, has now been very successfully refashioned into

TELEPHONE
041 241 1233
FAX
041 241 3812
INTERNET
www.locanda-sanbarnaba.com
CREDIT CARDS
AE, MC, V

RATES
Single 110€, double 170–180€,
junior suite 210€; extra bed
30% of room rate; excellent
lower off-season rates

BREAKFAST
Buffet breakfast included

ENGLISH
Yes

thirteen peaceful rooms, all with different names and decor. Many overlook a pretty walled garden where summertime breakfasts can be served. The Sposa Persiana room, which means the "Persian bride," is a junior suite on the first floor. Its main feature is a dazzling frescoed and inlaid-wood ceiling towering above a gold-and-blue bedroom and an upstairs sitting room. The bathroom includes a pair of sinks, three mirrors, and loads of marble sink space. Only slightly less sumptuous is Il Ventaglio, "the fan," again with a frescoed ceiling, a tranquil garden view, and a stall shower in the bathroom. In I Rusteghi, which means "the rustics," you have classic beams instead of frescoes on the ceiling, a nice garden view, plenty of living space, and both a tub and shower in the bathroom.

FACILITIES AND SERVICES: Air-conditioning, bar, direct-dial phone, no elevator (2 floors), hair dryer, in-room safe, satellite TV

NEAREST TOURIST ATTRACTIONS: Accademia, Peggy Guggenheim Collection, Ca' Rezzonico, Grand Canal

LOCANDA CA' FOSCARI ★ (¢, 38)
Calle della Frescade, 3887-B
11 rooms, 5 with shower or bath and toilet

TELEPHONE
041 710 401

FAX
041 710 817

INTERNET
www.locandacafoscari.com

CREDIT CARDS
MC, V

RATES
Single 65€, double 75–95€,
triple 92–116€, quad 114€

BREAKFAST
Continental breakfast included

ENGLISH
Yes, also French and Spanish

Valter and Giuliana Scarpa's hotel is located between Campos Santa Tomà and Santa Barnaba, an upper-middle-class area filled with locals going about their daily lives. You will find many small shops, bakeries, bars, *caffès,* and restaurants (see *Great Eats Italy*), but few are geared specifically to the tourist trade.

Locanda Ca' Foscari is a family-run place, where the rooms are well cared for and maintained regularly. The walls are covered half with fabric and half with white paint. Each room is different, but they are clean and do not have sleazy, shrunken chenille bedspreads or hodgepodge junk furniture. The top floors are filled with morning sunshine, and the beds are good, even though they look like army issue. Room 5 is viewless and requires serious steps, but the heated towel racks and stall shower with a door might be trade-offs for some. Number 6, colorfully done in cabbage rose wallpaper, has two windows on a private garden, which has a lovely green tree and exquisite lavender wisteria vines in springtime. The narrow bathroom is serviceable. Room 9 has corner window light and bubblegum-pink bed coverings that really don't go with the green tapestry covering the lower section of the wall. The hall facilities are excellent, so if you are trying to sleep very cheaply, a bathless room here is the ticket.

NOTE: The hotel is closed from November 15 to February 1. Also, if you are traveling in a large party of twenty-four or more, you can arrange a half-board for dinner, but you must arrange this in advance.

FACILITIES AND SERVICES: No elevator (3 floors), office safe

NEAREST TOURIST ATTRACTIONS: I Frari Church

LOCANDA MONTIN ★★ (44)
Fondamenta delle Eremite, 1147

12 rooms, 6 with toilet and shower

Exacting guests will probably want to look elsewhere, but those who thrive on nostalgia, funky charm, and character will adore the Locanda Montin for its refreshing change from antiseptic anonymity. The hotel, which is off Calle Lunga Santa Barnaba, has for years attracted artists, writers, and musicians on prolonged visits to Venice. Up the stairs and along the corridors is the hotel's collection of original art from the fifties and sixties, done by artists who were regulars at the hotel's restaurant, Antica Locanda Montin, when the hotel was in its glory days. Now it is somewhat of a cult hotel, appealing to modern-day bohemians who do not mind some hall plumbing and thin walls.

Despite its quirky quarters, it is becoming increasingly difficult to get a reservation. If you do succeed, rooms have either a canal or garden view and are filled to the brim with an assorted array of furnishings, original artwork and, in one case, history. Number 12, a double with a canal view and no bathroom, was occupied from 1915 to 1918 by war hero Gabriele d'Annunzio and actress Eleanora Duse. The same bed and armoire they used are there today. Other good choices are Nos. 5 and 11. All have canal views and private bathrooms, and in No. 5, there is the added bonus of a balcony.

The hotel is situated just off Campo Santa Barnaba, and it is not the easiest address to find. Once you are on Calle Lunga Santa Barnaba, take Calle delle Turchette, which becomes Fondamenta di Borgo and wraps around to Fondamenta delle Eremite. Once there, look for the black carriage lamp hanging over the front door with the name Locanda Montin marked on it.

FACILITIES AND SERVICES: Air-conditioning in rooms with bathrooms, bar, direct-dial phone, no elevator (3 floors), fan, hair dryer available, one in-room safe, office safe, reception open Mon–Sat 8 A.M.–11 P.M.

NEAREST TOURIST ATTRACTIONS: Campo Santa Margherita, Ca' Rezzonico

TELEPHONE
041 522 7151

FAX
041 520 0255

EMAIL
locandamontin@libero.it

INTERNET
www.locandamontin.com

CREDIT CARDS
V

RATES
Single 60–70€, double 110–140€, triple 170€, quad 190€; extra person 30% of room rate; lower off-season rates; 5% discount for cash, 10% discount for cash in the restaurant

BREAKFAST
Continental breakfast included

ENGLISH
Yes

PALAZZO GUARDI (46)
Calle del Pistor, 995

TELEPHONE
041 296 0725
FAX
041 724 1067
INTERNET
www.palazzoguardivenice.com
CREDIT CARDS
AE, DC, MC, V
RATES
Single 90–140€, double
100–150€, triple 150–180€,
quad 180–250€, five 200–
250€, junior suite 150–200€;
excellent low-season rates
BREAKFAST
Continental breakfast included
(if not taken, can deduct 5€ per
person, per day)
ENGLISH
Yes

16 rooms, 4 apartments, all with shower or bath and toilet

Palazzo Guardi is yet another example of a restored fifteenth-century noble palace. The rooms are reminiscent of over-the-top Venetian grandeur, and they are done up with damask-covered walls, factory-reproduction lacquered furniture, and framed copies of paintings by Guardi and Canaletto. The glass elevator and the television sets mounted on the ceiling in some rooms seem out of place, but not the rooftop views, or for convenience's sake, the mosaic-tile bathrooms. Most of the rooms are suite-size. One of the best from a space standpoint is No. 7, a two-room affair with view windows and a large bathroom. Room 8, a fifty-square-meter choice with a parquet floor, is done in soft blues and greens and certainly has space in its favor, just not in the small bathroom. Near the hotel is a seven-room *dipendenza* that is less formal; it has all the same hotel facilities and equally spacious rooms, but no elevator. No matter where you sleep, everyone meets in the morning in a beautiful breakfast room with an original ceiling and trompe l'oeil walls.

NOTE: One of the partners of Palazzo Guardi has several apartments for rent. For further information, email Michele Cicogna at cicognave@libero.it.

FACILITIES AND SERVICES: Air-conditioning, direct-dial phone, hair dryer, elevator, laptop loaner, minibar, 2 Jacuzzis in annex, in-room safe, satellite TV

NEAREST TOURIST ATTRACTIONS: Accademia, Peggy Guggenheim Collection, Grand Canal

PENSIONE ACCADEMIA (VILLA MARAVEGE) ★★★ ($, 43)
Fondamenta Bollani, 1058

TELEPHONE
041 521 0188
FAX
041 523 9152
INTERNET
www.pensioneaccademia.it
CREDIT CARDS
AE, DC, MC, V
RATES
Rates span low/high seasons:
single 85–135€, double 140–
290€, suite or garden cottage
"Thelma" 250€
BREAKFAST
Continental breakfast included
ENGLISH
Yes

27 rooms, all with shower or bath and toilet

The Pensione Accademia, occupying one of the most romantic settings in Venice just off the Grand Canal, offers charm and serene beauty, as well as low-season prices many can afford. It began as a villa in the seventeenth century, was occupied as a private mansion until the early 1900s, and was then used as the Russian consulate before World War II. It was also the fictional residence of Katharine Hepburn in *Summertime*. The stately villa is surrounded by wonderful gardens that give you the pleasant feeling of being a million miles away from central Venice, though you are actually only minutes away. On one side of the villa, a graceful patio faces the canal, with tables and chairs placed among flowering plants. Along the other side is a garden with wisteria vines, fruit trees, blooming roses, and a bubbling fountain.

The Accademia's interior is just as appealing, with classic Murano chandeliers, Victorian and Venetian furnishings, and polished wood floors. There is a cozy upstairs tearoom and a formally set breakfast room overlooking the rose garden. The adjoining bar has an ornamental fireplace. The reception area and main lobby open onto the large back garden. The rooms all vary and have either canal or garden views. Number 12, which overlooks the front garden, has a four-poster bed, polished hardwood floors, and a pretty floral-tile bathroom. Number 44, done in blue and yellow, can be pressed into service for three, but it is much better used as a double. It has an inlaid wood floor, three windows on the canal, a large bath with a tub, and a small entry framed with mirrors. Single travelers are not reduced to closet-size accommodations. Room 27 on the top floor is an exceptionally nice choice for solo travelers. I like the beamed ceiling, wood floor, pretty Art Deco lamp, and the view over the front garden and the canal. The shower has not only doors but a small seat.

While every room in the hotel has virtues to recommend it, my absolute favorite Accademia accommodation is "Thelma," the private garden cottage named in memory of a guest from Brighton, England, who died in an automobile accident. She came often to the hotel and especially loved the garden, so when the hotel built the cottage, they dedicated it to her. Isn't that a lovely thing to do? The beamed cottage has a spacious sitting room with Oriental rugs, a stone floor, and a comfortable sofa and chairs for pleasant lounging. The superior-class bedroom and bathroom have all the extras that make you want to stay forever. Outside, there is an inviting terrace set with a table and chairs, the perfect place to remember Thelma and admire the lovely gardens she so loved.

As you can imagine, reservations are essential—in some cases, a year in advance. The fiercely loyal clientele often reserve their favorite room or suite for the next year during their current year's stay.

NOTE: Also under the same ownership is the Hotel Ala (see page 284). As at Hotel Ala, guests from the Pensione Accademia are given discounts at the Ristorante da' Raffaele.

FACILITIES AND SERVICES: Air-conditioning (May 15– Sept 15), bar, direct-dial phone, no elevator (2 floors), hair dryers, guest Internet terminal, laundry service, in-room safe, satellite TV, 2 handicapped-accessible rooms, non-allergenic rooms

NEAREST TOURIST ATTRACTIONS: Accademia, Peggy Guggenheim Collection, Grand Canal

PENSIONE LA CALCINA ★★★ (53)
Fondamenta Zattere ai Gesuati, 780

28 rooms, 26 with shower or bath and toilet, plus 2 suites and 3 apartments

TELEPHONE
041 520 6466

FAX
041 522 7045

INTERNET
www.warmhospitality.com

CREDIT CARDS
AE, DC, MC, V

RATES
Rates span low/high seasons: hotel: single 55–106€, double 99–186€, superior doubles 161–239€; suites: 161–213€; apartments: 213–239€

BREAKFAST
Buffet breakfast included with all accommodations

ENGLISH
Yes

Beloved by British and American guests for over a century, La Calcina is the same pensione where the writer John Ruskin wrote *The Stones of Venice* during his 1876 stay in Venice. It has mellowed well with age, and today stands out as a delightful respite from modernity and as an excellent Great Sleep value with great character. Beautifully positioned on the Giudecca Canal, it provides guests with modern comforts while maintaining its Old World charm. On the ground floor is a small bar and formal dining room facing the lagoon that serves breakfast, as well as well-priced lunches and dinners (see *Great Eats Italy*). When the weather is warm, meals are served on a wide terrace built over the water. Guests are encouraged to enjoy this picture-perfect spot during the day, as well as the panoramic roof terrace with a million-dollar view of Venice. This terrace is so small it can accommodate only two people at a time, therefore guests are requested to reserve their time here.

The twenty-eight very comfortable rooms are individual in decor but uniform in amenities. All have been recently redone in light colors and fabrics with parquet floors and original furnishings. Rooms 37, 38, and 39 have terrace views and are especially appealing, and so is No. 2, with three windows and a balcony view of Giudecca, the lagoon, a small side canal, and the bridge over it.

Nearby, the owners have three exceptional suites and two apartments with equipped kitchens, all named after flowers. The very livable suites have a sitting room and are welcome choices for those who want more space but don't need a kitchen. The three apartments are wonderful. Dalia is built like a ship. It has three windows overlooking the Giudecca Canal, a small kitchen, and loads of sink and cupboard space in the bathroom, which also has a tub and shower. I like Rosa because it feels so much like a home. In fact it was where the owners lived until they moved to Lido. Viola is the largest apartment, and like the others, it has plenty of room to move in, enjoy your stay, and never want to leave.

FACILITIES AND SERVICES: Hotel: air-conditioning, bar, direct-dial phone, no elevator (4 floors), hair dryer, guest

Internet terminal, guest discounts at restaurant (lunch and dinner), light meals on the terrace during the day, in-room safe, satellite TV; apartments and suites: all of the above, plus washing machines, fully equipped kitchens, hotel maid service; all accommodations nonsmoking

NEAREST TOURIST ATTRACTIONS: Accademia, Peggy Guggenheim Collection, Giudecca Canal, Santa Maria della Salute

San Polo

The smallest *sestiere*, San Polo has one of the most important destinations for visitors and locals alike: the Rialto Market. For hundreds of years the Rialto Market was the center in Venice for buying and selling everything from the finest gold and laces to the humble potato. The area developed into a rabbit warren of shops, taverns, offices, and street stalls. Not much has changed today. The Rialto Bridge is lined with one stall after another, and at the foot, along the canal, are the famous fruit, vegetable, meat, and fish markets. For visitors, this is a must-see part of Venice. Also, two of the most important collections of art outside Piazza San Marco are in the Gothic I Frari Church, which contains important works by Titian, and in the Renaissance Scuola Grande di San Rocco, with paintings by Tintoretto.

HOTELS

OTHER OPTIONS
Student Accommodations

($) indicates a Big Splurge; (¢) indicates a Cheap Sleep

HOTEL GUERRATO ★ (¢, 19)
Calle Drio La Scimia, 240/A
20 rooms, 9 with shower and toilet; 3 apartments, all with shower and toilet

Between 1298 and 1747, San Lorenzo nuns occupied this building. When Napoleon came to Venice, the nuns were moved to the San Zaccaria Church, and the history of who lived here becomes murky, at least until 1960, when the Guerrato family bought the building and rented out

TELEPHONE
041 522 7131, 041 528 5927
FAX
041 522 7131
EMAIL
hguerrat@tin.it
INTERNET
www.tiscalinet.it/pensioneguerrato

CREDIT CARDS
MC, V
RATES
Rates span low/high seasons:
single 70–95€, double 90–
130€, triple 105–135€, quad
165–175€; rates for apartment
on request
BREAKFAST
Continental breakfast included
ENGLISH
Yes

rooms. Since 1994 it has been owned by two brothers, Roberto and Pierro. They had no hotel experience before taking it over, and they were quickly plunged into intensive on-the-job training as they resurrected it from the ashes and turned it into a spirited Great Sleep in the heart of Rialto and one of the best one-stars in Venice.

Fortunately, they had the sense to keep some interesting remnants of the past: an old upright organ (no pipes, however), a fresco here and there, a burled wood console radio, a funky ceramic dog collection, and a few pieces of antique furniture. If you land in No. 7, you will have a new bathroom and a peek at both the Grand Canal and Rialto Market from this large double. Space won't be an issue in No. 5, a corner room with an Art Deco mirrored dressing table. Another improvement project created five new top-floor double rooms that are geared to groups. Also available are three apartments, two in the hotel and a three-bedroom, two-bath apartment near Piazza San Marco.

A humorous sign displayed at reception clearly states the brothers' payment policy: "Make us happy, please pay cash. If not possible, we accept diamonds, gold, rubies, U.S. dollars, and also credit cards."

NOTE: The hotel is closed from January 9 to 30.

FACILITIES AND SERVICES: Air-conditioning, direct-dial phone, no elevator (2 floors), hair dryer available, office safe, in-room safe in 5 new rooms, nonsmoking hotel

NEAREST TOURIST ATTRACTIONS: Rialto Bridge and Market

HOTEL LOCANDA OVIDIUS ★★★ ($, 28)
Calle del Storione, 677/A (on some maps, Sturion)
15 rooms, all with shower or bath and toilet

TELEPHONE
041 523 7970
FAX
041 520 4101
INTERNET
www.hotelovidius.com
CREDIT CARDS
AE, DC, MC, V
RATES
Single 75–130€, double 210–
280€, extra bed 60€
BREAKFAST
Buffet breakfast included
ENGLISH
Yes

The Ovidius serves breakfast in a dazzling room overlooking the Grand Canal. The bright rooms, two of which share this fabulous view, are handsomely furnished in eighteenth-century Venetian style, each with a Jacuzzi bath or a power stall shower in a spacious bathroom. If your comfortable room doesn't directly overlook the Grand Canal, you can certainly appreciate it to your heart's content from a chair on the hotel balcony. The hotel prices fall into the Big Splurge category during high season. However, if you book through their Website, you will always get a discounted rate on rooms without a view. Room 203 is a good example. This double room has a street view, Jacuzzi bath, and typical painted Venetian furnishings. True, you can't see the Grand Canal from here, but the hotel balcony solves that problem nicely.

FACILITIES AND SERVICES: Air-conditioning, direct-dial phone, elevator, hair dryer, Jacuzzi in 4 rooms, minibar, in-room safe, satellite TV, nonsmoking hotel

NEAREST TOURIST ATTRACTIONS: Grand Canal, Rialto Bridge

LOCANDA CA' ANGELI (34)
Calle del Tragheto della Madonnetta, 1434
9 rooms, 6 with shower and toilet

Brothers Georgio and Matteo and their sister, Camilla, inherited this *palazzo* from their uncle, Angelo Scattolin, who was a noted architect, professor at the Academy of Fine Arts, and overseer of St. Mark's Church between 1960–70. In restoring it, the family kept the original layout intact and maintained respect for the classic Venetian style, while creating light and airy bedrooms offering all the comforts. They were able to incorporate their uncle's art collection and several pieces of fine furniture, most notably the chest of drawers in the junior suite and the secretary in the living room. The junior suite, the living room, and the breakfast room have wonderful views overlooking the Grand Canal; three others look onto a side canal, and the rest look over the private courtyard and small garden.

Almost all of the rooms are recommended, but watch out for the three on the top floor that share a bathroom. They can be reserved independently or as a family unit. One is a tiny single with no bedside light; another is a twin, again with poor lighting; and the third is a double-bedded room with great closets but nowhere to sit other than on the bed. The communal bathroom has a slanted ceiling with low beams, making it impossible for anyone over five-feet, eight-inches tall to stand upright in the shower. The remaining six rooms have none of these drawbacks, and the junior suite and No. 5 are quite special. The suite is furnished in family antiques and has a full Grand Canal view and a Jacuzzi. Number 5, a cozy eight-by-eight-foot room, has a monumental balcony that is twice the room size. This room is especially popular when the weather is warm and guests can stretch out on the wooden chaises and savor the view. Because there are only nine rooms, the staff can take a personal interest in each guest, and as a result, you will feel very much at home.

FACILITIES AND SERVICES: Air-conditioning, direct-dial phone, elevator, hair dryer, Jacuzzi in junior suite, laundry service, minibar, in-room safe, satellite TV, nonsmoking hotel

TELEPHONE
042 523 2480
FAX
041 241 7077
INTERNET
www.caangeli.it
CREDIT CARDS
MC, V
RATES
No singles; double as single 104–140€, double 120–180€, junior suite (1–3 people) 180–290€
BREAKFAST
Continental breakfast included
ENGLISH
Yes

NEAREST TOURIST ATTRACTIONS: Grand Canal, I Frari Church, Scuola Grande di San Rocco

LOCANDA SANT' AGOSTIN (20)
Campo Sant' Agostin, 2344

TELEPHONE
041 275 9414
FAX
041 275 3014
INTERNET
www.locandasantagostin.it
CREDIT CARDS
MC, V
RATES
Rates span low/high seasons:
single 60–178€, double 78–
198€, junior suite 110–280€;
baby cot and children under 3
years are free
BREAKFAST
Buffet breakfast included
ENGLISH
Yes

10 rooms, all with shower or bath and toilet

Everything is on one floor at this noble sixteenth-century *palazzo* located midway between the Rialto Bridge and the train station. I like it because the rooms and baths are newly done, the friendly hospitality of owners Leonardo and Federico is pleasing, and the location is just far enough from the usual tourist stomping grounds to keep the neighborhood real and local. The rooms are spacious, and like most boutique *locandas,* they have their own distinct Venetian style, with inlaid mosaic tile or hardwood floors, gold framed beds, Murano lights, and heavy draperies held back by multifringed tassels. The marble bathrooms are exceptional, with full mirrors, recessed lighting, and deep tubs in most. Two rooms have canal views from their balconies.

FACILITIES AND SERVICES: Air-conditioning, direct-dial phone, no elevator (one floor), hair dryer, minibar, office safe, satellite TV, nonsmoking hotel

NEAREST TOURIST ATTRACTIONS: I Frari Church, Scuola Grande di San Rocco

LOCANDA STURION ★★★ ($, 27)
Calle del Storione, 679 (on some maps, Sturion)

TELEPHONE
041 523 6243
FAX
041 522 8378
EMAIL
sturion@tin.it
INTERNET
www.locandasturion.com
CREDIT CARDS
AE, DC, MC, V
RATES
Single 160€, double 220–260€,
triple 280–320€; lower off-
season rates; promotions year-
round
BREAKFAST
Buffet breakfast included
ENGLISH
Yes

11 rooms, all with shower or bath and toilet

If you dream of a room on the Grand Canal but have nightmares about the truly astronomical prices most hotels charge, fret no more and reserve a room at the Locanda Sturion, a hotel with a history that dates back to the thirteenth century, when it housed merchants bringing their wares to the Rialto Market.

The best rooms are the two large ones that overlook the Grand Canal. Because these are the only two with canal views, they are extremely popular, so get your request in early. The walls in the rooms are covered in red or pink brocade that matches the bedspreads. Tea and coffeemakers with a packet of cookies are welcoming touches. The tiled bathrooms have lighted mirrors over the sinks bordered with artistic tile frames, a supply of toiletries, and heated towel racks. Guests either love or hate the two top-floor rooms, Nos. 9 and 10. Getting to them requires even more stair climbing, but both are romantic—one has a pitched dormer roof and a bird's-eye view; the other is a quiet two-room suite that works well for a family. No matter where your room is, you can be assured it will be nonsmoking. Breakfast is served in a dining room with a canal view. You will no doubt want to linger here over a second cup of coffee while scribbling a few cards to friends back home, suggesting you may never return from Venice.

NOTE: Warning! For most, the four flights of stairs (sixty-eight steps straight up) to the reception area and hotel proper will be a piece of cake. For some, however, they might pose a problem. Once you get to the reception, you could have more of a hike, depending on the room location.

FACILITIES AND SERVICES: Air-conditioning, bar, direct-dial phone, no elevator (4 floors), hair dryer, guest Internet terminal, minibar, parking (rates on request), in-room safe, satellite TV, special Venetian travel videos and children's Disney cartoon videos (in English and Italian) in the lounge, tea and coffeemaker in the room, nonsmoking hotel

NEAREST TOURIST ATTRACTIONS: Grand Canal, Rialto Bridge

Santa Croce

Named after the fourteenth-century Benedictine monastery of Santa Croce, this *sestiere* is located along the Grand Canal where, in years now past, the Fascist regime created the Piazzale Roma, the monstrous car park at the end of the bridge leading from Mestre to Venice.

HOTELS

Albergo Casa Peron ★ (¢)	**313**
Hotel ai Due Fanali ★★★	**314**
Hotel Airone ★★	**315**
Hotel Al Tolentini ★ (¢)	**316**
Hotel Falier ★★	**316**
Locanda Salieri ★ (¢)	**317**
(¢) indicates a Cheap Sleep	

ALBERGO CASA PERON ★ (¢, 35)
Calle Vinanti, Salizzada S. Pantalon, 84
11 rooms, all with shower and sink, 7 also with toilet

This heaven-sent retreat for economy-minded Great Sleepers is in an attractive neighborhood midway between Piazzale Roma and the Grand Canal. Gianrico Scarpa and his wife, Luana, put a great deal of effort into keeping their hotel in tip-top shape. This shows from the minute you step into the lobby and reach your tidy bedroom until you sit on

TELEPHONE & FAX
041 711 038

EMAIL
casaperon@libero.it

INTERNET
www.casaperon.com

CREDIT CARDS
MC, V

RATES
Single 48–72€, double 75–95€, triple 100–125€; 20% lower off-season rates
BREAKFAST
Continental breakfast included
ENGLISH
Yes

the peaceful upstairs terrace filled with vines and fragrant flowering plants and boasting a view of the nearby bell tower. The eleven nests are sunny, bright, and reasonably spacious, with simple furniture displaying not a nick or scratch. Seven have private bathrooms; the rest have only private showers and sinks. My top choice is No. 5, with a private shower and toilet and the bonus of a small terrace with white jasmine and red roses blooming on it.

The dining room is small, with only four tables and a poster of one of Gianrico's departed birds. Be sure to notice the wooden chest that Gianrico found in a trash heap and refinished himself. He is also an amateur painter and has hung his work in the dining area and in many of the bedrooms. The Scarpas live in the hotel and are dedicated to every detail of its operation. Offering colorful help is their beautiful talking and singing parrot, Perino, who considers himself the "assistant manager" and often rides on Gianrico's shoulder.

NOTE: The hotel closes in January. Gianrico takes guests out in his boat. Rates start around 60€ for two hours, and trust me on this...that is a steal!

FACILITIES AND SERVICES: Air-conditioning in 5 rooms, no elevator (3 floors), office safe

NEAREST TOURIST ATTRACTIONS: Interesting neighborhood, close to car parks at Piazzale Roma, I Frari Church, Scuola Grande di San Rocco

HOTEL AI DUE FANALI ★★★ (17)
Campo San Simeon Profeta, 946

TELEPHONE
041 718 490
FAX
041 718 344
INTERNET
www.aiduefanali.com
CREDIT CARDS
AE, DC, MC, V
RATES
Single 165€, double 205€, extra bed 25% of room rate; apartments from 181€, two-night minimum; lower off-season rates
BREAKFAST
Continental breakfast included
ENGLISH
Yes

16 rooms, 4 apartments, all with shower or bath and toilet

Beautiful rooms await guests at the desirable Hotel ai Due Fanali, which occupies the ancient school of the Church of San Simeon Grand—you can see a bas-relief of the saint inside the hotel portico. The location on a quiet square in Santa Croce, across the Grand Canal from the train station and Piazzale Roma, is convenient for many.

The handsome lobby has polished marble floors, intricate wood ceilings, and period furnishings. The friendly staff keeps everything right on the mark, and the rooms are well conceived and done with impeccable taste. The singles benefit from Grand Canal views, and the premier rooms on the top floors have splendid views, too. Of these, No. 301, a twin-bedded double, has the best view. Not to be overlooked is No. 201, in soft blue and yellow, which has the original wood ceiling beams, a French marble fireplace, and a view of the square in front of the hotel. The soft yellow bedspreads complement the painted headboard. The bathroom, like all the others, is exceptional, with chrome and gold fittings and marble fixtures, plus a water shield for the shower, ample shelf space and light, and plenty of towels. In the morning, a generous breakfast of juice, rolls, cereal, and yogurt is served either on the top-floor terrace or in the third-floor glassed-in breakfast room with a glimpse of the Grand Canal.

Also available through the Hotel ai Due Fanali are four handsome apartment suites near Piazza San Marco, at Calle del Cagnoletto, 4084. Three of the rooms have extraordinary views. From the windows facing the Riva degli Schiavoni you can overlook the San Marco basin and the island of San Giorgio Maggiore. The light, open apartments are decorated in the best of taste, employing just the right balance of tradition with whimsy. They sleep up to four persons, have fitted kitchens, require a two-night minimum, and have all the services offered at the hotel, including daily maid service and breakfast (for an extra charge), but if you need anything more, there's a direct telephone line to the hotel.

NOTE: The owners of Hotel ai Due Fanali will soon be opening a new property, the Hotel Cà Nigra, a four-star former residence of the Dilomatic Count Costantino Nigra. It is on the Grand Canal and has two gardens and a private boat dock. For further information, contact Hotel ai Due Fanali.

FACILITIES AND SERVICES: Hotel: air-conditioning, direct-dial phone, elevator, hair dryer, minibar, in-room safe, satellite TV; apartments: same as hotel, plus no elevator, kitchens, daily maid service

NEAREST TOURIST ATTRACTIONS: Across Ponte degli Scalizi from the train station, Piazzale Roma, Grand Canal

HOTEL AIRONE ★★ (18)
Fondamenta San Simeon, 557
13 rooms, 8 with shower and toilet

One of the redeeming features of this two-star roost near the train station and Piazzale Roma car park is that their four Grand Canal view rooms don't cost one euro more than the other nine that overlook trees or an elementary school on the back. The only room to avoid at all costs is No. 18. Its view is just too grim. Reaching the hotel requires a two-flight walkup. The style is stripped-down Ikea with no clashing fabrics to send color-sensitive guests groping for blinders. Another feather in its cap is that its bright rooms and bathrooms are very clean. The client

TELEPHONE & FAX
041 520 4991, 041 520 4800

EMAIL
albergoairone@libero.it

INTERNET
www.aironehotel.com

CREDIT CARDS
AE, DC, MC, V

RATES
Single 104€, double 96–160€, triple 208€, quad 238€; lower off-season and midweek rates

BREAKFAST
Continental breakfast included
ENGLISH
Yes

profile tends to be thrifty Europeans who have an early call at the train station, or who want to pick up their car and head out of town before the rush.

FACILITIES AND SERVICES: Air-conditioning in rooms with private bathrooms, direct-dial phones, no elevator (2 floors), fans, hair dryer, office safe, TV

NEAREST TOURIST ATTRACTIONS: Grand Canal, train station, Piazzale Roma

HOTEL AL TOLENTINI ★ (¢, 24)
Calle Amai, Corte dei Amai, 197/G
7 rooms, all with shower and toilet

TELEPHONE
041 275 9140
FAX
041 275 3266
INTERNET
www.albergoaitolentini.it
CREDIT CARDS
MC, V
RATES
Single 60€, double 100€, triple 120€; lower off-season rates
BREAKFAST
Not served
ENGLISH
Yes

The Al Tolentini is an all-purpose, nominally priced Great Sleep, where the clean rooms do not subscribe to the garage-sale-gothic school of interior decorating. Number 2 is a double with blond laminated furniture and space enough to add bunk beds for children. The old-fashioned half-bathtub has a curtain, but the sink is in the bedroom. In twin-bedded No. 8, a sunny corner room that is neat as a pin, the bathroom is outside the room, but private to it. Because space is at a premium, there is no dining room, so breakfast is not served.

FACILITIES AND SERVICES: No elevator, fans available, office safe, TV

NEAREST TOURIST ATTRACTIONS: Train station, Piazzale Roma, I Frari Church, Scuola Grande di San Rocco

HOTEL FALIER ★★ (30)
Salizzada San Pantalon, 130
19 rooms, all with shower or bath and toilet

TELEPHONE
041 710 882, 041 711 005
FAX
041 520 6554
INTERNET
www.hotelfalier.com
CREDIT CARDS
AE, MC, V
RATES
Single 150€, double 180€; lower off-season rates
BREAKFAST
Continental breakfast included
ENGLISH
Yes

Completely restyled from top to bottom in 1992, the Hotel Falier is close to Piazzale Roma (the enormous car park) and the train station. The area is not touristy, but it is lined with good neighborhood restaurants (see *Great Eats Italy*) and shops that are fun for browsing.

The stylish open lobby, complete with Doric columns, French furniture, and potted palms, faces a street and a canal. At the back of the lobby is a corner breakfast area with tufted red banquette seating, where you can watch the equivalent of *Good Morning, America* on the television with your strong coffee, rolls, and jam. The rooms are either singles or doubles, and though small, have uniform window curtains, flowered bedspreads, built-in furniture, luggage racks, and modern baths with good shelf space. Two little terraces for guests are brightened by potted flowers and rooftop views. One of the most requested rooms, No.

41, with a pitched roof, looks out onto one of these terraces. Unless drastic changes have occurred, forget Rooms 14 and 16 on the ground floor, complete with bars and chickenwire on the windows and no space to crawl around the bed. In the summer, insist on one of the sixteen rooms with air-conditioning, and why not, they cost the same as those with only a rotary fan.

NOTE: The owner, Salvatore Sutera Sardo, also owns the three-star Hotel American in Dorsoduro (see page 302).

FACILITIES AND SERVICES: Air-conditioning in 16 rooms, bar, direct-dial phone, no elevator (2 floors), fans, hair dryer, in-room safe, satellite TV in 17 rooms, 13 nonsmoking rooms

NEAREST TOURIST ATTRACTIONS: Train station, Piazzale Roma, I Frari Church, Scuola Grande di San Rocco

LOCANDA SALIERI ★ (¢, 29)
Fondamenta Minotto, 160
11 rooms, all with shower and toilet

If you can plan your trip during the middle of the week, stay at least two nights, and avoid being here during Carnivale or from September through October, this will be a great budget sleep. At these rates, you can't expect to find handsome furnishings, flamboyant fabrics, or rooms with space enough to house mountains of luggage and then hang their contents. However, each one has a little table and two chairs, and views on either a small garden or a walkway by a canal. Bathrooms are barely big enough to swing a cat, but they are new, tiled, clean, and have good towels and enclosed stall showers. There is no breakfast served in the hotel; instead guests go to Ribò, a very upscale restaurant next door, where they also receive discounts for lunch and dinner.

FACILITIES AND SERVICES: Air-conditioning, direct-dial phones, no elevator (3 floors), hair dryer, office safe

NEAREST TOURIST ATTRACTIONS: Piazzale Roma, I Frari Church, Scuola Grande di San Rocco

TELEPHONE
041 710 035
FAX
041 721 246
INTERNET
www.hotelsalieri.com
CREDIT CARDS
AE, DC, MC, V
RATES
Single 90€, double 120€, extra bed 25€; lower off-season and midweek rates
BREAKFAST
Continental included
ENGLISH
Yes

Hotels on the Islands

Giudecca Island

The biggest claim to fame on Giudecca Island—a mainly tourist-free zone—is the Hotel Cipriani, where rooms start around $850 per night and nearly triple to $2,120 for a suite—breakfast, taxes, and service included. Call the Cipriani at 800-223-6800 for reservations. You can also have a meal or a drink at Harry's Dolce, which is less pricey than Harry's Bar in San Marco. At the other end of the budget spectrum is a bargain-basement hostel that serves cafeteria-style meals and a holy hotel that is currently closed for renovation.

OTHER OPTIONS
Hostels
Ostello Venezia   **328**

Lido Island

Lido stretches for eleven kilometers between the lagoon and the Adriatic Sea. It is known for its beaches, its gambling casino, and the Venice Film Festival. It is the only Venetian island where cars are allowed (you must catch a car ferry from the mainland). You can get to Lido from San Zaccaria in Venice in about ten or fifteen minutes by vaporetto, but you will be light years away from the true spirit and unique romantic charm of Venice. The best way to explore Lido is on a bicycle, which you can rent at several locations. Lido also has many old-fashioned hotels, ones where families have come for generations and stayed for "the season," though the season is now probably only a week or ten days. Modern working life is one reason for the shorter stays, but another has to be the high prices charged during the high season. However, it you are willing to do Lido in the off-season, your hotel bill will be cut by 30 to 50 percent.

Tourists flock to Lido during the warm months, drawn by the casino, by nostalgic memories of society life during the heyday of the twenties and thirties, and by the long stretch of beach. Unfortunately, hotels control the best sections of the beach, and unless you stay at a hotel that rents beach cabanas, you will be relegated to the public beaches at the northern and southern ends of the island, where the water is not always clean. Even if you do not go to lounge on the sand, Lido is great: you can play tennis and golf, water ski, windsurf, parasail, ride horses, bicycle, walk, and drive. On Tuesday mornings, there is a large outdoor market that is patronized largely by Venetians, who are attracted by the prices and the quantity of stalls. In addition to the usual food stalls, there are scores of others selling ready-to-wear and household goods, making it a real window on local life.

HOTELS

($) indicates a Big Splurge

ALBERGO QUATTRO FONTANE ★★★★ ($)
Via Quattro Fontane, 16

58 rooms, all with shower or bath and toilet

The beautiful Albergo Quattro Fontane is on the site of the first casino on Lido, which was built in the late sixteenth century and was loftily "dedicated to country delights and learned conversations of the Venetian aristocracy." During the nineteenth century, the casino became a tavern where poet Robert Browning was a regular customer. In the early 1900s, it was reconstructed into a huge country-style chalet, keeping only the stately fireplace with the lion-shaped mantel and four columns in the dining room. The present owners, sisters Bente and Pia Bevilacqua, came here with their parents more than fifty years ago. Over time they have imaginatively decorated the hotel's bedrooms and public areas, mixing their splendid sense of whimsy with period furniture, old paintings, and unusual objects they have collected in their world travels. What they have created "is not a hotel," as Bente says. "It is a gracious country-house a few minutes from 'the stones of Venice.' Everything in the house, its rooms, public spaces, and quiet reading room, is created to let guests enjoy their days in a refined atmosphere."

It takes awhile to absorb everything in Albergo Quattro Fontane, and frankly it can't be done in just one visit. Everywhere you look, there is an object or display that catches your eye, whether it is something so simple as framed exotic sea shells, a quartet of Thai puppets, a bubbling fountain surrounded by lovely flowers, the collection

TELEPHONE & FAX
041 526 0227

INTERNET
www.quattrofontane.com

CREDIT CARDS
AE, DC, MC, V

RATES
Single 130–270€, double 160–400€, extra bed 50–100€; children 10 and younger 30% discount; half-pension 47€ per person; beach cabana 65–130€ per day

BREAKFAST
Buffet breakfast included

ENGLISH
Yes

of pipes in the intimate bar, or African masks hanging on the wall off the main dining room. Pia is an artist, and you can see her imaginative work hanging over the aqua blue sofa in the living room and displayed on the menu of the restaurant, which is known for its fine food, excellent wines, and old-fashioned service (see *Great Eats Italy*). The grounds of the property, lovingly tended by two full-time gardeners, are equally inviting, with places to sit and enjoy a candlelit drink or an al fresco lunch or late-summer dinner shaded by a three-hundred-year-old plantain tree.

The individually decorated rooms, many of which are named after Palladio villas, are distinctly arranged for guests to settle in for a long stay. A favorite is No. 1, which has the beds the sisters slept in when they were young. There is also a fifteen-foot armoire, Victorian chandeliers, carved armchairs, and in the bathroom, more towels and toiletries than you could ever hope to use. No matter which room is yours, you will be treated as a valued guest who is staying in a beautiful and very personal home. There is nothing like it in Venice, nor anyplace else for that matter.

NOTE: The Albergo is closed from November 10 to April 1. Rates quoted are for high season.

FACILITIES AND SERVICES: Air-conditioning, bar, no elevator (3 floors), hair dryer, data ports (in some rooms), laundry service, minibar, free parking, restaurant (for breakfast, lunch, and dinner), room service, in-room safe, satellite TV, tennis court, beach cabana

NEAREST TOURIST ATTRACTION: Lido, about a 15-minute walk to the vaporetto for Venice

HOTEL ATLANTA AUGUSTUS ★★★ ($, 118)
Via Lepanto, 15
31 rooms, all with shower or bath and toilet

The motto at the Hotel Atlanta Augustus is "Cleanliness, Professionalism, and Comfort." This promise is a reality thanks to owners Ricardo and Haji Polacco, their able assistant Marco, the superb cleaning staff headed for twenty-five years by Adriana, and Leonardo the cat, who gives every guest a warm welcome. With this unbeatable combination, it is no wonder it has such a loyal clientele. But that is only part of the package you get at this hotel on a quiet street in one of the best sections of Lido.

The Liberty-style villa has thirty-one modern bedrooms, six with balconies, two with small corner kitchens with microwave ovens, and four penthouse suites. A redecoration program is underway—it started with the first floor and is working itself up to the third— but with what I would

TELEPHONE
041 526 0569
FAX
041 526 5604
INTERNET
www.hotelatlanta.net
CREDIT CARDS
AE, DC, MC, V
RATES
Rates span low/high seasons: single 60–120€, standard double 65–190€, deluxe double 80–240€, junior suite 120–330€; beach cabana 20€ per person, per day
BREAKFAST
Buffet breakfast included
ENGLISH
Yes

consider mixed results. Most of the bathrooms in this first phase have been redone in a wild kaleidoscope of hot colors, which are highlighted with shimmering gold mosaic pieces. They are pretty but somehow over-the-top in this setting. Some rooms are calmer, and these have off-white wall coverings, carpeted floors, and copies of Tiffany lights, a welcome respite from the ubiquitous Murano style. Others, unfortunately, mix ornate furnishings with old-fashioned wall coverings, and have yards of mismatched fabrics that clash with those glowing bathrooms. If you check into Suite 105, wear dark glasses until your eyes get used to the bright Chinese red . . . which envelops the furniture and curtains and accents the gold-covered sofa. Plans are on the books to redo the lobby, and I can't wait to see how that turns out. Oh well, we all don't have the same taste.

However, the best spectacle is found in the four penthouse suites, which have such dynamic views that the hotel requests that guests in these rooms arrive at sunset for maximum impact. These suites have floor-to-ceiling windows and large, flower-bedecked terraces that allow guests to enjoy round-the-clock vistas of faraway Venice. Mezzanine bedrooms and Jacuzzi baths add to their appeal. A buffet breakfast served in the two-room dining area or in the garden provides energy enough for the entire day, or at least until you return to the American Bar, which features a nightly happy hour. During the day you can rent a bicycle from the hotel and pedal around the island, exploring all of its pretty neighborhoods, beaches, and parks.

NOTE: The hotel is closed in December and January.

FACILITIES AND SERVICES: Air-conditioning, bar, direct-dial phone, elevator, hair dryers, small kitchenettes in some suites, free parking, some in-room safes, office safe, TV, satellite TV in penthouse rooms, nonsmoking rooms, bicycle rentals

NEAREST TOURIST ATTRACTIONS: Lido Beach, 20- to 30-minutes to Venice via vaporetto and foot

HOTEL BELVEDERE ★★★ ($, 115)
Piazzale Santa Maria Elisabetta, 4
30 rooms, all with shower or bath and toilet

The Belvedere, owned and managed by the same family since it was built in 1857, is one of the mainstays on Lido Island, overlooking the lagoon and across the street from the landing stages for the vaporettos that take you to Venice. The dependably clean rooms have been modernized and are enhanced by dedicated upkeep and above-average bathrooms, all with showers. Fourteen of them have views

TELEPHONE
041 526 0115
FAX
041 526 1486
EMAIL
hbelve@tin.it
INTERNET
www.belvedere-venezia.com
CREDIT CARDS
AE, DC, MC, V

RATES
Rates span low/high seasons:
single 50–130€, double 90–
240€; half- or full-board 20€
per person per meal
BREAKFAST
Buffet breakfast included
ENGLISH
Yes

and rent for the same price as the viewless chambers. The hotel offers free beach cabanas and free parking. The hotel also operates a good restaurant and snack bar (see *Great Eats Italy*), but this part of the hotel operation is closed on Monday and from November until Carnivale.

FACILITIES AND SERVICES: Air-conditioning, bar, direct-dial phone, elevator, guest Internet terminal, restaurant and snack bar, in-room safe, satellite TV, free parking, free beach cabanas and bicycles, one nonsmoking room

NEAREST TOURIST ATTRACTIONS: Lido Beach, 10 to 15 minutes by vaporetto to Venice

HOTEL CRISTALLO ★★ (117)
Gran Viale Santa Maria Elisabetta, 51
24 rooms, all with shower or bath and toilet

TELEPHONE
041 526 5293
FAX
041 526 5615
EMAIL
cristallo@veneziahotels.com
INTERNET
www.veneziahotels.com
CREDIT CARDS
AE, DC, MC, V
RATES
Rates span low/high seasons:
single 50–180€, double 80–
180€; discounts for *Great Sleeps
Italy* readers
BREAKFAST
Continental breakfast included
ENGLISH
Yes

The Cristallo is on the wide boulevard that runs through the small commercial section of Lido from the ocean to the lagoon. Everyone likes manager Andrea Leone because he is helpful, considerate, friendly, funny, and treats guests like family. The hotel has other things going for it, including inexpensive parking and the use of the hotel beach cabanas on the posh Lido Beach. On the flip side, the bathrooms are either super or have downright hideous color schemes, but you can't fault their cleanliness.

All the bedchambers come with their own bathrooms, and four have front-facing balconies. Number 32 is a corner site with two windows looking onto a garden and over rooftops, and just wait until you see the new gray marble sink and tub in the bathroom. Of this and two other rooms, 12 and 22, Andrea said, "We should rent the bathrooms rather than the rooms." Not so No. 27, which has an ugly brown-tile bathroom and a pea-green toilet with a glaring white seat. The room itself is noisy, has prison-issue beds, and overlooks corregated metal roofs at the corner of the main drag. Down the hall, No. 28 has the same bilious bathroom but a better bedroom that can sleep four when the Murphy-bunk beds are pulled down. Number 34, one of the biggest and brightest, sleeps four and is on the street.

NOTE: The hotel is closed from November 15 to March 31, though it reopens for one week after Christmas and for Carnivale. Under the same ownership are the Hotel Pensione Wildner (see page 272) and Locanda del Ghetto (see page 262) in Cannaregio.

FACILITIES AND SERVICES: Air-conditioning, direct-dial phone, elevator, hair dryer available, in-room safe, satellite TV, parking (5€ per day), use of beach cabana (shared with other hotel guests)

NEAREST TOURIST ATTRACTIONS: Lido Beach, 10- to 15-minute vaporetto ride to Venice

HOTEL PANORAMA ★★★★ ($, 116)
Piazzale Santa Maria Elisabetta, 1
22 rooms, all with shower, bath, and toilet

For a century, there has been some sort of hotel here, but nothing anyone could label as smart or classy. All that changed in 2000 when the Panorama opened after a thorough renovation. Now the hotel comes across as confident and dressed to impress its seemingly endless stream of contented guests. The dark wood furnishings have a 1900s look, and floor-to-ceiling windows make the rooms seem larger and much lighter. Baths are great: they are all marble with stall showers and wide pedestal sinks. For the best views, request a corner room on the first or second floor; for more space, ask for a room on the third. These third-floor rooms are under a mansard roof and do have a peek-a-boo view from their ceiling skylights; bathrooms have a soothing Jacuzzi. If you are a beachgoer, the hotel has free umbellas and lounge chairs on loan, but you have to do the carrying, and it's over a mile to and from the beach—though you can always hail a cab or hop onto a bus if you don't have a car.

NOTE: The hotel is under the same ownership as Hotel Cà Formenta (see page 268) on Via Garibaldi in Venice.

FACILITIES AND SERVICES: Air-conditioning, bar, direct-dial phone, hair dryer, elevator, guest Internet terminal, laundry service, minibar, free parking, in-room safe, satellite TV, discounts at a bicycle shop, free beach umbrellas and lounge chairs

NEAREST TOURIST ATTRACTIONS: Lido, 10- to 15-minute vaporetto ride to Venice

TELEPHONE
041 276 0486
FAX
041 276 9805
INTERNET
www.hpanorama.com
CREDIT CARDS
AE, DC, MC, V
RATES
Single 110–150€, double 170–250€, triple 220–310€; children under 2 are free, children 3–10 get 20% discount; 2-night minimum on major holidays and weekends; discounts for *Great Sleeps Italy* readers, and Internet specials
BREAKFAST
Buffet breakfast included
ENGLISH
Yes

HUNGARIA PALACE HOTEL ★★★★ ($, 119)
Gran Viale Santa Maria Elisabetta, 28
82 rooms, all with shower or bath and toilet

After millions of dollars invested and more than a year of renovations, the Hungaria Palace Hotel is grand once again. Just one glance at its imposing Majolica tiled exterior and you will understand why this magnificent monument to Art Nouveau has been used in countless films and photo shoots. No matter where you turn, there is another wonderful piece of furniture, painting, or framed photographic reminder of the glory days of this Lido landmark. A graceful terrace wraps itself around the front of the hotel and serves as an al fresco dining area in

TELEPHONE
041 242 0060
FAX
041 526 4111
INTERNET
www.hungaria.it
CREDIT CARDS
AE, DC, MC, V

RATES
Rates span low/high seasons: single 178–220€, double 107–378€, suite 260–535€; half-board 30€ per person; beach chairs and umbrellas 25€ per day

BREAKFAST
Buffet breakfast included

ENGLISH
Yes

the spring and summer. Otherwise, guests are served in a glass-enclosed winter garden.

On the first through third floors, each carefully appointed room carries out the Art Nouveau theme in its original furnishings. Those on the fourth floor are done in muted tones with dressy rattan and bamboo furnishings. The computer data ports and modern bathrooms speak to its upmarket clientele, who want modern conveniences with their stylized surroundings. Children are welcome, and in fact there is a back garden play area just for them. For beachgoers, umbrellas and chairs are available. The restaurant, open only for dinner, offers a special fixed-price menu for hotel guests.

FACILITIES AND SERVICES: Air-conditioning, bar, children's play area, conference room, direct-dial phone, elevator, hair dryer, some Jacuzzis, laundry service, minibar, data port, free parking, in-room safe, satellite TV

NEAREST TOURIST ATTRACTIONS: The hotel itself, Lido Beach, 10- to 15-minute vaporetto ride to Venice

Other Options

There are times when alternatives to hotel stays make sense. The cheapest choice of all is a campground on the outskirts of Venice. If you are a student, there are a handful of student accommodations and two hostels. Those looking for an apartment can book one through a rental agency or contact one of the many hotels that maintain apartments in Venice (see the index, page 397, for a complete list).

Apartment Rentals

Before reserving any apartment in Venice, whether it be through an agency or in connection with a hotel, please refer to "Tips for Renting an Italian Apartment," page 15. Also, see the index for a complete list of Venice hotels that maintain apartments and/or suites with kitchens (page 397).

APARTMENT RENTALS

VENICEBLISS

TELEPHONE
02 454 89 438, cell 339 739
0377
FAX
02 738 0617
EMAIL
laura-crespi@fastwebnet.it;
venciebliss@fastwebnet.it
CREDIT CARDS
None
RATES
One-bedroom from 935€ per
week; 2-bedroom from 1,265€
per week; rates includes all
utilities except the phone and
weekly maid service; discounts
for longer stays and in
low-season
ENGLISH
Yes

Venicebliss offers a select number of delightful Venetian apartments in interesting neighborhoods that are geared to local life. It is owned and managed by Laura Crespi, a delightful lady who takes a very personal interest in pleasing all of her guests. I like her apartments because they are spotlessly clean, attractively decorated, and reasonably priced, especially if you can move in for a month in the off-season. I also like their sunny balconies, beautifully equipped kitchens, and clotheswashers. Venicebliss has no Website, but Laura will email you pictures of her apartments.

VIEWS ON VENICE (56)
Campo San Luca, 4267/a (San Marco)

TELEPHONE
041 241 1140
FAX
041 1241 5821
INTERNET
www.viewsonvenice.com
CREDIT CARDS
MC, V
RATES
From 900€ per week for a
studio; 10% discount in low
season and for stays of a month
or more; rate includes weekly
maid service and utilities
(except the telephone)
ENGLISH
Yes

The apartments offered by Views on Venice are nothing short of sensational. The company is owned by the Ferragamo family (see Windows on Tuscany, page 132), so you know right away these will be apartments that stand out from the rest of the competition. By consulting their Website and thumbing through their beautiful catalog, you will have no trouble finding the holiday home of your dreams, whether it be a sunny one-bedroom on a quiet *campo*, a villa with a swimming pool, or an ornate *palazzo* facing the grand canal. All of these properties are personally owned or selected by the family and managed by them, and rates are surprisingly affordable. They are beautifully furnished, extremely comfortable, perfectly located, and equipped with the best facilities. In short, no detail is overlooked to ensure an unforgettable stay. As Maria Ferragamo says of her apartments: "You will feel at home, surrounded by the magical atmosphere of Venice."

Camping

Forget white stretches of picturesque beaches where you can pitch a tent under the starry sky. That is just not happening in Venice. Most of the campsites are in dreary, drab Marghera or Mestre, and on the other side of Porto del Lido in Cavallino, which is on the water. The tourist office issues a long list, but don't expect too much beauty with your Bunsen burner. Another downer—campsites are relatively expensive. Rates quoted below include a per-person fee plus a site fee, whether you are staying in a tent, camper, or caravan; all rates are per day. If the focus of your stay is to see Venice, you are much better off in a centrally located budget bed and not stuck in the boonies, where the trek back and forth to Venice costs you not only valuable time but considerable money. Think about this hard before deciding on packing your tent.

CAMPING

CAMPING FUSINA
Via Moranzani, Mestre (outside Venice)

1,000 campsites

In summer, a boat connects the Fusina campground to Venice at a cost of around 5€ one way. Otherwise, you have to take the bus to Mestre and get to Venice from there. This translates to twenty minutes by boat to Venice or an hour and a half by bus, foot, and boat. There is a store, restaurant, bar, and Internet café, and the showers are free.

FACILITIES AND SERVICES: Bar, coin laundry, Internet access, small supermarket, pizza restaurant, free showers

TELEPHONE
041 547 0055
FAX
041 544 0050
INTERNET
www.camping-fusina.com
CREDIT CARDS
MC, V
RATES
Adults 7€ per day in all accommodations, children under 5 5€; tent 4€; cabin (no bathroom) 13€ per person; maxi-caravan (with bathroom and kitchen) 57€
ENGLISH
Yes

CA' PASQUALI
Via Poerio, 33 (outside Venice)

2,000 campsites

The campground has a store, a restaurant, laundry facilities, and a swimming pool. You will need a car or bus to go the five or six kilometers from the campground to the boat stop, which is Punte Sabbioni. The boat from here takes an additional forty minutes to get to Venice. In July and August, there is a bus from the campsite to the boat; at other times, unless you have wheels, you get off at Via Fausta and walk.

NOTE: The campground closes from late September to early April; call for exact dates.

FACILITIES AND SERVICES: Convenience store, bar, Internet access in bar, pizza restaurant, coin laundry, free showers, swimming pool; bikes and TVs for rent

TELEPHONE
041 966 1100
FAX
041 530 0797
INTERNET
www.capasquali.it
CREDIT CARDS
AE, MC, V
RATES
Adults 6.50€ in all accommodations, children 2–4 3.50€; tents on the beach 16.50€, off the beach 12.60€; caravans on the beach 47€
ENGLISH
Yes

Hostels

FORESTERIA VALDESE (82)
Calle Lunga Santa Maria Formosa, 5170 (Castello)

50 beds in 8 rooms, 3 dorms; plus 3 rooms and 2 apartments with bath and toilet

TELEPHONE & FAX
041 528 6797

EMAIL
veneziaforesteria@chiesavalde
se.org

INTERNET
www.chiesavaldese.org/venezia

CREDIT CARDS
V, 2% discount for cash

RATES
Dorm (8–14 beds) 24€ per bed first night, 23€ per bed each successive night; double room (2-night minimum) 58–76€; quad 106€; apartment (4–5 people) 106–118€

BREAKFAST
Continental breakfast included with dorms and rooms, not included with apartment

ENGLISH
Yes, but it can be limited

Housed in the crumbling Palazzo Caragnis at the end of Calle Lunga Santa Maria Formosa, the building dates back to the Doges and is now a national monument. In 1868, the Waldesian Protestant Church purchased the *palazzo*. The primary focus was to help needy children. In 1908, the grand hall was turned into a church for the Waldesian evangelical services. In 1925, the villa was opened to boarding guests, and today it operates as a hostel welcoming groups, families, and singles. The dorm rooms are basic, and so are the two flats with kitchens, which are good deals if there are several very dedicated cheap sleepers in your group and you only need a place to sleep and change clothes. No towels are provided for the dormitory rooms. Several rooms have balconies and views, the location is nice, and the rules are as follows: no smoking in the rooms, no outside guests, no booze, clear the table after breakfast, be out of your room from 10 A.M. to 1 P.M. You must make your bed, and there is no age limit or curfew. It is part of the same religious group that runs Istituto Gould in Florence (see page 120) and Casa Valdese in Rome (see page 203), but unfortunately it is a quantum leap behind them both.

The reception desk is open Monday to Sunday from 9 A.M. to 1 P.M. and 6 to 8 P.M., and on Sunday from 9 A.M. to 1 P.M. Reservations are accepted by phone only.

NOTE: Foresteria Valdese is closed for three weeks in November; call for exact dates.

FACILITIES AND SERVICES: Some TVs, Internet terminal in lobby

NEAREST TOURIST ATTRACTIONS: Piazza San Marco, Rialto Bridge

OSTELLO VENEZIA
Fondamenta di Zitelle, 87 (Giudecca Island)

250 beds, no private shower or toilet

TELEPHONE
041 523 8211

FAX
041 523 5689

EMAIL
vehostel@tin.it

This is the only hostel in Venice sanctioned by Hostelling International, and you must have or purchase a valid IYHF card to sleep in one of its 250 beds, divided into sixteen-bed rooms for men or women, plus two handicapped-accessible rooms. What to expect? Rules, rules, and more rules, including lights out (at the master switch) by 10:30 P.M., even though curfew is not until 11:30 P.M. The price of the room includes sheets and breakfast. Dinner is available for 10€, and if you are in a group, you can also request lunch, which is the same price. Guests cannot leave before 7 A.M., must be out of their rooms from 9:30 A.M. to 1:30 P.M., and can check in from 1:30 to 10:30 P.M. BYO towels, but leave the booze and cigarettes elsewhere. The office is open from 7 to 9:30 A.M. and from 1 to 11:30 P.M. Got that?

NOTE: The hostel is closed from December 12 to 28.

FACILITIES AND SERVICES: Internet terminal

NEAREST TOURIST ATTRACTIONS: Across lagoon from Venice; 15 minutes by boat to Piazza San Marco, 40 minutes to train station and Piazzale Roma

INTERNET
www.hostels-aig.org.

CREDIT CARDS
MC, V

RATES
19.50€ per person; dinner available for 10€; guests must have an IYHF card (17€ if purchased here)

BREAKFAST
Continental breakfast included

ENGLISH
Yes

Student Accommodations

In summer and during Christmas and other school vacation periods, accommodations to benefit most hardcore cheap sleeping budgets can be found in dormitories run by various schools. They are spartan at best. Some have strict rules and regulations, most have curfews and daytime lockouts, and a few serve low-cost meals.

Students interested in accommodation and other discounts in Venice should consider purchasing a Rolling VENICEcard (see page 248). All students and teachers should definitely purchase an ISIC card, which entitles them to significant savings almost across the board. For details, see page 29.

DOMUS CIVICA (23)
Calle d. Campazzo, 3082 (San Polo)
100 beds in 74 rooms, no private shower or toilet

Domus Civica is near the train station and open daily to all Great Sleepers looking for low-cost lodgings from June 15 to September 15. Most rooms are doubles with cold running water; showers, sheets, and towels are free; and breakfast is not served. There is a 20 percent discount with an ISIC card (see page 29) or a Rolling VENICEcard (see page 248). The reception desk is open from 7:30 A.M. to 11:30 P.M. Curfew is at 11:30 P.M.

NOTE: Domus Civica is closed to the public from September 15 to June 15.

FACILITIES AND SERVICES: Elevator

NEAREST TOURIST ATTRACTIONS: Train station

TELEPHONE
041 721 103

FAX
041 522 7139

EMAIL
catonello@hotmail.com

CREDIT CARDS
None, cash only

RATES
Singles 28.50€, doubles or triples 26€ per person

BREAKFAST
Not served

ENGLISH
Yes

Shopping: Great Chic

Fashion can be bought; style one must possess.
—Edna Woolman Chase

Throughout history, Italians have known and appreciated good taste and fine quality. The "made in Italy" label is recognized as signifying the best available the world over. The high quality of Italian life is evident everywhere you look, from gourmet food and fine wines to designer clothing, imaginative furniture, and unique handcrafts. In these days of standardization and mass production, Italian artisans are still creating original and beautiful objects. Italian ceramics, embroidery and lace, gold and silver jewelry, glassware, and paper and leather goods have established the country as a leader in the world market. Many believe that the Italians are some of the best-dressed people in Europe, if not the world. They dress with style, and they look with disdain at foreigners who wear shorts and T-shirts and the latest in athletic shoes, all in the name of "I am on vacation and will be comfortable at all costs."

Born shoppers simply cannot spend all of their vacation time taking in the sights, eating wonderful meals, and staying in quaint, charming hotels. To maintain their sanity, they have to go shopping. The good news is that the possibilities in Italy are endless. The bad news is that nothing comes cheap. It is sad but true that the days of finding one bargain after another in Italy are over. The dollar now buys about 30 to 40 percent less than it did just a few years ago. That, along with soaring inflation, has made shopping here almost prohibitive for many visitors, unless, that is, you know where to go, when to shop, and what to buy. This section devoted to Great Chic shopping will help you do just that, and in the bargain, you will certainly find keepsakes to bring home that you will enjoy for a lifetime.

Discounts are not easy to find. The government red tape has gone so far as to mandate the time and duration of major sales and the amount a store can discount its prices at these sale times. This is unbelievable to most Americans, but it is a fact of life for Italians. Two government-sanctioned sale periods take place each year: from mid-January until the end of February, and all of July. Prices tend to drop as the sales wear on. This is the time to buy, as prices are cut by as much as 50 percent on top-name and quality goods—not cheap items brought in especially for the sale. During nonsale times, look for shops with signs saying *sconti* (discounts) or *vendita promozionale* (promotional sale). These are not government-sanctioned sales, and the discounts will be minimal, but it is something.

The following list of shops in Florence, Rome, and Venice is by no means exhaustive, nor does it always represent the cheapest prices. These are eclectic choices that reflect good quality and value and are included to encourage you along your way to great shopping adventures of your own. Good luck and happy shopping!

Great Chic Shopping Tips

1. When shopping, if you like it, want it, and can afford it...buy it. Do not leave so that you can think it over, for an afternoon or a day, because you probably will not have time to get back, and even if you do, the item may be gone. Worse yet is leaving the store and not being able to locate it again.

2. Pack an empty, soft folding suitcase in your luggage so you can bring your purchases home with you—avoiding the expense and hassle of mailing and insuring. Even if the airline charges you an excess-baggage fee (usually around $125), it will be cheaper and much easier than mailing and insuring several separate packages.

3. Do some preliminary shopping research before you leave home. Make a list of sizes, and check prices in your local stores. That way you will be able to spot a bargain and be able to have a focus to your shopping excursions. However, do not get caught up in sticking to an exact list. Be flexible.

4. At flea markets and outdoor markets, despite the competition, you can expect only a 10 to 25 percent discount as a result of hard bargaining. You will always get the best price if you pay cash.

5. Never change money in a store. Go to a bank or an ATM for the best rate.

6. Bring a pocket calculator to avoid asking, "How much is that in dollars?"

7. Purchases are seldom returnable. Buy with care.

8. Sales are held from mid-January through February, and again in July. The price reduction can be as much as 50 percent—and this includes all the big-name designers.

9. Keep a list of your purchases along with the receipts to show when you return to the United States. It will make it much easier to fill out the forms for the EU tax refund; see "European Union Tax Refund" on page 332.

Customs

Every person, even a week-old baby, returning to the United States receives an $800 duty-free allowance. This applies only to purchases you carry with you. Family members can pool their purchases, so you can use what your spouse and children did not. (Remember, your spouse and children have to be with you...not waiting for you at home.) After the $800 per person limit, you pay a flat 10 percent duty on the next $1,000 worth of merchandise, and more as the amount increases. All food items you are carrying back to the United States must be declared. Most are cleared without problem; you just have to declare them. If you don't and you are caught, the food will be confiscated and you will be fined $1,000. Any purchase worth less than $100 can be shipped back to the States as an unsolicited gift. It is considered duty-free and does not count in your $800 limit. You can send as many of these unsolicited gifts as you wish, but only one per person for each mailing, and don't mail anything to yourself.

Some other things to keep in mind are that antiques must be over one hundred years old to be duty-free. A work of art is duty-free, and it does not matter when it was made or who the artist was. Most foodstuffs are illegal, but not coffee. If you bring with you expensive jewelry, cameras, piles of imported luggage, or fancy watches, carry the receipts for them, or you could be questioned about them and even forced to pay duty on them.

Finally, be aware that customs officials have seen and heard it all. Don't cheat or lie, as you will invariably be caught, you and your luggage will be searched completely, and you could be subject to stiff fines, even jail time. It is just not worth it.

For more information on U.S. customs rules and regulations, send for the free brochure "Know Before You Go," available from the Department of the Treasury, U.S. Customs Service, Washington, D.C, 20229; Tel: 202 354 1000; www.customs.ustreas.gov.

European Union Tax Refund (IVA)

European Union countries allow citizens from nonmember countries to buy goods and take them back to their nonmember countries tax free. This is only allowed when you leave the EU completely. In other words, it will not work if you leave Italy and go to Spain, but it will work if you leave Italy and return to the U.S. or Great Britain. Americans leave behind billions of dollars in these taxes in Europe every year. In many cases, maybe shoppers do not spend enough to qualify for a refund, or maybe they just don't know they are eligible for a refund. The amount you get back varies from country to country. In Italy it is around 15 percent.

Most Italian shopkeepers are not eager to promote this, but you should take advantage of the savings that the European Union tax refund, called the IVA, offers. It's very simple: You are entitled to a tax refund if you spend approximately 160€ or more at any one store. You can add up multiple purchases at a single store (sometimes adding them up over several days, sometimes only over the course of one day; ask, since store policies vary), but you cannot tally up purchases made at two or three branch locations, such as a sweater at a Benetton shop in Rome, three blouses at two of their Florence stores, and a coat from their store in Venice.

When you are paying for your purchase, show your passport and ask for a refund form (*fattura*) with a self-addressed, stamped envelope from the seller. Fill out the refund paperwork and keep all receipts. When you leave Italy, stop at customs, show them what you bought (it's not always required, but be ready), and get the refund forms stamped. Mail the stamped refund forms to the merchants; there is a mailbox at the airport specifically for this purpose. It is important to remember that the customs stamp must be obtained no longer than three months after purchase. The stamped refund form must be returned to the issuing store no later than four months after purchase. The merchant will mail you your refund, although maybe not right away (it sometimes takes up to three months). It is easier for both the store and you if you use a credit card for your purchases, and then the rebate can be credited back to your card. Easier by a long shot is getting an immediate cash refund. After the customs official has stamped your paperwork, go to the desk with the red, white, and green logo and the sign saying "Tax Free for Tourists."

Final word: Some stores will offer you a big discount to forget all about the IVA paperwork. Best advice: Take the *sconto* (discount) and run!

Size Conversion Chart

The charts below are just a guide. Keep in mind that sizing is not standardized in Italy as it is in the United States. Often you will find widely different fits in the same size. If you have the measurements of the absentee person you are shopping for, making a decision will be much easier, and certainly more of a sure thing. If shopping for yourself, take the time to try on the items.

Women's Dresses, Coats, and Skirts

American	6	8	10	12	14	16	18	
Continental	36	38	40	42	44	46	48	

Women's Blouses and Sweaters

American	6	8	10	12	14	16	18	
Continental	34	36	38	40	42	44	46	

Women's Hosiery

American	8	8½	9	9½	10	10½
Continental	1	2	3	4	5	6

Women's Shoes

American	5	6	7	8	9	10
Continental	36	37	38	39	40	41

Children's Clothing

American	3	4	5	6	6x
Continental	98	104	110	116	122

Men's Suits

American	34	36	38	40	42	44	46	48
Continental	44	46	48	50	52	54	56	58

Men's Shirts

American	14½	15	15½	16	16½	17	17½	18
Continental	37	38	39	41	42	43	44	45

Men's Shoes

American	7	8	9	10	11	12
Continental	39½	41	42	43	44½	46

Shopping in Florence

Florence has long been renowned for its wonderful shopping. First-time Great Chic shoppers may find the number of shops overwhelming, but take heart...the city's small size puts almost everything within walking distance. Florentine artists today maintain the same high level of originality and attention to detail that they did centuries ago. The specialties of Florence are hand-embroidered linens, gold, ceramics, leather, handmade paper goods, and bookbinding. Many families have worked in the same shops for generations and take enormous pride in the workmanship that bears their name and upholds their reputation for quality. Of course, this means that prices are often as high as the quality. So where does this leave the Great Chic shopper? First of all, it leaves you getting top quality for your money, which is worth spending a little more; when shopping for high-end merchandise, forget all about finding a "steal." For trinkets, not treasures, shop in the outdoor market stalls at the San Lorenzo Central Market and at the Straw Market, where you will find many imaginative items to accommodate even the slimmest budget. The competition is stiff in these two markets, but prices do not vary much from one stall to another. Sometimes you can bargain a few euros, but nothing significant. It all comes down to buying from the seller you like the best.

Shopping Hours

In Italy, store rules and Italian law do not necessarily coincide. New laws that relax the old rules continue to go into effect, and these have enabled shops in Florence to be open nonstop during the day, on Monday mornings, and if you can believe it, on Sundays. This law doesn't say stores must be open; it just gives them the right to be open if they so choose. Surprise! Florentine merchants have discovered that people like to shop after work and on their days off. Where only a few years ago it was impossible to make a purchase on a Monday morning or, heaven forbid, on a Sunday, now, thanks to these new laws, most stores have continuous hours during the week and stay open a few hours on Sunday. There are still a few holdouts, especially artisan shops and small mama-and-papa operations not on the tourist beat. Food shops are the main holdouts, and they still adhere to the old hours. In the dog days of August, many small shops close for several weeks, on Saturday afternoon, and all day Sunday. Things are still in a state of flux, and the hours given below for shops are more than ever subject to change. If you are heading for a specific shop, I suggest you call to double-check the hours, especially during August or during major holiday periods.

SHOPS: Mon–Sat 9 or 10 A.M.–7 or 7:30 P.M., Sun 11 A.M.–7 P.M.

FOOD SHOPS: Mon–Sat 9 A.M.–1 P.M., 3:30 or 4–7:30 P.M.; closed Wed afternoon in the winter, Sat afternoon in the summer, and all day Sun. August closing varies.

TYPES OF SHOPS IN FLORENCE

Artist Supplies

ZECCHI (66)
Via dello Studio, 19r (Il Duomo)

If you are an artist or art restorer, this is a must. The selection of materials is astonishing . . . even the selection of colored pencils is mind-boggling. If it is not here, chances are excellent it does not exist.

TELEPHONE: 055 211 470
FAX: 055 210 690
EMAIL: zecchifi@tin.it
INTERNET: www.zecchi.com
CREDIT CARDS: AE, DC, MC, V
HOURS: Mon–Fri 8:30 A.M.–12:30 P.M., 3:30–7:30 P.M., Sat–Sun 8:30 A.M.–12:30 P.M.
ENGLISH: Yes

Beauty Salons

MARIO (77)
Via della Vigna Nuova, 22r (Piazza Goldoni)

Mario is a full-service salon with cosmetics and perfumes on the street level and a beauty salon upstairs, where you can get a manicure, pedicure, massage, and facial, in addition to getting your hair cut, styled, and colored. Ask for Mario—he is the owner, and although he doesn't speak much English, he is assisted by people who do. He loves to give trendy, very short haircuts...be careful. Remember that all beauty services are à la carte, which means you pay separately for the shampoo, conditioner, hair gel, and spray, as well as for the base cut, style, and/or coloring. And please remember, in Italy you are expected to tip each person who works on you. How much will it be? About $50–75 for a cut, style, and color. The aesthetician prices are comparable to those in the States.

TELEPHONE: 055 294 813, 055 239 89 53
INTERNET: www.mariodiviadellavigna.it
CREDIT CARDS: AE, MC, V
HOURS: Tues–Sat 9 A.M.–6 P.M.
ENGLISH: Yes, and Mario speaks French

Bookstores

BM BOOKSHOP (74)
Via Borgo Ognissanti, 4r (Piazza Goldoni)

When it opened in 1963, the BM Bookshop was the first English-language bookshop in Florence. It is still going strong and features an excellent selection of books dealing with art, travel (including a large selection on Florence), fiction, cooking, design, rare books, and fashion. They also do mail-order and will ship your excess books back home for you, thus saving you not only schlepping the books to the post office but the red-tape nightmare of trying to figure out the post office's bureaucratic rules for this simple task. Also for sale is the antique bric-a-brac, displayed wherever there is extra space. In addition to running a great shop, owners Rossana Amoroso and Cosetta Boni and their staff are friendly and very welcoming.

TELEPHONE & FAX: 055 294 575
EMAIL: bmbookshop@dada.it
CREDIT CARDS: AE, DC, MC, V
HOURS: Mon–Sat 9:30 A.M.–7:30 P.M., Sun 10:30 A.M.–7 P.M.; Jan–Mar: closed Sun
ENGLISH: Yes

ENGLISH BOOKSTORE & PAPERBACK EXCHANGE (56)
Via Fiesolana, 3r (Piazza della SS. Annunziata)

This is the unofficial community center for English-speaking visitors and residents in Florence. They will trade their secondhand books for yours or give you a store credit. In addition to being one of the major university textbook suppliers for students in Florence, they specialize in new and used books on art history, humanities, Italian studies, political science, travel, and popular fiction. The store is owned by American Emily Rosner and her husband, and they are plugged in to everything going on in Florence.

TELEPHONE: 055 247 8154
FAX: 055 247 8856

INTERNET: www.papex.it
CREDIT CARDS: AE, DC, MC, V
HOURS: Mon–Fri 9 A.M.– 7:30 P.M., Sat 10 A.M.–1 P.M., 3:30–7:30 P.M.;
closed middle 2 weeks of Aug
ENGLISH: Yes

China and Ceramics

DINO BARTOLINI (46)
Via dei Servi, 30r (Il Duomo)

Dino Bartolini was voted the best houseware shop in Italy, and after one visit, you will know why. The big store is filled with every kitchen gadget and cooking necessity imaginable, and a spectacular selection of china, pottery, crystal, and silver. They have good sales at the end of January and February.
TELEPHONE: 055 211 895
FAX: 055 264 281
CREDIT CARDS: AE, MC, V
HOURS: Mon 3:30–7:30 P.M., Tues–Sat 9 A.M.–1 P.M., 3:30–7 P.M.; closed Sun and in Aug
ENGLISH: Yes

DITTA LUCA DELLA ROBBIA (116)
Via del Proconsolo, 19r (Il Duomo)

Since 1904 this family-owned ceramics shop and factory has been world-renowned for their Della Robbia–designed ceramics. One of the sons specializes in reproduction Renaissance paintings.
TELEPHONE: 055 283 532
CREDIT CARDS: MC, V
HOURS: Daily 10 A.M.–6 P.M.; Dec–Feb: closed Sun & Mon, except Sun before Christmas
ENGLISH: Yes

LA MAIOLICA (23)
Via Guelfa, 31r (Piazza del Mercato Centrale)

One of the friendliest ceramic shops (and certainly one of the most interesting) in Florence is La Maiolica. You can watch the artist/designer Salvatore Rabbene create his wares in the tiny shop window, where you can also see his kiln and displays of his work. Salvatore speaks English and is used to dealing with Americans. He will make things to order, personalize any of his designs, and have your purchases insured and shipped to your home. The quality is excellent, and so is his service. All pieces are dishwasher-safe and lead-free.
TELEPHONE: 055 280 029
FAX: 055 437 8677
EMAIL: lamaiolicafirenze@katamail.com

CREDIT CARDS: AE, DC, MC, V
HOURS: Jan–Mar: Mon–Sat 9:30 A.M.–1 P.M., 3:30–7:30 P.M.; April–Dec: Mon–Sat 9:30 A.M.–7:30 P.M.; closed: Sun and first two weeks in Aug
ENGLISH: Yes

SBIGOLI TERRECOTTE (68)
Via S. Edigio, 4r (Il Duomo)

This is the retail outlet for a wide range of traditional handmade Tuscan ceramic tableware, all lead-free. Much of the tableware in local trattorias comes from this factory. They will ship.
TELEPHONE & FAX: 055 24 79 713
CREDIT CARDS: AE, DC, MC, V
HOURS: Mon–Sat 9 A.M.–1 P.M., 3–7:30 P.M.
ENGLISH: Yes

Clothing

ALFREDA E MANUELA EVANGELISTI (117)
Borgo de Greci, 33r (Il Duomo)

Ties, scarves, and shawls are sold all over Florence, and the quality ranges from flea-market polyester to beautiful Gucci silks. For a happy medium, one that's still very high quality but with very good prices, let the mother-daughter duo of Alfreda and Manuela help you select a silk tie or scarf or a dramatic shawl.
TELEPHONE: 055 292 772
CREDIT CARDS: AE, MC, V
HOURS: Mon–Sat 9:30 A.M.–6:30 P.M.; closed: Sun and Aug
ENGLISH: Yes

BLUNAUTA (70)
Via del Pronconsolo, 69r (Il Duomo)

Blunauta (formerly known as Balloon) has shops in most Italian cities (see "Shopping" in Rome, page 360, and Venice, page 376). They specialize in a selection of affordable, pretty colored silk clothing. Many of the items are made in China, so check the quality carefully. This shop is small but still a good place to pick up a missing piece you wished you had packed.

They have a second location with the same hours at Borgo la Croce, 59 (80, Piazza Santa Croce), near Mercato San Ambrogio.
TELEPHONE: 055 212 460
CREDIT CARDS: AE, DC, MC, V
HOURS: Mon 3:30–7:30 P.M., Tues–Sat 10 A.M.–7:30 P.M.; closed: Sun, 2 weeks mid-Aug
ENGLISH: Yes

CHIANTI CASHMERE COMPANY
la Piensola Farm, Radda in Chianti, 53017 (midway between Florence and Siena)

Dr. Nora Kravis started her goat farm with two goats, purchased initially to munch on the weeds. This grew to over two hundred goats and is now the only cashmere goat farm in Italy, raising its goats naturally in the Tuscan countryside. The cashmere fiber is harvested and made into one-of-a-kind hand-woven articles of the highest quality. The goats are hand milked for the whole milk that makes the company's natural skin-care products uniquely rich, creamy, and oh so good for your skin.

No perfume or artificial coloring is ever used, and the skin-care products are created, formulated, and produced exclusively by Nora. Trust me, once you start using her wonderful products, you will never go near a department store skin-care counter again.

You can visit the farm in person (please call ahead for an appointment), stay in her farmhouse (see Villas in Tuscany, page 140), or order online any of her cashmere scarves, shawls, and blankets, or her soaps, creams, lotions, shampoos, and sunscreens.

TELEPHONE & FAX: 0577 738 080
INTERNET: www.chianticashmere.com
CREDIT CARDS: MC, V
HOURS: Daily 10 A.M.–6 P.M. (please call ahead)
ENGLISH: Yes

Cosmetics and Perfumes

DR. VRANJES—ANTICA OFFICINA DEL FARMACISTA (10)
Via San Gallo, 63r (Piazza San Marco)

The shop is a heaven-sent mecca for natural and organic cosmetic products, using essences of essential oils and precious perfumes. The range of products includes wonderful lotions, cosmetics, body oils, and the purest perfumes for you and your home. I love the home perfume Terra, which is emitted on sticks flowing out of a large jar of golden perfume. It lasts about three months and your house will smell wonderful. At the San Gallo address, Dr. Vranjes runs a cosmetic school that takes appointments for supervised student massages, facials, and other beauty treatment at a fraction of regular price, and of course, you will be rubbed and wrapped in the doctor's divine products.

There is a second location that is a shop only: Borgo la Croce, 44r (81, Piazza Santa Croce); Tel: 055 241 758; Hours: Mon–Sat 10 A.M.–1 P.M., 3:30–7:30 P.M.

TELEPHONE: 055 494 537
FAX: 055 471 113
CREDIT CARDS: MC, V
HOURS: Mon–Fri 9 A.M.–7 P.M.; closed: Sat, Sun, and Aug
ENGLISH: Yes

FARMACIA MUNSTERMANN (75)
Piazza Goldoni, 2r (Piazza Goldoni)

Clarissa Petruzzi is carrying on the tradition established by her parents in running this unique pharmacy and cosmetics shop. Here you can buy her handmade natural and homeopathic cosmetics, which have been carefully prepared and packaged in the old-fashioned manner. She has created a fine stock of products for body and skin care, sun lotions, hair preparations, fragrances for men and women, plus facial cosmetics. Whenever I am in Florence, I stock up, especially on the rich Crema Nutriente Olio d'Oliva and on body lotion, which can be custom scented. If you run out before your next trip to Florence, there is a catalog available in English, but you must place a minimum 100€ order. Clarissa and her shop have my highest recommendation, not only for her top-quality products, but for the care and consideration Clarissa extends to every customer, whether a first-time visitor or a sweet neighborhood couple who have been shopping here for decades.

TELEPHONE & FAX: 055 210 660
EMAIL: munstermann@tin.it
INTERNET: www.munstermann.it
CREDIT CARDS: DC, MC, V
HOURS: Mon–Fri 9 A.M.–1 P.M., 4–8 P.M.; closed: Sun, 2 weeks after Christmas and 2 weeks in Aug
ENGLISH: Yes

OFFICINA PROFUMO FARMACEUTICA DI SANTA MARIA NOVELLA (49)
Via della Scala, 16 (Piazza Santa Maria Novella)

This is not a pharmacy but an *erboristeria,* a shop selling natural herbal-based cosmetics and herbal remedies. It is absolutely worth a visit if only to view the spectacular frescoed vaulted ceilings of the magnificent chapel in the only thirteenth-century monastery pharmacy in Florence that still has its unaltered, preserved, original appearance. The Dominican Fathers who once ran the pharmacy have gone, but you can still purchase their medicinal liqueurs. They are also famous for their pomegranate soap and almond cream. All products are still made according to the Dominican Fathers' traditions and are not tested on animals. They now have branches in many other Italian cities as well as in London and Paris, but the prices are higher elsewhere than they are here...and that is saying something. They will ship.

TELEPHONE: 055 216 276
FAX: 055 288 658
INTERNET: www.smnovella.com
CREDIT CARDS: AE, MC, V
HOURS: Mon 3:30–7:30 P.M., Tues–Sat 9:30 A.M.–7:30 P.M., Sun 10:30 A.M.–6:30 P.M.
ENGLISH: Yes

Department Stores

COIN (89)
Via dei Calzaiuoli, 56r (Il Duomo)

This is Italy's answer to middle-market shopping for men, women, and children. I like it for cotton fashions in the colors of the moment. There is also an interesting housewares section.

TELEPHONE: Not available
CREDIT CARDS: AE, DC, MC, V
HOURS: Mon–Sat 10 A.M.–7:30 P.M., Sun 11 A.M.–7:30 P.M.
ENGLISH: Very little, but it depends on clerk

LA RINASCENTE (86)
Via degli Speziali, 117/21r, on Piazza della Repubblica (Il Duomo)

The Rome-based department store has a branch in Florence. The quality is good, but most of the merchandise you can find at home and for less money. The top-floor dining terrace has mediocre food but a sensational view over Florence. You can enjoy the view without eating.

TELEPHONE: Not available
CREDIT CARDS: AE, DC, MC, V
HOURS: Mon–Sat 9 A.M.–9 P.M., Sun 10:30 A.M.–8 P.M.
ENGLISH: Yes

STANDA (79)
Via Pietraplana, 42r (Piazza Santa Croce)

Standa is a large supermarket with everything you will need to set up temporary housekeeping.

TELEPHONE: 055 283 071
CREDIT CARDS: MC, V
HOURS: Daily 8:30 A.M.–9 P.M.
ENGLISH: Depends on clerk, but don't count on much

Fabrics and Trimmings

ANTICO SETIFICIO FIORENTINO (126)
Via Bartolini, 4r (Piazza del Carmine)

As you enter Antico Setificio Fiorentino through a historic garden, you are taken back in time to another world of ancient patterns and glorious silks, which are faithfully reproduced by a handful of skilled artisans on eighteenth- and nineteenth-century hand looms. Yards of these flowing silks have been made here since 1786 to fill the custom orders for papal vestments, to provide the costumes worn in the famous Palio in Siena, and to satisfy an international clientele where quality is the only consideration, never cost. A visit to their shop is a requirement for any person interested in fabrics and design. The staff is extremely helpful and will take time to sell you exactly the silk you need to redecorate a villa, or just a few yards of silk brocade to make into pillows. They also carry their own line of cashmere-lined shawls, throws, and scarves. None of their fabrics are available elsewhere.

TELEPHONE: 055 213 861
FAX: 055 218 174
INTERNET: www.anticosetificiofiorentino.com
CREDIT CARDS: AE, DC, MC, V
HOURS: Mon–Fri 9 A.M.–1 P.M., 2–5 P.M.; closed Sat, Sun, and Aug
ENGLISH: Yes

PASSAMANERIA TOSCANA (42)
Piazza San Lorenzo, 12r (Piazza del Mercato Centrale)

This store has the most amazing selection of fabrics, tassels, braids, tapestries, exclusive handmade cushions, curtain holders, fringes, borders, laces—even mosquito netting—under one roof. It's worth a visit even if you just buy some decorative braid.

TELEPHONE: 055 214 670
INTERNET: www.ptfsrl.com
CREDIT CARDS: AE, DC, MC, V
HOURS: Mon–Sat 9 A.M.–7:30 P.M., Sun 10 A.M.–7:30 P.M.
ENGLISH: Yes

PASSAMANERIE VALMAR (103)
Via Porta Rossa, 53r (Il Duomo)

For a very Florentine gift that is easy to tuck into even the smallest piece of luggage, don't miss this colorful shop on a side street off of the main road leading from the Ponte Vecchio to Il Duomo. It offers one of the most complete assortments of *passamanterie,* which are tassels for keys and tieback curtains, drawer sachets, hand-embroidered cushions, and a dizzying collection of cords, ribbons, and fringes.

TELEPHONE: 055 284 493
FAX: 055 218 957
CREDIT CARDS: AE, DC, MC, V
HOURS: Mon–Fri 9 A.M.–7:30 P.M., Sat 10 A.M.–7:30 P.M.; closed 10 days in mid-Aug
ENGLISH: Yes

Gifts and Handicrafts

CARTOLERIA ECOLOGICAL LA TARTARUGA (78)
Borgo degli Albizi, 60r (Il Duomo)

This happy place sells an unusual selection of paper goods and hand-painted wooden toys to delight the child in all of us. Everything is made from natural ingredients, and all the paint is nontoxic. Prices are within every budget, even a child's.

TELEPHONE & FAX: 055 234 0845
CREDIT CARDS: DC, MC, V

HOURS: Mon 12:30–7:30 P.M., Tues–Sat 9:30 A.M.–7:30 P.M.
ENGLISH: Yes

CERTINI (147)
Via di San Niccolò, 2r (San Niccolò)

Walter Certini's name is already known to shoppers in the United States from Gump's in San Francisco and through the Horchow, Smithsonian, Bergdorf Goodman, and Neiman-Marcus catalogs. These references alone should tell you that this is very good merchandise. What is it? Beautifully crafted pieces made from painted wrought iron and metal. Walter is a master, and he has created everything from massive chandeliers to pieces of furniture, picture and mirror frames, light fixtures, wine carafes, candle-holders, and much, much more. You will just have to go to his combination studio/shop/factory and see for yourself. Walter is delightful, he will ship, and his English is excellent. He is not in the shop on Tuesday.

    TELEPHONE & FAX: 055 234 2694
    EMAIL: certini@tin.it
    CREDIT CARDS: MC, V
    HOURS: Mon–Fri 8 A.M.–noon, 3–6 P.M.; closed Aug
    ENGLISH: Yes

MANDRAGORA (65)
Piazza del Duomo, 50r (Il Duomo)

This is a treasure trove of local artists' work, copies of famous objects from Florentine museums, in addition to guidebooks, prints, catalogs, and art books, all under one roof for easy, one-stop shopping.

    TELEPHONE: 055 292 559
    FAX: 055 271 7800
    INTERNET: www.mandragora.it
    CREDIT CARDS: AE, DC, MC, V
    HOURS: Mon–Sat 10 A.M.–7:30 P.M., Sun 10:30 A.M.–6:30 P.M.
    ENGLISH: Yes

Gourmet Food and Wines

BOTTEGA DELLA FRUTTA (72)
Via dei Federighi, 31r (Piazza Goldoni)

Bottega della Frutta is sheer heaven if you appreciate fine fruits and vegetables. It is run by a friendly, outgoing husband and wife, Francesco and Elizabetta, who offer the bounty of Tuscany, and of the world, in their two-room shop piled high with the freshest, highest quality produce you are likely to see anywhere. Wines, olive oils, balsamic vinegar, cheese, Tuscan herbs, seasonings, and condiments . . . you name it, they have it. After two visits, you will feel like a regular. More important, you will be treated as one. On top of this, their prices are very fair, and Elizabetta speaks wonderful English, offers easy-to-follow recipes using their magnificent products, and rightfully says, "If we don't have what you want, it is to be 'discovered.'"

TELEPHONE: 055 239 8500
CREDIT CARDS: MC, V
HOURS: Mon–Tues, Thur–Sat 8 A.M.–7:30 P.M., Wed 8 A.M.–1:30 P.M.; closed Aug
ENGLISH: Yes

CHERUBINO (39)
Via Sant' Antonino, 4r (Piazza del Mercato Centrale)

Why is Cherubino better than scores of pasta shops like it in Florence? The hospitable owner, Maria, is the reason I shop here for fresh ravioli and her array of dried pastas in all shapes, sizes, and flavors. She also sells good olive oil, balsamic vinegar, limoncello, biscotti and *vin Santo,* and local wines.

TELEPHONE: 055 210 901
CREDIT CARDS: MC, V
HOURS: Mon, Thur–Sun 10 A.M.–8 P.M., Tues–Wed 3–8 P M.; closed July 10 Aug 10
ENGLISH: Yes

FIASCHETTERIA ZANODINI (55)
Via Sant'Antonino, 47r (Piazza del Mercato Centrale)

If you are a wine buff, this is a reqired stop in Florence. The mind-boggling selection of wines includes wines from their own vineyards, including a fine Chianti Classico. The owner is very knowledgeable and will spend time with each customer. Also available are grappas, old Italian liqueurs, and limoncello.

TELEPHONE: 055 239 6850
FAX: 055 296 708
EMAIL: zanovini@tin.it
INTERNET: Lelame.com
HOURS: Mon–Sat 8:15A.M.–2 P.M., 3:30–8 P.M.; closed Sun
ENGLISH: Yes

LA BOTTEGA DELL' OLIO (110)
Piazza del Limbo, 2r (Ponte Vecchio)

The shop is located on a tiny square, next to S.S. Apostoli Church, one of the oldest in Florence and the place where the Easter Day parade starts. A visit to La Bottega dell' Olio is a very pleasant education in the joys of olive oil. Almost everything in the pretty shop has something to do with olives or olive oil, and owner Andrea will patiently explain the virtues of his large stock of extra-virgin olive oils or let you browse to your heart's content. I like the olive-motif kitchen linens, his olive oil–based skin care products and soaps (ask about *sa di sapone*), olivewood cooking and serving implements, and wonderful array of flavored vinegars, including carob, honey, fig, and of course, raspberry. Best of all you can taste before you buy.

TELEPHONE & FAX: 055 267 0468
INTERNET: www.labottegadellolio.it

CREDIT CARDS: DC, MC, V
HOURS: Mon–Sat 10 A.M.–7 P.M.
ENGLISH: Yes

Hats

GREVI (71)
Via della Spada, 115r (Piazza Goldoni)

Grevi hats and bags are sold at Neiman-Marcus, Bloomingdales, Barney's, and Saks Fifth Avenue at three times the price you will pay in Florence. Their hats are all handmade and can be sized to fit. The personnel is willing to take as much time as necessary to see that you walk out with a wonderful hat.

TELEPHONE: 055 876 223
FAX: 055 873 2053
INTERNET: www.grevi.com
CREDIT CARDS: AE, DC, MC, V
HOURS: Tues–Sat 10 A.M.–7:30 P.M.
ENGLISH: Usually

Jewelry

ANGELA CAPUTI (111)
Borgo Santi Apostoli, 44/46 (Ponte Vecchio)

The striking jewelry is all designed by Angela Caputi and sold exclusively in her shop in Florence, which is overseen by her sister, Paola. Whenever I wear one of her designs, I am always asked, "Where did you find that wonderful necklace (or that marvelous pin or beautiful earrings)?" The prices are reasonable when you consider you are getting one-of-a-kind pieces that you will wear and love for years. She also sells a line of clothing designed to complement her stunning jewelry.

TELEPHONE: 055 292 993
FAX: 055 211 315
EMAIL: angelacaputi@hotmail.com
INTERNET: www.angelacaputi.com
CREDIT CARDS: AE, DC, MC, V
HOURS: Mon 3:30–7:30 P.M., Tues–Sat 10 A.M.–1 P.M., 3:30–7:30 P.M.
ENGLISH: Yes

THE GOLD CORNER (121)
Piazza Santa Croce, 15r (Piazza Santa Croce)

The gold here is sold by weight, which makes it work out to be slightly less expensive. In addition to their huge selection of gold jewelry, which fits almost every budget and taste, I like the Roman bronze coins set in 18-carat gold (certificate of authenticity included) and the white or yellow gold necklace scarves that sell here for much less than they do at Tiffany's.

Many of the designs are exclusive to this shop. A 20 percent discount is given for payment with cash or traveler's checks; 15 percent for credit cards; and an additional 12 percent is taken off for the IVA (see page 332).

TELEPHONE: 055 241 971
FAX: 055 247 8437
EMAIL: goldcorner@fol.it
CREDIT CARDS: AE, DC, MC, V
HOURS: Winter: Tues–Sat 9 A.M.–6 P.M.; summer: daily 9 A.M.–7:30 P.M.
ENGLISH: Yes

I FALSI GIOJELLI (34)
Via de' Ginori, 36r (Piazza del Mercato Centrale)

For great costume jewelry that is affordable, unusual, wearable, and great fun, pick up a piece or two of the imaginative baubles designed by the owner, Sylvia, and made here with a combination of plexiglass, buttons, colored string, and hemp chord.

TELEPHONE: 055 287 237
EMAIL: falsigioielli@yahoo.it
CREDIT CARDS: MC, V
HOURS: Mon–Sat 10 A.M.–7:30 P.M.; closed Sun, middle 2 weeks in Aug
ENGLISH: Yes

MARIELLA INNOCENTI (108)
Loggo del Mercato Nuovo, 32, across from Straw Market (Il Duomo)

If you can't bring yourself, or your pocketbook, to spend serious money in the Ponte Vecchio jewelry shops, just keep going north on Via Por Santa Maria until you come to this treasure trove of fabulous fakes, which cost a mere fraction of the high-priced spread on the bridge. The quality and selection are impressive, especially the copies of pins from the forties and fifties and those worn by the Duchess of Windsor and Jackie Kennedy.

TELEPHONE: 055 239 8531
FAX: 055 264 6063
CREDIT CARDS: AE, DC, MC, V
HOURS: Daily 9:30 A.M.–7:30 P.M.
ENGLISH: Yes

SEZIONE AUREA (139)
Via Guicciardini, 49r (Pitti Palace)

This shop offers a beautiful selection of handmade, hand-painted, Florentine Renaissance–inspired fiberglass jewelry at affordable prices. These are one-of-a-kind pieces you will not see back home.

Second location: Via dei Servi, 46r (43, Piazza della SS. Annunziata); Tel: 055 239 6143; Hours: Mon–Sat 10:30 A.M.–1:30 P.M., 3:30–7:30 P.M., Sun 10:30 A.M.–1:30 P.M., closed 15 days in Aug.

TELEPHONE & FAX: 055 288 132

EMAIL: sezione.aurea@inwind.it
CREDIT CARDS: AE, DC, MC, V
HOURS: Daily 10:30 A.M.–7:30 P.M.
ENGLISH: Depends on sales personnel

Leather

When shopping for leather, many tourists head for the shops that line Borgo dei Greci off Piazza Santa Croce or to a stall at the Straw Market or San Lorenzo Market. As far as I'm concerned, there is more junk than quality at these places, so shop carefully, because after a while it all blurs together.

FURLA (88)
Via Calzaiuoli, 47r (Il Duomo)

Furla is fabulous for well-priced handbags and color-coordinated accessories geared to fashion-conscious, young-at-heart women. The quality is high, and the prices in Italy are much lower than they are in the States. They have franchises in Rome, Venice, and major cities worldwide. In Florence, there is a second, smaller location at Via della Vigna Nuova, 28r (76, Piazza Goldoni); Tel: 055 282 779.
   TELEPHONE: 055 238 2883
   CREDIT CARDS: AE, DC, MC, V
   HOURS: Daily 10 A.M.–7:30 P.M.
   ENGLISH: Yes

MADANI (122)
Lungarno Acciaiuoli, 28r (Ponte Vecchio)

I am a big fan of this company's attractive leather handbags, belts, and small accessories, which are all exclusive to this boutique.
   TELEPHONE: 055 294 650
   FAX: 055 265 6292
   EMAIL: madanisrl@virgilio.it
   CREDIT CARDS: AE, DC, MC, V
   HOURS: Mon–Sat 9 A.M.–7 P.M.; closed Sun, 2 weeks mid-Aug
   ENGLISH: Yes

MADOVA GLOVES (138)
Via Guicciardini, 1r (Pitti Palace)

This shop, in business since 1919, sells only leather gloves made in its factory, which is the only one in Florence. The quality is unsurpassed. They can make a pair of gloves from the tracing of a hand, or for hands that are difficult to fit. The gloves come in every type of leather and color and are lined in cashmere, silk, sheepskin, or wool. Believe it or not, they are handwashable. The company prints directions in which the six easy washing steps are pictured and written in English. You could not possibly go wrong. The prices in the catalog (sent free of charge or on the Internet) include shipping.

TELEPHONE: 055 239 6526
FAX: 055 210 204
INTERNET: www.madova.com
CREDIT CARDS: AE, MC, V
HOURS: Mon–Sat 9:30 A.M.–7:30 P.M.; closed Sun
ENGLISH: Yes

PAOLO CARANDINI (99)
73, Via de' Macci (Piazza Santa Croce)

Paolo Carandini uses contemporary, clean lines in designing his unusual boxes, frames, bags, desk accessories, and folders, which come in vibrant shades of yellow, orange, and bright red leather. If you buy one of his leather-covered boxes because you love it, you put your fantasy inside.

TELEPHONE: 055 245 379
FAX: 055 400 570
EMAIL: paolocarandini@hotmail.com
CREDIT CARDS: MC, V
HOURS: Mon–Sat 9 A.M.–1 P.M., 3–7:30 P.M.; closed Sun
ENGLISH: Yes

SCUOLA DEL CUOIO (THE LEATHER SCHOOL) (118)
Piazza Santa Croce, 16r (Piazza Santa Croce)

Bags, belts, boxes, briefcases, frames, loads of little gifty items, handbags, suitcases, and more are sold at this commercially run leather store in the old dormitory of the Franciscan monastery, next to the sacristy of Santa Croce Church. You can also enter through the garden behind the church, at Via Giuseppe, 5. The Leather School was founded by the friars at the end of World War II to renew the tradition of leather tooling and gilding, which had been done centuries earlier at the monastery. Everything is still made on the premises and can be customized or personalized. The first American shopper was General Dwight D. Eisenhower, who ordered things from here. Since then, they have designed a bag for Diana, Princess of Wales, and the Emperor of Japan. Some of the smaller merchandise can be shopworn, so look over several pieces of the same item before you buy it. They also have an Internet catalog and can ship worldwide. Staff attitude and customer service have improved.

TELEPHONE: 055 244 533/4
FAX: 055 248 0337
INTERNET: www.leatherschool.it
CREDIT CARDS: AE, DC, MC, V
HOURS: Winter: Tues–Sat 9:30 A.M.–12:30 P.M., 3:30–6 P.M.; summer: daily 9:30 A.M.–6 P.M.
ENGLISH: Yes

TADDEI (91)
Via S. Margherita, 11r (Il Duomo)

The third-generation, family-run Taddei leather workshop is recognized as one of Florence's finest. Just one of Simone Taddei's leather boxes takes fifteen days to make, requiring thirty-two steps from start to finish. As you can see, this is handcrafting at its best, and the privilege of ownership is the high-quality box that displays no designs...it stands alone in its perfection and purity. You will find this workshop tucked in an alley across from Dante's church.

TELEPHONE & FAX: 055 23 98 960
CREDIT CARDS: AE, MC, V
HOURS: Mon–Fri 8:10 A.M.–7:45 P.M., Sat 8:10 A.M.–7 P.M.; closed Sun
ENGLISH: Yes

Linens

LE TELLERIE TOSCANE (144)
Sdrucciolo dè Pitti, 15r (Pitti Palace)

Tuscan textiles, with country themes and fine Renaissance motifs, are reproduced by this wonderful family-owned textile company. Their shop displays luxurious jacquard table linens, matelassè bedding in American sizes, and 1,000-thread-count, pretty, and easy-to-pack kitchen towels and accessories. Prices are moderate, considering the exceptional quality. Other shops are in Siena and Cortona. They will ship fabric samples, and you can order directly.

TELEPHONE & FAX: 055 216 177
EMAIL: ttt@ttt-firenze.it
CREDIT CARDS: AE, DC, MC, V
HOURS: June–Sept: Mon–Fri 10 A.M.–1:30 P.M., 2:30–7 P.M.; in Sept–June closed Sun–Mon, open Sat; closed Aug 10–31, one week in winter (dates vary)
ENGLISH: Yes

Markets

In this section are Florence's markets, antique, food, flea, and otherwise. There are no telephone numbers to call, English is limited, and even when you can find a seller who takes credit cards (and few do), you will always get a better deal with cash. In addition, always be on the alert for pickpockets.

FORTEZZA ANTIQUARIA (5)
Piazza della Indipendenza

From September through June, on the third Saturday and Sunday of the month, this is a large antiques market. The quality is good, and the sellers are there rain or shine. No market is held in July or August.

HOURS: Third Sat–Sun of month, 9 A.M.–7 P.M.

MERCATO CENTRALE DE SAN LORENZO (SAN LORENZO CENTRAL MARKET) (28)
Piazza del Mercato Centrale

A visit to this colorful indoor market is a required experience, even if you aren't a foodie. Two floors display every type of edible you can imagine. On the ground floor are stands selling meat and fish, cheese, baked goods, household items, groceries, wines, olive oils, spices, and Tuscan gourmet items that make great gifts. There are places to grab a cappuccino and a pastry with the sellers if you arrive early, or eat a sandwich washed down with a beer or a glass of sturdy red wine. Upstairs you will find stand after stand of fruits and vegetables. Around the outside, hundreds of vendors hawk leather, Florentine paper goods, scarves, umbrellas, bags, T-shirts—you name it. The prices outside are sometimes negotiable. Always watch for quality and hope the seller is honest. Stand No. 4 has fake Gucci scarves. This entire shopping experience is part of a trip to Florence. Plan to come for the morning and have lunch at the sandwich stall in the market or at one of the nearby trattorias (see *Great Eats Italy*).

HOURS: Indoor food market: Mon–Sat 7 A.M.–1 P.M.; outside stalls: daily 9:30 A.M.–7 P.M., in winter Tues–Sat 10 A.M.–6 P.M.

MERCATO DELLA CASCINE (47)
Cascine Park (western edge of Florence)

If you can eat it, wear it, water it, feed it, or dust it, chances are it is for sale at the Mercato della Cascine. This weekly outdoor market on Viale Lincoln along the Arno River is a mix of outdoor food stands and endless clothing and houseware stalls pitching everything from aprons to underwear. It is very local, as most tourists don't venture out this far. Go early for the best selection. Maybe you will get lucky and unearth a great bargain, as I did when I found cashmere turtleneck sweater for $15. I should have bought every one they had, because an hour after I bought mine, the pile was reduced to one lone chartreuse number with a hole in the sleeve. Watch your wallets and purses, and take your own shopping bags. Few sellers speak English. If you don't feel like walking, hop on Buses 1, 9, or 12. Otherwise, walk west along the Arno on Lungarno Amerigo Vespucci to the Piazza Della Vittoria Veneto and follow the crowd.

HOURS: Tues 7 A.M.–1 P.M., but most stalls don't get really going until 8 A.M.

MERCATO DELLE PULCI (97)
Piazza del Ciompi (Piazza Santa Croce)

On the last Sunday of the month, a large antique market with over one hundred sellers sets up hawking everything from old postcards and prints to genuine antiques and collectables small enough to tuck into a suitcase. During the week regular dealers open their doors along a block-long row of permanent covered stalls. Forget them. The quality is terrible, and the prices are ridiculous.

HOURS: Varies by stall; usually Tues–Sat 10 A.M.–1 P.M., 3–6 or 7 P.M., last Sun of month 9 A.M.–6 P.M.

MERCATO DI SANTO SPIRITO (135)
Piazza Santo Spirito (Pitti Palace)

On the second Sunday of the month, it's a combination hippie flea market, flower market, organic food market, and general junk sale. On the third Sunday, it is a biological market, with lots of ethnic crafts. It might be worth your time if you are a swap-meet fan, or if you want a change of pace. Plan on lunch at one of the restaurants around the piazza (see *Great Eats Italy*). There is also a dry goods and small produce and flower market on the piazza during the week, but the quality is spotty.

HOURS: Tues–Sat 8–11 A.M.; second Sun of month 10 A.M.–7 P.M.; third Sun 9 A.M.–4 P.M.; no Sun markets in Aug

MERCATO NUOVO (STRAW MARKET) (107)
Loggia del Mercato Nuovo, Via Por Santa Maria (Il Duomo)

When I first came to Florence years ago, this was a bargain paradise. Not anymore. Although you can find some straw products (chiefly hats), most stalls sell the same things you can find at the San Lorenzo Central Market (see above) and for about the same price. They have the same fake designer bags, jewelry, linens, and tourist kitsch. The stall owners speak English and are not about to reduce their prices, but it is still worth a look. Be sure you touch the boar's nose in front and make a wish. It will bring you good luck, and may bring you back to Florence.

HOURS: Daily 9:30 A.M.–7 P.M., sometimes later in summer

MERCATO SANT' AMBROGIO (98)
Piazza Sant' Ambrogio, at Piazza Ghiberti (Piazza Santa Croce)

This is a lively indoor/outdoor neighborhood market selling to the locals. If you patronize a stall three or four times, you will be treated just like one of the natives. Here you will find all the same meats, fish, dairy products, fruits, and vegetables found at the Mercato Centrale, but at slightly lower prices. The flower stalls are much better here, especially the selection of seasonal plants and blooms. The Tavola Calda da Rocco across from the coffee bar is a great place for lunch. The dry-goods stalls outside have some worthwhile buys in cotton underwear and socks. The best day to go is Saturday.

HOURS: Mon–Sat 7 A.M.–1 P.M.

Outlet Stores (Outside Florence)

I have gone on this shopping safari using three modes of transportation: with a private car and driver; by train, taxi, and foot; and finally by air-conditioned bus. Believe me, the bus is fast, efficient, cheap, and easy. After all, you need to save your strength and money for shopping! One of the best bus tours is run by Caf Tour and Travel. The trips run year-round on Monday, Tuesday, Friday, and Saturday; they pick you up and drop you off by the train station and give you plenty of time to go broke. There are two choices:

a Gucci and Prada Outlets tour lasts five hours and costs 20€, and a second tour includes Gucci, Prada, Fendi, and Dolce & Gabbana, lasts nine hours, and costs 27€. One warning: When you book, make sure you get a paid receipt and that your name is on the printed list for the day and time you are going. If you're not on the printed list, you might not get a seat.

Caf Tour & Travel (38): Via S. Antonino, 6r (Train Station); Tel: 055 283 200, 055 210 612; Fax: 055 238 2790; Internet: www.caftours.com.

THE MALL/GUCCI
Via Europa 8, 50066 Leccio-Reggello

Would you be interested in a Gucci handbag, pair of shoes, golf bag, dog frisbee and matching leash, bobsled (no kidding!), or wonderful accessory for 30 to 50 percent less than you will pay in the main shop in Florence? If the answer is yes, all this and more is yours at the Gucci outlet mall about a forty-five minute drive from Florence. Don't forget to stop at the IVA tax refund desk on your way out (see page 332). Other designer outlets here include Salvatore Ferragamo, Veneta Bottega, Valentino, La Perla, Tod's/Hogan, Ungaro, Armani, and more. There is a nice *caffè*/bar where your nonshopping pals can hang out until the Caf Tour bus is ready to leave.

TELEPHONE: 055 865 7001, 055 861 7007

FAX: 055 865 7149

INTERNET: www.gucci.com

CREDIT CARDS: AE, DC, MC, V

HOURS: Mon–Sat 10 A.M.–7 P.M., Sun 3–7 P.M. (hours can vary, call to check)

ENGLISH: Yes

PRADA
Localita Levanella, Montevarchi

Be still my shopping heart . . . I found a pair of the current season's Prada shoes for the equivalent of $59, the same ones I saw three months later on display in the shoe department of Neiman-Marcus for $289! I am still jumping for joy. That was just one of the drop-dead bargains I scooped up the day I shopped until I dropped at Prada. There are other brands besides Prada, such as MiuMiu, Jil Sander, and Helmut Lang. Saturday crowds can be lethal. Best time to go is on a weekday, another reason to take the afternoon Caf Tour bus. Once here, you can't just walk in. You have to take a number and wait until it is called; groups of ten are allowed to enter at mystery intervals. There is no place to sit while you wait, unless you plop down on the asphalt in front, sit in your car, or try and get a seat in the smoky *caffè*. But you have to be careful and not wander off or get distracted—if they call your number and you don't hear it, tough luck. You must go to the end of the line and start over. Be sure you bring an umbrella, since it could rain, as it did once for me. The good news is that once inside, you can stay as long as your shopping energy holds up, or until the bus leaves. The store is well laid out, and the drill is simple. You select your items, get another number, and present it at the checkout desk, where you pay, get your goodies, and go home one very happy shopper. Reminder: Don't forget the paperwork for the IVA tax refund; see page 332.

TELEPHONE: 055 91 901
CREDIT CARDS: AE, DC, MC, V
HOURS: Mon–Sat 9:30 A.M.–7:30 P.M., Sun 2–7:30 P.M.; last entrance at 7 P.M. (hours can vary, call ahead)
ENGLISH: Yes

Paper and Stationery

FANTASIE FLORENTINE (133)
Borgo Sant' Jacopo, 50r (Pitti Palace)

All of the gift items here are covered in marbleized paper by Eliana and her sister, Julia, who have been doing this for more than thirty years, twenty in this location. The prices are low and the selection limited, but it is a great source for gifts that are inexpensive, light, and easy to carry.

TELEPHONE: 055 210 436
CREDIT CARDS: None
HOURS: Mon–Fri 10:15 A.M.–6 P.M., Sat 10:15 A.M.–2:30 P.M., Sun 11 A.M.–2:30 P.M.; closed last half of Aug
ENGLISH: Yes

GIULIO GIANNINI & FIGLIO (143)
Piazza Pitti, 37r (Pitti Palace)

Six generations of the Giannini family have been creating marbleized paper in their factory/shop across from the Pitti Palace. No matter where you look in Florence, you will see marbleized paper, the origins of which can be traced back to this family, who were the first to produce it in 1856. Today, they are still at work upstairs turning out a variety of high-quality marbleized paper and leather goods, which are sold downstairs. Free morning appointments are taken two days in advance for small groups to visit their workshop.

TELEPHONE: 055 212 621
FAX: 055 28 83 29
INTERNET: www.giuliogiannini.it
CREDIT CARDS: AE, DC, MC, V
HOURS: Mon–Sat 9 A.M.–7:30 P.M., Sun until 6:30 P.M.; closed Sun in winter
ENGLISH: Yes

IL TORCHIO (141)
Via de' Bardi, 17r (San Niccolò)

Anna Anichini, who is now ably assisted by her daughter, is a true Florentine craftswoman and artist who works with marbleized paper and leather, two of Florence's specialties. All of her pieces are designed and made here in her workshop, which doubles as a showroom. Because everything is made here, she is able to offer some of the best prices and a wonderful selection. She does everything from photo frames to wedding and photo albums, diaries, address books, jewelry boxes, and papered pencils to match a covered scratch-paper holder. If you do not see what you want, she can make up sets to order. She is very friendly and easy to work with and offers fast service.

TELEPHONE: 055 234 2862
FAX: 055 263 9014
CREDIT CARDS: AE, DC, MC, V
HOURS: Mon–Fri 9 A.M.–7:30 P.M., Sat 9 A.M.–1 P.M.; closed Sun, 2 weeks in mid-Aug
ENGLISH: Yes

SCRIPTORIUM (53)
Via dei Servi, 5/7r (Il Duomo)

In this fast-paced, technology-driven world, some of us have not forgotten the joys of a beautifully accessorized desk. Scriptorium has everything for that beautiful desk, either at the office or at home. The luxurious leather-bound boxes, diaries, and specialized handmade writing papers are created by the owner, Fernando, and his wife. The prices are very reasonable when you compare the quality of this work to that of most of the competition.

TELEPHONE: 055 211 804
FAX: 055 238 2681
INTERNET: www.scriptoriumfirenze.com
CREDIT CARDS: AE, DC, MC, V
HOURS: Mon–Sat 10 A.M.–2 P.M., 3:30–7:30 P.M.
ENGLISH: Yes

Prints

L'IPPOGRIFO (132)
Via di Santo Spirito, 5r (Pitti Palace)

This interesting shop (with no outside sign), not far from the Ponte Vecchio, makes and sells beautiful, original etchings engraved by hand on copperplate and printed one at a time without mechanical processes and colored in watercolors. The technique is the same artisans have been using for five hundred years. Everything is guaranteed, numbered, and signed by Gianni Raffaelli, the artist.

TELEPHONE & FAX: 055 213 255
INTERNET: www.stameippogrifo.com
CREDIT CARDS: AE, DC, MC, V
HOURS: Mon 4–7:30 P.M., Tues–Fri 10 A.M.–1 P.M., 3–7:30 P.M.
ENGLISH: Yes

Shipping

MAIL BOXES ETC. (51)
Via Della Scala, 13r (Piazza Santa Maria Novella)

If you can't take it with you, give those bulky purchases to Caroline Lauder and her friendly, English-speaking crew and let them wrap and send everything for you...including suitcases, which are bubble-wrapped for extra protection. They will provide you with packing materials, pack for you, prepare customs documents, and provide a tracking number. Other services include Western Union, sending and receiving faxes, and photocopies.

Florence has another Mail Boxes Etc.: Via San Gallo, 26r; Tel: 055 463 0418. However, I know from personal experience how competent Caroline is and how satisfied I was with the services she provided.

TELEPHONE: 055 268 173
FAX: 055 212 852
EMAIL: mbe212@mbe.it
INTERNET: www.mbe.it
CREDIT CARDS: MC, V
HOURS: Mon–Fri 9 A.M.–1 P.M., 3:30–7 P.M.
ENGLISH: Yes

Shopping Streets and Areas

Almost every street and area in Florence has interesting shops of some sort. This very short list is only meant to get you started. I encourage you to wander about and discover your own special Florentine shopping finds.

BORGO LA CROCE (82, PIAZZA SANTA CROCE)

This is an interesting street in that it is filled with the type of shops Florentines frequent in their day-to-day lives. One of the most interesting is Mesticheria Mazzanti at Borgo la Croce, 101r, a hardware/household store stocking everything for your home with the exception of linens and furniture. On Saturday morning you can't squeeze down the aisles. Also on the street are branches of Blunauta (see page 338) and Dr. Vranjes—Antica Officina del Farmacista (see page 339).

VIA DE' CALZAIUOLI (85, IL DUOMO)

This crowded pedestrianized stretch of retail opportunities includes a Disney store.

VIA DELLA CONDOTTA (105, IL DUOMO)

This interesting collection of stores includes stamp dealers, print shops, bookstores, one shop devoted to artistic lampshades and wastepaper baskets, and another selling weird herbal concoctions.

VIA DE' SERRAGLI (128, PITTI PALACE)

This area between Santo Spirito and San Frediano is very local, filled with age-old workshops run for decades by furniture restorers. Antique shops line Via de' Serragli and the side streets surrounding it.

VIA DE' TORNABUONI (101, PIAZZA GOLDONI)

This is the premier shopping street in Florence, with all the big-name international designers. If you have young children or are a doting grandparent, be sure to see the Loretta Caponi shop that sells the most magnificent children's clothes this side of heaven, and with equally high prices. Side streets worth strolling are Via della Vigna Nuova, Via delle Spada, and Via delle Sole.

VIA GUICCIARDINI AND BORGO SANT' JACOPO (142, 134, PITTI PALACE)

Via Guicciardini continues after the Ponte Vecchio and leads to the Pitti Palace and Boboli Gardens. Naturally almost every tourist hits this section of Florentine pavement and encounters the shops along it. In front of the Pitti Palace, local artists of varying abilities sell their paintings. Just across the bridge, parallel to the river, is Borgo Sant' Jacopo, another prime shopping territory.

Shopping in Rome

Rome is not the shopper's paradise you will find in Milan, Florence, and Venice. There are many beautiful shops, but the prices are very high, unless you are lucky enough to be in Rome during the twice-yearly sales that take place from around mid-January to the end of February and again in July through August. For the best buys, look for leather, knits, jewelry, and shoes. If you want religious items, head for Via Conciliazone, which leads to St. Peter's Square. Leather goods used to be available for next to nothing at street markets. Today, cheap leather is just that: cheap. Be sure that any leather you buy is stamped *vero cuoio,* a sign that means the leather is real, not imitation.

An occasional visitor to Rome never makes it to the Vatican at all, but no one misses the Piazza di Spagna (Spanish Steps). This is the heart of the city's best shopping, where deluxe boutiques and big-name designers beckon crowds to admire and buy, especially during the sales, when shoppers snap up $150 silk scarves as if they were napkins. Just two blocks from these shops is Via Frattina, where you will find the same high-quality merchandise, but the designer names are not as famous and the prices are slightly less. Great Chic shoppers will like the neighborhoods around Campo de' Fiori and the winding, narrow streets of Trastevere. Less-expensive shops are across the Tiber on Via Cola di Rienzo and Via Ottaviano, but you will get what you pay for here, as the quality is not always tops. Dedicated bargain hunters will want to check out the Sunday morning flea market at Trastevere, but don't expect to find any hidden bargains... go for the fun of it, and if you find something you like and want, all the better. If you are looking for knock-off designer bags and accessories, follow Ponte Sant' Angelo across the Tiber River all the way to Via Conciliazone, a route lined with hawkers touting their wares. Look carefully before you buy because the quality can vary greatly. Don't pay the first quoted price; bargaining is part of the game plan. The shopping possibilities in Rome listed below are only meant to get you started. There is much more, and I predict that after an hour or so on the job, you will be off on your own, discovering all sorts of wonderful places.

Shopping Hours

Shopping times in Rome are hardly set in stone and are subject to change according to the whims of shop owners. During August, the closings can range from a week to a month, so if you are going to a specific shop, it is always wise to call ahead before making the trip and finding it *chiuso per ferie* (closed for holiday). Department stores and a growing number of shops on the tourist trails stay open nonstop throughout the day, during August, and on Sundays. The following hours are for small shops.

WINTER: (Oct–June): Mon 3:30–7:30 P.M., Tues–Sat 9:30 A.M.–1 P.M., 3:30–7:30 P.M.

SUMMER: (June–Sept): Mon–Fri 9 A.M.–1 P.M., 4–8 P.M., Sat 9 A.M.–1 P.M.

FOOD SHOPS: Mon–Wed, Fri–Sat 8:30 A.M.–1 P.M., 5–7:30 P.M., Thur 8:30 A.M.–1 P.M. These hours are observed year-round.

HOLIDAYS: If a holiday falls during the week, many shops stay open on Monday and close on the holiday, but this does not apply to food shops.

TYPES OF SHOPS IN ROME

Bookstores

THE ALMOST CORNER BOOKSHOP (81)
Via del Moro, 45 (Trastevere)

Dermot O'Connell's delightfully crowded Almost Corner Bookshop is a well-known fixture in Trastevere. The shop specializes in worldwide fiction in English and in Italian literature translated into English. At least 11,000 books are in inventory at any time, but on the off chance they do not have what you want, it will be ordered.

TELEPHONE & FAX: 06 583 6942

EMAIL: almostcorner@libero.it

CREDIT CARDS: AE, MC, V

HOURS: Mon–Sat 10 A.M.–1:30 P.M., 3:30–8 P.M., Sun 11 A.M.–1:30 P.M., 3:30–8 P.M.; closed Sun in Aug

ENGLISH: Yes

ANCORA BOOKSHOP (45)
Via della Conciliazione, 63 (The Vatican)

This Catholic bookshop also sells some of the better religious souvenirs. Look upstairs for the English-language titles.

TELEPHONE: 06 687 7202, 06 53 49 630

FAX: 06 683 3050

EMAIL: libreria.roma@ancora-libri.it

CREDIT CARDS: AE, DC, MC, V
HOURS: Mon–Fri 9 A.M.–7 P.M., Sat 9 A.M.–12:45 P.M.
ENGLISH: Generally

ANGLO AMERICAN BOOKSHOP (40)
Via della Vite, 27 (Piazza di Spagna)

This English-language bookshop is loaded with guidebooks, art histories, architecture books, and paperback fiction. The prices are high, but the selection is good.

TELEPHONE: 06 679 5222
FAX: 06 678 3890
INTERNET: www.aab.it
CREDIT CARDS: AE, MC, V
HOURS: Winter: Mon 3:30–7:30 P.M., Tues–Sat 10 A.M.–7:30 P.M.; summer (July–Sept): Mon–Fri 10 A.M.–7:30 P.M., Sat 10 A.M.–2 P.M.; closed 2 weeks mid-Aug
ENGLISH: Yes

ECONOMY BOOK AND VIDEO CENTER (114)
Via Torino, 136 (Train Station Area)

The Goldfield family runs a great bookshop. Bring in your used English-language books, and you will receive store credit toward your purchases. If you are in Rome for any length of time and love to read, then you might be interested in renting hardback best-sellers (10.33€ deposit, plus 2.50€ weekly fee). There is a wide selection of cards, children's books, videotapes, books on tape, travel books, and some local art and crafts.

TELEPHONE: 06 474 6877
FAX: 06 483 661
EMAIL: books@booksitaly.com
INTERNET: www.fineideas.it
CREDIT CARDS: AE, DC, MC, V
HOURS: Mon–Sat 9 A.M.–8 P.M.
ENGLISH: Yes

THE ENGLISH BOOKSHOP (5)
Via di Ripetta, 248 (Piazza del Popolo)

This is a small bookshop specializing in English-language books on Italy and worldwide architecture and interior design. They also have some interesting handcrafts from Kenya.

TELEPHONE: 06 320 3301
FAX: 06 320 3300
EMAIL: theenglishbookshop@katamail.com
CREDIT CARDS: AE, DC, MC, V
HOURS: Mon 3:30–7:30 P.M., Tues–Sat 10 A.M.–7:30 P.M.; closed 2 weeks mid-Aug
ENGLISH: Yes

Clothing and Accessories

BLUNAUTA (33)
Piazza di Spagna, 35 (Piazza di Spagna)

A clothing store with many outlets in Italy, Blunauta (formerly Balloon) has good prices on tailored clothes for men and women, most of which are silk, designed in Italy and made in China. This means you must look carefully for poor workmanship and flimsy silks. Items are color-coordinated, and it is easy to put together an outfit complete with accessories. Racks hold one piece in every style, and then you choose the color you want from a bin or wall display. I have two words to say about most of the clothes: they wrinkle. To keep the stock looking its best in this store, two full-time ironing ladies are employed.

To find the store, look for the hot-air balloon hanging over the rear courtyard entrance, about two doors down on the left side of the American Express office. There are benches in the courtyard for your nonshopping companions, or they can look for step space and join the crowds people-watching on the Spanish Steps. I am not even going to mention that one of the best McDonald's you will encounter is right here on the Piazza di Spagna.

For discounted Blunauta clothes, visit their stock shop near Campo de' Fiori, page 362.

TELEPHONE: 06 696 421
FAX: 06 6964 2388
CREDIT CARDS: AE, DC, MC, V
HOURS: Mon–Sun 9:30 A.M.–7:30 P.M.
ENGLISH: Yes

FFI–FATTA FABBRICA ITALIANA (25)
Via Vittoria, 53 (Piazza di Spagna)

I am a fan of FFI's wonderful, brightly colored, affordable bags made in durable materials. One of my favorites is the bright orange nylon canvas bag that unfolds from its two-inch-square size in my purse to a sturdy fourteen-inch-square shopping bag.

TELEPHONE: 06 691 90 882
INTERNET: www.ffitalia.it
CREDIT CARDS: AE, MC, V
HOURS: Mon 3:30 A.M.–7:30 P.M.; Tues–Sat 10:30 A.M.–7:30 P.M.
ENGLISH: Yes

IL BACO DA SETA (26)
Via Vittoria, 75 (Piazza di Spagna)

The 100 percent natural fabric linens, cottons, silks, and cashmeres are custom designed and made into beautiful, comfortable outfits you will wear and enjoy long after you have recovered from sticker shock. To ease this, go in January and July when the merchandise is on sale.

TELEPHONE & FAX: 06 67 93 907
EMAIL: baco.seta@tiscali.it
CREDIT CARDS: AE, DC, MC, V
HOURS: Mon 3:30–7:30 P.M., Tues–Sat 10 A.M.–2 P.M., 3:30–7:30 P.M.;
closed Aug 15–25
ENGLISH: Yes

LARA (29)
Via delle Carrozze, 21 (Piazza di Spagna)
Sweet dreams are yours when wearing one of the luscious nightgowns from Lara. Don't overlook the lacy lingerie, high-thread-count sheets, towels, and table linens. Sale prices can be inspiring.
TELEPHONE: 06 678 24 72
CREDIT CARDS: AE, DC, MC, V
HOURS: Daily 10 A.M.–8 P.M.; closed mid-August, call to check dates
ENGLISH: Yes

Cosmetics and Perfumes

OFFICINA PROFUMO FARMACEUTICA DI SANTA MARIA NOVELLA (60)
Corso Rinascimento, 47/49 (Piazza Navona)
This is a branch of the famous Florentine company, which does not sell pharmaceuticals but natural cosmetics and perfumes. The staff here is exceptionally helpful. For details, see page 340.
TELEPHONE: 06 687 2446, 06 686 9498
FAX: 06 687 9472, 06 686 9586
CREDIT CARDS: AE, DC, MC, V
HOURS: Mon–Sat 9:30 A.M.–7:30 P.M.
ENGLISH: Yes

Department Stores

COIN (18)
Via Cola di Rienzo, 173 (The Vatican)
This is the K-Mart of Italy, with clothing for the whole family, a small cosmetics department, housewares, a basement supermarket, and a great toilet on the second floor. There is another very nice Coin department store (no cosmetics or supermarket) on Piazza Alessandria, in a nontouristy, up-market neighborhood north of the Train Station.
TELEPHONE: 06 324 3319
CREDIT CARDS: AE, MC, V
HOURS: Mon–Sat 10A.M.–8 P.M., Sun 10:30 A.M.–8 P.M.
ENGLISH: Yes

LA RINASCENTE (55)
Via del Corso, 189 (Trevi Fountain)
By American standards, this is a very small store, but it is the best department store game in town. Ask for the Hostess Tourist Service, which will help you locate what you want to buy. Don't forget to get the IVA (tax rebate) if you spend 160€ or more (see page 332).

TELEPHONE: 06 679 7691
FAX: 06 679 6886
CREDIT CARDS: AE, DC, MC, V
HOURS: Mon–Sat 9:30 A.M.–10 P.M., Sun 10:30 A.M.–8 P.M.
ENGLISH: Yes, depends on clerk

STANDA/OVIESSE (85)
Viale di Trastevere, 60 (Trastevere)
Oviesse is a far cry from fashionable, but it is fun to look at what the average Italian buys. Every once in a while you will find something great . . . especially in the underwear department. The basement supermarket (Standa) is good, especially the cheese and deli sections.

Two other branches of this department store/supermarket are located near the Vatican (on Via Cola di Rienzo) and at Viale Regina Margherita, on the outskirts of Rome.

TELEPHONE: 06 589 5342
CREDIT CARDS: AE, DC, MC, V
HOURS: Mon–Sat 8:30 A.M.–8 P.M., Sun 9:30 A.M.–1:30 P.M., 4–8 P.M.
ENGLISH: Limited

UPIM (50)
Via del Tritone, 172 (Trevi Fountain)
This store sells utilitarian housewares and clothing, a few with a hint of style, plus basic cosmetics. Handy to know about in a pinch.

TELEPHONE: 06 678 3336
CREDIT CARDS: AE, DC, MC, V
HOURS: Mon–Sat 9 A.M.–8 P.M., Sun 10 A.M.–8 P.M.
ENGLISH: Limited

Discount Shopping

BLUNAUTA STOCK HOUSE (71)
Via dei Chiavari, Largo del Pallaro19a (Campo de' Fiori)
End-of-season clothes and household accessories can be found here at dramatically lower prices than what you will pay at the Piazza di Spagna store. There are lots of boxes and bins, each one priced and some sorted according to size, so be ready to dig for your treasures.

TELEPHONE: 06 687 6671
CREDIT CARDS: MC, V
HOURS: Mon 3:30 A.M.–7:30 P.M., Tues–Sat 9:30 A.M.–7:30 P.M.
ENGLISH: Limited

DRESS AGENCY (8)
Via del Vantaggio, 1-B (Piazza del Popolo)
The shop attracts women who want to dress well and spend less for designer clothes that are barely worn. It probably is not worth a taxi trip across Rome, but if you are in the neighborhood, it is worth a look. The clothes are reasonably current, in good condition, and fairly priced. They also carry shoes (three-and-a-half-inch stilettos, anyone?) and bags. Look for such drawing cards as Valentino, Versace, Armani, Gucci, and Prada, plus lots of minor designers.

TELEPHONE: 06 321 0898
CREDIT CARDS: AE, DC, MC, V
HOURS: Mon 4–7:30 P.M., Tues–Sat 10 A.M.–1 P.M., 4–7:30 P.M.; closed Aug
ENGLISH: Yes

IL DISCOUNT DELL'ALTA MODE (11)
Via Gesù e Maria, 14/16-A (Piazza del Popolo)
This must be the last-chance spot to buy dated, shopworn overstocks of designer labels such as Giorgio Armani, Jean-Paul Gaultier, and Claude Montana at about 50 to 70 percent off. The selection and quality varies, but it seems better at the men's store two doors down at No. 14. If you are in the neighborhood, give it five minutes. Who knows? You may hit pay dirt.

TELEPHONE: 06 361 3796
CREDIT CARDS: MC, V
HOURS: Mon 2:30–7:30 P.M., Tues–Sat 10A.M.–7:30 P.M.
ENGLISH: Yes

LEONE LIMENTANI (78)
Via del Portico di Ottavia, 47 (Jewish Quarter)
This is a huge discounted china store selling almost every pattern known at discounts ranging from a few cents to big bucks. The displays of Wedgewood, Richard Ginori, Lalique, and Baccarat are what you would expect in any major department store, but the rest is not for the delicate shopper clad in pastels. Most of it is stacked on shelves in a big, dirty, dusty barnlike space; clerks are scarce; and you must do the searching on your own. Bring gloves and a rag to wipe the dust off the plates to see if there are any defects. If you are trying to match a specific pattern, bring a small item of it. In addition to china, look for crystal, silver, pots, pans, and kitchenware. Plan on one hour just to case the store, then go back and make your selection. It is a good place to fill in your own china pattern, but don't forget to calculate in shipping charges if you do not carry your purchases yourself. Unless you like long waits, try to avoid Saturdays when it is filled with prospective brides and grooms and with women who have finally convinced their husbands that they do need new china. When ready to buy, ask for an English-speaking clerk.

TELEPHONE: 06 6880 6686/6949
FAX: 06 689 2598

CREDIT CARDS: AE, DC, MC, V

HOURS: Mon 3:30–7:30 P.M., Tues–Sat 9 A.M.–1 P.M., 3:30–7 P.M.; closed Aug 6–27

ENGLISH: Yes

MAS (122)
Piazza Vittorio Emanuele (Train Station Area)

If you love Pic-n-Save or Tati in Paris and never pay retail, you are a candidate for Mas. There are bins and bins of clothes, shoes, suitcases, sundries, umbrellas, hats, scarves, some seriously ugly Dr. Martens, sweaters (even cashmere if you look hard enough!), fur coats, camouflage camping gear, bedding, zippers, and much more, for everyone from toddlers to seniors, at prices you won't believe. There are dressing rooms and clerks. It is all the luck of the draw. The first time I was here, it was a gold mine. The last time, I struck out. In between it has been worth the trek, if just from a curiosity standpoint.

If you approach on Via Carlo Alberto, you pass one fake jewelry and hair ornament shop after another. On the sidewalks around Mas are merchants with their wares displayed on sheets, which can be rolled up for quick getaways should the *polizia* come around. Clearly, this is not a Rodeo Drive shopping experience. This shopping excursion takes time and is recommended only for the hard-core Great Chic shopper. Your nonshopping mate/significant other will go absolutely crazy here. The square in front, Piazza Vittorio Emanuele, was the site of a huge outdoor market. The market has moved indoors (see page 369), just beyond the square, and in its place a neighborhood park has been built with benches and playground equipment for the children. However, please watch out for the gypsies who ply the area and swarm the market as it is about to close. They are fast and clever and can (and will if you are not careful) take your purse and wallet in a heartbeat.

TELEPHONE: 06 486 8078

CREDIT CARDS: MC, V

HOURS: Mon–Sat 9 A.M.–1 P.M., 3:45–7:30 P.M., Sun 10 A.M.–1 P.M., 3:45–7:30 P.M.

ENGLISH: Don't count on it

Gifts

AI MONASTERI (63)
Corso Rinascimento, 72 (Piazza Navona)

Ai Monasteri was established in 1892 and since that time has been managed by the Nardi family, who sell products made in Italian monasteries. They offer a variety of natural cosmetics, creams, and beauty products (including one to tone up the body and chest), wines, grappas, liqueurs, natural elixirs, jams, honey, extra virgin olive oil, vinegars, chocolates, essential oils, soaps, and more. The products are nicely displayed with English explanations of what they are made of, and in the case of the cosmetics, what miracles they will do for you. They also produce a catalog in English. The staff is personable, and the prices are reasonable.

TELEPHONE & FAX: 06 688 02783
INTERNET: www.monasteri.it
CREDIT CARDS: MC, V
HOURS: Mon–Sat 9 A.M.–7:30 P.M.; closed part of Aug, call to check
ENGLISH: Yes

Gourmet Food and Wines

BUCCONE (7)
Via di Rippeta, 19 (Piazza del Popolo)

Buccone has an amazing selection of wines, spirits, liqueurs, olive oils, and balsamic vinegars, all of which can be shipped to any address on the planet. Please see *Great Eats Italy* for a description of their wine bar and restaurant.

TELEPHONE & FAX: 06 361 2154
CREDIT CARDS: AE, DC, MC, V
HOURS: Mon–Thur 9 A.M.–8:30 P.M., Fri–Sat until midnight; closed Sun except in Dec.
ENGLISH: Yes

CASTRONI (21)
Via Cola di Rienzo, 190, 196, 198 (The Vatican)

Castroni is Rome's answer to Fauchon in Paris. It is a wonderland of regional specialties, plus they offer the largest selection of imported foods in Rome, which they will pack for you but not ship. A second store sells small bottles of olive oil, truffle oil, and different types of dried pastas that make great gifts to take home to lucky friends. It is located at Via Ottaviano, 55, at the corner of Via Germanico, 66; Tel: 06 3972 3279; Fax: 06 3972 3251.

TELEPHONE: 06 687 4383
FAX: 06 687 4382
INTERNET: www.castronigroup.it
CREDIT CARDS: MC, V
HOURS: Mon–Sat 8 A.M.–8 P.M.; closed few days mid-Aug (call to check)
ENGLISH: Yes

ENOTECA COSTANTINI (24)
Piazza Cavour, 16 (The Vatican)

If you are a serious wine lover and connoisseur, the Enoteca Costantini should be on your A-list. The shop is on two levels, the first of which is devoted to an expensive restaurant and a wine bar where you can happily munch your way through a variety of cheeses and bar snacks while drinking a glass or two of wines from Italy or from around the world. It also has shelf after shelf of distilled spirits and bins of bargain—and not-so-bargain—wines.

Downstairs is where the serious business of wine-tasting and wine selling takes place. Every Tuesday through Friday, the family holds wine-tasting seminars here amid rows of bottles of magnificent wines they have been collecting for thirty years. These tastings (held in Italian, unfortunately) are not for the casual tourist, but for real aficionados who pay 185€ for a visit to a winemaker and seven two-hour wine-tasting lessons, where four wines are tasted and discussed. However, anyone can buy their wines, which range from 3€ a bottle to more than 550€, or stand at the bar upstairs and enjoy a glass or two of a fine vintage.

TELEPHONE: 06 320 3575
FAX: 06 32 13 210
INTERNET: www.pierocostantini.it
CREDIT CARDS: AE, DC, MC, V
HOURS: Mon 4:30–8 P.M., Tues–Sat, 9 A.M.–1 P.M., 4:30–8 P.M.
ENGLISH: Yes

FRANCHI (20)
Via Cola di Rienzo, 204 (The Vatican)

A rival to Castroni, Franchi has a deli of your dreams, with wonderful antipasti and roast meats to make up gourmet picnics, fresh coffee ground to order at their coffee bar, and an enormous selection of ham, cheeses, and wines from all over Italy.

TELEPHONE: 06 686 4576
INTERNET: www.franchigift.com
CREDIT CARDS: AE, DC, MC, V
HOURS: Mon–Sat 8:15 A.M.–9 P.M.
ENGLISH: Yes

LA BOTTEGA DEL CIOCCOLATO (125)
Via Leonina, 82 (Colosseum)

Looking for a replica of the Colosseum, the Vatican, or Buddha in white or dark chocolate? Here is your source, an amazing little shop making and selling all sizes and shapes of chocolate replicas, including Carnivale masks and Mickey Mouse in white chocolate. A small Colosseum is 12€, a large one will set you back 32€. Everything can be gift wrapped, and you can design your own basket of chocolate goodies.

TELEPHONE: 06 482 1473
CREDIT CARDS: AE, DC, MC, V
HOURS: Mon–Sat 9:30 A.M.–7:30 P.M.; closed June, July, and Aug, or if it is too hot
ENGLISH: Limited

TRIMANI (99)
Via Goito, 20 (Train Station Area)

Trimani has been considered one of Rome's premier wine and liquor shops since it opened in 1821. Naturally you can buy a vintage *cru* that could cost more than your trip to Rome, but they also stock a good selection of wine at affordable prices and ship worldwide. They also have assorted dry pasta, jams, jellies, honey, dried fruits, and olive oils. To sample a few wines before you buy, go around the corner to their wine bar and restaurant, also called Trimani, at Via Cernaia, 37b (see *Great Eats Italy*).

TELEPHONE: 06 446 9661

FAX: 06 446 9630

INTERNET: www.trimani.com

CREDIT CARDS: AE, DC, MC, V

HOURS: Mon–Sat 8:30 A.M.–1:30 P.M., 3:30–8 P.M., Sun 10 A.M.–1:30 P.M., 4–7:30 P.M.

ENGLISH: Yes

VOLPETTI (91)
Via Marmorata, 47 (Testaccio)

Volpetti is recognized as one of the best food shops not only in Rome but in all of Italy. At first glance, you may wonder why, but if you speak with Claudio, you will see how it earned its deserved high reputation. Let's start with their cheeses, most of which come from Norica in Umbria and are stored in a climate-controlled cellar. Every day Claudio washes the rinds with whey and turns them, the way his mother did, to keep the cheeses clean and uniform. Claudio is passionate about his cheese and works twelve hours a day. He says, "Cheese is like a child, it changes every day. Climate, terrain, and the hand of man make a cheese. The animal is the means to the cheese, but the land is the source." He can explain the cheeses, tell you what wine and foods to serve with them, offer samples, and put your choices in vacuum packs for the trip home. In addition to the fabulous cheeses, Volpetti sells a tremendous variety of meats, breads, aged vinegars, and interesting salsas. For a real taste of their foods and products, treat yourself to lunch at their cafeteria-style restaurant, Volpetti Piú, around the corner at Via Alessandro Volta, 8/10. If you can't get to Rome to shop at Volpetti, shop online and have your order delivered to your door.

TELEPHONE: 06 574 2352

INTERNET: www.fooditaly.com; www.volpetti.com

CREDIT CARDS: AE, MC, V

HOURS: Mon–Sat 8 A.M.–2 P.M., 5–8:15 P.M.; Tues–Sat 8 A.M.–8 P.M.

ENGLISH: Yes, ask for Claudio

Hairdressers

ELLEFFE—LF (84)
Via di San Calisto, 6/6a, near Piazza Santa Maria in Trastevere (Trastevere)

This modern full-service salon is in the heart of Trastevere. It was recommended to me by an American hairdresser who did not steer me wrong. Fabio gave me the best haircut I have ever had in Italy, and I will definitely be calling for an appointment on my next visit to Rome. Manicures, pedicures, massages, and an array of beauty services are available.

TELEPHONE: 06 583 43 483
FAX: 06 583 33 875
EMAIL: elleffehair@virgilio.it
CREDIT CARDS: MC, V
HOURS: Tues–Sat 9:30 A.M.–7 P.M., Thur until midnight; closed one week mid-Aug
ENGLISH: Yes

Housewares

HOUSE AND KITCHEN (65)
Via del Plebiscito, 103 (Piazza Venezia)

As the name of the store says, here is a beautiful selection of unusual items to enhance your home and kitchen.

TELEPHONE: 06 679 4208, 06 678 7965
FAX: 06 679 4133
CREDIT CARDS: MC, V
HOURS: Mon 4–8 P.M., Tues–Sat 9:30 A.M.–8 P.M., Sun 10:30 A.M.– 2:30 P.M., 3:30–7:30 P.M.
ENGLISH: Yes

SPAZIO SETTE (76)
Via dei Barbieri, 7 (Campo de' Fiori)

Look no further than Spazio Sette for Rome's best showcase of contemporary design for the home. Allow plenty of time . . . the beautiful merchandise, displayed on two floors, seems to go on forever.

TELEPHONE: 06 686 9708
FAX: 06 6830 7139
CREDIT CARDS: AE, DC, MC, V
HOURS: Mon 3:30–7:30 P.M., Tues–Sat 9:30 A.M.–1 P.M., 3:30–7:30 P.M.
ENGLISH: Yes

Leather

FURLA (31)
Piazza di Spagna, 22 (Piazza di Spagna)

This is just one of a dozen Rome locations for this popular leather handbag and accessory shop. Designs are ahead of the curve, the quality excellent, and prices affordable. There are also shops in Florence, page 347, and Venice, page 382.

TELEPHONE: 06 6920 0363
INTERNET: www.furla.com
CREDIT CARDS: AE, DC, MC, V

HOURS: Daily 10 A.M.–8 P.M.
ENGLISH: Yes

IBIZ (73)
Via dei Chiavari, 39 (Campo de' Fiori)

Everything is made by hand in a factory next door by the Nepi family of artisans, who have been working here for three decades. I resisted the temptation to have a leather desk chair (195€) shipped home and have been sorry ever since. Smaller items that you can easily tuck into a suitcase include natural or hand-colored leather belts, bags, and briefcases, all at very fair prices.
TELEPHONE & FAX: 06 6830 7297
CREDIT CARDS: AE, DC, MC, V
HOURS: Mon–Sat 9:30 A.M.–7:30 P.M.; closed 2 weeks mid-Aug
ENGLISH: Yes

Markets

As usual, there are no telephone numbers to call for these markets, nor are credit cards generally accepted. You will find very little English spoken, though it varies by stall. As in all markets, beware of pickpockets.

CAMPO DE' FIORI (68)

This is the most photographed outdoor market in Rome. The market begins around 7 A.M., except Sunday, and closes between 1 and 2 P.M., when everyone escapes to nearby restaurants for lunch. Life on the *campo* picks up in the early evening, and by midnight it is filled with people spilling out of the *caffès* around it.
HOURS: Mon–Sat 7 A.M.–1 P.M. (or thereabouts)

MERCATO DI PORTA PORTESE—TRASTEVERE (88)
Between the Tiber and Viale di Trastevere, from Ponte Sublicio to Ponte Testaccio (Trastevere)

All roads on Sunday lead to this huge open-air flea market, which runs from Ponte Sublicio to Ponte Testaccio. Over a thousand sellers offer everything you can imagine and some things you cannot: some fakes, some hot, some authentic. The Piazza Ippolito Nievo side has the antique sellers. Watch out for pickpockets and try to bargain down (about 10 to 20 percent). To get there, take Bus 75 to Porta di Portese, or take Via Ippolito Nievo off Via di Trastevere.
HOURS: Sun dawn–2 P.M., sometimes earlier

MERCATO ESQUILINO (123)
Via Principe Amadeo and Via Ricasoli (Train Station Area)

This large indoor market replaced the one that stood for decades on Piazza Vittorio Emanuele. The piazza is now a neighborhood park, complete with benches for seniors and play equipment for their grandchildren. It's a big improvement in this rather mixed, immigrant-heavy neighborhood. Because of the cultural mix, you can expect to find a wide variety of ethnic food in the market. The stalls are jammed with every edible product from the animal, vegetable, and fruit worlds...as well as some things that do not look edible. Watch out for pickpockets, especially when the stalls are beginning to close down and the gypsies swoop in for their handouts.

HOURS: Mon–Sat 7 A.M.–1 P.M.

MERCATO PONTE MILVIO
Ponte Milvio (northern edge of Rome)

The antiques dealers are here on the first Sunday of every month in a market that runs along the river under the bridge. It is considered the best market for serious antiques shoppers. Some sellers take credit cards.

HOURS: First Sun of month, 9 A.M.–6 P.M.

PIAZZA FONTANELLA BORGHESE (38)
Piazza Fontanella Borghese (Piazza di Spagna)

The stalls at this small market at the end of the Borghese Square sell prints, stamps, old postcards, books, some jewelry, medals, and assorted knickknacks. The items are not cheap, but there may be an old print that will catch your eye. You can bargain for 10 to 15 percent off, and cash helps.

HOURS: Mon–Sat 9 A.M.–6 P.M.

PIAZZA TESTACCIO (89)
Off Via Aldo Manuzio (Testaccio)

This is a small but interesting market in a solid working-class area of the city. There are also a few clothing stalls and countless ones that sell shoes. On the third Sunday of the month there is a flea market selling antiques and assorted kitsch.

HOURS: Mon–Sat 8 A.M.–1 P.M.; third Sun of month, 9 A.M.–4 P.M.

Shopping Streets

The following streets are lined with beautiful shops and are well worth a stroll. You will not be alone in your *passeggiata* (stroll), especially late in the afternoon or on Sunday, when it seems as though all of Rome is out browsing and window-shopping. Most of these stores are expensive, but now and then you will find something you can afford, especially during the January and July sales. Besides...looking and dreaming cost only time.

VIA BORGOGNONA (37, PIAZZA DI SPAGNA)

Chic and expensive shops with lovely displays.

VIA COLA DI RIENZO (19, THE VATICAN)

Be sure to stop in Castroni, a gourmet grocery store, at No. 191 (page 365). This street has some of Rome's more modestly priced shops but is a serious dining desert.

VIA CONDOTTI (34, PIAZZA DI SPAGNA)

Probably the most famous shopping street in Rome, Via Condotti is Rome's answer to Rodeo Drive, lined with very expensive boutiques, though not always the most famous names.

VIA DEI CORONARI (52, PIAZZA NAVONA)

One of the premier shopping street for antiques.

VIA DEL BABUINO (27, PIAZZA DI SPAGNA)

Designers, some antiques, and art.

VIA DEL CORSO (57, PIAZZA VENEZIA)

An endless string of hip shops with blaring music and clothing aimed at youthful shoppers with buffed bods to match.

VIA DEL GOVERNO VECCHIO (59, PIAZZA NAVONA)

Clothing with style and attitude.

VIA FRATTINA (39, PIAZZA DI SPAGNA)

More famous and near-famous designers.

VIA MARGUTTA (12, PIAZZA DI SPAGNA)

Art galleries and antiques.

VIA SISTINA (36, PIAZZA DI SPAGNA)

From the top of the Spanish Steps to Piazza Barberini: small shops, high prices, excellent quality.

Shopping in Venice

The Venetians say, "the first handsome woman that ever was made, was made of Venice glasse."
James Howell, Familiar Letters, *June 1621*

Beginning with Marco Polo, the Venetians controlled trade with the East, bringing silks and spices to the European continent. The trading spirit continues to this day, as millions of visitors flock to the city not only to enjoy its unique beauty and art but to purchase handmade lace, beautiful glassware, and papier-mâché Carnivale masks.

The maze of winding streets crisscrossed by canals and bridges will prove frustrating for the shopper with limited time and patience. It is easy to get turned around in Venice, but this is not the same as being lost. Please do not worry about getting a little mixed up; everyone does, even the natives, and it is part of the charm and adventure of Venice. Besides, who knows? You may discover some sumptuous restaurant, the perfect hotel, or a hidden shop you otherwise would have missed.

Venice is divided by the Grand Canal, which winds like an S through the most famous parts of the city. Every *sestiere* (district) has its main shopping street, with little alleyways wandering off of it, so you are almost guaranteed to find wonderful treasures no matter where you look. The Grand Canal, the Piazza San Marco (St. Mark's Square), and Rialto Bridge are the best-known landmarks. Shopping is concentrated in these areas: the Mercerie, a succession of streets winding from Piazza San Marco to the Rialto Bridge; the Frezzeria, prime shopping between the far end of Piazza San Marco from the Basilica and La Fenice; and Salizzada San Lio, leading away from Rialto through Castello. Calle della Mandola (San Marco) is filled with glass bead and paper shops, and the streets around Campo Santo Stefano are known for antique dealers. There are no shopping complexes in Venice. For this type of shopping, you have to go to Mestre.

Shopping Hours

The larger the shop, the longer the hours. During high season, the majority of shops are open daily, from around 10 A.M. to 7:30 P.M. In the winter, it is a toss-up. During August, expect to find service-oriented shops (such as cleaners, pharmacies, and hairdressers) and some small shops closed for a week or so. The following hours are reasonably dependable, but this is Venice, so if you are going to a specific shop, it pays to call ahead.

WINTER: Mon 3:30–7:30 P.M., Tues–Sat 10 A.M.–1 P.M., 3:30–7:30 P.M.

SUMMER: Mon–Sat 10 A.M.–1 P.M., 4–7:30 P.M., some open Sunday afternoon

FOOD SHOPS: Mon–Tues, Thur–Sat 9 A.M.–1 P.M., 5–7 P.M., Wed 9 A.M.–1 P.M.

TYPES OF SHOPS IN VENICE

Antiques

ANTICHITÀ BROCANTE (120)
Via L. Mocenigo, 5/A, off Via Lemanto (Lido Island)

Catherine Alary has successfully transformed her hobby of collecting furniture, lace, linens, and small objets d'art from the 1800s to the 1900s into a business on Lido. Her charming shop is just far enough from the tourist trail to keep it authentic. In other words, she depends on locals as customers, not on the tourist trade Lido experiences about six months of the year. Of course, you probably won't buy one of her armoires, but she has plenty of other collectables that fit easily into a suitcase. For instance, she has a large collection of early cigarette cases that would make perfect business-card holders, and some great old compacts. I also like her vintage clothing dating from 1900 to 1950.

TELEPHONE: 041 526 5189; cell 339 6864 538

EMAIL: caalary@tin.it

CREDIT CARDS: None, cash only

HOURS: Winter: Sun, Mon & Thur 10 A.M.–1 P.M., Wed, Fri–Sat 10 A.M.–1 P.M., 4–7 P.M.; summer (June–Sept): Mon, Wed–Fri 5–8 P.M., Sat–Sun 10 A.M.–1 P.M.; closed Jan–Feb

ENGLISH: Yes, and French

Art Galleries

GALLERIA LIVIO DE MARCHI (64)
San Samuele, 3157/A (San Marco)

Roderick Conway Morris, writing in the *International Herald Tribune,* summed up Livio de Marchi's work very well: "Livio de Marchi is the world's greatest living surrealist. Applying ancient Venetian woodcarving techniques, beautiful materials, notably pine and cherry wood, he crafts ephemeral and everyday objects such as flowers, ties, handbags, umbrellas, shoes, shirts, jackets, balloons, books and teddy bears, giving them permanent form in wooden sculptures that make amusing and pleasing works of art." I will add only this: you have to see it to believe it. The Studio Livio de Marchi is at Calle del Dose, 2742/A (San Marco).

TELEPHONE: 041 528 5694
FAX: 041 523 9159
INTERNET: www.liviodemarchi.com
CREDIT CARDS: AE, MC, V
HOURS: Mon–Fri 9 A.M.–noon, 1:30–9 P.M.; Sat by appointment; closed Aug
ENGLISH: Yes

MADERA (41)
Campo San Barnaba, 2762 (Dorsoduro)

Madera is an art gallery showcasing the work of contemporary Italian designers and artists. In addition to rotating shows, it represents some artists permanently. One of these is jewelry designer Ninfa Salerno, who is gaining well-deserved recognition for her unusual Papuni (aboriginal-inspired) art jewelry made from metal and glass beads. Be sure to see her necklaces.

TELEPHONE & FAX: 041 522 4181
INTERNET: www.maderavenezia.it
CREDIT CARDS: AE, DC, MC, V
HOURS: Mon–Sat 10:30 A.M.–1 P.M., 3:30–7:30 P.M.; closed Aug, Jan (call to check)
ENGLISH: Yes

Art Supplies

CARTOLERIA ACCADEMIA (47)
Rio Terrà della Carità, 1044 (Dorsoduro)

Everything an artist could possibly need is in these two locations. The Rio Terrà store is behind the Accademia. The second is on Campo Santa Margherita, 2928; Tel: 041 528 5283; Open: Mon–Fri 9 A.M.–12:30 P.M., 3:30–7:30 P.M., Sat 9 A.M.–12:30 P.M.

TELEPHONE: 041 520 7086
CREDIT CARDS: None, cash only

HOURS: Mon–Fri 8 A.M.–1 P.M., 3:30–9:30 P.M., Sat 9 A.M.–noon, 3:30–7:30 P.M.; closed middle 2 weeks of Aug
ENGLISH: Yes

Bookstores

FANTONI LIBRI ARTE (55)
Salizzada San Luca, 4119 (San Marco)

This family-owned bookshop is known for its large selection of illustrated books on art, architecture and design, Venice, and photography. It is the only place I have found in Venice that carries a detailed street map in book form (similar to Thomas Brothers) with sequential address numbers given for every *sestiere* and the islands. It is also packed with interesting and useful information about all the addresses, and it is in both Italian and English. I consider it a real find. Ask for *Calli, Campiellie e Canali, Guida di Venezia e Delle Sue Isole* by G. Paolo Nadali and Renzo Vianello (Edizioni Helvetia).
TELEPHONE: 041 522 0700
CREDIT CARDS: AE, DC, MC, V
HOURS: Mon–Sat 10 A.M.–8 P.M.
ENGLISH: Yes

LIBRERIA LINEA D'ACQUA (58)
Calle de la Cortesia, 3717, after Campo Manin (San Marco)

There is a good selection of books about Italy and Venice, first editions, rare and out-of-print books, and English-language books.
TELEPHONE & FAX: 041 522 4030
INTERNET: www.lineadacqua.it
CREDIT CARDS: AE, DC, MC, V
HOURS: Mon–Sat 10:30 A.M.–7 P.M., closed Sun, Nov
ENGLISH: Yes

Ceramics and Porcelain

GIULIANA ROLLI (32)
Calle del Tagiapietre, 2599/A/B, at corner of Calle secondo dei Saoneri (San Polo)

Giuliana Rolli is the only artist in Venice who does hand-painted porcelain. When I first found her, she was working out of a space not much bigger than a closet. Success has brought her to this new, larger location where she has space to paint and fire her work, and then to display it after it is completed.

All the porcelain you see in the shop is hers, and there is bound to be some special piece you will find to give as a gift, or to take home as a keepsake of your trip, and she can personalize any item. She also carries work from other artists and craftspeople, and as a result the shop is crowded with lots of other things of various quality. Her English is excellent, and she is a delight. Be sure to tell her hello from me.

TELEPHONE: 041 524 0789
FAX: 041 720 393
EMAIL: giulianarolli@virgilio.it
CREDIT CARDS: AE, MC, V
HOURS: Mon–Sat 10 A.M.–1 P.M., 4–7:45 P.M.; closed first 2 weeks in Aug (dates vary); call ahead to verify hours
ENGLISH: Yes

Clothing

ARABESQUE (96)
Ponte de Greci, 3403 (Castello)

If I had time to go to only one shop in Venice for clothing, Arabesque would be at the top of my list, not only for the wonderful merchandise but for the charming Adelia, who will wrap you in silk and velvet scarves, shawls, and throws you will adore. She also carries a beautiful line of silk and linen separates for women and ties for men. She is absolutely charming and willing to take time to be sure you have just the beautiful piece you want. You won't leave empty-handed... that would be an impossibility.

TELEPHONE & FAX: 041 522 8177
CREDIT CARDS: AE, DC, MC, V
HOURS: Mon–Sat 10 A.M.–12:30 P.M., 3:30–8 P.M.
ENGLISH: Yes

BLUNAUTA (91)
Campo della Guerra, 513 (San Marco)

This store sells affordable silk clothing, designed in Italy and made in China. There are also shops in Florence (see page 338) and Rome (see page 360).

TELEPHONE: 041 522 9096
CREDIT CARDS: AE, DC, MC, V
HOURS: Mon 3:30–7:30 P.M., Tues–Sat 9:30 A.M.–12:30 P.M., 3:30–7:30 P.M.; closed one week mid-Aug
ENGLISH: Yes

VENETIA STUDIUM (93)
Mercerie San Zulian, 723 (San Marco)

The fabulous fabrics here are displayed in an Ali Baba's fantasy world of Fortuny-style silks in every color and shade imaginable. The firm is known around the world for its exclusive production of the original Fortuny lamps, and for a creative range of pillows, scarves, drawstring purses, and other glorious accessories—all inspired by cosmopolitan fashions at the end of the nineteenth century. You will see countless copies... but don't be fooled.

There are three other locations: Calle Largo XXII Marzo, 2043 (72, San Marco), Tel: 041 522 9281; the corner of Campo dei Frari, 3006 (31, San Polo), Tel: 041 713 393; and Calle de la Ostreghe, 2428 (80, San Marco), Tel: 041 520 0505. All four shops have the same hours and fax number.

TELEPHONE: 041 522 9859
FAX: 041 522 7353
INTERNET: www.venetiastudium.com
HOURS: Mon–Sat 9:30 A.M.–7:30 P.M., Sun 10:30 A.M.–6:30 P.M.
ENGLISH: Yes

Department Stores

COIN (79)
Salizzada San Giovanni Grisostomo, 5787 (Cannaregio)

This nationwide department store chain was founded in Venice after the end of World War II. It sells middle-of-the-road clothing for the entire family as well as home furnishings. There is a second location that sells only lingerie, cosmetics, and perfumes at Calle del Magazen, Campo San Luca, 4546 (54, San Marco).

TELEPHONE: 041 520 3581
CREDIT CARDS: AE, DC, MC, V
HOURS: Mon–Sat 9:30 A.M.–7:30 P.M., Sun 11 A.M.–7:30 P.M.
ENGLISH: Yes

Fabrics and Trimmings

BEVILACQUA (99)
Fondamenta Canonica, 337/B (San Marco)

The pope, heads of state, and royalty buy Bevilacqua's magnificent brocades, braids, tapestries, velvets, and trims. This is the smaller of the two shops, but by far the most picturesque . . . who wouldn't be thrilled to be in a shop along a canal next to a rendezvous point for gondolas? The second location is also in San Marco (79) on Campo Santa Maria del Giglio, 2520; Tel: 041 241 0662, Fax: 041 241 5133; Hours: Mon–Sat 9 A.M.–2 P.M., 3–7:30 P.M., Sun 9:30 A.M.–2 P.M., 3–6 P.M.

TELEPHONE: 041 528 7581
FAX: 041 241 7196
INTERNET: www.bevilacquatessuti.com
CREDIT CARDS: AE, DC, MC, V
HOURS: Mon–Sat 10 A.M.–7 P.M., Sun 10 A.M.–5 P.M.; closed 2 weeks in Aug
ENGLISH: Yes

Glass

For more on Venetian glass, see Murano, page 387.

FRATELLI TOSO (114)
Fondamenta A. Colleoni, 7 (Murano Island)

If you love glass, do not miss Fratelli Toso.

The Toso brothers are carrying on their family tradition, begun in 1854, of creating exquisite glass. Theirs is not only one of the most recognized factories, but the oldest on Murano. The dusty, rather cluttered shop is obviously not there to attract the casual glass buyer of beads or glass objects—in fact, they don't do beads at all. If you go upstairs to their museum, you will see wonderful examples of their work, starting from the early days and continuing to the present, and you will quickly realize that everything they do is a handcrafted work of art, aimed toward serious buyers. Ask to see their collector's line, called Maestro Glasses, and you won't leave without at least two for yourself. They also design beautiful lights, can make anything to order, and ship worldwide.

TELEPHONE: 041 739 060, 041 739 089
FAX: 041 739 688
CREDIT CARDS: AE, MC, V
HOURS: Mon–Fri 9 A.M.–noon, 2–5 P.M., Sat 9 A.M.–1 P.M.
ENGLISH: Yes

Glass Beads and Jewelry

ANTICLEA ANTIQUARIATO (102)
San Provolo, 4719-A (Castello)

Gianna and her husband, Lucciano, are carrying on a family business started more than twenty years ago by her parents. They specialize in antique jewelry and beads, beaded bags, and beaded flowers. They sell their pieces in a tiny shop that is a treasure chest of wonderful things. The shop sits along a canal and is filled with all sorts of interesting nuggets besides beads and beaded objects, including old postcards, maps, prints, and a few antiques. It takes a while to absorb it all, so plan time to just look at what they have before you decide.

TELEPHONE & FAX: 041 528 6946
CREDIT CARDS: AE, MC, V
HOURS: Mon–Sat 10 A.M.–7:30 P.M.; closed Sun, 10 days in Aug (dates vary)
ENGLISH: Yes

GENNINGER STUDIO (39)
Calle del Traghetto, 2793 (Dorsoduro)

Leslie Genninger, a designer from Cincinnati, Ohio, has demonstrated what imagination, American drive, and hard work can do to make a dream come true. In 1988, she left a career as an investment banker and came to Venice, where she fell in love with Murano glass and at the same time was sad to realize that few new designs were being made. So she started her own design studio, and now her exclusive, custom-made glass and jewelry designs are selling as fast as she can produce them. She uses some old beads as well as her own creations to make the most wearable necklaces, bracelets, earrings, cufflinks, pins, buttons, and stickpins I've seen in Venice.

There is a second location next to Campo San Fantin on Calle del Fruttariol, 1845 (62, San Marco); Tel: 041 523 9494; Hours: Mon–Sat 10 A.M.–1:30 P.M. 3–7:30 P.M.; special appointments available

TELEPHONE & FAX: 041 522 5565
INTERNET: www.genningerstudio.com
CREDIT CARDS: AE, DC, MC, V
HOURS: Mon–Sat 10 A.M.–1:30 P.M., 2:30 P.M. –7 P.M.
ENGLISH: Yes

NINFEA (83)
Calle Lunga Santa Maria Formosa, 5228 (Castello)

For many years, Francesca Alessandri has been acquiring "Venetian pearls" dating from the end of the last century to 1940. Her collection of originally designed necklaces, bracelets, and accessories made with these antique beads are unique. She also has a good selection of yesterday's things—Bakelite, paperweights, little antique items. All are interesting, and all are crowded into a very tiny space.

TELEPHONE & FAX: 041 522 2381
INTERNET: www.ninfeavenezia.it
CREDIT CARDS: AE, MC, V
HOURS: Tues–Sat 11 A.M.–12:30 P.M., 4:30–7:30 P.M.; closed Aug 1–20
ENGLISH: Yes

RIALTO 79 (22)
Ruga degli Orefici, 79 (San Polo)

Venetian glass jewelry can be a dime-a-dozen bauble. Everywhere you look you will see strand after strand of cheap necklaces and gaudy earrings. Nowhere is the selection any tackier than along and around the Rialto Bridge, with, that is, the exception of this shop and Segreti Veneziana, their second shop, described on page 380. Armando and his wife, Luisa, stock an excellent selection of handmade glass beads, many of which are designed by Luisa and made in the shop. I especially like her silver and gold necklaces strung so they appear to be floating around your neck. There is something for every budget, and there are no hard-sell tactics. Look for their shop on the right side as you walk away from the Rialto Bridge toward Campo della Pescheria (the fish market).

TELEPHONE & FAX: 041 522 0647
EMAIL: rialto79@aruba.it
CREDIT CARDS: AE, DC, MC, V

HOURS: Daily 9:30 A.M.–7 P.M.; closed Sun in Nov; closed Dec and Jan
ENGLISH: Yes

SEGRETI VENEZIANI (25)
Near Campo San Bartolomeo end of Rialto Bridge, 5335 (San Polo)

Matteo Belardinelli—the son of Armando and Luisa, who own Rialto 79 (see page 379)—has branched out on his own in this attractive shop. He also sells loose beads and can do custom work. You are certain to find something wonderful here or at Rialto 79.

TELEPHONE: 041 523 8483
EMAIL: rialto79@aruba.it
CREDIT CARDS: AE, DC, MC, V
HOURS: Daily 10 A.M.–7 P.M.; closed Jan
ENGLISH: Yes

Gourmet Food and Wines

BOTTIGLIERA COLONNA (84)
Calle della Fava, 5595 (Castello)

It is a little shop with a good selection of Italian wines from small producers. They also have a good supply of grappa, speak English, ship worldwide, and take credit cards.

TELEPHONE & FAX: 041 528 5137
EMAIL: botcol@libero.it
CREDIT CARDS: MC, V
HOURS: Mon–Sat 9 A.M.–1 P.M., 4–8 P.M.; closed Jan 15–31
ENGLISH: Yes

GIACOMO RIZZO (78)
San Giovanni Grisostomo, 5778 (Cannaregio)

One of the best gourmet food shops in Venice is Giacomo Rizzo, which has been dispensing its handmade pastas (in all sizes and shapes), balsamic vinegars, truffles, extra-virgin first-pressed olive oils, honeys, and dried mushrooms since 1905. The dried pastas are made without preservatives or colors and range from a simple spinach tagliatelle to others flavored with radicchio, smoked salmon, cuttlefish, and beetroot.

TELEPHONE & FAX: 041 522 2824
CREDIT CARDS: AE, DC, MC, V
HOURS: Mon–Tues, Thur–Sat 8:30 A.M.–1 P.M., 3:30–7:30 P.M., Wed 8:30 A.M.–1 P.M.; closed a few days in Aug
ENGLISH: Yes

MASCARI (21)
Rugha Orefici, 381 (San Polo)

In the front, it looks like a gourmet grocery store with bags of *funghi porcini,* bottles of specialty olive oils and aged balsamic vinegar, spices, jams, jellies, hard candies galore, and even jars of Dijon mustard. The best part about Mascari is its large Italian wine selection, which you see when you go into the back rooms. Ask for Gabriele, one of the sons; he speaks English and can help you select just what you want. They do not ship.

TELEPHONE: 041 522 9762
EMAIL: iginioma@tin.it
INTERNET: www.imascari.com
CREDIT CARDS: None
HOURS: Mon–Sat 8 A.M.–1 P.M.; 4–7:30 P.M.; closed Aug 1–17
ENGLISH: Yes

RIZZO VENEZIA (105)
Calle dei Fabbri, 933/A (San Marco)

Rizzo Venezia is a high quality gourmet food store with three locations. In addition to their well-known breads and pastries, vast selection of candies, a deli section, and fresh ground coffees, they stock all the Italian foods, condiments, and spices you need to set up your own Italian kitchen. The location at Rio Terra San Leandro, 1355 (4, Cannaregio), is the biggest, but the two in San Marco, which are very close to each other, are more central.

TELEPHONE: 041 522 3388
INTERNET: www.rizzostore.com
CREDIT CARDS: MC, V
HOURS: Mon–Sat 9 A.M.–7 P.M.
ENGLISH: Yes

VINO E...VINI (113)
Fondamenta dei Furlani, 3301 (Castello)

Be local and bring your own plastic bottles and fill them with table wines dispensed from the tubs (2–3.20€, depending on wine). Or, upgrade to one of the best choices of Italian and international wines in Venice. In addition, the shop stocks sixty French champagnes, ninety different grappas, sweet dessert wines, whiskey, olive oils, and balsamic vinegars.

TELEPHONE & FAX: 041 521 0184
CREDIT CARDS: MC, V
HOURS: Mon–Sat 9 A.M.–1 P.M., 5–8 P.M.; closed 2–3 weeks in Aug (dates vary)
ENGLISH: Yes

Hats

ANTICA MODISTERIA (88)
Campo San Salvador, Calle del Lovo, 4813 (San Marco)

The motto here: "Crown yourself with one of Giulana Longo's hats." At the little hole-in-the wall shop owned by talented hatmaker Giuliana Longo, every hat you want can be found—from the fantasy one of your dreams to a simple straw hat. The shop has been in her family for over one hundred years and is known for trimming and making hats for gondolieri, pilots, and vintage car enthusiasts. Giuliana and her beagle, Muccy, are here every day to serve clients, and they do so with a smile and great enthusiasm.

TELEPHONE & FAX: 041 52 26 454
EMAIL: giul.longo@tiscali.it
CREDIT CARDS: AE, DC, MC, V
HOURS: Mon–Sat 10 A.M.–7 P.M.; closed Mar
ENGLISH: Yes

Leather

FURLA (86)
San Salvador, 4833 (San Marco)

Furla sells smartly designed leather handbags and coordinated accessories that complement almost all wardrobes and budgets. There are also shops in Florence (page 347) and Rome (page 368).

TELEPHONE: 041 277 0460
CREDIT CARDS: AE, DC, MC, V
HOURS: Mon–Sat 9:30 A.M.–7:30 P.M., Sun 10:30 A.M.–7 P.M.
ENGLISH: Yes

Linens, Lace, and Vintage Clothing

For more on lacemaking, see Burano, page 387.

ANNELIE PIZZI E RICAMI (42)
Calle Lunga S. Barnaba, 2748 (Dorsoduro)

A wonderful selection of antique and new linens, laces, lingerie, blouses, curtains, baby clothes, and table coverings are sold here. The sachets made from old scraps of lace and the monogrammed lingerie bags with pretty pastel satin ribbon ties are charming gifts that take up no space in your suitcase. Monogramming is available, and the prices are very good.

TELEPHONE & FAX: 041 520 3277
CREDIT CARDS: AE, MC, V
HOURS: Mon–Fri 9:30 A.M.–12:30 P.M., 4–7:30 P.M., Sat 9:30 A.M.–12:30 P.M.
ENGLISH: Yes, and German

CAPRICCI E VANITÀ (37)
San Pantalon, 3744/43 (Dorsoduro)

The ironing board in front serves as a reminder of the care required for the lovely lace and vintage clothing sold here. The charming one-of-a-kind shop specializes in Italian and imported laces, old folk costumes, and clothing and jewelry from the forties, fifties, and sixties. There is also a beautiful line of Orient-inspired bags and separates.

TELEPHONE: 041 523 1504
CREDIT CARDS: AE, MC, V
HOURS: Mon 4–7:30 P.M., Tues–Fri 10 A.M.–1 P.M., 4–7:30 P.M., Sat 10 A.M.–1 P.M.; closed Sat in June–July and all of Aug
ENGLISH: Yes

JESURUM (87)
Mercerie del Capitello, 4857 (San Marco)

Exquisite linens and laces are sold by this company, which has been famous for more than a century for its magnificent handiwork. Ask to see what is on sale.

TELEPHONE: 041 520 6177
FAX: 041 520 6085
INTERNET: www.jesurum.it
CREDIT CARDS: AE, DC, MC, V
HOURS: Mon–Sat 9:30 A.M.–7:30 P.M., Sat 10:30 A.M.–6:30 P.M.
ENGLISH: Yes

LA FENICE ATELIER (66)
Ponte dei Frati, 3537, between Campo San Stefano and Campo San Angelo (San Marco)

Christina Linassi's La Fenice Atelier carries a wonderful selection of beautiful handmade and hand-embroidered linens that remind us of the past. Her shop is the only place in Venice where you can find these hand-woven textiles made from historical patterns. All the linens and 100 percent cotton laces are machine washable (please do not spin).

TELEPHONE: 041 523 0578
FAX: 041 522 6840
EMAIL: lafeniceatelier@libero.it
INTERNET: www.lafeniceatelier.it
CREDIT CARDS: AE, MC, V
HOURS: Mon–Sat 10:30 A.M.–1 P.M., 2–7:30 P.M.; closed Dec & Jan until Carnivale (dates vary)
ENGLISH: Yes

Markets

The most famous food markets in Venice are alongside the Grand Canal by the Rialto Bridge. You will probably get your Venetian T-shirts here, but with few exceptions, don't count on it as a quality stretch of merchandise. Traditional outdoor fairs are held during the major Venetian festivals. A week before Easter, the whole length of Strada Nuova, Campo Santa Bartolomio, and Campo San Luca are filled with market stalls selling clothes, leather, sweets, and some craft items. Just before Christmas and Easter there is an antiques market in Campo San Maurizio (see below). Year-round, there are also outdoor food markets at Campo Santa Margherita (Dorsoduro), on a barge off Campo Santa Barnaba (Dorsoduro), on Campo Santa Maria Formosa (Castello), along Via Garibaldi (Castello), and in a cluster of stalls along Strada Nova (Cannaregio). The market on Lido is on Tuesday mornings.

They are all open in the mornings and sometimes in the afternoon. Generally speaking, the hours are Monday to Saturday 8:30 A.M.–12:30 P.M., and afternoons, except Wednesday, 3:30–7:30 P.M.; closed Sunday.

MERCATINO DELL'ANTIQUARIATO (77)
Campo San Maurizio (San Marco)

An antique market is held here on Palm Sunday weekend, the first weekend in June, and the weekend before Christmas. Lots of sellers, and definitely worthwhile if you are a collector or just a dabbler.

HOURS: Three times a year, Fri–Sun 10 A.M.–7 P.M.

RIALTO BRIDGE (26)

Rialto is *the* market in Venice, as it has been for hundreds of years. The *erberia* (fruit and vegetable stalls) sells everything the *pescheria* (fish market) does not. This is definitely worth a trip, and don't forget your camera.

Lining the Rialto Bridge and along Ruga degli Orefici, the street leading away from the bridge, are scores of cheesy tourist traps selling plastic gondolas, plates with pictures of the Doge's Palace, imitation gondolier hats, and more. However, there is the occasional item of quality, and if you are shopping for T-shirts, here's the place. Bargains are rare.

HOURS: Fish market: Tues–Sat 7 A.M.–1 P.M.; fruit and vegetable market: Mon–Sat 8 A.M.–1 P.M.; other stalls: winter Mon–Sat 10 A.M.–7 P.M., summer daily

ENGLISH: Usually

Masks

LA VENEXIANA (63)
Frezzeria, 1135 (San Marco)

The streets of Venice are lined with one mask and costume store after another, very few of them selling the real thing—that is, handmade, hand-painted masks and hand-detailed costumes. Every piece you see at

La Venexiana is handmade exclusively for their stores. At their two shops you will find papier-mâché masks of everything from famous opera characters to Mickey Mouse, and fabulous costumes to wear at Carnivale, to your next masked ball, or to wow your friends at Halloween.

The second location is at Ponte Canonica, 4322 (100, Castello); Tel & Fax: 041 523 3558.

TELEPHONE & FAX: 041 528 6888
INTERNET: www.lavenexiana.it
CREDIT CARDS: AE, DC, MC, V
HOURS: Daily 9:30 A.M.–7:30 P.M.
ENGLISH: Yes

TRAGICOMICA (36)
Calle dei Nomboli, 2800 (San Polo)

If you ever wanted to know how Venetian masks are made, enroll in one of the full- or half-day classes held in their workshop and . . . you get to keep the mask you make. The selection of masks and costumes is awe-inspiring.

TELEPHONE: 041 721 102
FAX: 041 524 0702
INTERNET: www.tragicomica.it
CREDIT CARDS: AE, DC, MC, V
HOURS: Mon–Sat 10 A.M.–7 P.M., Sun 10 A.M.–6 P.M.; closed Christmas–New Year's
ENGLISH: Yes

Paper and Stationery

EBRÛ (67)
Campo San Stefano, 3471 (San Marco)

There are many imitators, but few can compare with the beautiful handmade marbleized papers, classical book binding, handmade silks, and home accessories found in this shop.

TELEPHONE & FAX: 041 523 8830
EMAIL: avalese@iol.it
INTERNET: www.albertovalese-ebru.com
CREDIT CARDS: AE, DC, MC, V
HOURS: Mon–Sat 10 A.M.–1:30 P.M., 2:30–7 P.M.; closed 2 weeks mid-Aug
ENGLISH: Yes

GIANNI BASSO (77)
Fondamenta Nuove, Calle del Fumo, 5306 (Cannaregio)

Anyone who appreciates the fine art of hand printing should consider a visit to Gianni Basso a required stop on a trip to Venice. Gianni Basso is a master craftsman who designs and prints every piece he turns out the old-fashioned way, by hand. He is well-known and loved not only in Venice but by clients who come to him from around the world. His business cards are nothing short of fabulous, as is all of his printed stationery. He also does a limited edition of Pinocchio cards and scenes of Venice. He works in his shop every day but Sunday, occasionally assisted by his wife and their vagabond dog, Lilly.

TELEPHONE: 041 523 4681
CREDIT CARDS: None, cash only
HOURS: Mon–Fri 8:30 A.M.–1 P.M., 2–7 P.M., Sat 8:30 A.M.–1 P.M.; closed July 20–Aug 20, Dec 23–Jan 6
ENGLISH: Yes

LEGATORIA PIAZZESI (78)
Campiello Feltrina, 2511 (San Marco)

Piazzesi is the oldest paper shop in Italy still using the wood-block printing method. I like the boxes, albums, and flat-folding wastebaskets covered with block prints of Venice.

TELEPHONE & FAX: 041 522 1202
EMAIL: olavi@tin.it
CREDIT CARDS: AE, DC, MC, V
HOURS: Mon–Sat 10:30 A.M.–1 P.M., 3–7 P.M.
ENGLISH: Yes

Woodworking

GILBERTO PENZO (33)
Calle II dei Saoneri, 2681 (San Polo)

The owner of this fascinating shop is passionate about his cause: to preserve the maritime heritage and save the traditional, old boats of Venice. In this workshop he restores and replicates historical boats by hand. He points out that the gondola is only one of one hundred types of Venetian boats. You, too, can be a ship or gondola builder if you buy one of his model kits.

TELEPHONE & FAX: 041 719 372
EMAIL: gilbertopenzo@bigfoot.com
INTERNET: www.venetia.it/boat
CREDIT CARDS: MC, V
HOURS: Mon–Sat 9:30 A.M.–12:30 P.M., 3–6 P.M.
ENGLISH: Yes

The Islands

LIDO

Antichità Brocante sells interesting vintage clothes, furnishings, accessories and objets d'art. See page 373.

BURANO

The island of Burano is as charming and homespun as Murano is touristy and hard-sell. You can do both islands in a day, and that is what I recommend. Burano is known primarily for two things: fishing and lace. Artisans still make the lace by hand, and the prices are astoundingly high. However, you should be able to find beautiful hand-done hankies, sachets, and other little gifts at affordable prices. The lace-making school began in 1872 and is open to the public, selling goods from their stunning modern and traditional collection of table and bed linens. There is also a museum that displays magnificent pieces of old lace. I recommend going there first, before shopping, so you will be able to recognize the hand-sewn from the machine-made when you hit the shops. When you start your shopping, browse first, then go back and buy, all the time trying not to be too confused by the endless selection, most of which unfortunately originates in Hong Kong or the Philippines. But Burano is also known for its rich, eggy cookies and its gaily painted houses. Bring your camera and allow time to wander... this is a photo opportunity for sure.

How to get to Burano: If you are already on Murano, get the No. 12 vaporetto to Burano. If you are leaving from Venice, you can get the No. 12 from the Fondamenta Nuove (in Cannaregio).

MURANO

Though Venice's major glass makers have shops around San Marco, it is much more interesting to see them all together on Murano. The prices are somewhat competitive. You may be able to negotiate on large purchases but not on the little souvenirs. Do not fall for the many hawkers touting a "free trip to Murano." These con artists prowl the wharf along the Grand Canal and the streets leading to it with offers of free boat trips to the island. Once you are on one of these boats, you are steered to the shops these guys represent, and they get a kickback on whatever you buy. Be assured that buy you will with these high-pressure salesmen, who make the worst used-car salesman at home look like a cupcake. You can go by yourself from vaporetto stop No. 5 along the Grand Canal at San Zaccaria in front of the Danieli Hotel, or at No. 12 from Fondamenta Nuove in Cannaregio. You will need to allow at least three hours, or longer if you combine this with the worthwhile and interesting trip to the island of Burano (see above). Sunday is a good day to make the Murano-Burano trip because almost all the shops and restaurants are open.

Glossary of Italian Words and Phrases

It is forbidden to steal towels, please. If you are not person to do such is please not to read notice.
> —*Sign in a hotel room, quoted in* Holiday, *May 5, 1969*

Not throw nothing of windows.
> —*Sign in Venetian hotel room*

Well, the hotels are trying, and you definitely get their messages!

Although the staff of most hotels speak English, you will occasionally run across people working in smaller pensiones who have a limited command of the language. Thus it is important to try to master a few words of Italian to get by in a pinch. Before your trip, buy some Italian language tapes, or check them out from the library, and listen to them whenever you can. You will be amazed at how much you will absorb. Your efforts will be warmly rewarded by smiles and appreciation—and like the signs quoted above, even if what you say is a little garbled, you'll probably get your message across.

General Phrases

Good morning	*Buon giorno*
Good afternoon/evening	*Buona sera*
Good night	*Buona notte*
Hello/good-bye (informal)	*Ciao*
Good-bye	*Arrivederci*
Yes/No	*Si/No*
Please	*Per favore*
Thank you	*Grazie*
You are welcome	*Prego*
All right/okay	*Va bene*
My name is . . .	*Mi chiamo . . .*
What is your name?	*Come si chiama?*
How are you?	*Come sta?*
I am fine, thank you	*Bene, grazie*
And you? .	*E lei?*
today	*oggi*
tomorrow	*domani*
yesterday	*ieri*
See you tomorrow/Saturday	*A domani/a sabato*
Have a good weekend	*Buona domenica*
Do you speak English?	*Parla inglese?*
I do not speak Italian	*Non parlo italiano*
I understand	*Si, capisco*
I do not understand	*Non capisco/Non ho capito*

I do not know	*No lo so*
Can you please repeat slowly?	*Può ripetere lentamente?*
Excuse me	*Mi scusi/Prego*
Excuse me (in a crowd)	*Permesso*
I am sorry	*Mi dispiace*
here/there	*qui/la*
good/bad	*buono/cattivo*
big/small	*grande/piccolo*
cheap/expensive	*economico/caro*
hot/cold	*caldo/freddo*
vacant/occupied	*líbero/occupato*
Help!	*Aiuto!*
Stop!	*Alt!*
Look out!	*Attenzione!*

At the Hotel

hotel	*hotel/albergo*
annex	*dipendenza*
Do you have a room?	*Ha una cámera?*
I would like a (quiet) room . . .	*Vorrei una cámera (tranquilla) . . .*
for one/two/three people	*per una/due/tre person(a/e)*
for one/two/three nights	*per una/due/tre nott(e/i)*
for one/two weeks	*per una/due settiman(a/e)*
with a double bed	*con un letto matrimoniale*
with two beds	*con due letti*
with a private shower/bath	*con una doccia/un bagno privata(o)*
with a balcony	*con una terrazza*
How much is it?	*Quanto costa?*
It is expensive	*È caro*
Is breakfast included?	*È compresa la prima colazione?*
Do you have anything cheaper?	*Ha qualcosa che costa di meno?*
Do you accept credit cards?	*Si accettano le carte di credito?*
full-board/half-board	*pensione completa/mezza pensione*
Can I see the room?	*Posso vedere la camera?*
I will take it	*La prendo*
I would like to reserve a room	*Vorrei prenotare una camera*
I have a reservation	*Ho una prenotazione*
a key	*un chiave*

Getting Around

North, south, east, west	*nord, sud, est ovest*
Where is . . . ?	*Dov'è . . . ?*
a hotel/the station	*un albergo/la stazione*
Is it near/far?	*È vicino/lontano?*
left/right	*sinistra/destra*
straight ahead	*sempre diritto*
It is on the right	*È alla destra*
post office	*ufficio postale*
postage stamp	*francobollo*
bus stop	*fermata dell'autobus*
train station	*stazione ferroviaria*

subway	*metropolitana*
airport	*aeroporto*
one-way ticket	*biglietto di solo andata*
round-trip ticket	*biglietto di andata e ritorno*
first class	*prima classe*
second class	*seconda classe*
Could you tell me the time?	*Mi può dire l'ora?*
What time is it?	*Che ore sono?*
When does it open?	*A che ora apre?*
When?	*Quando?*
What?/What is it?	*Cosa?/Cos'è?*
Why?	*Perché?*
How?	*Come?*
Which?	*Quale?*
Where are the restrooms?	*Dov'è il bagno?*
Does it close for lunch?	*Chiude per pranzo?*
Where is an Internet café?	*Dov'è si trova l'Internet point?*

Changing Money

Is there a bank near here?	*C'è una banca qui vicino?*
Is there an exchange bureau?	*C'è una cassa di cambio?*
Can I use my credit card?	*Posso usare la carta di credito?*

Telephone

I want to buy a phone card	*Voglio comprare una scheda telefonica*
I want to make a call to . . .	*Voglio fare una chiamata a . . .*

Signs

Aperto/Chiuso	*Open/Closed*
Ascensore	*Elevator*
Chiuso per ferie	*Closed for holidays*
Chiuso per restauro	*Closed for restoration*
Divieto di sosta	*No parking*
Entrata/Uscita	*Entrance/Exit*
Gabinetto	*WC*
Guasto	*Out of order*
Ingresso líbero	*Free entrance*
Livero	*Vacant*
Non toccare	*Do not touch*
Occupato	*Occupied*
Perícolo	*Danger*
Scale	*Stairs*
Senso unico	*One-way street*
Signori/Signore	*Gentlemen/Ladies*
Strada senza uscita	*Dead-end street*
Suonare il campanello	*Ring the bell*
Tirare/Spingere	*Pull/Push*
Vietato	*Forbidden*
Vietato fumare	*No smoking*
Zona pedonale	*Pedestrian zone*

Days of the Week

Monday	*lunedì*
Tuesday	*martedì*
Wednesday	*mercoledì*
Thursday	*giovedì*
Friday	*venerdì*
Saturday	*sabato*
Sunday	*domenica*
today	*oggi*
tomorrow	*domani*
day after tomorrow	*dopodomani*
yesterday	*ieri*
in the morning/this morning	*di mattina/stamattina*
in the afternoon	*nel pomeriggio*
in the evening	*di sera*
tonight	*stanotte*

Months

January	*gennaio*
February	*febbraio*
March	*marzo*
April	*aprile*
May	*maggio*
June	*giugno*
July	*luglio*
August	*agosto*
September	*settembre*
October	*ottobre*
November	*novembre*
December	*dicembre*

Numbers

1	*uno*	20	*venti*
2	*due*	21	*ventuno*
3	*tre*	30	*trenta*
4	*quattro*	40	*quaranta*
5	*cinque*	50	*cinquanta*
6	*sei*	60	*sessanta*
7	*sette*	70	*settanta*
8	*otto*	80	*ottanta*
9	*nove*	90	*novanta*
10	*dieci*	100	*cento*
11	*undici*	101	*centuno*
12	*dodici*	110	*centodieci*
13	*tredici*	200	*duecento*
14	*quattordici*	500	*cinquecento*
15	*quindici*	1,000	*mille*
16	*sedici*	10,000	*diecimila*
17	*diciassette*	50,000	*cinquantamila*
18	*diciotto*	1,000,000	*un milione*
19	*diciannove*		

Index by City

FLORENCE

ROME

ACCOMMODATIONS

BIG SPLURGES

VENICE

ACCOMMODATIONS

Readers' Comments

Every effort has been made to provide accurate information in this edition of *Great Sleeps Italy,* but as seasoned travelers know, there are no guarantees. With the passage of time, hotel owners and managers may change, policies undergo revision, and due to inflation and currency fluctuations, prices will probably increase by at least 10 to 15 percent by the next edition. The publisher and author, however, cannot be held responsible for changes that do occur, or any inconveniences the reader may experience because of them.

Great Sleeps Italy is updated and revised on a regular basis. If you find a change before I do, or make an important discovery you want to pass along, please send me a note stating the name and address of the hotel or shop, the names of the people you dealt with, the date of your visit, and a description of your findings. Or if you prefer, visit my website (www.greateatsandsleeps.com) and leave your comment on my message board. As hundreds of readers who have written to me know, your comments are very important to me, and I respond to as many as possible. Thank you, in advance, for taking the time to write.

Please send your written comments to Sandra A. Gustafson's *Great Sleeps Italy,* c/o Chronicle Books, 85 Second Street, Sixth Floor, San Francisco, CA 94105. For more about all the books in the *Great Eats/Great Sleeps* series, and updates as I travel, please visit my website at www.greateatsandsleeps.com.

Make the most of your trip to Europe with
Sandra Gustafson's Great Eats and Sleeps guides.

Also available

Great Eats Paris

Great Sleeps Paris

Great Eats London

Great Sleeps London